Dimensions of Library and Information Science

CONCEPTS IN COMMUNICATION, INFORMATICS & LIBRARIANSHIP (CICIL)

General Editor: **S.P. AGRAWAL**

CICIL-1	Development of Library Services in India: Social Science Information **S.P. Agrawal**	Rs. 150
CICIL-2	Development of Documentation in India: Social Science Information **S.P. Agrawal**	Rs. 250
CICIL-3	UNESCO and Social Sciences: Retrospect and Prospect **S.P. Agrawal** and **J.C. Aggarwal**	Rs. 250
CICIL-4	INDIANA : A Bibliography of Bibliographical Sources **M.K. Jain**	Rs. 200
CICIL-5	Dimensions of Library and Information Science: Kaula Festschrift **V. Venkatappaiah** (Eds.)	Rs. 600
CICIL-6	Book Numbers: Some Indian Methods **M.P. Satija** and **S.P. Agrawal**	Rs. 100
CICIL-7	National Policy for University Libraries in India: Problems and Perspectives **N.B. Inamdar** and **L.S. Ramaiah** (Ed.)	Rs. 250
CICIL-8	Media Utilisation for the Development of Women and Children **B.S. Thakur** and **Binod C. Agrawal**	Rs. 150
CICIL-9	Terrorism: An Annotated Bibliography **Susheela Bhan** (Ed.)	Rs. 275
CICIL-10	Transnational Library Relations: The Indo-American Experience **M.B. Konnur**	Rs. 175
CICIL-11	Geography of Marketing and Commercial Activities in India (Documentation on Research Information) **R.S. Dixit**	Rs. 130
CICIL-12	Information India 1988: Global View **S.P. Agrawal** and **J.C. Aggarwal**	Rs. 200
CICIL-13	Women's Education in India: Historical Review, Present Status and Perspective Plan **S.P. Agrawal** and **J.C. Aggarwal**	(in press)
CICIL-14	Cultural Communication in India: Role and Impact of Phonograms **J.M. Ojha**	(in press)
CICIL-15	Second Historical Survey of Educational Development in India: Select Documents 1985-1989 **S.P. Agrawal** and **J.C. Aggarwal**	(in press)
CICIL-16	Documentation Encyclopaedia of UNESCO and Education **J.C. Aggarwal** and **S.P. Agrawal**	(in press)
CICIL-17	Attitude Towards Information: A Study of Post-Graduate Teachers and Researchers in Social Sciences **N.G. Satish**	(in press)
CICIL-18	Librarianship and Bureaucratic Organisation: A Study in the Sociology of Library Profession in India **P.K. Jayaswal**	Rs. 175
CICIL-19	Literature Search **K.A. Isaac**	Rs. 150
CICIL-20	Child Education in India: Index to Scholarly Writings in Indian Educational Journals and Newspapers since independence **S.P. Agrawal** and **Naresh Kanta**	Rs. 100
CICIL-21	Lok Sabha and Vidhan Sabha Elections in India 1989 & 1990: Process and Results with Comparative Study of Manifestos **S.P. Agrawal** and **J.C. Aggarwal**	Rs. 250
CICIL-22	Islamic Studies in India: A Survey of Human, Institutional and Documentary Sources **Mohamed Taher**	(in press)
CICIL-23	Panchayati Raj: An Annotated Bibliography **N.B. Inamdar, N.G. Satish** and **Anil Takalkar**	(in press)
CICIL-24	Information India 1989-90: Global View **S.P. Agrawal** and **J.C. Aggarwal**	Rs. 500

Concepts in Communication Informatics & Librarianship-5

General Editor: S.P. Agrawal

Dimensions of Library and Information Science

Kaula Festschrift

(Papers contributed in honour of Prof P N Kaula on his Sixty-first Birthday)

Editor
Dr Velaga Venkatappaiah

Associate Editors
Dr S R Gupta
Sister M Esperanza, AC
Dr S Fazle Rab

CONCEPT PUBLISHING COMPANY, NEW DELHI 110059

ISBN 81-7022-240-0

First Published 1990

Published and Printed by
Ashok Kumar Mittal
Concept Publishing Company
A/15-16, Commerical Block, Mohan Garden
New Delhi 110059 (India)

Lasertypeset by
Microtech Advance Printing Systems (P) Ltd.
H-13, Bali Nagar
New Delhi 110015

Prof. P N Kaula

General Editor's Introduction

CICIL is a new series launched by the publishers covering communication, information technology and librarianship fields which are inter-related and which, at the same time, in themselves include in their scope a very wide range of topics for investigation, research and study.

Communication is a quality of sentient. Homo-sapiens high up in the evolutionary order had fashioned many modes and mediums of expression. Of late, technology has armed man with dynamics and effecting communication. All this necessitates us to reflect on the role of the librarian in the emerging scenario. Librarianship, the grand discipline with the art and science of management, in a sense, lords over all the subjects. The present series will look at ideas, old and new, in all the allied areas.

The present publication, exhaustive in its treatment of library science and information technology merging with each other, offers an interesting and useful bill of fare to a large range of readers. It deals not only with the current stage of development or knowledge on the subject it has taken up, but goes back to the genesis and moves upwards to the latest phase to present the entire gamut of facts, both basic and peripheral. The communication revolution has transformed the library science and movement into a higher exercise of documentation with a view to giving the readers what they want almost instantly as if the entire network of libraries has been invested with the magic powers of Aladin's Lamp.

This volume, *Dimensions of Library and Information Science*, owes its inspiration to Professor P N Kaula and comprises papers dedicated to him as a bouquet on his 61st birthday. Son of a school teacher, Kaula performed actively on the stage called "information science and technology" for about four decades. He started his career humbly as a librarian in DAV College at Srinagar (Kashmir) on the strength of a testimonial that he had been a student-member of the college library committee. His pursuit of knowledge soon took him to Madras, where he found his "Guru" in Dr S R Ranganathan, who had retired from the University of Madras. From that point onwards, he moved from success to success and enriched professional literature so much that his contributions have been acknowledged by leading lights in the profession.

The legend of Kaula, therefore, is the motivation factor for an assessment of library science and information technology spanning the past and the present in this birthday volume. The papers have been classified under themes from 'A' to 'V' alphabetically, dropping 'I' and 'O'. Out of the numerous significant points emerging from the various papers, a few should bear mention to emphasise the value the present publication has for those who want to profit from its study. Our country has reached a milestone, where isolated library collections in our universities should belong to the past. The ever-increasing number of Indian Universities should pool their resources and coordinate their holdings to serve readers, who are anxious to sample them, wherever they might be based. Without this network, we would find that teaching, learning and research would soon lose their relevance.

One of the writers emphasised the fact that information science, like any other branch of knowledge, cannot be taught in isolation or out of the framework of the social, cultural, economic, political, scientific and technological environment in a particular country or region. The way of teaching information science in a country may be different from the situation elsewhere. We should, therefore, keep in view the dictum "unity in diversity" by holding the same goal everywhere, namely, that information science education should serve the entire mankind uniformly, whether or not some countries are way behind the developed ones.

It is important to remember, in conclusion, that a librarian's motto should be : "Learn to Give". We must pass our professional knowledge and skill to library users to enable them to pursue their quest of knowledge. And this volume should inspire every one of us to follow in the footprints of Kaula, with a prayer that he be around us, as before, for many years to come.

S P AGRAWAL

Contents

Theme B : Research and Technical Libraries

Theme C : Indological Libraries

Theme E : Library Automation

Theme F : Computer-based Library System

Theme G : Information Technology

Theme H : Information Systems

Theme N: Union Catalogues

Theme P: Users' Education

Theme Q: Library Associations

Theme R: Role in Library Development

Theme T: Impact and Reflections

Theme U: Impressions and Reminiscences

List of Contributors

ARORA, Jagdish: Documentation Officer, National Institute of Immunology, New Delhi-110065

BGOYA, Walter: General Manager, Tanzania Publishing House, Dar-es-Salaam, Tanzania

BURAGOHAIN, Alaka: Reader, Department of Library and Information Science, Gauhati University, Guwahati-781014

CHADHA, Ravinder Kumar: Librarian, The British Library, Lucknow

CHANDEL, A S (Dr): Reader, Department of Library & Information Science, NEHU, Shillong-793003

CHANDRA, Harish: Assistant Librarian, Central Library, IIT, New Delhi-110067

CHAUDHARY, Poonam: Shaheed Bhagpat Singh College (Eve), Govindpuri, New Delhi-110019

CHOPRA, H R (Dr): Reader, Department of Library & Information Science, Panjab University, Chandigarh-160014

COMAROMI, John P : Editor, Dewey Decimal Classification, Placid Club Education Foundation, New York (USA)

CURRAS, Emilia (Dr) (Prof): Directora, Gabinete de Documentaciaon Cientifica, Universidad Autonoma de Madrid, Madrid-3 (Spain).

DOSA, Marta: Syracuse University School of Information Studies, 200 Huntington Hall, Syracuse, N Y 13210 (USA)

EBINUMA, Yukio: Director, Department of Technical Information, Japan Atomic Energy Research Institute

ESPERANZA, M (Sister) (AC): Librarian, Patna Women's College, Patna-800001 (Bihar)

GRIKHANOV, G A : Department Head, Theory and Methodics of Formation and Use of Library Stocks, The V I Lenin State Library of the USSR, Moscow (USSR)

GUPTA S R (Dr): Lecturer, Department of Library and Information Science, University of Delhi, Delhi-110007

GURTU, Arvind: Times of India, New Delhi-110002

HAVARD-WILLIAMS, P : Professor of Library & Information Studies, Loughborough University

JANAK Raj (Dr): Librarian, Thapar Institute of Engineering & Technology, Patiala - 147001 (Punjab).

JOHN, B : Documentation Unit, INCOR, Andhra University, Waltair-530003

KASIVISWANADHAM, S : Officer-in-Charge, INSDOC Regional Centre, CSIR Complex, Taramani, Madras-600113

KHURSHID, Anis (Dr)(Professor): Chairman, Department of Library & Information Science, University of Karachi, Karachi (Pakistan)

KHURSHID, Zahiruddin: Head of Cataloguing, King Fahd University of Petroleum & Minerals, Dahran, 31261 (Saudi Arabia)

KONNUR, M B (Dr): Lecturer, Department of Library & Information Science, Poona University, Pune-41100 (Maharashtra)

KUMAR, Narinder (Dr): Reader and Chairman, Department of Library & Information Science, Kurukshetra University, Kurukshetra-132119

KUMAR, P S G (Dr): Head, Department of Library & Information Science, Nagpur University Campus, Nagpur-440010

KUNDU, A K : Assistant Librarian, NEHU, Nagaland Campus, Kohima-797001

KUNZE, H C Horst (Dr) (Prof): Former Director General, Deutsche Staatsbibliotek, Berlin (GDR)

LAHKAR, Narendra: Lecturer, Department of Library & Information Science, Gauhati University, Guwahati-781014

LAZAR, Peter (Dr): Former Director General, Hungarian Central Technical Library and Information Centre; Former Chief of Division and Field Expert of UNESCO; Honorary Fellow and Former Vice-President of the International Federation for Information & Documentation (FID), Former Secretary, International Advisory Committee on Documentation, Libraries and Archives of UNESCO, H-1035, Budapest (Hungary)

LUNDU, Maurice C (Dr): Librarian, Univerisity of Zambia at Ndola, P O Box 21692, Kitwe, Zambia

MALHAN, Inder Vir (Dr): Reader, Department of Library Science, University of Jammu, Jammu-180001.

MISHRA, Bhawanath: Campus Librarian, Bihar Veterinary College Library, Rajendra Agricultural Univerisity, Patna-800014

MOHAN KRISHNA, P : Documentation Unit, INCOR, Andhra Univerisity, Waltair-530003

MURTHY, S S : Director, DESIDOC, Delhi-110054 (India)

NAYEEM, M A (Dr): Librarian, T N B Law College, (Bhagalpur University), Bhagalpur-812001

PRASAD, A R D: Documentation Unit, INCOR, Andhra University, Waltair-530003

RAB, S Fazle (Dr): Head, Library & Documentation Division, A N S Institute of Social Studies, Patna-800001

RAJU, P Soma (Dr): Reader, Department of Library & Information Science, Andhra University, Waltair-530003

RAMAIAH, L S : Librarian, Central Institute of English and Foreign Languages, Hyderabad-500007

RANGRA, V K : Assistant Director (Training), DESIDOC, Delhi-110054

RUDICH, Salomon M Dorf (Dr): Former Chief of Medical Documentation Medical Publications Department, Scientific Council, Ministry of Health at Havana (Cuba)

SAPRE, S B : Technical Teachers Training Institute (Western Region), Bhopal-962013 (MP)

SARAF, Veena: Lecturer, Department of Library and Information Science, NEHU, Shillong-793003

SATIJA, Mohinder Partap: Department of Library & Information Science, G N D University, Amritsar-780014 (Punjab)

SAXENA, R S : University Librarian, Allahabad University, Allahabad-211002 (UP)

SHUKLA, Bana Bihari (Dr): Head, Department of Library & Information Science, S B Women's College, Cuttack-753001

SINGH, Sukhdev : Assitant Librarian, Bhai Gurdas Library, G N D University, Amritsar-780014 (Punjab)

SINHA, Arun K : Senior Officer, Library & Information Services, Tata Engineering & Locomotive Co. Ltd., Jamshedpur-831001 (Bihar)

SUBBARAO, C V : Senior Librarian, Institute of Defence Studies and Analysis, New Delhi-110001

THAKUR, U M (Dr): Reference Librarian and Lecturer, Library & Information Science, Patna University, Patna-800015 (Bihar)

TREHAN, G L : Former Secretary, Punjab Library Association; Founder Chandigarh Library Study Circle, 859/15-B, Chandigarh -160015

VENKATAPPAIAH, Velaga (Dr): Secretary, Professor Kaula Endowment for Library & Information Science; Secretary, Zilla

Granthalaya Samstha, Library Building, Elluru-534006 (AP)

VERMA, Sahib Singh: Librarian, Shaheed Bhagat Singh College (Eve), Govindpuri, New Delhi-110019; Secretary, Indian College Library Association (Regd); Municipal Councillor (Municipal Corporation of Delhi), 150 Madhav Kunj, Keshav Puram, Delhi-110035

VIJAYA LAKSHMI, B (Dr): Department of Library & Information Science, Andhra University, Waltair-530003 (AP)

Introduction

V Venkatappaiah

1. Recorded Knowledge and Information

The thirst for knowledge and information has been one of the enduring characteristics of mankind; and with that thirst has gone the irrepressible and inquisitive urge to record information. As knowledge stores, consisting of innumerable documents embodying already known or newly created thought, have grown in the form of libraries and information centres, so have the problems of recording and finding out information which is already known and recorded in some specific document.

We have moved from a concept called library where the emphasis has been on book study to documentation where the emphasis is on an item of information. The newly created documentation activity has been replaced by information activity. The change has been significant, and today in the fields of education and research, economics and sociology, science and technology, humanities and environmental psychology, information is sought, exploited, assessed, synthesized, interpreted and analysed to give the desired results for the progress of humanity.

1.1 *Change Caused by Information and Technology*

There is no doubt that the traditional library with which we worked for centuries for dissemination of knowledge has attained during the past few decades, new dimensions and have got engulfed or transformed into an Information Resource Centre. During the past two decades, information industry has become the world's fastest growing : not only micros, software, work stations, data bases, but journals, newsletter books, every form of printed and televised message. Desktop publishing threatens another surge forward. Information and technological revolutions have brought about a considerable change in libraries and their working. Today it is a common practice to talk about information analysis, information transfer, information handling, information processing, information retrieval. In India, the transformation is slow but it is bound to change the structure, techniques, working and services of libraries.

2. Honoured on Fiftieth Birthday

Prof P N Kaula, who has grown with the development of libraries and the theory and practice of library science with an appreciable record of 44 years (1944—1988), has worked through this evolution as a worker in all humility, with devotion, understanding, through sun and shade and has carved out a distinct place for himself. It was in 1974 that an International Festschrift Volume Committee consisting of 215 members from 30 countries and several international bodies prepared *Kaula Festschrift* in honour of his completing 50 years of dedicated life and three decades of professional work. The essays contributed to the present *Festschrift-2* cover a number of topics covering library science and its extension into what is called information science and technology.

3. Struggles and Hard Work

3.1 *College Library Committee*

Kaula came from a humble family, his father was a school master with a large family. His schooling and college career went through a difficult period particularly when his father wanted him to take up a job to supplement his income. Providence helped him to save this situation as he would have become a teacher and ended his career in that way. In his college career he was elected a student-member and later secretary of the college library committee which job he took up seriously. This created in him an interest in the "world of books" which gradually developed and fully matured in his future life.

3.2 *Outstanding Beginnings*

Kaula started his career as a librarian in DAV College, Srinagar, based in the certificate he had earned as a student-member of the College Library Committee. This made him to go to Madras and later to Banaras to obtain a Diploma in Library Science. At Madras he came in contact with Dr S R Ranganathan who had retired from Madras University prematurely. His first encounter with Ranganathan is already referred to in several places. Ranganathan took a liking for Kaula and Kaula found in him his *Guru* or guide for his future life. After obtaining his diploma, Kaula went back to Srinagar to serve his college library where he introduced Colon Classification, open access system, longer hours of work and offered personalized service as a do-all librarian. He also wrote articles in Urdu for daily and weekly papers and occasionally a piece of rhyme too. This to the surprise of everyone, numbered over 100 within a span of 18 months. It was the beginning of the feat of passion or a mission for the cause of libraries. He also published a booklet entitled *Kashmir Men Ilmi Inqalab* (Educational Revolution in Kashmir).

3.3 *Unusual Sacrifice*

Kaula then went to Pilani to work as the Chief Librarian of Birla Central Library under the Birla Education Trust. Here he reorganized the library introducing new services to the extent that the Secretary, Birla Education Trust, granted 18 months' leave of absence to Kaula when he was called by Ranganathan to join the Delhi University Library on a Junior Library Assistant's scale of Rs. 100-10-200. Kaula was then in a lecturer's scale and had served under the Trust for about 3 months only. But the impact of hard and dedicated work even during this short period made the Secretary of the Trust not to accept the resignation of Kaula and granted him the leave against the normal rules of service since Kaula was still on probation. This goes to show that Kaula worked with dedication and competence wherever he worked. He had the courage to take the risk even when the Secretary discouraged him by calling him the "wisest fool".

3.4 *Varied Tasks*

Kaula worked only at the Delhi University Library in a junior subordinate capacity. Otherwise he has held the top positions everywhere. Even in this junior subordinate capacity, Kaula set an example to others by his hard and dedicated work. During this period

(1948—51) Kaula worked in the Library, became Managing Editor of *ABGILA* (*Annals, Bulletin* and *Granthalaya* of Indian Library Association) started by Dr Ranganathan, worked for the journals and on the works of Ranganathan in and outside the printing press, studied for M.Lib. Sc. which he joined in the very first batch when it was instituted in 1948, served on several Committees of the Indian Library Association as a Council Member, wrote three books on Kashmir — *Tasvir-e-Kashmir, Kashmir Speaks* and *Kashmir Darshan* and also many papers and attended All-India Library Conferences on his own and made a mark on the national scene. He also worked with Ranganathan in the evenings for the Union Catalogue of Learned Periodicals for South Asia — Pilot Fascicule, distribute the copies of *Abgila* on his bicycle to the subscribers in Delhi, and yet remained with Ranganathan till mid-night. Kaula displayed enormous capacity for hard work, devotion to duty, unusual interest in professional work and dedication to the cause of libraries.

3.5 *Up on the Ladder of Leadership and Fame*

Kaula slowly but surely moved up in the hierarchy of the disciples of Ranganathan. He had gained admiration and recognition from his senior colleagues including Prof S Das Gupta, the University Librarian and Head of the Department of Library Science. Das Gupta wrote on February 16, 1951, about the competence of Kaula in the following words :

> ". . . a great burden of the work of reorganizing the Delhi University Library was borne by Kaula and this unique opportunity of building up diverse types of library services right from the beginning has given him a rich and varied experience. Among his colleagues he distinguished himself as much by his keenness and enthusiasm as by his ability, application and industry. . . . Shri Kaula's professional qualifications and technical competence are of a very high order. . . . He is one of the three or four persons in the country who have received systematic practical training in Documentation and organization of specialized library service.
> Mr Kaula's contribution to professional literature has been quite varied and some of his works have been noted for their merit by distinguished professional colleagues in the West. . . . He has firmly established himself as a specialist particularly in the field of Research and Business Libraries."

This is another example of Kaula as a subordinate of unusual capacity, honesty, integrity and competence. Kaula then moved to Delhi College, now Zakir Husain College, on deputation and organized its library, designed its counter and furniture and earned a reputation from the academic community. In June 1951 Kaula moved to the Ministry of Labour, Government of India, and introduced for the first time systematic documentation work in the Government of India libraries in November that year. His work at the Ministry of Labour is recorded elsewhere and I need not mention it here. But Kaula besides his work at the Ministry brought out a number of documentation/microbibliographies, drafted syllabus for the Certificate course in library science at Aligarh Muslim University at the invitation of Prof S Bashiruddin and regularly delivered lectures at week-ends from 1951—58 thereby establishing himself as an inspiring teacher. The record lecturing was done during this period in Aligarh for six and a half hours in a single day. Besides this, he continued working for Union Catalogue of Learned Periodicals for South Asia by paddling the distance of 14 km each way from his office in New Delhi to the residence of Dr Ranganathan. He also founded Delhi Library Association and started its activities in various directions like starting its journal *Library Herald* in 1958, established its school of library science in 1955, drafted its Library Bill in December 1954 and organized conferences, exhibitions, etc. In the words of Prof Das Gupta Kaula became the "soul" of DLA. The Association recognized the talent and organizing capacity of Kaula by presenting him an Address of Tribute at the Constitution Club in July 1960. This aspect of work further demonstrated the infinite capacity of Kaula to work hard for the profession with single-mindedness.

4. Passion for Work and Service

Kaula shifted to Varanasi at the invitation of the Banaras Hindu University. The Vice-Chancellor, Dr V S Jha came to Delhi to negotiate the terms of Kaula, offering him professor's scale with a higher start and with no probation period. This is perhaps unique in the service of that University. At BHU Kaula changed the classification system and cataloguing to that of Ranganathan's systems as a missionary to a collection of about 500,000 volumes with no additional staff. This was considered a "miracle" by those who knew the magnitude of work involved in it. He also introduced a number of services, constructed 64 research cubicles and introduced open access, long hours of work and only three days' closure of the library in a year. He introduced B.Lib. Sc. in 1963 and M.Lib. Sc. in 1965, the second University in India to start this advanced teaching in library science. He also extended the activities of the library and made it more serviceable, establishing service wings like study centres in the city, publication programmes were introduced including documentation in anticipation of demand.

Against all these manifold activities, Kaula had to face some problems which had arisen from his passion for the profession. He had reached the pinnacles of fame, was respected, admired, loved and surrounded by groups who revered him in the true spirit of *guru-shishya* relationship as we find in the Sanskrit classics; on the other hand, a few of these who gained favours initially became overambitious, and later got involved in politics to run Kaula down.

4.1 *Price for Upholding Professional Standards*

Much of the trouble started with Kaula having advocated Ranganathan's system, Ranganathan's celebrations, Ranganathan's Festschrift. This came to surface when under the influence of the former Director of National Library, the Vice-Chancellor, who was known to him, decided to change the Ranganathan system of classification to outdated Decimal Classification. Kaula was away in Cuba on a Unesco assignment. This became handy for the then Director of Insdoc who had waited for an opportunity to change the system of classification. A huge sum of Rs. 40,000 was spent in inviting eight so called experts, four from the National Library and four from Insdoc to reclassify the huge collection as a vengeance against Dr Ranganathan. Kaula returned and fought against it to the great annoyance of the establishment. Similarly when Kaula became full-time Professor of Library Science in 1971, the then Vice-Chancellor appointed the Head of the Department of Geography as Honorary Librarian of the University Library. Kaula fought the battles both in the Academic Council and outside, arguing that the University would be ridiculed if a Professor of some other subject was made the Superintendent of Sir Sunderlal Hospital instead of a qualified medical specialist; similarly if some non-agricultural faculty member was put in charge of dairy and farm in the institute of Agriculture; or even a non-technologist was put in charge of the water and electric supply department of the Institute of Technology, why the

University Library alone should have a non- library science man as its librarian. This argument though logical and forceful, irritated the then Vice-Chancellor and Kaula had another battle to fight which he did, untiringly.

4.2 *Mental Composure and Complete Detachment*

When Kaula was in conflict with some in authority, it was amazing to find him working for his defence at one moment, following it up immediately after with sitting down with saintly composure, writing a professional article for his journals and for others; correcting proofs received from the press; and attending correspondence to his professional calls like lectures, meetings, seminars and others. Without his knowing it, it was a state of complete detachment about which we read in books on religion. This has been a great quality in Kaula and has given him greater strength to pursue his chosen subject.

4.3 *Formidable Record of Contributions*

Much of the work in the profession by Kaula is known and there are papers in this volume which give one aspect or the other of his contributions. What is not much known is Kaula as a man.

Years ago, Edison said that genius is one part inspiration and 99 parts perspiration. This applies to Kaula. Of course, he makes no bones about this in saying this with disarming humility. His world is a world of his own subject which has now gained a substantial dimension. His success comes from his one-track mind, his obsession with his own field of work. When he talks about it in meetings, lectures or in conversation, he talks with authority and confidence. He is a dedicated worker and as self-sacrificing soul. He has no pride of being an intellectual and an internationalist. He says that he is still a learner of his subject which shows his humility and greatness. He still wants to master the subject though he has at the cost of physical pain and suffering to his family attained a *front rank* position having written more than four dozen books and monographs, edited 43 bibliographies on diverse subjects, about 1100 articles and book reviews, designed 18 depth classification schedules besides designing buildings and furniture of several libraries and has been editing professional journals with international circulation; is on numerous committees and professional bodies; is known the world over with love, respect and affability, and never ignored when the world of libraries is on the anvil.

4.31 *Recognition in Press*: Leading newspapers with wide circulation have acknowledged the impact of the contributions of Kaula. *Amrita Bazar Patrika* named him under Spotlight—a teacher of repute. *The Statesman*, New Delhi, stated that he is one of the two persons who have made their impact the world over (the other being Dr Ranganathan), and called him Prophet of Library Power. *Daily Telegraph* referred to him as "very tall library scientist" under "Librarians sans Libraries". The *National Herald*, New Delhi, called him "Doyen of Library Science".

5. Judging as a Man

No one can say that obscurity is Kaula's fate. Behind this man who stands out with commanding posture in the world of learning is a humble child-like man at home. Happily married with five children, he is not the master of the house but a member. Mrs Asha Kaula understands him for she is herself a trained librarian. His concern in the home is the food that he takes. He is informal to a fault. If someone knocks at his door, Kaula will come out barefooted to receive him. If the servant or his wife is not around, he will himself briefly leave the conversation and prepare tea for him.

In interpersonal relations, Kaula is dependable and responsible. If he says he will do a thing, he will go out of his way, and occasionally to an embarrassing and surprising degree, to help the other. He expects others too to be equally responsible to him. That is the trait that he has possibly picked up from his mentor. He loves his students and showers bundles of affection on them. It is no wonder he has ardent disciples among his students in many parts of India.

5.1 *Endearing Qualities*

Let me confess that I was not fortunate to be a student of Kaula. I became his admirer and indirect disciple when I found that he had contributed more than anyone else, after his *guru* Ranganathan, which has given him an abiding place in the profession. It is for the profession to judge him as a library scientist. I profess to him like many others who have known him at close quarters, as a man. And as a man Kaula has impressed me, and many others apart from his students, as one who will live in the hearts of those whom he knew as a friend or colleague till they breathe. His colleagues in coming years may forget him but his friends and disciples will pass the legend of his absence of social snobbery, his modesty, his anxiety to help others, his courage, his fortitude, his capacity to suffer in adversity with equanimity, refusal to let success go to his head, his infinite capacity to work hard and to encourage younger people to come up in the profession, will pass as parables for a normal lesson-book.

6. Move for Festschrift-2

Completion of 60 years has been another milestone in the career of Prof Kaula. His friends, admirers, students and colleagues decided to bring out "*Kaula Festschrift-2*" as a token of gratitude to what he has done and achieved. The 61st Birthday Celebration Committee was formed with Prof Iqbal Narain, the then Member Secretary, Indian Council of Social Science Research, as Chairman to invite contributions on various aspects of library and information science. It was felt that Kaula being a versatile professional having mastery over several branches of the subject, contributions should be on a great variety of subjects and we tried to find contributors who had some relationship with Kaula and who represented diverse aspects of librarianship. So the International Committee issued an appeal inviting contributions.

7. Selection of Contributions

Seventy-two contributions were received. The work of sorting them out and puting them into some shape was done by Sister M Esperanza and Dr S F Rab and we found 50 of such contributions worthy to be included in the Festschrift. Dr S R Gupta looked through the editorial details and saw it through the press. The Committee regrets that it has not been possible to include all the papers in the volume due to its various limitations. The Committee feels grateful to the contributors who have sent the papers.

8. World-wide Representation

8.1 *Geographical Scatter*

Geographical scatter of the contributors to the *Festschrift-2* is as under :

Sl. No	Countries	Representation
1.	Cuba	1
2.	GDR	1
3.	Hungary	1
4.	India	40
5.	Japan	1
6.	Pakistan	1
7.	Saudi Arabia	1
8.	South Africa	1
9.	Spain	1
10.	Tanzania	1
11.	UK	1
12.	USA	2
13.	USSR	1
14.	Zambia	1

8.2 *Vocational Analysis of Contributors*

Vocational analysis of the contributors whose papers have been included in the *Festschrift Volume* is as under :

Sl. No.	Vocation	No. of authors
1.	University Teachers (20):	
	Professors	6
	Readers	8
	Lecturers	6
2.	Special Libraries	5
3.	University Libraries	6
4.	Professional Colleges	3
5.	Documentation Centres	4
6.	Research and Technical Libraries	4
7.	National Libraries	2
8.	Information System	1
9.	College Libraries	3
10.	Journalism	2
11.	Editorial Specialist	2
12.	Publisher	1

The contributions have been grouped into 21 themes and the treatment of the papers contributed has been given in Conspectus.

9. Everlasting Personal Qualities

Kaula is known to the profession as a multifaceted personality. He loves the profession and likes the people who work in it. He has constantly been in touch not only with the subject and its dimensions but also with the colleagues, seeking their ideas and opinions. He has therefore a wide circle of friends and colleagues. His generosity, encouragement, and assistance to friends and colleagues has been extraordinary and his support for younger colleagues and students remarkable. The papers contributed to the *Festschrift* will not only enrich the subject with all its facets and phases but will also help in understanding more about a colleague who has earned a name for the profession not only in India but beyond its frontiers. The *Festschrift* is a humble token of gratitude that we owe to this noble and dedicated and yet very humble person — Kaula.

Conspectus

This volume is divided into 21 Themes numbered (Theme A — Theme W). Each of these contains chapters relating to the topic mentioned. Each chapter represents a paper contributed to this volume.

Theme A is on Academic Libraries. It has chapters A1-A3. They cover Academic librarianship in perspective, the introduction of modern technologies in the management of academic libraries, the bibliographical control in academic libraries, and the analysis and growth of international cooperation in manpower development. Theme B deals with Research and Technical Libraries. Chapter B1 discusses their role and problems. Chapter B2 identifies the problem in human resource development and proposes practical solutions.

Theme C gives an account of Indological Libraries in India. It identifies their problems and specifies their new dimensions.

Theme D deals with Library and Information Science Education. It has chapters D1-D3. Chapter D1 describes the environment factor and the information science programmes in SADCC Region (Southern African Development Coordinating Conference). Chapter D2 gives a historical narration of library science education in India and evaluates the training programmes at various levels. Chapter D3 lays emphasis on research work and suggests introduction of quality improvement programmes for working librarians.

Theme E covers Library Automation. Chapter E1 brings forth the scenario of automation programme in Saudi Arabia, Kuwait and Sultanate of Oman and the efforts to introduce it in some other libraries.

Theme F brings out the computer-based library system. It has three chapters. Chapter F1 is devoted to on-line data base technology, its components and suggests a network model. Chapter F2 highlights the advantages of implementing computer-based systems and discusses the areas in which it can be introduced. Chapter F3 introduces the computers in general.

Theme G is devoted to Information Technology. It has chapters

G1-G2. Chapter G1 discusses the use of personal computers (PCs) in library and information systems. Chapter G2 brings out the trends in information technology including telecommunications and telecommunication-based systems.

Theme H encompasses various Information Systems. It has chapters H1-H7. Chapter H1 is devoted to explaining the special aspects of INIS operations in Japan. It describes the input and use pattern of INIS data base. Chapter H2 discusses the commercial data bases for information retrieval services and emphasizes on the need for creation of data bases at institutional level. Chapter H3 discusses computer based network and its relevance for on-line information retrieval systems. It gives also a brief account of internal on-line services. Chapter H4 is devoted to describing the role of INFOTERRA as a referral system in organizing environmental information. Chapter H5 presents an account of data base management systems and their functions and capabilities. Chapter H6 makes a comparative analysis of papers in science, social sciences and humanities based on citations. It evaluates the citation of articles in a specific library science journal. Chapter H7 narrates the growth and development of information systems and documentation work in social sciences.

Theme J comprises studies of International and Comparative Librarianship, forming chapters J1-J6. Chapter J1 narrates the impact of the works of Dr S R Ranganathan on American librarianship. It refers to the tributes paid to the work of Ranganathan as "World Librarian". Chapter J2 discusses international librarianship and the impact of the work of Prof P N Kaula. It brings out the difference in librarianship and information science and projects the views of Prof Kaula on the subject. It also presents the dichotomy created in the field. Chapter J3 covers some aspects of international documentation and the impact of Prof Kaula by his works, views, meetings and personality. It also expresses admiration of Prof Kaula for his oratory and the depth of knowledge on the subject. Chapter J4 covers the development of the Soviet libraries based on the culture of Soviet society. It also describes the literacy activities and the programme of library development in the USSR originally initiated, planned and worked out by V I Lenin. It also states the increasing role of libraries. Chapter J5 describes the development of library and information services in Cuba and the work of Prof Kaula as Unesco Expert. It also gives an impact of his activities. Chapter J6 gives an account of the libraries in Tanzania describing rural libraries, university and special libraries, children's libraries and the work of Tanzania Library Association.

Theme K consists of two chapters. Chapter K1 discusses library marketing, evaluates all aspects of marketing strategy and presents the marketing promotion programmes. Chapter K2 deals with the specific issues pertaining to marketing phenomena as applied to library services.

Theme L deals with book promotion activities particularly with illustrated works. It describes the development of illustrations and illustrated works in Germany stating also its significance and advantages.

Theme M pertains to organization of Knowledge and Analysis of Subjects. Chapter M1 discusses Dewey Decimal Classification, its expansion, influence, limitations, covering also its international and Indian aspects. Chapter M2 describes the developments in Colon Classification through its various editions, particularly its Edition 7. It presents the features of this edition in conceptual and notational aspects.

Theme N discusses the role of Union Catalogue in Resource Sharing. It presents the problems and prospects of Union Catalogue work for 21 countries in the Arab region.

Theme P deals with Users' Education. Chapter P1 describes the overview of user education and training programmes conducted in scientific and technical libraries in India.

Theme Q is devoted to discussing the Role of Library Association. Chapter Q1 describes the foundation, structure, activities and achievements of the Delhi Library Association which was founded and nursed for several years by Prof P N Kaula. It also refers to the Address presented to Kaula by the Association.

Theme R gives a brief account of Library Development in two States of India. Chapter R1 mentions the work of Prof Kaula in the development of libraries in Assam. Chapter R2 states the work of Prof Kaula in the promotion of library legislation and library education in Bihar. It also refers to the Address of Tributes presented by 22 organizations at Patna.

Theme S deals with Professional Journalism and Teaching. Chapter S1 presents an account of the editing work of journals by Prof Kaula. It evaluates the work of journalism specifying the features and standards set out by him. Chapter S2 is a description of genius of Prof Kaula as exhibited in his activities of teacher-educator and his contributions to his discipline of L & IS. It portraits Kaula as an educator and assesses his work covering the span of 34 years. Chapter S3 refers to the missionary devotion of Prof Kaula which makes him an ideal Librarian and an inspiring Teacher. It also speaks about his other activities in other related fields.

Theme T contains five chapters. They describe the impact and reflection of the work and activities of Prof Kaula. Chapter T1 is an appreciation from a distinguished colleague (of Prof Kaula) from Pakistan. It gives briefly the admirable record and influence of the work of Kaula who is referred to as a multifaceted internationalist. Chapter T2 presents a critical appreciation of Prof Kaula projecting him as a faithful disciple of Dr S R Ranganathan and admiring his courage, fortitude, competence, standards and an ideal of his own. Chapter T3 evaluates the work of Prof Kaula narrating some of the episodes from his life. It also highlights his views on the slow development of libraries. Chapter T4 presents an analysis of the work of Kaula and that of Dr S R Ranganathan pointing out latter's impact on Kaula as Librarian, Teacher, Editor and Project Designer. It also refers to the work that Kaula did for Dr Ranganathan in popularizing his ideas. It also records the views of Ranganathan on Kaula mentioning him as an Educator of Library Science. Chapter T5 describes several aspects of the work of Prof Kaula and their impact on national and international librarianship.

Theme U records Impressions and Reminiscences. It contains chapters U1 and U2. Chapter U1 projects the profoundity of his knowledge and willingness to help researchers. Chapter U2 makes an intimate study of Kaula's work as Unesco Expert, as Journalist, as Learner and as Leader of the profession. It gives a personal glimpse of Kaula as a man with tremendous courage, fortitude and ever willing to help others.

Theme V contains two poems given as chapters V1 and V2. Chapter V1 describes the profile of Kaula stating various facets and phases of his life and work. Chapter V2 is the tribute paid to Kaula on his completing six decades of a dedicated life.

Theme W is a record of the achievements made by Prof Kaula. Chapter W1 enlists the works of Prof Kaula. Chapter W2 mentions felicitations and honours conferred and works on Prof Kaula. Chapter W3 is a chronology of events in Kaula's life.

The contents pages show in a fairly significant way detailed headings of topics covered in the Conspectus.

—Editors

A 1

Teaching Role of Academic Librarians: Fact or Assumption

AS Chandel and Veena Saraf

0. Introduction

The library profession even today could not get its due recognition and status. It is only some developed countries like the USA, UK, etc., which could place the library profession in the right perspective and appropriate hierarchy of status. In developing countries including India, the struggle for status and recognition of services is still continuing. Even the academic community does not consider the academic librarians as colleagues and co-partners in learning and teaching process. What the librarians have to offer the faculty and students in educational process is still not recognized? When this is the situation in the academic world, what could be expected of a society which comprises illiterate and neo-literate population. The potential role of an academic library is still not established and recognized. The profession is unable to demonstrate the importance of library services to the patrons. The academic activities are being continued without much involvement of libraries. Teaching seldom had been library oriented. The student community is not motivated for library use. The society also does not demand what librarianship can give. Therefore, the traditional librarianship which is desired by the patron is still continuing. The professional, non-professional and semi-professional activities of librarianship are so thickly intermingled that the user is unable to make the differentiate between the three activities.

1. Emphasis on Semi-Professional Work

In such circumstances, we simply show more of our inferior status of clerical and house-keeping jobs. A professional knowledge, competence and skills remain unexplored and latent. The underutilization of professional capacities has been described by Eldred Smith[1] as under:

> "The . . . functions that librarians perform are, more often than not, so circumscribed by regulation and routine, so lacking in autonomy, individual judgement and expertness as to qualify for more as bureaucratic rather than professional activity. There is little professional about an acquisition librarian who spends his time in bibliographical verification or even on the routine review of a national bibliography or blanket order shipment. There is little professional about a cataloguer who rather automatically applies the principles of the Library of Congress or Dewey to a given number of books each day — usually trying to maintain an acceptable volume of productivity without real knowledge of the field in which he is cataloguing or of the needs of the library's clientele and how they use the catalogue; there is little professional in a reference librarian who answers routine and substantive questions with equal indifference to and lack of knowledge of the questioner and his library needs. Such librarians are guided primarily by institutional routines, regulations and values. Their relations to their clientele are at best indirect or fragmentary. Their involvement with any subject or area of the collection is incidental and usually through the medium of book trade list or catalogue rules."

It is quite obvious from the above statement that we do more peripherial activity rather than core activity.

In such a situation, we have to re-examine our role and take initiative to change the existing situation.

2. Looking at Ourselves: Status Dilemma

We rightly or wrongly always blame the authorities for inadequate funds, staff and non-recognition of our status and services. But at the same time we also do not look at ourselves whether we are doing the desired services as prescribed in our profession or not. After all, why our own colleagues and equals in teaching faculty are hesitant and reluctant in recognizing us as faculty members? They do not welcome us as teachers. The profession is at the crossroads where we are able to claim neither academic status nor faculty status authoritatively and convincingly in spite of the fact that both these are intrinsic in librarianship. We should ask ourselves whether we are performing the teaching role of faculty or have we been claiming this status on the basis of assumptions. We may agree to a certain extent with the opinion given by Amitia Etzioni[2] who says that, "claiming to be a faculty, are these typically associated with persons who press for what they are not, guilty feelings for floating a status claim without sufficient and legitimately". Faculty status for librarians is defined by McAnally[3], "the profession of all or most of the privileges of the classroom teaching faculty including faculty rank. Academic status is held to be the possession of some but not all usual faculty privileges, with definite classification as academic but always without faculty rank". "The faculty status entails complete equality with academic faculty in regard to rank and titles, promotion criteria, tenure, subbatical leave, rates of pay, holidays and vacations, representation in faculty, government and fringe benefits."[4]

In India, the status of University and College librarians was recognized as early as in 1959 when the UGC constituted a committee under the Chairmanship of Dr Ranganathan. The committee defined the status of library staff as "The high academic and professional qualifications, the combination of academic and administrative responsibilities and the practice of the Universities all the world over indicate that the status and salary of the library staff should be same as those of the teaching and research staff". The UGC accepted the recommendations in 1961 and upgraded the salary scales of academic librarians working in Universities and colleges. Since then the parity is being maintained. There are still many States which have not implemented the recommendations even after 30 years.

3. Teaching Role

If we are able to perform and demonstrate the core activities of organizing and retrieval of world knowledge and information with conceptual framework, the academic status for such personnel becomes quite obvious. If the profession also takes up the teaching work which has gained much importance in recent years, it can have the privileges of academic as well as faculty status without claiming.

The teaching role of librarianship is not merely a claim to get status but it is the basic function of an academic library today. It is the part of the professional duty to educate the academic community including faculty members enabling them in identification, retrieval and use of information resources required for their study. The teaching library activity is today considered as the 4th R of pedagogical process and essential for every literate. The teaching responsibility of the 4th R exclusively lies on the library profession. This is the central role to be performed by the academic library staff. As librarians it is our duty to develop library-oriented teaching and programme of instruction in the use of library.

4. Library Instruction

Teaching activity of library staff on library resources (4th R) is represented by different terms, viz., Library Instruction, Library Education, or User Education and Library Use Instruction and Bibliographic Instruction. The general objective of the instructional programme in academic libraries as stated by ACRL[5] is, "a student by the time he, or she completes a programme of undergraduate studies should be able to make efficient and effective use of available library resources and personnel in the identification and procurement of materials to meet the information needs". It has further given the service standard regarding library instruction that "it is a routine work closely with teaching faculty in identifying instructional needs and teach the use of library resources to meet their needs". The academic librarians have to involve themselves in library instruction programmes more seriously in order to justify their claims for professionalism and faculty status, thereby performing their basic functions.

In spite of so much emphasis and unanimous agreement on the needs of instructional programme, no step has been taken so far by the academic librarians to do anything in this line in India. This programme has become very important and popular especially in the USA, where the work in this area had started as early as in 1930 at the conceptual level.

A National Orientation Conference was held at Eastern Michigan University on May 7-8, 1971, with the stated purpose as "to explore a number of practical solutions to such problems as: how to motivate students to use the library, how to teach the proper method of research, and how to assist teaching faculty in maximum use of library resources for curriculum planning". This was the emphasis on the important role of librarians in teaching and learning process. Dr Ranganathan was well aware about this programme which is evident in his book on Reference Service where he has emphasized on "*Initiation of Fresh Man*". The genesis of the concept lies in reference service which only Dr Ranganathan had foreseen much ahead of time.

How could the goals of the academic libraries given by Travis G White[6] be achieved without initiating and activating the instructional programme? Hence we have to:

(a) Maximize the user needs satisfaction
(b) Minimize the time loss in supplying the user's needs
(c) Increase actual number of users.

The probable problems which the librarian may have to face and solve in initiating this programme could be summarized as follows:

5. Staff Inadequacy

It is quite possible that librarians may face some difficulties in initiating the programme due to lack of staff and other facilities, but he cannot postpone this responsibility. It may be argued that this programme is more important for libraries which are understaffed because the users become independent in library use and may not need staff assistance in the future. Once they know how to use the library, they may not much depend upon the reference service or any other such assistance which needs more staff.

6. Faculty Cooperation

The faculty attitude towards the library professionals is important. The cooperation of faculty and administration is essential for the implementation of this programme. The librarians have to convince the faculty and the administration that library instruction is of primary importance and students should be given sufficient time for learning the use of library and its resources. This is only the joint effort of all the three which can make this programme a success. It is important for the faculty staff to de-emphasize the teaching methods which do not necessitate them to use the library. Unless this programme is made need oriented, it is difficult to motivate the students. Unwillingness on the part of the students cannot bring any result. Librarians have to convince both the faculty and the students that their teaching role is essential in the educational process, and that their partnership in the education of students is equal.

7. Problems in Teaching

The library instruction is not a piecemeal activity of reference desk where the librarian simply assists the user in finding the information. Some librarians due to some reasons or the other may not like formal classroom teaching work and if this assignment is enforced on unwilling librarians, the programme would be far from being effective. In the beginning a librarian may find it difficult to teach but gradually he may acquire the confidence and competence of communication and may also start enjoying the work at a later stage. The comment made by one of the librarian could being well be quoted here. He says, "I certainly intend to continue to seek librarians who can and want to teach, especially because of the benefits the students have gained from the library instruction and tremendous enhancement it has given traditional reference work."[7] The librarian cannot evade this responsibility. The teaching competence has to be developed because there is neither any option nor any alternative to this function of librarianship.

8. Designing of Instructional Programme

It is not an easy task to design a viable course based upon conceptual framework. The varied information needs of the students have to be determined. The instructional programme has developed to an extent that some of the professionals associated with the teaching work feel that it has its own bulk of knowledge, its own theory and framework. The search strategy has to be worked out which brings all information sources under its purview. It has to develop its own teaching methods and apply the suitable media of instruction based upon the course contents and instructional objectives. The guidelines emerging out of various researches done in this area would help in the designing of the course. The guidelines given by ACRC[8] may also be referred to while going in for a course design. The following factors may be useful in planning the programme:

(1) To ascertain the information needs of users;

(2) To assess the skill and knowledge required for the purpose;
(3) To know what assistance and resources would be needed;
(4) To visualize the possible problems which shall have to be encountered;
(5) To find out the possible solution to the problem;
(6) To apply suitable teaching media.

9. Conclusion and Suggestions

A librarian's motto should be "learn to give" which implies that we ought to pass our professional knowledge and skill to the users of library for their problem-solving in educational pursuits. This can be achieved by introducing a regular library instruction programme in every academic library. This would satisfy our patrons, convince authorities about the important role of libraries, assist faculty members in their teaching assignment, bring recognition to the profession and ultimately improve the education standard as a whole. Therefore, all academic librarians should initiate the programme, may be in the form of orientation. Unless the librarians start contributing in research and teaching, they cannot justify their claim of faculty status. They have to keep pace with the faculty members with regard to their qualifications and nature of duties.

To provide universal access to higher education to all and to enlarge the creative capacity of our society, it is essential that there be universal access to library resources and their effective use. The profession has to meet the challenge to improve higher education where students get an opportunity to think, sharpen their intellectual curiosities and develop an independent attitude in academic work. There is an appropriateness of integrating library work with teaching work. We librarians have also to fulfil our role as educators.

REFERENCES

1 Smith, Eldred: Service and Housekeeping: Changing Professional and Non-Professional Responsibilities in the Academic Research Library. Paper delivered at the Indiana University Library Dedication, Oct. 9-10. 1970, pp. 59-60, Quoted by Millicent D Abell: The Changing Role of the Academic Librarian: Drift and Mastery. *College and Research Libraries*, Vol. 40, (L) 1979, pp. 100.

2 Etzioni, Amitai, Ed: The Semi Professions and Their Organisations. New York, Frers Press, 1969. pp. vi-vii. In: Pauline Wilson: Librarians as Teachers: The Study of An Organisation Fiction. *Library Quarterly*, Vol. 49, 1979, pp. 146-62.

3 McAnally, Arthur M: Status of the University Librarian in the Academic Community. In John N. DePew: The ACRL Standards for Faculty Status: Panacea or Placebo, *College and Research Libraries*, Vol. 44, (6), 1983, p 410.

4 Madan, Raj et al: The Status of Librarians in four years State Colleges and Universities. *College and Research Libraries*, Vol. 29 (5), 1968, 382.

5 Towards Guidelines for Bibliographic Instruction in Academic Libraries. *College and Research Libraries News*, No. 3, 1975, p. 138.

6 White, Travis G: Quantitative Measures of Library Effectiveness. *Journal of Academic Librarianship*, Vol 3(3), 1977, p. 130.

7 Burroughs, Carol: Library Instruction — Column Opinion. *Journal of Academic Librarianship*, Vol. 8(2), 1982, p. 97.

8 Towards Guidelines... op. cit. (see footnote 5 above).

A 2

Modern Management in Academic Libraries

P Havard-Williams

1. Effects of World Recession

All libraries are suffering today from the effects of the world recession. Some are suffering more than the others. In West Africa, in particular, libraries are suffering from the fact that most books are published in other countries, and hence need external currency and, in the great majority of cases, hard currency. Lack of money does not affect developing countries alone. The Royal Library in Brussels, the Belgian national library, is in dire financial straits, with staff positions unfilled, periodical subscriptions cancelled, and a lack of recent acquisitions. Even the British Library, considered to be well founded, has published a "strategic plan" which is aimed at rationalizing services so as to able to provide an effective service on less money.

2. Funding of Libraries

But the change in circumstances is due not only to a lack of money. There is a widespread lack of confidence both among librarians and their users in the value of libraries. This has come about because of the universal concern with management values rather than professional values. Secondly, because of the development of computerized information and that of the new technologies and their opportunities of converging with automated processes. The extent of automation in science, technology and commerce enhances its importance, and the result is that the book is under pressure to assert its importance. Thirdly, libraries tend to be at once isolated from other units within an overall structure, and also to be relatively small in relation to the overall size of the organization. Libraries in most universities, for instance, represent between 1.5% and 5% of the total cost. Moreover, they do not usually require sudden high increases. Libraries to operate efficiently need consistent funding to support a whole series of small tasks and a succession of relatively small cost materials (books, journals, microfilms, etc). It is a commentary on library provision today that a university library could do without buying books for a year, but could fund a computer installation for the library in the same year. International funding bodies are wary of funding libraries comprehensively because of the necessity for continuing funding: this may not be maintained, they consider, by the "home" funding body which will take off when the international funding has finished. Libraries, then, do not rank highly for funding, because

(a) their requirements are not great, but continuous;
(b) they do not emit "glamour"; and
(c) they also tend to be inward looking.

3. Librarian as Manager

The new brand of librarian therefore aims to be a manager rather than a scholar — and the danger is that having failed as a scholar, he may yet fail as a manager. A great deal depends on the current race of academic librarians.

One of the enduring problems of librarians is to maintain their position within the overall environment of their institutions. A library is, after all, a service to a service and, unless there is a constant awareness of rendering to the university or college, this service which is relevant, wanted and useful, the library is all too likely to see itself as an end in itself. One must therefore be aware of the constraints of the institution within which one is working. These will be widely different in different kinds of institutions — a large research university will have greatly different expectations of its library from a small university with a mainly technological or educational bias. Within that context, it is important that the academic librarian not only has an awareness of the broad direction in which his institution is going, but also knows the direction in which he is setting the library within that overall context. Different people will of course react to situations in different ways, but he needs to be sure that he is sensitive to what is going on around him, and that he is aware of having found his own management style. The role of a professor used to be to know more and more about less and less: the role of a university librarian might be said to know less and less about more and more; or, to put it more usefully, to know something about everything, and everything about something. He or she needs to know what is going on in the university (how else can he/she make his/her library serve?) and serve, or be represented on, boards of faculty/studies, as well as ensuring that he or she is well placed to take part in the corporate management of the university by serving on major committees. Equally, it is important to know what is going on within the library, with a broad knowledge of the different centres of activity.

3.1 *Management of Personnel*

The management of personnel is perhaps the major key to this. Personnel now takes up to 60% of the library budget, and in mere terms of resources is an important item. More than that, it is the people who make the atmosphere of the library and can create the service *ambience* mentioned at the beginning of the paper. For the more a systems approach is adopted, the more important a service approach becomes as a counterbalance. Personnel have to be well motivated in a situation which today gives rise to greater use at the same time as budget reductions — more service is expected for less money. Moreover, because of the lack of posts, there is low mobility, little to offer in terms of promotion, a great deal of technical change involving quite fundamental changes in staff expertise and structures. If one is unlucky, there may be poor personal relations among sections of the staff within the library, diminishing energy and a lack of personal initiative.

4. **Change in Libraries**

Because of the speed at which change is taking place in libraries there is not time enough to restructure staffing models, so that existing staffing structures are inappropriate and grades no longer make sense in a new environment. Institutions — certainly institutions in Europe — are insufficiently flexible to provide changes quickly enough. Staff dissatisfaction leads to unionization which adds a new dimension to negotiation for change.

4.1 *Impact on Staff Development*

In the present fluid situation, where one may not be sure of the budget for the current year, where uncertainty abounds, it is important to be clear about one's own management style, and share as much information as one possibly can: open budgeting entails open management in order to provide the basis for sound motivation with decisions shared and management demystified. Delegation has to be done thoroughly, within carefully defined parameters and with a corresponding accountability for action. Shared decision-making still has to leave the "buck" where the boss is, but also gives his or her greater insight into the qualities and deficiencies of his/her colleagues. Directors of libraries will be in a better position to identify staff development and training needs. Indeed, it is through the creation of new initiatives and thrashing out the need for change, and the consequent training required that adequate motivation can be maintained. It will, of course, be necessary to build on the most secure staff members in order to maintain overall morale, and provide both adequate training programmes appropriate to their needs and a spirit of adventure in contemplating projected innovation. One of the most important, though most unspectacular, ways of maintaining morale is to go round regularly to listen to what staff have to say, and hence pick up the state of the working climate within the library.

If the library has clearly defined objectives with which to serve its institutions, the training programme too needs clearly defined objectives, conceived within the overall directional plan of the institution as a whole and the library itself. This needs to take account of the changing nature of the library itself; objectives have to be rethought constantly, but the "vision" of the librarian as to how the library will continue to grow and develop as a service (not necessarily in terms of materials) is still important. That concept has to be conveyed to staff so that they will see their work, their division in the library in the context of the institution of which they are part.

5. Management of Change

Indeed, the management of change is a crucial element in management, though it has to be emphasized, it is not the only element. Management must also signify continuity, for the psychological benefit of the institution, of the library and of its staff.

Change is occurring not only in the library: it is also occurring outside it. With the reduction of numbers of the teaching staff, there is likely to be less teaching, and with the reduction in the number of students, their quality is likely to rise. As the result of both, and the development of teaching aids, there may well be more video instruction and the greater development of distance learning. As the budgets of libraries become smaller, less in multiple copies may be bought, while students will be less able to buy the necessary textbooks. There may well be a greater need for information staff with specialist degrees as well as information science education, and less in the way of the "general practitioner". Furthermore the proportion of professional/non-professional staff is likely to change, and their will be a four-tier staff — "expert professionals", "general practitioners", "technicians" and "library assistants". Academic libraries since the 1960s have had a three staffing tier system.

5.1 *Role in Developing Services*

Information scientists will not only have an important role in developing services for undergraduates (study skills and learning methods) but also in the development and maintenance of information services for research projects, providing on-line services, SDI files, and helping teaching staff to maintain research files on their own personal computers. They will also attempt to provide information services for industry. Much of all this will be on a cost-recovery basis since libraries will expect payment for all services outside the activity not financed by the University Grants Committee or the Research Councils (and even that could change).

6. **Leadership Qualities**

This scenario may be satisfactory as a look into the future, but the problem remains that a library is "a service to a service". The institution of which it is part, university, polytechnic or college, finally determines what part the library will play. The uncertainty of where tertiary education institutions see their roles is one of the greatest difficulties for the director of any general service within them. Hence leadership qualities within the library are of paramount importance. Outside the library, it is important for the library director to identify the leaders of opinion within the institution: these will be not only the leading professors who play a part in the committee structure but also others — the lecturer or technician who is also a county councillor, the reader who just happens to be important in the "power group". For the new director, there are the "honeymoon" benefits. But in the long term, the library director needs to be informed on local university information, on *Hansard*, on national sources of information, and be ready to adjust his policy and service to take account of shifts of policy and thinking within his/her institution. He or she has to maintain the credibility of the library within the institution and be aware of the peculiarities of the local culture. Indeed, at every professional level it is important that the staff talk the same language as senior administrators and the senior academics, but he or she also needs to challenge some erroneous assumptions — centralization saves money, automation or cooperation saves money.

The task of being a university polytechnic or librarian is as difficult as it has ever been. The holder needs professional integrity, considerable managerial competence, flexibility and a personal vision of the service he or she wants to provide in order to create the appropriate "*ethos*" within the library suitable and in harmony with the institution of which the library is a part. No wonder libraries are suffering from a lack of identity.

7. Situation in Developing Countries

The situation is even more pronounced in developing countries, when the need is greater, the resources less. Management training is also frequently lacking and professional staff are at a premium. Part of the problem lies in poor staff salaries, even where these are comparable with those of the teaching staff. Frequently library salaries are less favourable, and if the *anget* which is affecting libraries in developed countries is extended to developing countries, salaries may even relatively get worse. Nor will their frequently be external currency to buy the traditional library materials, let alone sophisticated equipment for the new media and automation. Access to data bases seems even more far away. Yet the crucial role played by information today cannot be ignored, and some means must be found to make politicians, government and university administrators and university governing bodies appreciate its importance.

8. Responsibility of LIS Departments

This can be done, first and foremost, only by the profession itself. A heavy responsibility lies on the shoulders of library and information science departments to encourage the most able and dedicated students to read the Master's degree in library science, and to encourage the most able to take doctorates not only for teaching posts but also for library and information posts: so that from among these candidates there may come a leader who is able to give new direction to library and information service.

There would seem to be a case for establishing an international library and information science school where the most able people from a number of countries could come together. Here, fundamental problems of library and information provision could be discussed, and advanced students could receive a thorough training research and good practice to return to their countries and provide new impetus to library management and service. This kind of school would be expensive ($750,000 per annum and a capital grant of $1,000,000) but it would provide a think-tank for an area of activity which appears to be essential to the development of a modern society, and yet which is so often little understood in developing societies.

Modern teaching techniques, especially if the teaching is to be spread over large numbers, needs modern technology, needs innovation practices which do not merely imitate those of the developed countries, but use the techniques and technologies available creatively applied to the particular circumstances of particular countries.

9. The Future Librarian

This brings us back to practice in the academic library. Education and training must produce the kind of librarian who is confident in his management practice, confident in handling staff, and on top of the best professional practice so that he (or she) may use his (or her) knowledge in the service of the users who are the people for whom the service is provided. Modern management education must include therefore personal management with attention to interpersonal relations, financial and resource management, professional subjects (indexing, information sources, database management, expert systems) some educational method and a general course sitting library and information work both in a country's culture and in history. As an educated man, a scholar, a manager and a real member of the academic community, there is still a very important role for the university librarian and the Director of Information services, but it is a demanding role which calls for a long preparation, sterling integrity of character and a commitment to university service with a greater degree of interior commitment than has been required in earlier generations.

library director needs to be informed on local university information (the Harvard) or national sources of information, and be ready to adjust his policy and strategy to take account of shifts of policy and thinking within his/her institution. He or she has to maintain the credibility of the library within the institution and be aware of the peculiarities of the [illegible]. At every professional level it is important that the staff talk the same language as senior administrators and the senior academics, but he or she also needs to challenge some erroneous assumptions — centralization saves money, automation or computers [illegible] saves money.

The task of being a university or polytechnic librarian is as difficult as it has ever been. The librarian needs professional integrity, considerable managerial competence, flexibility and a personal vision of the service he or she wants to provide in order to create the appropriate 'climate' within the library service and in harmony with the institution of which the library is a part. No wonder libraries are suffering from crisis of identity.

7. Situation in Developing Countries

The situation is even more pronounced in developing countries, where the needs are greater, the resources less. Management training is also [illegible], teaching and professional staff are at a premium. Part of the problem lies in poor staff salaries, even where these are compared with those of the teaching staff. Frequently library salaries are unfavourable, and it is the [illegible] which is affecting librarians in developing countries. [illegible] developing countries, salaries may even [illegible] go worse. Nor will there frequently be external currency for the institution to obtain materials, let alone sophisticated equipment for the new media and automation. [illegible] that raises some examples [illegible]. So the crucial role played by information [illegible] recognised and sometimes must be fought to make politicians, government and university administrators as university governing bodies [illegible].

8. Responsibility of LIS Departments

Much can be done. It is the concern of not only the profession but also [illegible] responsibility lies on the shoulders of library and information [illegible]

A3

Bibliographical Control among Indian University Libraries: The Need for an IULNET to Improve the Quality of Services to the Academic Community

L S Ramaiah

1. Status of Higher Education

India has a large system of higher education in terms of absolute numbers. In the years after Independence there has been rapid proliferation in the establishment of universities/colleges in the country. Higher education was given due *priority* in National Planning. The role and importance of higher education has been stated in the Government of India policy frame document, "Challenge of Education", in the following terms:

> "Higher education has been given a place of special importance because it can provide ideas and men to give shape to the future and also sustain all the other levels of education. The quality of life and pace of development of any nation depends on the ideological climate; the widespread perceptions of history, culture, tradition and values; and the feeling of confidence in human capability to overcome material, social and spiritual problems of living. Higher education and the intelligentsia nurtured by it have a special role in determining the quality of the overall environment. Higher education also supplied a wide range of increasingly sophisticated and ever-changing variety of manpower needed in industry, agriculture, administration and services."

1.1 *Quantitative Growth*

Today, in our country there are around 150 universities and institutions deemed "to be" universities and about 6,000 colleges. It is estimated that the total strength of the university/college faculty are around 210,000 and students are about 40 lakhs, which include 40,000 research scholars and three and 250,000 post-graduate students.

This vast academic community need and use information in one way or another.

2. Importance of University Libraries

The need and the importance of university libraries was well emphasized by the Radhakrishnan Commission (1948). Kothari Commission (1964) and various UGC Committees in the past. Due to liberal UGC grants under the chairmanship of late C D Deshmukh and effects of the recommendations of Education Commissions, majority of the university libraries have good physical facilities and moderate document collections.

2.1 *Escalation of Prices*

But during the past decade and a half due to escalation of prices of books, periodicals and other items and shrinking purchasing value of rupee, the university libraries have been finding it difficult to keep their collections up to date. They have lost their buoyancy and gradually their collections are becoming inadequate for research. Further, the volume of printed material is doubling every 10 to 15 years. It is impossible now for any single library to collect and house all the relevant printed material. University libraries cannot any longer stand alone like islands and this is even more so in a developing country like ours with limited book resources. The material in all university libraries in India must be linked together and made available in each of them as the need arises.

3. National Policy Initiated

University libraries have so far been planned and organized individually. There is no National Policy till now. Their planning is, therefore, a planning without policy at the national level. A National Policy for university libraries is important because such a policy formulation means definition of objectives. The initiative, therefore, taken by the AIU to formulate a National Policy for the university libraries in the country is a timely one in the right direction.

The report of the AIU Committee "National Policy on University Libraries — Policy Outline" has stated in the objectives, among other things, the need for networking and resource sharing among the Indian universities. To quote in their own words it is like this. The report says: "*Networking and resource sharing among university libraries should be practised by each institution towards utilization of all resources*". But the report has failed to spell out in clear-cut terms what should be such a network, may be, the report is only a policy outline, and the Committee might not have felt the need to elaborate it.

4. Networking for Resource Sharing

Any networking for resource sharing should satisfy the following conditions. They are:

1. An understanding of the necessity to cooperate;
2. An acceptance of the responsibilities involved in such cooperation;
3. The formal network within which to cooperate; and
4. The tools with which to cooperate.

4.1 *Necessity to Cooperate*

It is estimated that the total holdings in the universities as well as in those of the institutions deemed to be universities was about 125 lakhs. The annual intake of books is about 9 lakhs and of periodicals 1.1 lakhs. These should not remain like goods sheds. In order to become "locomotives of progress" and to meet the growing general demand and need in the years to come and to the maximum use of their holdings, the Indian university libraries should be linked together by a network system for cooperation. Individually, the university libraries can no longer meet the requirements of the faculty and research scholars. Their modernization and rejuvenation, in order to make them buoyant and virile as instruments of service, brooks no delay. Fast developing technologies in information transfer at the international level demand change in the institutions where information is handled. The Indian university libraries are on the threshold and they should prepare themselves to accept this challenge for a change to usher themselves into the 21st century.

4.2 *Acceptance of Responsibilities*

The participants of the IULNET should accept the responsibilities involved for the network. They are the Union and State Governments, AIU, UGC and the University authorities. Such a network should be backed by legislation, otherwise it will not work efficiently. Education being the common subject for the Central and State Governments, the Union Government may come forward with an enactment for a network cooperation among the Indian universities. The legislation should be based on the principle of coordination rather than control.
The financial component involved for such network both software and hardware may be met by the centre.

5. IULNET

The network should consist of three units. These are:

1. Central Unit;
2. Specialized Subject-based Centres; and
3. University Libraries.

The Central Unit can be located either in the UGC or AIU. It will store consolidated information in computer. It should be linked with the university libraries and Specialized Subject-based Centres with telex and other fast telecommunication facilities.

There should be Specialised Subject-based Centres for (1) Natural Sciences; (2) Applied Sciences/Technology; (3) Social Sciences; (4) Humanities; and (5) Arts. These centres have to be established in various parts of India coordinating activities in their field of specialization on the model of the Science Information Centre established by the UGC at Bangalore. Already the establishment of such centres for Humanities and Social Sciences at S N D T Women's University, Bombay, and M S University, Baroda, have been announced. These centres should be liberally provided with funds to coordinate activities and to provide various referral services.

The university libraries should be equipped to automatize some of their in-house operations and services. They should be provided with microfilming facilities, xeroxing equipment and microprocessors.

6. Tools and Operations

6.1 *The Central Unit*

(a) The Central unit should maintain a Central Union Catalogue of the total document holdings of Indian university libraries for facilitating the location of materials. Locating devices are certainly important in mobilizing the resources of the university libraries for the purpose of resource sharing.

(b) It also should have central union catalogue of periodical holdings in the university libraries. It should publish a consolidated *Indian Union Catalogues of Periodicals* (IUCOP) on the model of BUCOP and also bring out *Supplements* periodically.

(c) It should be the deposit centre for all M.Phil, Ph.D. Dissertations. A copy of all Dissertations produced in all universities should be deposited in the centre. They should be available for consultation for Indian and foreign research scholars. At the time of deposit the permission of the research scholars may be obtained to xerox for the research purposes as is the practice in the UK and USA.

(d) The Centre should publish the *Indian Dissertation Abstracts* on the model of *Dissertation Abstracts International*. It can be a quarterly or half-yearly, if not a monthly publication.

(e) The Centre should also publish *Research in Progress*. It can be an annual volume of all research topics registered for research in various universities in India.

(f) The Centre should also publish "Index to Theses" yearly as done by the ASLIB for the British University Dissertations. This is at present done by the AIU but it is not an annual feature.

(g) The Centre should be able to get Xerox copies of periodical articles not available in its own network and within India on the request of university libraries.

(h) The Centre should strive for the standardization of procedures and practices in university library operations.

(i) The Centre should conduct short courses and workshops to the university libraries from time to time in the ever changing library advances and technology.

6.2 *The Specialized Subject-based Centres*

(a) These centres should do indexing and abstracting of the documents in their specialization and supply them to university libraries.
(b) The Centres should prepare subject bibliographies for the benefit of users in the field.
(c) They should provide referral services to users.
(d) They can provide translation facilities for foreign and Indian languages wherever they are needed by the users.
(e) They should keep microfilm or microfich copies of core documents published within India and abroad in their specialised fields.
(f) They should provide SDI services to individual and corporate users.
(g) They should prepare directories of special groups and "who is who" in their specialized fields.
(h) They should help various university libraries in planning the cooperative acquisition schemes.

6.3 *University Libraries*

(a) They should agree for resource sharing liberally.
(b) They should prepare check-lists, shelf-lists, etc., of their holdings.
(c) They should equip themselves with automatic xeroxing equipments.
(d) They should bring out their list of additions, current awareness bulletins and distribute them to various university departments, and colleges and university libraries.

7. Conclusions

1. Time have arrived to sing the requiem to the isolated library collections in the Indian universities. The collections of all these libraries should be linked up to a network in order to have proper resource sharing.
2. The resource sharing implies resource acquisition by various university libraries for proper utilization of their slender resources.

3. Advances in Library and Information Science make the network system as a pre-emptive technology. The Indian university libraries should not lag behind in coordinating their holdings and adopting latest technology to render efficient and effective services, to the academic community.
4. Without the help of the network, the teaching-learning processes and the research activities in the temples of wisdom are greatly hampered and it is not on a comparable level with research in other advanced countries.

REFERENCES

1. ANDERLA, Georges: *Information in 1985: A Forecasting Study of Information Needs and Resources*. Paris, OECD, 1973.
2. ATHERTON, Pauline: *Handbook for Information Systems and Services*. Paris, Unesco, 1977.
3. INDIA, Association of Indian Universities: *National Policy on University Libraries*. Report. New Delhi, AIU.
4. INDIA, Department of Science and Technology: National Information System for Science and Technology: *Systems Analysis for Information Sciences*. New Delhi, NISSAT.
5. INDIA, Education (Ministry of,) : *Challenge of Education — A Policy Perspective*. New Delhi, 1985.
6. INDIA, Planning Commission. Working Group: *Report of the Working Group of the Planning Commission Modernisation of Library Services and Information for the Seventh Five Year Plan, 1985—90*. New Delhi, 1984.
7. THOMPSON, James : *The End of Libraries*. London; Clive Bingley, 1982.
8. WEISMAN, Herman : *Information Systems, Services and Centres*. New York; Becker and Hayes, 1972.

B 1

Research and Technical Libraries: Their Role and Problems

R S Saxena

0. Introduction

Libraries, which in the modern sense of the term are called as Human Resources Centres or Information Centres, play a significant role in improving educational standards and quality of research. Librarians traditional role and function of collecting and storage of knowledge in a helpful, systematic and scientific manner for posterity is fast changing to that of disseminators of knowledge to potential users at the time of its emergence and need without any loss of time. In other words speedy and timely access to knowledge or information to scientists, researchers and technologists is the call of the day and librarians have to meet this demand by taking the help from modern gadgets, mechanical devices and scientific inventions in electro-magnetism, photography, audio-visuals and telecommunications. The impact of this fast changing concept of library and its function is most apparent in research and technical libraries.

1. Role of Technical Libraries

"Knowledge or information is power." Information today is considered to be a basic resource for national development and for socio-economic and industrial development process. The importance of scientific and technical information hardly needs any elaboration as it has boon fully established that mere presence of technology, skill and manpower does not constitute technological progress.

The useful social goals can be achieved only if the technological hardware, the operational skills and brainwave are adequately supported by services like management of information. It is true that for the healthy growth of any industry and raising its productivity, the scientists, engineers and technologists serving in industry must be kept well informed about the latest technological advancements in that particular industry and how to overcome the problems such as market competition, labour problems, better and cheaper methods of production. Libraries, particularly those of technical universities and research organizations, which are repositories of latest knowledge and information, play a significant role in the dissemination of information among scientists and technologists.

2. Era of Information Explosion

In the modern age of science and technology documents are being published in each field with a rapidity unheard of in the past, and knowledge is doubling within a span of 10 years. According to UNESCO statistics about 600,000 documents are published each year. The annual output of information is expected to be 12 to 14 million documents which according to a recent estimate would contain nearly 72 billion pieces of information. The learned periodicals in the field of science and technology alone has now swelled to 60,000 and is increasing at the annual rate of nearly 1,000 periodicals to the existing list of periodicals, i.e., with an average of seven periodicals per day, containing over 3 million documents. Since need for information also grows at the same approximate rate as the increase in the generation of information, proper and effective information transfer devices and medias must be thought of for conserving the research potential of scientists, technologists and research workers.

2.1 *Devices for Meeting the Challenge*

For meeting the challenge of the explosion of knowledge the Librarians and Information Scientists have forged several mechanical devices, new tools and new techniques as well as resorted to resource sharing by setting up data bases and data banks on special subjects and also linking the data bases with other local, national and international data bases. Assistance of modern electro-magnetic devices such as computers, circuit T.A. telex, satellite communication, etc., is being taken for storage, quick and timely retrieval and dissemination of information to the needy and potential users.

2.2 *Modern Developments in India and Abroad*

Most of the advanced countries of the world have modernized their libraries by mechanizing their library services and introducing computerized library services such as Alert Service and Current Awareness Service, Selective Dissemination of Information Service, Information Analysis Serivce, etc. They have set up Data Bases and Data Banks on specialized subjects and hooked them with national and International Data Bases and Data Banks of other countries such as INLS (Paris), VINITI (Russia), UNISIST (UNESCO). In the USA an information industry run by commercially operated agencies which maintain their own data bases on specialised fields serves a $ 10 billion plus industry with an annual growth rate of 20 to 30 per cent. Information on or about any topic or field of specialization can be had in no time against charges depending upon the nature of service rendered or desired. In India too a humble beginning in this direction has been made under NISSAT (National Information System for Science and Technology) and agencies like INSDOC, DESIDOC, Department of Science and Technology of Government of India are making frantic efforts in setting up sectorial information centres, regional information cells and local information units and linking them with other national and international data bases and data banks with the cooperation and active support of UNESCO and UNISIST programme. Centres such as National Information Centre, Bangalore, National Social Science Documentation Centre, New Delhi, National Information Centre for Drugs and Pharmaceuticals (CDRI), Lucknow, National Information Centre for Leather Technology, Madras, National Food Information Centre, Mysore, National Information Centre for Aeronautics, Bangalore, are achievements in this direction. Presently, there exists no Engineering Information Service Centre in the country and the University of Roorkee is already trying for the same. A proposal for the same has been submitted to the UGC (Appendix). Besides the Government sponsored information dissemination agencies several private agencies like Constellate Consultants (CONCON) Allied Pub. Ltd., New Delhi; Higgen Bothain, Madras, etc. have started this activity as a commercial industry like those in the USA.

3. **Elements Responsible for Problem**

Owing to the basic difference in the role and functions of research and technical libraries from those of public and general academic libraries, the structure, set-up and services to the clientale are of a specialized nature in the former. The three basic elements constituting a library, namely; books, readers and staff, pose uniaue problems and need special solutions depending upon time, situation, occasion and place.

Let us examine each of these elements one by one and study the possible special problems posed by them in research and technical libraries and how such problems could be resolved.

3.1 *Books*

With the explosion of knowledge, the physical form in which the knowledge or information is now-a-days appearing is no more confined to the traditional form, i.e. books but is appearing in varied forms, such as periodicals, seminar or symposia proceedings, research reports, M.E. and Ph.D. theses, house journals, brochures, monographs, technical codes and standards, unpublished government sponsored research projects, engineering reports and analysis reports, microfische, micro-cards, micro-films, maps, charts, tables, gramophone records, video cassetts, tapes, computer-based information lines, etc. Since research and technical libraries mostly deal with nascent micro-unit of thoughts clothed in the aforesaid physical forms, their procurement, storage, preparation for use and dissemination to users they face special problems.

Problem		*Solution*
(A) Acquistion:	(i) Limitation of funds and cost factor	Judicious & equitable distribution of funds among different Departments and Laboratories, set principles and formulae may be evolved.
	(ii) Selection	Selection Committees may be set up in the organization
	(iii) Difficulty in procurement	Approved panel of vendors and direct ordering to publishers
	(iv) Yearly rise in cost	Budget provision proportionate to the rise in price index

(Contd.)

(Contd.)

Problem			Solution
	(v)	Price verification	Price proof from suppliers including proforma invoices
	(vi)	Accessioning of material due to language and format	Separate accession registers may be maintained
	(vii)	Duplication avoidance	Proper maintenance of order files & thorough checking prior to ordering
(B) Classification	(i)	Highly technical and specialized nature	Assistance of specialists should be sought
	(ii)	Inter-disciplinary subjects	Priority to ordering department or laboratory
	(iii)	New subjects or topics not provided in the scheme	Redesigning or modifying the scheme
	(iv)	Lamination or fusion of subjects	Selection of analytico-synthetic scheme of classification capable of hospitality in chain as well as in array
	(v)	Rapid increase and change in knowledge	Reclassification of material
(C) Cataloguing	(i)	Reports, symposia seminars	Selection of standard cataloguing code
	(ii)	Choice of subject-headings	Chain procedure and self-designed list of subject headings
	(iii)	Book No. Assignment	Physical form of the material to be mentioned
(D) Physical Preparation		Physical form and size	Each publication needs special treatment
(E) Display		Fragile and expensive	To be displayed by special means and avoid chances of losses and mutilation.
(F) Maintenance and Upkeep		Size, cost and nature of publication	To be shelved in specially designed drawers, cabinets, etc.
(G) Circulation		Size, cost, recency and nature of publication	Personnel ledger system may be designed
(H) Binding and Preservation		Size, cost, fragile nature, fast deterioration	Special binding and Preservation techniques such as fumigation and lamination of material and keeping in air-conditioned rooms.

3.2 *Readers*

The type and nature of clientele vary a lot in the technical institution and research organisation libraries. Their needs and aims in using a library also differ a lot. Since a library exists to meet the need of its all readers irrespective of their age, sex or social status the onus of serving the clientele to the maximum extent lies on the shoulders of the Librarian and this function he performs through judicious selection and acquisition of expensive and rare technical books and periodicals of their need, providing essential library services beneficial to them and even making them available the material of their demand, but not available in the library, through Inter Library Loan and Library Cooperation.

Broadly speaking, the library clientele may be divided into the following category:

(A) Undergraduates
(B) Post-graduate and Research Scholars
(C) Scientists and Technologists
(D) Faculty Members
(E) Non-Technical staff including Administative Officers

(A) *Undergraduates*: Owing to the technical books and periodicals being very expensive, their high cost compells the undergraduates to depend mostly on the resources of the libraries of their institutions. In order to familiarize the undergraduates with the library collections, its resources varied types of services and for proper use of the library, the below mentioned techniques and procedures may be adopted by technical libraries to properly serve the clientele:

(i) To run library orientation courses of long and short term duration for the undergraduates. Besides this, lectures from time to time on "How to use Library" and "Latest Library Tools, Techniques and Equipments" may be arranged by the library.
(ii) Library Guide and Library Bulletin may be published by the library.
(iii) Multiple copies of prescribed textbooks and supplementary reading books given in sylabii should be purchased by the library depending upon the number of users.
(iv) Textbook Reference section should be established where copies

of textbooks should be made available to students for consultation within the library.

(v) Book Bank or Textbook Loan Scheme be introduced for long-term loan of textbooks.

(vi) Book Reservation Facility should be provided.

(vii) A system by which library users may be informed about the loan of any book to an individual and the date of its return should be introduced in the circulation procedure.

(viii) Reference Desk should be provided in each library.

(ix) Bibliographical services should be made available.

(x) Reprographic Services at nominal cost should be provided.

(xi) The Library should remain open on holidays and its reading room should be kept open for longer hours especially during examination period depending upon the need of students.

(xii) Books on varied subjects and tastes should be made available to students so as to satisfy their curiosity and provide them recreation and a change.

(B) *Postgraduate and Research Scholars:* The need of this category of clientele is some what of a specialised nature and the library can satisfy their urge for mental food by adopting the techniques, mentioned below:

(i) To acquire latest books of specialized nature dealing with their field of the research topics of research scholars and those of specialists need.

(ii) Current and back volumes of periodicals of interest to research scholars and scientists should be acquired.

(iii) Inter-Library Loan facilities should be made available.

(iv) Resource sharing should be practised to the extent feasible in all technical libraries as an economy measure.

(v) Union Catalogues of holdings of neighbourhood libraries should be maintained.

(vi) Routing of periodicals should be done periodically.

(vii) Circulation of Accession lists among research scholars and faculty members should be done regularly.

(viii) Reproduction circulation of table of content-pages of core journals, subscribed by the library, should be done on weekly or fortnightly basis.

(ix) Documentation service should be introduced to the extent feasible.

(x) Intensive Reference and Bibliographical service should be provided to all postgraduate students and research scholars.

(xi) Library Bulletin giving information about latest acquisitions and new services of the library should be published periodically.

(C and D) *Scientists, Technologists, Specialists and Faculty Members*: This category of clientele needs special treatment. Cubicles may be provided in libraries for such category of readers and in several cases library services at their own desks should be made available to them. The following specialized services in addition to those provided to postgraduate students and research scholars should be provided to this category of library users:

(i) Current Awareness or Alert Services.

(ii) Selective Dissemination of Information Service.

(iii) Information Analysis Service.

(iv) Documentation Service including Reprographic and Translation Services.

(v) To maintain close liaison with the local, national and international data bases and Data Banks and assist the specialists and scientists with the vast resources of such agencies.

(vi) To provided modern communication system facilities such as telex, satellite communication On-Line services etc.

(E) *Non-Technical Staff Including Administrative Officers*: In order to serve this category of clientele the Library should acquire sufficient number of books of general and recreational nature like books on banking travel, description of fiction, biographies, income-tax, law etc.

4. Staff

The success or efficiency of any technical or research Library depends largely upon the quality and extent of interest in the Library work taken by the staff recruited in the libraries. Unless the services of adequate qualified staff both technically and academically are available to the library the mere presence of rich collection in the library or the availability of the latest gadgets, tools and equipments can hardly produced the desired results and render high quality of service to the clientele. Besides this library staff should work with a missionary zeal and develop a spirit of service and an attitude of open mindedness, free from conservatism and ready to adopt new and better techniques and procedures. To attract qualified youngmen full of zeal and enthusiasm to technical and research organization libraries, their status and salary should be commensurate with their qualification and experience. The existing staff should be provided ample opportunities for increasing their qualifications and brushing up their knowledge by attending refresher courses, continuing education courses, orientation lectures, seminars, conferences and visits to foreign countries.

5. Gadgets, Tools and Equipments

The technical and research libraries should not lag behind in acquiring and using the latest modern equipments, gadgets and mechanical devices. The advances of modern developments in the fields of electro-magnetism, photography, audio-visuals and telecommunication system should be fully exploited and used in such libraries so as to provide high quality of service to library clientele and to conserve the research potential from fruitless search of material or working on problems already solved elsewhere. Gadgets, like personal computers, latest models of computers with enough storage and retrieval capacities, electro-stat photo-copiers, micro-films and micro-fische reader-cum-printer, equipments for micro photography, preparation of micro-films, etc., should be made available to these libraries. Plants for preservation of documents such as fumigation and lamination plant are a must for research organization libraries. Electronic typewriters are necessary for research libraries for releasing bibliographies, etc. Air-conditioning plants should be fitted in library reading rooms and stacks so as to provide calm and cool atmosphere conducive to serious study and research. Telex, Teleprinters, Satellite Communication System facilities should be extended to library users in research organization libraries. Browsing rooms and cafetaria facilities should be provided to serious readers in all technical and research organization libraries.

6. Tribute to Prof Kaula

It is a matter of great pleasure for me to get an opportunity of expressing my sentiments and feelings about Prof P N Kaula, one of the most outstanding personalities among library scientists of the present generation and a stalwart of library profession in India. Besides being an eminent scholar of library science, he is a wonderful teacher and a fine orator. He may be called a true disciple of our Father of Library Science in India, Prof S R Ranganathan. Like Shivaji, the disciple of Swami Samarth Ram Das and Shri Narender Swami Vivekananda, the disciple of Swami Ramakrishna Prof Kaula the disciple of Prof Ranganathan, has succeeded in accomplishing the mission of his master and glorifying the image of India in the library world. Prof Kaula through his sincerity to the profession, devotion to duty and hard work has kept India's flag flying in the field of library science and filled the vacuum caused by the passing away of Dr Ranganathan. Prof Kaula has served three university libraries and college libraries, these are Birla Central Library, Delhi University Library and Banaras Hindu University Library, besides Delhi College and DAV College, Srinagar. In all these academic libraries, he has left his impact by his hard work, dedication and innovation. Much can be written by what he did and achieved in these libraries. He has set an example to be followed by others.

I happen to be in contact with Prof Kaula for the past three decades, i.e. from 1951 when I joined Delhi University and worked with Prof Kaula on a joint project of UNESCO and ILA of compilation of Union Catalogue of Scientific Periodicals in South Asia. Prof Kaula is a very hard working person with a great stamina and strong will-power. Whatever work he takes up, he never leaves it unfinished in spite of all odds, hinderances and difficulties in its completion. He strictly adheres to the principle of work-chastity enunciated and followed by Dr Ranganathan. The saying of his master, "Take up an idea, make that idea of your life, think of it, live on it and dream of it," is being rigidly followed by Prof Kaula and I think this is the key to his success in the profession and in all ventures of his life. There are very few persons in our profession who can undergo such travails and tests of life through which Prof Kaula has passed and has never lost his spirits and enthusiasm towards his profession or his assignments. Each test was an *Agni Pariksha* and proved a boon to him and he came out successfully through it. Now he is at the fag-end of his career's journey after retirement from the university service but still his zeal, interest and enthusiasm towards the profession know no bounds. I pray to God Almighty that he may live many more years of active life and keep on contributing to the enrichment of the profession. I wish him a long fruitful life free from struggles and impediments.

7. Conclusion

Libraries of research and technical institutions help in generation and dissemination of new knowledge and conservation of research potential as well as saving valuable time and energy of scientists and research workers in literature-search or doing repetitive jobs. They play a distinctive role in the communication system and through their timely dissemination of relevant and potential information to the persons concerned leads to socio-economic and industrial development of the country.

A well-equipped and well-managed library run on modern scientific lines making full use of modern scientific developments by adequately qualified librarians with a missionary zeal, enthusiasm and progressive outlook is a must for all technical institutions. The status, salary and service conditions of librarians of such libraries should be on a par with those of other scientists and technologists. At least 10% of an institution's total budget allocation should be provided for its library so that it can play its role to the fullest extent. Possibilities of resource sharing among technical and research libraries should be fully exploited so as to meet the need of each and every potential reader at the least cost.

BIBLIOGRAPHY

Saxena, R S: Periodical Section and Its Problems. *Libra*, Vol 15, 177-78, pp. 39-46.

Saxena, R S: Impact of Exponential Rate of Growth of Periodicals and Their Cost on Scientific and Technical Libraries. (In: *Seminar Papers at 26th All India Library Conference*; New Delhi, ILA, 1980).

Saxena, R S: Sectorial Information System for Science and Technology in Uttar Pradesh: A Plan. (In: *28th All India Library Conference Papers*; New Delhi, ILA, 1982, pp. 223-34).

Saxena, R S: Sharing of Resources Among Libraries. (In: *Perspective in Library and Information Science* edited by S N Aggarwal et al, Vol 2. Lucknow, Print House, 1982, pp. 19-28).

Saxena, R S: Resource Sharing Among Universities and Research Organizations Libraries in Uttar Pradesh. (In: *Fifty Years of Librarianship in India, Past, Present and Future*: Seminar Papers at 29th All India Library Conference, New Delhi. New Delhi, ILA, 1983, pp. 104-11, 231-34).

Saxena, R S: Importance of Continuing Education for Librarians and Information Scientists. (In: *Continuing Education for Librarians*: Seminar Papers New Delhi,

ILA, 1984, pp. 58-65).

Saxena, R S: Ethics of Collection Development in University Libraries. (In: *Building Library Collections and National Policy for Library and Information Services*: Seminar Papers at 30th All India Library Conference, Jaipur. New Delhi, ILA, 1985, pp. 145-53).

Saxena, R S: Librarians' Role as Guide and Stimulator to Research. (In: *Dimensions in Library and Information Science* edited by G Bhargava and A Tejomurty. Indore, Anamita Publications, 1986, pp. 70-79).

Saxena, R S: *Information Retrieval Techniques and Reference Sources and Tools in Pure and Applied Sciences*. Agra, Y K Publishers, 1987.

Saxena, R S: Quality Improvement in Library Staff. (In: *Quality in Libraries*: Seminar Papers at 32nd All India Library Conference, Anantpur. New Delhi, 1987, pp. 344-48).

APPENDIX

FORMULA FOR ALLOTMENT OF FUNDS BEING FOLLOWED AT ROORKEE UNIVERSITY

(A) **No. of Teachers/Scholars/Students**

1 No. of Faculty Staff (sanctioned strength) x 2
2 No. of Research Scholars x 2
(may be counted on the basis of actual enrolment in a year).
3 P.G. Diploma students (sanctioned strength).
M.Sc./M.Tech./M.Phil.
M.E./M.Arch ....x 1.5
4 U.G. Students (sanctioned strength)
B.E. x 1
B.Arch. x 2

(B) **Initial Funds**

1 Major departments: Rs. 50,000
2 Minor departments: Rs. 25,000
(continuing education)

More weightage to newly established departments.

B 2

International Cooperation in Human Resource Development

Marta Dosa

1. Human Resource Capability

Societal and human problems such as adequate nutrition, agricultural innovation, rural conditions of life, and access to health care need the problem solving and information production/use are determined by complex cultural and other factors. Information professionals play an important role in this process, and their effectiveness may be further enhanced by strengthening certain aspects of human resource development.

The building of human resource capabilities must move ahead simultaneously on several fronts:

(1) basic, applied and problem-focused research;
(2) formal and non-formal education;
(3) professional ethics and standards;
(4) information policies;
(5) technological skills and the abilitv to assess and select appropriate methods; and
(6) communication capacity.

1.1 *Science of Humanity*

Rene Dubos says, "Scientists must give greater prominence to large human concerns when choosing their problems and formulating their results. In addition to the science of things, they must create a science of humanity, if they want the intellectual implications and practical applications of their efforts to be successfully woven into the fabric of modern life".

The idea of "a science of humanity" is a conceptual bridge with the potential of connecting different disciplines as well as different cultures. It holds the promise of bringing together researchers, educators and decision-makers in a joint enterprise of enhancing the quality of life wherever people believe in human development.

2. Role of Human Resources

One needs to understand the role of human resources in mitigating problems of the world through the generation, transmittal and use of knowledge. In economic terms, resources are considered factors of production and basic inputs used to produce goods and services. Human resources include all forms of labour from the least skilled worker to the most highly skilled professional. The economics of information and knowledge is concerned with the optimum allocation of resources. Depending on the assumptions upon which investigations are based, human resources for the production and servicing of information and knowledge may encompass occupations ranging from telephone operators through office workers to information managers.[1]

Although the above mentioned approach to the workforce aptly reflects the vast scope of information handling in modern society, both tradition and research provide us with a more usable description of a multiprofession of information. Accordingly, information professionals include information managers, librarians, archivists, records managers, and a few other categories of information specialists. Information scientists, on the other hand, represent the theory-oriented branch of a science of information.

2.1 *Role of Practitioners*

In rapidly changing fields of professional practice, the roles of practitioners tend to diversify and branch out to the extent that the scope of each original profession is increasingly difficult to discern. In the case of such social phenomena, it is often professional education that urges upon us the self-discipline of definition and clarity. The International Symposium on Harmonization of Education and Training Programmes in Information Science, Librarianship and Archival Studies, convened by UNESCO on October 8-12, 1984, in Paris, has generated an Action Plan, noting: "There was a consensus that a conscious effort should be made towards the realization of harmonization of education and training programmes for the information professions, beginning with the library, documentation/information and archives management professions".[2]

2.2 *Agricultural Information Professional*

A delineation of the agricultural information professional (AIP) evolved from discussions at the 1980 IAALD Conference in Manila. The scope of the description includes, in addition to the above-listed information handling roles, agricultural extension officers. According to Ronchi Martinelli, " . . . we represent a cluster of professions rather that only one . . . ".[3] She supports her statement with an extensive overview of reports, documents and papers leading toward a formulation of a policy for agricultural information education.

Today, we centre on the contributions of information professionals to the dissemination and application of knowledge in several major areas of world problems. This objective in itself presents an extremely broad spectrum of information activities and policies. My paper, however, will approach this compelling perspective from a very specific point of view. It proposes an international cooperative programme to strengthen information science research and its use for problem solving in agriculture, food production and nutrition.

3. **Professional Practice, Education and Research**

The proposal is based on the following premises:

In the wake of the 1983 IAALD Conference in Nairobi, the education and training of agricultural information professionals received in-depth attention. The multiplicity of recommendations was synthesized and made widely available by Ronchi Martinelli.[3] Highlights of the conference were captured also in a report by Russell.[4] The conference papers serve as a broad foundation for implementation. Therefore, it may be efficacious to turn our thoughts to research upon which many long-range developments in professional education, practice and policy rest.

There are numerous national and international organizations which are engaged in information science and communication research bearing upon rural development and agriculture. Some are developing networks of investigators and consultants to facilitate interdisciplinary projects and the dissemination of R & D work. Examples are the International Network for Educational Information (INED) created by the International Bureau of Education (IBE) and the Transnational Network for Appropriate Technology (TRANET), which operates the TRANET Clearinghouse in Rangeley, Maine, USA. The European Coordination Centre for Research and Documentation in Social Sciences (ECSSID) in Vienna, Austria, and UNESCO's Data Retrieval System for the Social Sciences (DARE) represent resources which are highly complimentary to the specialized research information emanating from the FAO information systems. The international information community is the beneficiary of the current awareness service *R & D Projects in Documentation and Librarianship*, jointly produced by FID and UNESCO.

These are only a few examples drawn from a vast array of resources, but they readily point to two problems. Indigenous research in information science is still a rare phenomenon in developing countries. Moreover, rapid access to the right information at the right time from these rich resources is still difficult for information scientists and professionals in developing countries. There is a need for an information sharing network in the area of agriculture, food and nutrition that would address these particular problems. Instead of duplicating any of the existing collaborative programmes, it would establish links between key subject specialists in each international programme, system or network, and make this information widely known in the developing areas of the world.

4. Some Issues in Human Resource Development

From farmer education to comprehensive rural development, information in many disguises plays a key role. Using quantitative data from eighteen studies carried out in low-income countries, Lockheed, Jamison and Lau were led to the conclusion that farm productivity increased as a result of farmer education.[5]

The necessity of effective management of innovation and data in rural development projects has been widely discussed.[6,7,8] Information as a basic decision-making tool in the analysis and management of agricultural programmes was emphasized by Kulp.[9] Schubert described agricultural marketing information systems in Brazil, India and Tanzania.[10]

In the face of such diversification in the form and handling of information and data, a fundamental question arises: Where are the specialists who will not only design and manage information and data systems but will also be capable of linking systems with each other and making them accessible? Who are these professionals and what kind of education do they need?

More than a decade ago Schein's study of the professions noted incisive changes in educational trends. He recorded the "The values and needs of professional students are . . . changing as they seek ways to engage in challenging projects in their careers, as they advocate extending professional services to clients who have been historically underserved, and as they demand flexible timing for their education and a different pacing and organization of the curriculum" (p. xi).[11] The directions in professional practice which emerged in response to these educational trends in the 1970s included an increase of interdisciplinary cooperation among professionals, a tendency to emphasize social consciousness, and reforms in professional preparation (p. 7).[11]

4.1 *Professional Attitudes*

In recent years, the rate of change in professional attitudes has quickened and become more controversial. Commercial advertisement of services, collective bargaining, fear of malpractice suits, and conflicting values within the same profession became household words in the United States and are making inroads in professional practice in some other countries. With the growth of computer and telecommunication technologies, practitioners in information-related activities find themselves in the midst of new ethical questions concerning information equity, the privacy of records, computer security, intellectual property, and the exchange of scientific information.

4.2 *Professionals in Developing Countries*

While professionals in technologically advanced countries have been struggling with the complexities of changing values and client-practitioner relationships, the professions in many developing countries still face the basic problem of producing the necessary human resources. Although there is certainly no scarcity of potential practitioners, the international literature reflects grave concern about appropriate education and training programmes. Low-income societies have been hindered in developing their professional work force by the unavailability of educational opportunities, resources constraints, and the slow rate of change in curricula. Even where educational innovation has been introduced in spite of economic and technological barriers, problems of recruiting qualified teaching staff, establishing research programmes, and producing or acquiring educational materials are monumental.

These differences in professional concerns between developing and industrialized countries make the question "who are the information professionals and what kind of education do they need?" even more urgent. I would like to suggest two answers.

First, information professionals everywhere in the world are indispensable resources for national development. They are both generators and conduits of interdisciplinary knowledge and, as such, they have a momentous responsibility. Second, the education information professional's need is composed of theory and skills. Since the only activities that link theory with practice are research and dissemination, we must concentrate our energies on *Education for Creative Problem Solving*. In this sense, there are no differences between developing and technologically advanced countries.

5. **Problem Solving in Interdisciplinary Areas**

Research is often discussed as either basic or applied mode of investigation, its goal being either abstract knowledge or immediate utility. However, there is a third approach that has been neglected in the literature: problem-focused research. "In this area, the desire for knowledge is to a certain extent, linked with the desire for action" (p. 578).[12] Problem-focused research provides an appropriate framework for the study of information needs in rural development, agriculture, food and nutrition. Where the joint work of several disciplines and professions is needed to attempt solutions, the information professional can be an equal partner. This role demands not only information handling skills, but also the ability to formulate and carry out research on information problems.

A problem, suggested Bartee, may be defined as "an unsatisfied need to change a *perceived present situation to a perceived desired* situation" (p. 439).[13] The key concept here is "perception", leading to an almost intuitive identification of a problem. At least two consequences flow from this recognition. Original problem formulation, treatment and — if achieved — solution are subjective and culturally determined processes, because they depend on human assumptions about "how things are" and "how they should be". For this reason, investigation of problems in a developing country ideally should be conducted by indigenous researchers or teams which include investigators from the local culture. Because of the dominance of subjective perspectives on problems, data collection, analysis and interpretation are especially important. Apart from the possibility of data misuse or manipulation, these are objective and universal processes. Atinmo and Akinyele stated in their major nutrition policy study in Nigeria: "In particular, empirical data and conceptual frameworks are needed for understanding the social, economic, and historical determinants of malnutrition and the consequences for nutritional standards of different development strategies, public policies, institutional arrangements and technological changes.[14] The same is true for nutrition information infrastructures.

5.1 *Four Phases*

A further argument for the development of an indigenous research corps in each country can be found in Bartee's concept of a "problem solving chronology" (pp. 443-447).[13] This developmental view contains four phases:

(1) Personalization or individual problem solving;
(2) Collaboration or data exchange and joint use;
(3) Institutionalization or problem-related decision-making in organizations; and
(4) Socialization or the introduction of changes in social attitudes and norms. To this sequence, Bartee added the process of Diffusion (p. 446).[13]

Each of these dimensions of research requires an understanding of cultural assumptions in the given social environment. In information science research of either the applied or poblem-focused variety, the need for taking the cultural context into consideration is further heightened. Information professionals cannot possibly base their principles and practices on imported and unadjusted models.[15] We may conclude that true international collaboration in human resource building will be achieved only by the *Establishment and Continuous Enhancement of Research Capability* in developing countries.

5.2 *Information Science Research*

How can this be done? Education and training for information science research, sponsorship for new investigators, support of team research, increase availability of journals and conferences addressing research needs, and programmes for the transfer of research methodologies and experience come readily to mind. All are beneficial prospositions, but none assures ongoing two-way communication between researchers in developing and industrialized countries.

We can choose an approach which would effectively supplement the above methods. An international network of researchers in agricultural, food, and nutrition information would, above everything else, highlight the social significance of research. In developing countries, one of the direst problems information practitioners and educators who want to engage in research face, is working in isolation. This has been the experience of investigators, not only in information science, but also in other fields. For example, in a study of agricultural research, Murphy wrote about the training of agricultural researchers by programmes of the U.S. Agency for International Development that "the basic problems did not lie with training *per se* but with keeping the returned trainees working in research.[16]

The network would strengthen the role of information researchers in developing countries *vis-à-vis* (a) researchers in other fields and (b) researchers in other countries.

6. **The Proposal**

The purpose of international collaboration is to assure that the building of human resource capacity in each country is moving ahead simultaneously on several fronts: (1) basic, applied and problem-focused research; (2) formal and non-formal eduaction; (3) professional ethics and standards; (4) information policies; (5) technological skills; and (6) communication capacity. But it is cross-national cooperation in research that can be expected to stimulate all other activities. Therefore, the proposal is submitted as follows:

1 In cooperation with other international associations and organizations, IAALD may find it timely to initiate an international network of information professionals who are engaged in research in agricultural, food and nutrition information.

2 Using existing media such as the Quarterly Bulletin of IAALD, potential research topics, innovative methodologies, suggestions for collaboration, current projects and recent findings may be announced. For example, the "Idea Flash" column of the FID Education and Training Committee (FID/ET) Newsletter carries ideas and addresses of individuals rather than only organizations.

A data base of information (experts, projects, addresses, research reports and papers, etc.), identified by a survey and extracted from the announcements, may be created. The FID/ET Clearinghouse and other sites may be used in a cooperative pattern.

7. Conclusion

Rather than claiming to be a "first-time-ever", this proposal builds on the recommendations and experiences of experts and organizations in both collaborative research and information exchange.[17-25]

The problems in terms of funding, staffing, time constraints, different interests and different information formats cannot be denied. However, these barriers may be eliminated if three principles are observed:

(1) the network would serve knowledge and experience sharing by researchers rather than data or document sharing by formal systems;
(2) the network would not duplicate the work of any existing information system, programme or network, but will link them and researchers through contact persons; and
(3) the network would connect information professionals who are specializing in research in agricultural, food and nutrition information and thus it would not get too general and unwieldy.

Experience and research have shown that international peer networking strengthens the creative work of individuals, opens the way to alternative modes of technology transfer, cuts across different formal programmes, enhances the dissemination of research, and forestalls duplication of effort.

REFERENCES

1 ORGANIZATION FOR ECONOMIC CO-OPERATION AND DEVELOPMENT (OECD): *Information Activities, Electronics and Telecommunications Technologies.* Paris; OECD, 1982. 2 vols.

2 UNESCO, *International Symposium on Harmonization of Education and Training Programmes in Information Science, Librarianship and Archival Studies, Paris, 8-12 October 1984, Final Report.* Paris; UNESCO, 1984. (PGI-84/CONF. 801/COL. 4).

3 RONCHI Martinelli, M T: Education and Training for the Agricultural Information Professions. (*Quarterly Bulletin of IAALD*, Vol 28(3), 1983, pp. 126-151).

4 RUSSELL, H M: *Education and Training for Agricultural Library and Information Work.* Melbourn, Australia, Victoira. Department of Agriculture. 1983 (Study Tour Report Series no. 90).

5 LOCKHEED M E, JAMISON D T and LAU L J: Farmer Education and Farm Efficiency: A survey (*Economic Development and Cultural Change*, Vol 29(1), October 1980, pp. 37-76).

6 FEDER, Gershon, *et al: Adoption of Agricultural Innovation in Developing Countries, A Survey.* Washington, D C; The World Bank, 1982. (Staff Working paper 542).

7 DEBOECK, GUIDO and KINSEY Bill: *Managing Information for Rural Development: Lessons from Eastern Africa.* Washington, D C; The World Bank, 1980. (Staff working paper 379).

8 SRINIVASAN, T N: *Malnutrition: Some Measurement and Policy Issues.* Washington, D C; The World Bank, 1980. (Staff working paper 373).

9 KULP, E M: *Designing and Managing Basic Agricultural Programs.* Bloomington. (In: International Development Institute, PASITAM, 1977).

10 SCHUBERT, Bernd: *Market Information Services.* Rome; Food and Agriculture Organization, 1984 (FAO Agricultural Service Bulletin, 57).

11 SCHEIN, E H: *Professional Education: Some New Directions*, with D W Kommers. New York, N Y; McGraw-Hill, 1972.

12 BIE, Pierre de: Problem-focused research (In: UNESCO, *Main Trends of Research in the Social and Human Sciences*, Part I, Paris, 1970).

13 BARTEE, E M: A Holistic view of problem solving. (*Management science*, Vol 20(4), December, Part I, 1973, pp. 439-448).

14 ATINMO, Tola and LAOLU Akinyele: *Nutrition and Food Policy in Nigeria.* Kuru, Jos; Nigeria, National Institute for Policy and Strategic Studies, 1983.

15 CUSACK, D F: The transfer of Computer-based Technology in Agroclimate Information Systems. (*Interciencia*, Vol 6(4), July/August 1981, pp. 261-267).

16 MURPHY, Josette: *Strengtheing the Agricultural Research Capacity of the Less Developed Countries: Lessons from AID Experience.* Washington, D C; U S Agency for International Development, 1983 (Programme evaluation report 10) S18.52/4:10.

17 ABOYADE, B O: Towards a Rural Development Information System. (*Quarterly Bulletin of IAALD.* Vol 28(2), 1983, pp. 63-70).

18 DOBROV, G M, RANDOLPH R H, RAUCH W D: International Research Co-operation: The Role of Computer Assisted Communication. (*UNESCO*

Journal of Information Science, Librarianship and Archives Administration, Vol 2(2), April/June 1980, pp. 78-88).

19 FURTADO, A M: The International Network for Educational Information (INED) and the Latin American/Caribbean Participation (*UNESCO Journal of Information Science, Librarianship and Archives Administration*, Vol 5(2), April/June 1983, pp. 82-85).

20 MELKOTE, S R: In search of alternative communication strategies for rural development in the Third World: A critique of the diffusion of innovations research. July 1982 (Paper presented at the Annual Meeting of the Association for Education in Journalism, Athens, Ohio, 1982) (ERIC ED 219 754, microfiche).

21 METCALF, J R: Secondary services for developing countries (*Aslib Proceedings* Vol 36(7/8), July/August 1984, pp. 299-307).

22 MARKS A I: Some problems of networks: The case of CILO (*International Forum on Information and Documentation*, Vol 8(4), October 1983, pp. 23-26).

23 ROZSA, Gyorgy: International co-operation and trends in social science information transfer. (*UNESCO Journal of Information Science, Librarianship and Archives Administration*, Vol 2(4), October/December 1980, pp. 234-239).

24 WILDE, G R: An Educational and informational delivery network for rural intermountain communities. (*Bulletin of the American Society for Information Science*, Vol 10(5), June 1984, pp. 20-22).

25 WOOLSTON, J E: Information Exchange in a North-South Context: Is There More to Gain Through Cooperation Than in Trying to Establish New Markets ? (*Aslib Proceedings*, Vol 36(1), January 1984, pp. 7-15).

C 1

Indological Libraries: New Dimensions

Narinder Kumar

1. Scope

The subject under study is "Indological Libraries: New Dimensions". Further contemplation with the import of the canon of context leads one to the amplified title "Libraries specializing in Indology and changes therein due to new library technology or the new objectives of "Library" as a social institution." Thus in the amplified subject, the following kernel terms require explanation in detail:

(1) Library;
(2) Indological subjects;
(3) New Technology; and
(4) New Dimensions.

1.1 *Library*

The advent of "democratic" ideal in the contemporary society has given new import to "Library" as a social institution. It is at present a public utility institution meant for the improvement of the intellectual health of the community where it is located. It is no longer a storehouse of books meant for the selected few. Its portals are open to one and all.

1.2 *Indology*

The term is formed out of two constituents "Indo" and "logy" wherein "indo" is a prefix used in the sense "of India" and "logy" is a suffix being derived from the word "logos", meaning "science", "doctrine" or "theory". Further contemplation upon the word reveals that it is not only a science, it is also an art. It is a comprehensive term that includes everything related to India or having Indian origin. The subjects generally included in Indology are:

(a) Indian Astronomy, Mathematics, Chemistry and Ayurveda
(b) Indian mysticism with all its branches
(c) Indian classical literature
(d) Indian Linguistics
(e) Indian Religions
(f) Indian Philosophy
(g) Indian Art, Architecture, Culture, History, Epigraphy, Numismatics and Archaeology
(h) Indian Political and Economic Thought
(i) Indian Law Codes

Besides above-mentioned disciplines, there are certain "source exploitation" subjects, such as manuscriptology, etc., that are to be brought under the focus of the present study.

1.3 *New Technology*

The nascent technology is largely based upon convergence of interest between electronics, computing and communication with a thrust from rapid development of micro-electronics. Electronic message system can revolutionize the office activity if it is hooked with conventional activities such as telephone, telex, telegram, post offices as well as internal mail and meetings into voice store, digital exchanges, telex, teletex, computer-based electronic mail view data system, teleconferencing, etc. In document preparation activity, dictation can be passed on to central recording system, for typing, correcting, editing and producing multiple copies through word processor. The photocopying technique is the best process to follow. The new technology has made it possible to modernize the traditional activities and transform the ordinary office into that of electronic office. Satellites have also made a great impact on communication systems because of their wide-band-width with large information capacity and multiport networking. The Department of Electronics is in a process to get INSAT-1B channel dedicated to transmitting, computer data at high speed, and have asked Indian Telephone Industries to design roof-top earth stations to link government office computer terminals with

INSAT-1B. It is with this background of new technology that the Indological libraries need to be discussed afresh.

1.4 *New Dimensions*

Indological libraries have their origin as manuscript libraries started in princely States as a mark of dignity or as store houses of religious traditions attached to temples. Their collections were not open to public and the common man has no access to such materials. In free India these libraries have either become government property or part of philanthropist trusts. Another current of Indological libraries originated as a part of academic libraries at university level. This part was enriched through the University Grants Commission during the Second to Sixth Five Year Plans. In the present context, these libraries are either predominated by manuscripts or by rare and out-of-print costly books. As such these libraries have strict restrictions in use of their reading material. The new dimensions, in this context, refer to the desirable changes in the functioning of these libraries because of change in library philosophy under new environments — social as well as political — and the introduction of new information technology.

2. Indological Manuscript Libraries

The Manuscript Libraries are those libraries that have handwritten old books as their stock. These libraries started as repositories of manuscripts with a solitary function of preservation of manuscripts for posterity and also the organization of these manuscripts for modern library services. The traditional manuscript libraries have mostly been concerned with the collection and preservation of manuscripts and, as such, the organizational activity has mostly been subjective and very little has been done for maximum use of their holdings. Such libraries are concerned with the acquisition of rare manuscripts/books either through purchase or gratis. In the early stages their handwritten copying, as and when the base of the old book became brittle, was also considered the function of the library. But with the development of microfilms, microfitche techniques and reprographic machines these libraries have now enriching their collections easily by getting copies of old and rare manuscripts and books from different institutions and individuals in order to promote their maximal use.

2.1 *Indian Scene*

From the perusal of the published catalogues of manuscript libraries we find that the manuscripts in large quantities are available from Mithila (Bihar), Bengal, Orissa, Andhra, Nepal and Kashmir and in a moderate number from Maharashtra, Gujarat and Rajasthan. From other States manuscripts are available in a very small number. For their search and acquisition substantial grants are being provided by the Central Government. The prominent of the Manuscript Libraries are located in Mithila Sanskrit Shodha Samsthana (Dharbhanga), K P Jayaswal Research Institute and Bihar Research Society (Patna), in Uttar Pradesh — Akhil Bharatiya Sanskrit Parishad (Lucknow) and State Archives (Allahabad), in Maharashtra — Bharatiya Vidya Bhavan and Asiatic Society (Bombay), in Andhra Pradesh — State Art Gallery and Archives (Mylapur); in Tamil Nadu Government Oriental Manuscript Library (Madras), manuscript collection of Madras University Library and Adyar Sanskrit Library; in Bengal — Calcutta Sanskrit College, Asiatic Society, Bangiya Sahitya Parishad, Sanskrit Sahitya Parishad and in Jammu — Raghunath Temple Library. The Central Sanskrit Vidya Peeth in Allahabad, Tirupathi, Delhi, etc., is also developing manuscript collection through its regional centres spread all over India. In Varanasi Sarswati Bhawan Library is also developing manuscript collections with the assistance from University Grants Commission. In many university libraries UGC Manuscript Sections are also being developed. In manuscript of Persian scripts the noted libraries are Raza Rampur Library, Khuda Baksha Library, Patna, etc.

2.2 *Present Functioning*

In this context manuscript libraries which is a combination of the trio namely, (1) collection of handwritten old books, (2) the librarian busy in augmenting his/her stock through acquisition, then busy in preservation through different techniques and also engaged in such services which make them usable without any harm to the originals and (3) the institution of user's services where the user-scholars are busy in publishing them either in original form or comparative editions, or their transliterations and translations into favoured languages, or critical study of these works, either to propound their theories or to restore their text.

As such the manuscript libraries are not only preservers of the cultural remains of humanity but also of social institutions promoting dissemination of knowledge included in these rich remains of humanity with the help of all the modern techniques and scientific advances at the services of the scholars scattered all over the world. It is in this context that we are to conceive and promote integrated development of Manuscript Library System for the entire nation. It is not starting of a new library but to have new national and regional institutions equipped with latest machines and gadgets to integrate the stock and services of the individual libraries for the service of the entire nation.

3. Analysis

Before closing the description of Indological manuscript libraries, we must clarify the dimensions of the science of manuscripts, manuscriptology and its offshoots requiring attention by Indological librarianship. Manuscripts, unquestionably, are invaluable sources for the reconstruction of the history and culture of a country. These reveal the contemporary society and provide vital links to culture and knowledge.

3.1 *Manuscriptology*

Further contemplation upon the subject of manuscriptology reveals that it is not only a science, it is also an art. It is a comprehensive term that includes everything related to a systematic scientific study of manuscript, i.e. handwritten old books. It includes within its purview searching and acquisition as well as preserving and publishing of handwritten old books. The basic emphasis of the subject is to make individual collection of handwritten old books accessible to one and all. The methods involved are: to search and to acquire and then to preserve and disseminate through publishing. Descriptively speaking manuscriptology concerns collection, collation, critical and comparative editing by going through the variant readings (pathantras), also subject wise classification, conservation and chemical treatment, purging of the interpolations, rectification of errors (grammatical, metrical or otherwise), tracing the missing portion or changes caused intentionally or inadvertently, deciphering the script properly, understanding the abbreviations and symbols used in manuscripts, ascertaining the purpose of writing (such as presentation to or patronage of somebody or for the continuance of knowledge), establishing the chronology or date of composition of the original work and the copyist (by means of evolutionary cycle of alphabets, linguistic developments and quotations from the earlier or contemporary authors cited in the text concerned), and many other tasks for judicious utilization of the handwritten old books.

As we view the subject today it may include the following branches:

(1)	Acquisitions:	(i) Search (ii) Purchase (iii) Gratis (iv) Deposits (v) Loan
(2)	Repair and Care:	Two agencies – National Archives of India, New Delhi and National Laboratory for Preservation and Restoration of Arts, Lucknow.
(3)	Processing for use:	Classification, Cataloguing, Ecology, Inter Library Loan, etc.
(4)	Augmenting user activities:	Transcription, Transliteration, Photocoyping, Microcopying, etc.
(5)	Publishing:	In original form or transliteration in favoured scripts, critical edition based upon different recensions, commentaries and critical studies of these.

The first four branches are within the purview of the Manuscriptology for libraries, the fifth branch is related entirely with the "Scholar and the Manuscript". The latter discipline is looked after by the formal education being imparted at postmaster and pre-research degree by some of the universities, i.e. in M.Phil. courses in classical literature departments. It is relevant also because it includes interdisciplinary highly technical subject in its portals such as epigraphy including paleography and calligraphy, linguistics and poetics as well as dramaturgy. But, it is the former four branches that require due consideration at Library Science education level.

4. Services

It is lamented by scholars that the Indological libraries are reluctant to allow them to handle these manuscripts for fear that their pages may be stolen or damaged. The solution suggested by the scholars themselves is to make several photo-copies of each manuscript and these can be made available to scholars. This can also help the collection of all such manuscripts (writings) and rare as well as out of print costly books in one place.

Transliteration facilities are the second prerequisite for proper utilization of these libraries. Even transcribing of a manuscript on demand in a current and favoured script can help the research activities based upon manuscripts. The acquisition of manuscript is not like an ordinary activity, it is rather a literary detective work which is difficult one and requires special acuemanship.

5. Purpose, Goals and Objectives

The Indological libraries as obtainable at present have now extended their areas of activities to:

(a) Collection and selection of reading material appropriate for library use.
(b) Preservation of reading material for posterity.
(c) Organization of reading material for modern library services.

The traditional Indological libraries have mostly been concerned with the collection and preservation of material and as such the organization activity has been subjective. The basic function of the modern library as a constituent of social education in a democratic form of government is the socialization of reading material for study and research. However, while planning for their new dimensions, we may have to make them responsible for their cooperative contribution towards benefiting the society as their clientele all over the country.

5.1 *Role of Government*

At present the role of Government towards the healthy growth of Indological libraries is passive. It is mainly the Central Government as well as the State governments who provide grants for the maintenance and growth of supporting materials. But, the grants for the organizational staff are not compatible with the role that these libraries are supposed to play. Some of the Indological libraries with insufficient funds are passing through a crisis for survival. At present there is no national policy for the utilization of the reading material being acquired or being maintained by the individual Indological libraries, or the manuscript collections of university libraries.

In India, there is no national policy of exchange of information regarding availability of Indological Literature from one library to another nor is there any governmental agency engaged in such a communication policy which is vital for integration of services in these libraries. There are no separate figures available for the total amount spent on manuscriptology and Indological research in the country, for it is always merged into total budget outlay for education. In finance it has no independent existence and as such the resources are scattered, indefinite and non-ascertainable.

5.2 *Service to Users*

The only service available to users, and that too only in case of nationalized manuscript Indological libraries is free consultation of material within the library premises. Some of the libraries are having the service of supply of transcripts of manuscripts and of rare reading material at cost rates. Recently a few libraries having acquired reprographic apparatus have started the supply of reprographs on demand against cost rates. The provision of reprographic units to the individual libraries, at least one in a town, providing reprographs at subsidized rates, is the basic need. Another important service that requires immediate addition is transliteration facilities.

5.3 *Staffing Pattern and Development*

The available staffing patterns are differential and partial. The librarian appointed is usually a graduate in library science supported by non-professional staff having some oriental qualifications, e.g. the Madras Government is providing the librarian-incharge, a professionally qualified person supported by a few posts of pandits having oriental qualifications. The need is that an Indological manuscript library should be charged with the functions of the provision of all modern library services, there should be a set of norms for providing an input of. professional, semi-professional and non-professional staff as per workload of services acquisition as well as organization of reading material.

One of the basic suggestions that may be included among new dimensions is founding of five specialized regional training schools of manuscript librarianship. The trainees be offered financial assistance to undergo the specialized courses. At the apex there should be a national centre engaged in research activity to harness the benefits of new information technology and which is most relevant and useful for the organization of reading materials and modernization of the various functions of Indological libraries. It may be conditioned as an ecological study in global development of new information technology. To attract proper manpower, the trained graduates must be provided with proper financial compensation while being on job with benefits in service conditions as well as bright promotional avenues while working in the field.

6. Problems of New Dimensions of Indological Libraries

On the basis of foregoing discussions, we may recognize the following issues:

(1) The problem of acquisition, organization and use of collections in Indological libraries are formed with the following facets in view:

  (a) Subject area specialization,
  (b) Multilingualism; and
  (c) Lack of reference tools for selection of Indological materials

(2) Lack of knowledge of the ecology and preservation of Indological reading material.

(3) Lack of uniform standardization of terminology in documentation, preparation of descriptive cataloguing and classification (subject headings) of Indological literature.

(4) Lack of automation and bibliographical control of Indological reading material in all forms, nascent as well as old, with the help of new information technology.

(5) Lack of norms and standards for Indological libraries for

  (a) Staff
  (b) Finance

(c) Reading Material
(d) Building
(e) Library Services

(6) Lack of curriculum innovations in Indological librarianship in schools of library science.

(a) Teaching
(b) In service training programme both core and advanced types.

(7) Lack of uniform national policy of Integrated National Indological Library system with a network of regional centres for feeding the needs of States with the cooperation of NICNET or INDONET.
(8) Lack of determination of priorities and planning strategies; coordination between Indological library services, manuscript research; and publication materials of the existing Indological Libraries in the country.
(9) Lack of self-evaluation methodology for the Indological libraries.
(10) Lack of identification of area studies in researches.
(11) Lack of computerized users orientation programmes.
(12) Lack of national policy of documentation and information retrieval system.
(13) Lack of inclusion of manuscript librarianship in All-India Oriental and Indian Library Association Conferences.
(14) Lack of Fellowships in Indological librarianship under Cultural Exchange Programmes.

Broadly speaking, the above-stated problems can be classified into five major heads:

(a) Acquisition
(b) Processing
(c) Circulation and Reference
(d) Management
(e) Education and Training

7. The Solutions

The first two National Conventions of Oriental Libraries recommended:

(1) A central agency for the promotion of Oriental Libraries be established by the Government of India with an objective to:

(a) make National and Statewise survey of manuscripts resources and devise a programme for their proper utilization.

(b) bring out a comprehensive directory of Oriental collections scattered inside and outside India.

(2) An Integrated National Oriental Manuscript Library System be evolved:

(a) by enacting a suitable law to get all the scattered Oriental manuscript material deposited with the nearest centre of the system. It is suggested that the Government of India, Ministry of Education and Culture be requested to enlarge the scope of the Indian Antiquities Act to ensure the collection of manuscripts.

(b) by encouraging the private owners to get their collections deposited voluntarily with the nearest centre of the system or with any institutions they desire.

(c) by acquiring the privately managed libraries or collections through the purchase of original manuscripts or their reprographs deposited with the nearest centre of the system.

(d) It is suggested that the Government of India, Ministry of Education and Culture, be requested to provide funds for workshops at suitable institutions for specialized training of manuscripts librarianship.

(3) Special training for manuscript libraries be conducted at the following levels:

(a) National Archives of India be requested to conduct special short-term courses in manuscripts preservation techniques for manuscript libraries.

(b) National Archives of India be also requested to produce necessary literature on care, repair and preservation of manuscripts and rare books, etc., through indigenous and modern techniques in all the Indian languages.

(c) The Department of Library Science in Indian universities, especially universities pledged for the Indological studies, may include a special paper on administration of Oriental Libraries and Manuscriptology.

(d) It is suggested that the Union Government may be requested to provide funds for workshops at suitable institutions for specialized training of Oriental manuscript libraries.

Thus, Indological Librarianship provides for a vast area of library development, application of modern technology, unearthing of the past with vital dynamic services in an integrated mode of development and human resources through concerted efforts and proper planning and of course substantial financial input.

8. Conclusions

Thus, we arrive at a point where from we can visualize the areas of application of new technology in the Indological librarianship providing new dimensions to this highly specialized field.

8.1 *For Published Catalogue of Manuscripts*

Manuscript catalogues are usually published and require uniformity in standards to arrive at the stage of developing a Union Catalogue through machine readable information techniques, especially for the descriptive one. Therein, the reprographs of the first and the last page of the manuscript, if given, shall provide for the actual feel of the script as well as the language of the enlisted manuscripts. This will definitely help the researcher located at distance. Further, placement of these libraries in a computer-aided network shall further augment the use of manuscript collection of Indological libraries.

8.2 *Indological Classification Scheme*

There is a need for an analytico-synthetic depth classification scheme for individual Indological subjects which has computer compatibility to utilize modern subject indexing techniques with the help of machines.

8.3 *Critical Editing*

The boredom of repetitive job of copying all the recensions of a manuscript must be done away with through "word processor" especially designed for the purpose of better speed, efficiency and accuracy.

9. INMALIS

The author proposed as early as 1973 an Integrated National Manuscript Library and Information System (INMALIS) and published his views in "Library and Librarian", Raipur (1977). For "Indological Libraries: New Dimensions" in the present context, the idea can be further developed to include all the Indological libraries thus creating an Integrated system wherein resource sharing among member libraries is more practical. In order to realize this objective the Indological library system with national library at the apex be linked with NICNET/INDONET and terminals in regional as well as individual large Indological libraries.

The suggestions regarding "Resource sharing among Manuscript Libraries" are available in *I.L.A. Bulletin*, Delhi (1978). Points to add are application of computer as well as reprographic technology to the concept of resource sharing exploiting electronic communication techniques.

D 1

Teaching of Information Science in the Southern African Development Coordination Conference (SADCC) Sub-region: Conformity or Diversity ?

Maurice C Lundu

1. Introduction and Emphasis

I am writing on this topic with no pretensions at all because I have no first-hand experience of teaching Information Science in the Region under review, let alone anywhere in the world. The most I can claim is that I have, during the past 15 years or so, given serious thought to this subject in the face of current trends taking place in the field somewhere else and their implications to our own peculiar situation. I can also claim familiarity with the Region in which I have been working as an academic librarian for the past 15 years — a period in which I have risen from a trainee librarian to University librarian at the University of Zambia.

During this period, I have tried to maintain some acquaintance with colleagues, both at home and abroad, engaged in the study and teaching of Information Science; one of such distinguished colleagues happens to be Prof P N Kaula who is being honoured by the publishing of this volume. At the outset, therefore, I would like to pay tribute to all those who have devoted their energies to studying all aspects of Information Science and to searching ways of applying its theories to the problems of African development. At this juncture, I would like to single out some national and international agencies, notably the International Development Research Centre (IDRC), Information Division (Canada) which has a regional office in Nairobi, Kenya; the German Foundation for International Development (DSE); the British Council; the American Information and Cultural Centres; UNESCO, IFLA, FID, and ICA all of which have been contributing positively to the understanding of what Information Science is in the context of SADCC Sub-region.[1]

2. The SADCC Sub-Region: The Information Environment

According to the Lusaka Declaration signed by the Heads of States and Governments in April 1980, nine independent countries of Southern Africa formed what is now known as the Southern African Development Co-ordinating Conference (SADCC). These countries are: Angola, Botswana, Lesotho, Malawi, Mozambique, Swaziland, Tanzania, Zambia and Zimbabwe. Namibia is expected to be the tenth member once she becomes independent from South Africa. Two of these States namely; Angola and Mozambique are former Portuguese colonies; while the other seven are Brittish colonies. This means that two foreign languages, i.e., English and Portuguese, are the languages used in official communication and deliberations.

2.1 *The Development Objectives of SADCC*

The development objectives of SADCC are stated as follows :

(1) The reduction of economic dependence, particularly, but not only on the Republic of South Africa;
(2) The forging of links to create a genuine and equitable regional integration;
(3) The mobilization of resources to promote the implementation of national, interstate and regional policies; and
(4) Concerted action to ensure international cooperation within the framework of our strategy for economic liberation.[2]

While it is true to some extent to suggest that the nine countries making up SADCC appear to exhibit similar levels of development or underdevelopment since they are all referred to as "developing countries of the Third World", it will certainly be a flagrant exaggeration of the real development environment. These countries are not certainly a homogeneous development block.

2.2 *Urbanization*

For example, in terms of urbanization, one tends to view both Zambia and Zimbabwe as being more urbanized than say Botswana, Lesotho, Malawi, Swaziland and to some degree Tanzania. The reason is simply that Zambia and Zimbabwe engage in mining economic activities that require a large concentration of population in one area. The other countries (with the exception of perhaps Angola and Mozambique) do largely depend on agricultural economics. Hence, their populations are scattered throughout the rural areas. In a way Zimbabwe is involved in more intensive farming than Zambia is. This state of affairs means, therefore, that even economic, social, scientific and technological development will tend to follow a similar pattern, although at the moment Zambia is trying very hard to diversify her economy from 90% dependence on copper to agro-industries and tourism. I believe that other SADCC States are involved in drawing up new developmental priorities to perhaps emphasize current resource mobilization — human, financial and natural — so as to achieve genuine economic self-sufficiency, the SADCC member States realize that other factors such as education, international assistance, political education, utilization of such resources as technical and scientific information and knowledge generated from within and outside the region will play a crucial role in the Region's desire to bridge the gap between the rural poor and the relatively urban rich. In other words, the priority in SADCC's development effort is to reduce the imbalance between rural and urban areas. How will Information Science Education contribute to this balancing act between rural and urban areas?

2.3 *Attitudes and Beliefs*

This very important question brings me to another aspect deemed to be critical in the teaching of Information Science (however defined) in this Sub-region. It has to be stated very vigorously that the idea of regarding information as a national resource or a commodity capable of transforming social, economic, scientific and technological structures has not strongly been recognized by decision- and policy-makers in particular. The current attitudes, thinking, beliefs, values, etc. are all rooted in the ancient past whose tradition did not encourage the utilization of recorded knowledge. The library was introduced in this type of society as supporting a foreign culture dominated by a colonial power which tended to degrade any type of ancient African knowledge perhaps because such knowledge was never recorded and transmitted to the present generation in any permanent records. In the process, the modern African information specialist within our Region has now come to depend more on information and knowledge generated, processed and organized for him outside his own immediate environment. Even contemporary African belief system appears to continue mystifying such African knowledge and practices as witchcraft, herbalism, traditional medicine, peasant farming and oral exchanges of ideas especially among the rural population. It is this kind of conditioning that must be addressed to in our attempts to teach Information Science in the kind of environment that I have tried to emphasize up to this point.

This then leads me into an area that everyone listening has some idea about. We are all supposed to be Information Scientists and that is why we are attending the American Society for Information Science Convention here in Las Vegas. However, we must accept that we have all come with our own individual conception of what we believe Information Science is and how it should be taught in our own respective environment. It is not my intention to try to sway anybody to my own thinking and understanding of Information Science. Suffice to underscore the point that I have very good reasons — reasons that will be made clearer in the course of this paper — for subtitling my paper : *Conformity or Diversity?* The emphasis given to the SADCC environment in the preceding section in which my kind of Information Science Education should take place is indeed deliberate because I am convinced that the teaching of Information Science can never take place in vacuum and in the isolation of the prevailing socio-economic, cultural, political, scientific, technological infrastructure of a particular region and a specific stage on a time scale.

3. Information Science: What is It?

Reading innumberable articles in journals and books discussing issues relating to this topic, I get the feeling that there is something called Information Science. In fact, the presence of a professional body like the ASIS is a clear testimony that Information Science as a field of study does indeed exist. However, I have discovered that there is something on which there has been no universal agreement among experts; and this is what constituted the body of knowledge that we refer to as Information Science. Is it a body of facts? Is it a methodology? Is it a conflict between Western discipline and belief system and what I would like to refer to as "African Liberation Librarianship" which is currently attempting to stress its relevance to and relate itself to African cultural, psychological and monistic conception of the World? As it happens, the Americans, Germans, Russians, English, French, Chinese, Japanese and Africans in general all have different ideas about what that something they want to call Information Science in fact is. This is a very critical issue on which I am not at the moment qualified to comment.

For the purpose of this presentation though, I intend to confine my comments on Information Science as a personal thing — meaning essentially that each one of us conceptualizes Information Science from his/her own personal standpoint which in many cases is influenced by what Sereno and Bodaken [3] refer to as "the Internal System" and "the External System". In their own words, "The Internal System is composed of all those elements that taken together make up a unique individual. Examples of elements making up the Internal System are an individual's personal traits, his past experiences — the whole inner psychological and intellectual complex".

While "the External System is composed of those elements that exist in the environment outside the individual. Examples of elements in the External System are such things as the particular words used in a message, the physical gestures of the communicators, the sound and scents surrounding the communicators, even the temperature of the room".

3.1 *Environmental Factor*

Those of you with searching minds will immediately perceive the kind of limitations and restrictions imposed upon how Information Science as a body of knowledge should be interpreted and taught in different socio-economic, political, cultural, technological and even in particular institutional environments of the world (the External System). In any case, the environment I am concerned with at the moment is the Southern African Development Coordinating Conference (SADCC) briefly described in the first section of this paper.

Armed with the reality of this particular environment which I believe provides the "External System" and my own "Internal System" as conditioned by my own experiences, intellectual orientation and professional education and training, I am now in a position to attempt the definition of Information Science as I perceive it and as it is currently being taught at two institutions in the Region under review.

These institutions are: the University of Zambia and the University of Botswana.

3.2 *Meaning*

Out of the multitude of definitions of Information Science one comes across in the literature, I think the one that meets the purpose of this paper is the following :

> "Information Science is the systematic study of information production or generation, its organization and transfer from a source to an actual or potential user regardless of the nature and character of such information and without undue emphasis on the channel through which such information is being transmitted or transferred."

Admittedly, this definition is not without its own flaws. Just like any other scientific concept, it may have its limitations in its universal interpretation and application. Indeed, that is the point I want to stress in this paper. Diversity of opinion and conceptualization contributes very much to what T S Kuhn refers to as "Scientific Revolution" which is the cornerstone of the growth of knowledge.[4] In so far as the teaching of Information Science at both the University of Zambia and the University of Botswana in the SADCC Region is concerned, I intend to concentrate my analysis on the interpretation of this definition.

4. Information Science Programmes in the SADCC Region

As indicated in the opening paragraph of this paper, my competence to discuss this issue stems from my familiarity with the Region. This familiarity is not only confined to my own native country, Zambia, for at various time in my professional career so far, I have managed to visit Tanzania, Kenya, Uganda, Malawi and Zimbabwe; and in the course of preparing this particular paper, I will able to visit Botswana and Lesotho under the sponsorship of the International Development Research Centre, Information Division (Ottawa, Canada), which has a regional office for Eastern and Southern Africa in Kenya. The only countries I have not been to in this Region are the two Portuguese-speaking countries: Angola and Mozambique, and the other one being Swaziland. In addition, I have met and shared ideas with most professional colleagues in the Region at various forums.

In the context of SADCC Region, the first institution to establish anything close to what can be called Information Science Department was the University of Zambia in 1967. The author is proud to inform the readers that he was the first product from this programme in 1969. Since then, several countries within the Region have expressed interest in mounting Library and Information Sciences programmes at both national and regional levels. At the moment, however, only Botswana has set up her own programme explicity to cater for Botswana, Lesotho and Swaziland. This programme came into existence in 1978.

On the Regional level, I can only think of a post-graduate school being proposed to be established in Ethiopia at the University of Addis Ababa. Again, IDRC and Unesco are directly involved. However, Ethiopia is, for the purpose of this paper, outside the Region under consideration and therefore I intend to say no more about this proposed programme. Consequently, the remarks that follow relate strictly to the situation currently obtaining at the Universities of Botswana and Zambia.

Before plunging myself into a detailed discussion on the analysis of the type of information science education being offered at these two institutions, perhaps, a word of warning at this juncture would be in order. Although according to my letter of invitation to present a paper at this session I was warned not to focus on library science education (as probably opposed to Information Science), I am certainly in great difficulty in trying to completely keep away from any temptation to fall into the trap of talking about Library Science instead of Information Science Education for three very good reasons :

(a) I am myself a product of Library Science education from the University of Zambia.
(b) The founders of these two programmes were themselves products of the traditional library Science Education (which is now under close scrutiny) in their own countries, e.g., Britain and America.
(c) Traditionally, the information environment is one that has relied very much on oral exchange of information and knowledge. The kind of Library Science Education worth talking about is basically an imposition from developed social, economic and technological External Systems. Hence, Information Science Education in such an environment does inevitably revolve

around questioning the value and relevance of Traditional Library Science Education in an emerging and changing value system with its attendant, new social, political, cultural, economic, scientific and technological problems.

It is in the light of these three relevant reasons that I am inclined to concur with Saracevic, Braga and Afolayan pertinent observation when they write :

> "The formal, academic teaching of information science in developing countries is provided almost exclusively within the framework of library schools and library curricula. Where information science is taught, it is represented mostly by one or two survey courses; there are very few programmes of specialization in information science providing any array of courses in the subject"[5].

Those information science educators well acquainted with developing countries teaching programmes will no doubt agree that this observation describes objectively and poignantly the kind of Information Science programmes assoicated with academic institutions in most developing countries. The two institutions under discussion are certainly no exception to this general rule. We begin with the programme at the University of Zambia.

4.1 *University of Zambia, Department of Library Studies*

Estabilshed in 1967 with the assistance of UNESCO, this is the oldest department in the Region. It is a department within the Faculty of Education. It is not a School or Faculty on its own as is the case in American system of higher education. It is obviously modelled on the British pattern. That is a major limiting factor in the way one defines the scope, content and development of the subject field in so far as the teaching of Information or Library Science is concerned.

As a department within a faculty, it boasts of only five full-time lecturers, three of whom are Zambians who obtained their first degrees at the University of Zambia itself and then went for their masters degrees in the United States. In fact, two of the Zambian lecturers are currently in the United States pursuing their Ph.D. degrees. Unfortunately, none of these lecturers appears to have a natural science subject background.

According to the 1984-85 Department of Library Studies handbook, the scope of what is taught there is defined thus :

"Librarianship relates to those activities which are concerned with the selection and acquisition of reading materials appropriate for libraries; preservation, organization, storage, interpretation, retrieval, dissemination and exploitation of such materials for the purpose of acquiring and assimilating the knowledge contained in them. This, in a nutshell, is what librarianship is all about."[6]

Does this definition of librarianship fall short of my definition of Information Science given earlier? Perhaps it does especially that it says little on the production or generation of information and confines itself to the selection and acquisition of "*reading materials*". However, in terms of retrieval, dissemination and exploitation of such materials in order of satisfy Zambia's varying information needs, this definition of librarianship is broad and flexible enough to include aspects relating to Information Science Education. It is the unique pedagogical approaches and the needs of the region that are the major constraints in attempting to introduce typical Information Science courses into what seems pure Library Science programmes.

The other point worth noting here is that the Department of Library Studies offers two programmes, namely, the semi-professional non-post-graduate diploma and the first degree programme which has been expanded to make it possible for one to major in library studies as well as in another subject field such as economics, sociology, chemistry, etc. We have a Bachelor of Arts or Science with Library Studies (B.A.L.S or B.Sc.L.S).

According to the handbook quoted above, graduates from such a programme are expected to work in various types of libraries : public, academic, special and school libraries and in any other types of libraries not readily identified with the traditional ones mentioned above. This is the market that seems to offer prospects to those graduating with B.A.L.S. Again, such a situation imposes its own restrictions on suitable pedagogical approaches to the teaching of information science in this Region. The kind of pedagogical approaches being used in countries like Europe, USA, Canada, USSR or Japan will appear to the totally out of context in a Region whose cultural, economic and above all technological base is totally different and rather evolving. Zambia is gradually accepting this view especially at the time when there is such a dearth of reading material in the country due to its poor state of economy.

4.2 *University of Botswana Department of Library Studies*

According to the 1984-85 handbook, the Department of Library Studies at the University of Botswana came into being in 1978 within the Faculty of Humanities. The location of this Department within the Faculty of Humanities seems to be a major departure from the usual arrangement found in many Universities especially in Britain where Library Studies Departments are found within the Faculty of Education.[7]

Apart from this particular observation, one tends to think that the Department of Library Studies at the University of Botswana follows patterns similar to the one at the University of Zambia. Both of them began with the certificate and diploma programmes although the University of Zambia dropped its certificate programme in 1971.

The Department of Library Studies at the University of Botswana currently offers two programmes, namely, a certificate programme lasting one year and a non-graduate diploma programme lasting two years. During my visit there, I was informed that the Department has plans to introduce a Postgraduate Diploma Programme to last one academic year and indications are that some library science elective courses will be introduced at the undergraduate level.

However, the logic of introducing a Postgraduate Diploma Programme instead of a Master's Programme at the time such a Postgraduate Diploma programme is gradually being phased out in most institutions in developed countries and it could probably be debatable. The department of Library Studies in Botswana should well be advised to reconsider this move and introduce a Masters' Programme right from the start. It is important that the Programme attracts good graduates so as to earn academic recognition in an environment that tends to emphasize academic credentials rather than what one can do with such credentials.

Currently, only Library Science courses similar to ones being taught at the University of Zambia are included in the two programmes. However, if the proposal to mount the Postgraduate Diploma Programme this academic year (1986-87) materializes, it is anticipated that courses with "Information Science" content will formally be introduced.

Meanwhile, the Department of Planning to include an aspect of Information in the title of the Department. It is intended to have the Department read as follows: either Department of Library and Information Studies or simply Department of Information Studies.

It is gratifying to note that my former University in England changed its title from Postgraduate Department of Librarianship to the Department of Information Studies, University of Sheffield, in 1981. This trend of associating information to any department or school dealing with all aspects of human communication, information and the growth of knowledge appears to augur well for the profession of Information Science. As I pointed out in the definition of Information Science above, it is the generation or production, organization, dissemination and utilization of information that defines the scope of Information Science, however, one cares to interpret it. The Department of Library Studies at the University of Botswana is on the right track despite the fact that its information technology infrastructure is not as developed as the one in the United States or Europe.

5. General Observations on these Two Programmes

Looking at the scope and content of the programmes being offered in the two Departments of Library Studies, one perceives the following general observations and conclusions :

(1) Both these two programmes have their grounding in the traditional Library Science education introduced and imposed upon them by circumstances dictated to by the institutions from outside both in terms of personnel and philosophical perspective. Their is very little Information Science content as understood in more technologically developed countries of the Northern Hemisphere.

(2) There are peculiar problems relating to obtaining the necessary educational resources to support these programmes due mainly to the general storage of financial resources and qualified personnel. There is also a great deal of dependence upon outside resource materials, human and financial. Saracevic *et al* have ably identified these problems in their paper referred to earlier.[8]

(3) The introduction of Information Science Education is

considered as an evolutionary trend that must have its roots in and links with the traditional Library Science Education. However, the Department of Library Studies at the University of Botswana seems to be more dynamic and ready to move into a new era by accepting that the information component must form the basis of an emerging new concept of Information Science Education in this Region; while the Department of Library Studies at the University of Zambia still remains conservatively clung to the same traditional ways of teaching the subject.

(4) Both these two institutions look like being totally aware of the fact that whatever new approaches to the teaching of information Science may be introduced, they will inevitably be hampered by the overriding absence of appropriate technological infrastructure and by the general lack of appreciation of the role of Information Science in the development of this Region.

(5) To keep current with developments in the field with the rest of the world is a major obstacle – one that perhaps will make it almost impossible for these two institutions to steadfastly move away from the traditional Library Science Education. Certainly, an infusion of new ideas from outside should be accepted as an important and crucial aspect of keeping up to date with new knowledge. At the moment, these two institutions are almost isolated from one another and from what is happening overseas unless one has a chance to attend a conference or short course outside the Region. That is why my presence here offers me such a unique opportunity to exchange ideas with colleagues from other parts of the world. This type of get-together is certainly lacking in my own environment.

(6) Training of indigenous personnel seems to be foremost among the priorities of these two institutions. This is a recommendable policy and one that must be encouraged at all cost.

The reason is simply that unless trained local manpower is available, it will be difficult to introduce Information Science programmes that will be relevant and responsive to the needs of the Region. Only indigenous experts will be able to interpret and apply knowledge acquired from foreign institutions in the best interest of the Region. However, it is urged that such programmes must put emphasis on flexibility that will encourage ready response to new situations or problems. Flexibility will offer a variety of approaches toward the solution of information problems. The new Information Science teacher and the Information Science student must all be flexible, have an open mind and be able to apply their knowledge to new ideas emanating from within and outside the Region.

6. Summary

The subject I have been trying to tackle is so wide and so involving that I cannot claim to have exhausted it or done justice to it. However, my emphasis has been on the environment in which the Information Science as defined in this paper is meant to be taught because I am totally convinced it is this environment that determines the scope, methodology and curricula of the field. Information Science or any other branch of knowledge is never taught in isolation or in complete oblivion of the social, cultural, economic, political, scientific and technological conditions currently obtaining in a particular environment. I hope that his nebulous and amoebic body known as Information Science is not a new philosophy to be forced upon cultures, in the SADCC Sub-region. I hope instead that out of the people, the culture the Library and Information Science institutions and the community at large will become a synthesis of the indigenous philosophy augmented and contributed to by relevant research and inventiveness created from individual's and society's needs — the local brand of Information Science.[9]

My plea in this paper has been to accept and to advance the now universally tested view that there is "unity in diversity". Our approach to the teaching of Information Science in different Regions of the world may appear divergent, but our goal must inevitably be seen to be the same — Information Science Education in the service of all mankind regardless of our stages of development. Perhaps, the introduction of a Master's Programme being contemplated at the University of Zambia would incorporate this philosophy into the overall objective of teaching this field of knowledge in a developing environment.

REFERENCES

1 Southern African Development Co-ordinating Conference. Blantyre, 1981.

2 SADIS : a study report on the feasibility of a Southern African Documentation and Information System. Unpublished report of a study mission undertaken from February 19 to April 12, 1983 at the request of the Government of Zimbabwe on behalf of SADCC States.

3 SERENO Kenneth K and BODAKEN Edward M: *Trans-Per: Understanding Human Communication.* Boston, Houghton Mifflin, 1975.

4 KUHN, Thomas S: *Structure of Scientific Revolutions.* Chicago, University of Chicago Press, 1970.

5 SERACEVIC, T BRAGA G M and AFOLAYAN M A : Issues in Information Science Education in Developing Countries. (*Journal of American Society for Information Science,* Vol (3), May 1985, pp. 192-199).

6 University of Zambia, Department of Library Studies Handbook 1984/1985, Lusaka, 1984.

7 University of Botswana, *op cit* Gaborone, 1984.

8 SARACEVIC T, *et al. op cit*, pp. 196-97.

9 GILBERT P G S and LOVEGROVE M N Ed. *Science Education in Africa*; a report of . . . London, Heinemann, 1972.

D 2

Evaluation of Library and Information Science Courses in India

Bhawanath Mishra

0. Introduction

Library and Information Science has become an important branch of education in our modern age. Various universities and institutions in the world have recognized its importance and have started training programmes in this important field of education at different levels. Thousands of students now seek admission to this field of education every year.

1. Pre-Independence Period (1911–47)

1.1 *In-Service Training*

The first formal course for training in librarianship in India was started in 1911. Prior to this there was some sort of In-service Training in Library routines in some of the larger libraries, such as the university libraries, established in the 19th century. However the existence of such training in the Imperial Library (Now the National Library), organized by John Macfarlane, the first Librarian from this Library from 1901 to 1906. In subsequent years the training programme was opened to the staff of other libraries and even to non-librarians.

1.2 *Baroda School*

Baroda and its enlightened ruler Maharaja Sayajirao Gaekward has the credit for initiating a programme of free public library service throughout the State in the first decade of this century. The credit for starting the first formal training course in library routine also goes to this State. In 1910, William Alanson Borden, an American Librarian – a student of Melvil Dewey, who was trained under the guidance of Charles Ammi Cutter at Boston Athenaeum was appointed Director of the State Library Department. In 1911, Borden started a Library Training Course in order to support the library development programme of the State with trained personnel. The course was begun at the Central Library, Baroda. The first batch consisted of 10 men and women of "high ability". They received training "in the theory and practice of Librarianship" for a year. This was followed by another year of practical work in the Central Library. In 1913, Borden started a summer school in Baroda city for the benefit of the city librarians. The course was of five months duration, with those trained in the first batch as instructors. The expenses of the 25 members who joined the summer school were paid by the State. Some Librarians from outside Baroda State also joined the course. After 1924 the course was discontinued.

1.3 *An Unsuccessful Attempt*

In 1912, an attempt was made to start a two-year postgraduate course in Librarianship at the Baroda College, but the attempt was far from being a success and, hence, very soon the course was discontinued.

1.4 *Punjab School*

A Library Training Course was started in 1915, when Don Dickinson, another American Librarian and a student of Melvil Dewey, was appointed Librarian of the Punjab University, Lahore. Dickinson's assignment specifically required him to train working Librarians in "Modern Library Methods". The first batch consisted of 30 working Librarians from the University Library itself and the local college libraries. The subjects taught were cataloguing, classification, bibliography, book selection and library administration. The course consisted of about 25 lectures. The educational qualifications of the trainees varied from non-matriculates to those holding a Bachelors's degree or Honours in Oriental Languages. An oral examination was also conducted as admission test. A small manual on library routines written by Dickinson himself served as a teaching aid.

In 1921, Lala Labhu Ram, a student of the Dickinson School, was appointed as Assistant Librarian of the Punjab University. He brought about some changes in the syllabus by including a number of additional subjects. The number of lectures was increased from 25 to 72. Several Librarians from outside this school were invited to deliver a series of lectures on a variety of subjects like:

Book Selection
Law of copyright in England and India
Oriental Bibliography
Sources of Provincial Histories of India
Library Buildings, their design and equipment
Open Access
Technical Libraries
Study of Foriegn Languages
Linguistic Survey of India
Milestones of English Literature
From Tennyson to Bernard Shaw, Anglo-Indian Literature

From 1928 onwards only the graduates were admitted to the course and from 1931 the study of either German or French was made compulsory. The Punjab Library School continued till the partition of India in 1947.

1.5 *Andhra Desa Library Association School*

In 1920 the Andhra Desa Library Association started a Library School at the Rama Mohan Granthalayam in Vijayawada. The duration of the course was one month. No qualifications were prescribed for admission. Lectures were delivered by scholars on various topics in Literature and sociology, which also included lectures on library movement. The course was thus oriented to the education of social workers rather than to that of the librarians. In 1934 the syllabus was modified to include more subjects on library work.

1.6 *Madras School*

The Madras Library Association was founded in 1928 through the efforts of Dr S R Ranganathan. After a course of training in librarianship in London Dr Ranganathan returned to India in 1925 to take up the position of Librarian of the Madras University Library. He had gained much experience while in England regarding the use of library service for social good. He applied the scientific methods to library practice. He propounded his ideas in a series of lectures before an audience of about 1,000 teachers at the conference of the South Indian Teachers' Union in 1929. The Madras Library Association established an Annual Summer Course in Librarianship. The lectures for this course were delivered by Dr Ranganathan himself.

In the beginning the objectives of the course were to spread the ideas of the value of a good library service and modern library methods among potential users of the library. Hence, teachers from schools and colleges were admitted during the first three years of training. Later practising librarians in colleges and other institutions were also admitted. The subjects included Laws of Library Science, Classification, Cataloguing, Issue Method and Library Routine.

In 1931 the course run by the Association was taken over by the Madras University. In 1937 it was converted into a full-time post-graduate course of one academic year's duration leading to the Diploma Course in Library Science. (In 1960 the Diploma Course was discontinued and the course of B.Lib.Sc. (Bachelor of Library Science) degree was started. The same year the University also started the M.Lib.Sc. (Master of Library Science).

Dr Ranganathan taught in Madras Library School until his retirement from the Madras University in 1944. Under his dynamic and distinguished leadership, the Madras Library School attracted students from other parts of India. Many of the students trained in this school were instrumental in starting the Library training courses in India.

It is worth mentioning here that with the conception of the Five Laws of Library Science in 1924 and their formulation and publication in 1929 and 1931, respectively, a unifying theory for all library practices and services, and a set of guideliness for dynamic development and study of Library Science as a whole, became available. Postulates, canons and principles based on the Five Laws for guiding the development and study of each of the branches of library could be derived.

1.7 *Imperial Library School*

In 1935, Khan Bahadur Asadullah, an alumni of the Punjab Library School, sponsored and organized a regular full-time Diploma Course in Librarianship in the Imperial Library (now the National Library), Calcutta. The course was drawn up on the patterns of the Punjab Library School. These two Library Schools cooperated with each other by offering courses every alternate year from 1944-46. These were discontinued after the partition of India in 1947.

1.8 *Bengal Library Association School*

During the 1930s, the library movement in the West Bengal received its stimulation from the Bengal Library Association under the inspiring leadership of its President Kumar Muninder Deo Rai. In 1935 the Association arranged for a Library Training Camp at Bansberia under the auspices of the Hooghley District Library Association of which Rai Muninder Deo was the President. The Bengal Library Association started a regular certificate course in Librarianship in 1937. This continues to the present day.

1.9 *Andhra University School*

In 1935, Andhra University started a Diploma Course on the pattern of the Madras University. Unfortunately it was suspended between 1937 and 1947. But in 1970 the B.Lib.Sc. course was started.

1.10 *Other University Library Schools*

Courses in Library Science patterned on the Diploma Course at Madras were started in four more Universities. They were :

(a) Banaras Hindu University, 1941
(b) Bombay University, 1943
(c) Calcutta University, 1946
(d) Delhi University, 1947

Thus, on the eve of Independence, there were six University Library Schools offering Diploma courses in Library Science.

2. **Post-Independence Period**

In 1972, India celebrated the Silver Jubilee of her political independence. During the twenty-five years period their have been significant and sustained efforts at promoting the development of scientific, educational and social institutions necessary to accelerate the economic development of the country. The number and variety of educational and research institutions at various levels have increased to a great extent since then. Some data indicative of this growth of educational institutions are given here. To the available data on the growth in the number of educational institutions should be added the data on research institutions. From 27 in 1900 the number of Research Institutes rose to 220 in 1947 and today this number about 1,500. They are still growing at the rate of 30 per year.

With the growth in the number of institutions there has been an increase in the percentage of literacy, the number of persons reaching higher levels of education and the number of specialists in different subjects. Consequently, the number of potential users of libraries and the number of libraries of various categories — School, College, University, Special and Public – have also increased. In turn, this has created a potential demand for a larger number of professional librarians. To meet this demand there has been a rapid increase in the number of Library Schools during the post-Independence period. Between 1947 and 1956 no new Library Schools were established, then seven schools were established from 1956 to 1959. In the 1960s, 18 University Library Schools were established. The periodic growth of Library and Information Science training programmes by various Indian Universities is given in Table 1.

2.1 *Industrial Development*

Till 1940 India was mainly known as an agricultural country. After Independence, the Five Year Plans aimed at creating the base for more rapid economic and industrial advance. The Second Five Year Plan (1956-57 to 1960-61) aimed to achieve self-sufficiency in foodgrains and expansion of basic industries like steel, chemicals, fuel and power and establishment of machine based industries to meet the requirements of further industrialization. To progress the work of industrialization a need was felt for Documentation work to hasten the information for development of industries.

2.2 *Government Interest in Documentation*

"The need for documentation was felt in India after the Independence and for the first time the Library of the Ministry of Labour and Employment, Government of India, started systematic documentation service in 1951. This was the result of the training of its Librarians with the M.Lib.Sc. courses of the University of Delhi (1957). As a result, Libraries in the Government of India were induced to start systematic documentation and bibliographical works for their respective departments with the establishment of INSDOC in 1952. Documentation in the field of the natural sciences received great impetus and the demand for Documentalists arose in several institutions. With the setting of a chain of scientific libraries Research Institutions and productivity drive in business organizations and industrial establishments, the emphasis on documentation is being laid asking for trained documentalists today".

The Government's interest and concern in information service as a necessary support to the accelerated developmental activities in the country were setting up of committees to consider the matter. The Krishnan Report (1955), the recommendations of the Working

Table 1: *Number of Universities providing Library/Information Science Courses*

Before 1950s	1950s	1960s	1970s	1980s
Andhra*	Aligrah*	Andhra Univ	Army Corps	Patna
Banaras[1]*	Nagpur	Rewa	Admn. College	Saugar*
Bombay[1]*	Usmania*	Baroda	Bangalore*	Magadh
Delhi[1]**	Pune*	Burdwan*	Bhagalpur	
Madras[1]*	Punjab[1]*	Gurjarat	Gulbarga	
	Vikram*	Gwalior	GN Dev	
	Calcutta[1, 2]*	Jabalpur	Kashmir	
		Jadhavpur	L N Mithila	
		Jaipur[1]*	Lucknow	
		Karnataka[1]*	Madurai[1]*	
		Kerala[1]*	Ravishankar	
		Kurukshetra	Sambalpur	
		Punjabi		
		Sanskrit Univ.[3]		
		SNDT Women's Univ*		
		Udaipur		

* Universities offering M.Lib.Sc: M.L.I.Sc. degree along with B.Lib.Sc.

** University offering M.Phil with M.Lib.Sc., M.L.I.Sc. and B.Lib.Sc.

1 Universities offering Ph.D. degree LIS

2 Universities offering two-year M.Lib.Sc. degree.

3 Universities offering Granthalaya Vijnan Shastri degree.

Committee (1959), the Thacker Report (1958), the Ranganathan Report (1959), the recommendations of the working group on Scientific Research of the Planning Commission (1959), the Kothari Committee Report (1960), the Lazar Report (1964), and the Ray Committee Report (1967), all have considered the problem of organizing scientific information activities at a national level. The significant development in the Indian scene of documentation was the establishment of INSDOC in 1952 by the Government of India with the cooperation of UNESCO. Since then this Centre has worked as an agency for bibliographical control, indexing and abstracting services and compilation of directories and union catalogues.

2.3 *INSDOC Courses*

In 1956 INSDOC organized a six-week training course for librarians and documentalists in South Asia. Seven librarians from Ceylon, Burma, Thailand and India were sponsored by UNESCO. The programmes of training were as follows :

(1) Sources of Information (Local, National and International).
(2) Practice in Literature search and compilation of bibliography.
(3) Use of Union catalogue and reference materials for locating scientific documents.
(4) Control of receipt of current periodicals using the three-card system as well as visible indexing.
(5) Working of different sections of INSDOC, particularly the photography, photo-offset and translation sections.

During 1957-58 INSDOC provided a four-week practical training programme for librarians working in the National Laboratories of the Council of Scientific and Industrial Research (CSIR). It also arranged for short term practical training on a specific request from different organizations.

In 1959 the Planning Commission also took interest in documentation. Its working party of scientific matters appointed Dr Ranganathan as one-man Committee to make proposals for the development of INSDOC during the Third Plan period. One of his recommendations was the establishment of training school for documentalists and research unit in INSDOC itself.

2.4 *DRTC Course*

The Documentation Research and Training Centre (DRTC) was established at Bangalore in January 1962. It started its functioning as a centre of training and research in documentation from April 1962. The initial planning of the work of the centre was done by Dr Ranganathan. He also took an active part in teaching, research and administration of the Centre during its first three years and thereafter he confined himself to guiding research work at the centre.

During the four decades of its existence, the Indian Statistical Institute has developed several facets of national and even to some extent of international importance. It has in its several aspects the character of :

(1) A Learned Society devoted to the enhancement of national knowledge in Statistical Science;
(2) A Professional Organization extending recognition to professional statisticians in various employments;
(3) A Commercial non-profit distributing corporation capable of carrying out, on economic terms, projects of fact finding and analysis for State and Central Governments and for Commercial and Industrial Organizations;
(4) A Teaching Centre for pure and applied statistics at under-graduate and post-graduate levels.
(5) A Publishing House corresponding with the University Press of many Western Universities.

3. **Evaluations of Training Programmes**

The need for studying and evaluating the programmes of different courses for librarians or library scientists in this country has never been greater than it is today. Every year one or the other university starts degree courses as part of its teaching programmes. The University Grants Commission has also considered equating the pay-scales of librarians with those of university teachers, provided the qualifications of the former are equated to those of the latter. Even government departments and various public corporations under them have shown increasing awareness of the necessity of having the professionally qualified librarians, although comparatively on lower pay-scales. Both the universities and governmental organizations require qualified personnel with a Master's or Bachelor's degree in Library Science at least for better paid posts. At this juncture a much pertinent question arises: – Do the existing institutions impart instructions suited to the services required of the personnels at different levels and to the services in different types of libraries? The University departments may tempt to answer the first part of the question in affirmative. But the fact remains that the basic need for educating librarians according to the need of different types of libraries yet remains to be realized and provided for.

4. Observations

Dr Ranganathan lately expressed, "Great misgivings are developing in me about the training given to librarians in our country of late. These misgivings emanate from my experience as a member of the several selection committees. The candidates seem to have got through the examination by studying a few notes. They have very little foundation. They are not even trained in systematic thinking. No doubt such a sudden expansion we are having. But my feeling is that dilusion is far more than what is healthy to the profession."

The University Grants Commission's Review Committee Report mentions that "There is no uniformity in regard to the pattern of papers, admission qualifications, scope of practical training, quality of teaching, etc. There is an urgent need for improving standards of teaching and research in the Department of Library and Information Science in the Universities. The Pattern of Library Education which has evolved in the country is not quite suited to the requirements of the new environment that has developed."

Prof S Bashiruddin has remarked, " . . . our search for norms of education for Librarianship must include a search for a pattern. . . . Librarians must receive a training oriented to the needs of different types of libraries that have emerged as our society undergoes changes. We follow the traditional system unmindful even of the changes that are taking place in the Libraries with which we have been familiar for quite a long time."

Prof P N Kaula has observed at the International Conference on Information Science held in Tel Aviv (Israel) from August 29-Sept 3, 1971, " . . . that the M.Lib.Sc. in India was a full two-year post-graduate training programme provided, the first year leading to B.Lib.Sc. programme . . . M.L.S. of the US which was a one-year postgraduate training programme had to be equated with B.Lib.Sc.

programme."

4.1 *M.Lib.Sc. Programme*

The M.Lib.Sc. course of the Indian universities does not follow a uniform pattern. The admission requirements differ from university to university, the duration of the course is also different and there is a vast difference in the syllabii of the M.Lib.Sc. course of various universities and institutions in India. An evaluation of the courses had been made in 1966 by Prof P N Kaula.

The UGC Review Committee 1965 entitled "Library Science in Indian Universities" made certain recommendations regarding Certificate, Diploma, B.Lib.Sc., M.Lib.Sc. and Ph.D. courses. Certain changes took place as recommended by the UGC panel on Library Science in the year 1978.

Though the duration of the M.Lib.Sc. course at the University of Calcutta is of two years, all other Universities are conducting one-year M.Lib.Sc. course. However, one-year is too short a duration keeping in view the importance and scope of the course. It shall, therefore, be in the fitness of things if the duration of the M.Lib.Sc. course is raised to two academic years with a slight modification and additions in the syllabii. Two most important subjects which are required to be included for the M.Lib.Sc. study are : (1) Computer Application in Libraries; and (2) Library Systems Analysis and Elements of Statistical Methods. For a two years M.Lib.Sc. course, there should be two projects, each one having maximum marks for evaluation equivalent to any other course included.

4.2 *M.Phil. Programme*

The M.Phil. programme should be a full-time programme, keeping in view its contents. This programme should be of one year's duration. Another category of M.Phil. students viz., working librarians, etc., may be allowed to join M.Phil. programme as part-time students and facilities in terms of finances, reading materials, etc., should be made available to them. The duration of the course for this category should be of two years.

4.3 *Accrediting Agency*

Prof P N Kaula has voiced his opinion that "UGC should be the accrediting agency for granting recognition to Library Science courses in the country. This would stop the unhealthy practice of opening new courses or new schools and thus help the improvement of standards of the existing courses." Similar is the decision taken by the UGC Panel on Library and Information Science at its meeting held on February 10, 1978, regarding Library and Information Science courses in India. Prof Kaula has urged upon the JOCLAI to take up this task.

4.4 *Curriculum*

The curriculum is a means of achieving the objectives. The curriculum is the predetermined measure of the quantum of knowledge to be acquired at each level of the discipline studied. According to Alfred North Whitehead education is the acquisition of the art of utilization of knowledge. This implies that the responsibility of the student is to learn rather than be taught. Therefore, the curriculum is meant to include only those aspects of a subject that are considered necessary to give a proper orientation to the student in pursuit of the subject. The curriculum, therefore, prescribes the measure of the minimum quantum of knowledge to be acquired. In the context of the tremendous growth of knowledge in every field, this seems to be the only rational guiding manual.

In planning the curriculum, careful thought is to be given as to what can be reasonably covered during the period fixed for the course. The period itself would vary depending on the prescribed entrance qualifications and the pre-entrance academic standard of the students. If the student does not come up to the mark and is deficient into general education and the desired subject specialization, that deficiency should be sought to be remedied to the extent possible in a professional course.

There seems to be an all-round agreement that the curriculum should include the traditional core of subjects like classification and cataloguing, organization and administration, book selection, reference service and bibliography, library and society including history of books and libraries. The difficulty and the lack of concensus leading to diversity of practice is with regard to the subjects outside the professional core. Librarianship is an inter-discipline subject. Therefore, some knowledge of the fundamentals of other disciplines, there history and methods should be a necessary part of a librarian's professional study. The idea is that the library education programme be concerned with the education of only those who have had a sound liberal education programme with specialization in a discipline or group of disciplines that would enable them to participate in the programme intelligently and with a full intellectual involvement. So the basic curriculum should supply a capital of concentrated knowledge which a librarian can apply later in a variety of circumstances. This consideration has given rise to some rethinking on the much advocated diversity in training and to a trend towards its yielding ground before the necessity for a sound basic training programme common to all, so that a Library Science student should be able to widen his/her horizon by adding the other elements that are necessary for his/her effective functioning with an awareness of one's total environment.

The curriculum for library education should also provide for a variety of collectives by types of Libraries, types of materials and library operations calling for specialized skills. The special needs of librarians working in a special library should be kept in view in formulating a Library School curriculum. The education of special librarianship, as part of the Library Schools programme, has of late received increasing attention and some guiding principles have been developed. It has been recognized that the valuing of the special courses meant for Special Librarianship be added to the Library School curriculum with an awareness of the fundamental problems relating to their organization and use. This requirement implies the provision in the Library Schools, either by themselves or in collaboration with other departments, of facilities for specialized training in sophisticated techniques in various engineering skills.

4.5 *Admission Requirements*

The present qualification of a Bachelor's degree prescribed for admission to the B.Lib.Sc. course is assumed to equip the students adequately to undertake the professional education programme. An enhancement of the entrance qualification to Master's degree does not seem desirable for the following reasons :

(1) Experience has shown that Master's degree holders are not necessarily better in respect of competence and aptitude than Bachelor's degree holders.

(2) Many promising Bachelor's degree holders may get eliminated

in favour of mediocre Master's degree holders.

4.6 *Recruitment of Students*

How are the students to be recruited? Can we go by their previous academic performance alone as marks or grades obtained by them in the qualifying examination? With the University course content the variations in standard and, above all, the defective evaluation system that exists today, this cannot be a completely reliable index of the competence of the students for the Library Science Course. Some schools prescribe an entrance test or an interview. Schools in the West attach importance to recommendations being produced by the students from their previous teachers. Each one of these individually taken has its own strength and weakness, and perhaps a reliable method is to be evolved from a combination of the elements of some or all these to suit individual situations. In India where the unemployment problem is so serious, students rush to programmes that hold out promises of some prospect of employment. In India, Library Science today has the distinction of being a discipline that attracts the largest number of applicants for admission, perhaps next only to medicine and engineering. Hence, it must be much more the responsibility of the teachers to inculcate a sense of vocation in the students.

It would be proper to emphasize here that before introducing any innovation in the curriculum, it would be necessary for a Library School to make proper plans so that the revised programme is implemented in the best possible manner. In addition, the Library School must acquire required books and other reading materials so as to facilitate the plans to introduce various changes in the curricula. Teachers must also be given sufficient time and facilities to get themselves prepared for teaching new courses in the programme.

D 3

Quality Improvement Programmes for Working Librarians

S B Sapre

1. Identifying the Work Done

Librarians and others concerned with providing information found a useful lesson in the story of an American organization which spent many thousands of dollars on a piece of research, only to discover too late that the work had been done elsewhere and was recorded in a five-cent pamphlet in their own library. All research into library affairs accordingly begins with a study of existing literature and every student writing a dissertation is expected to outline this initial exploration.

2. Emphasis on Research

Man appears to be universally beset by problems which must be met and solved. These problems are as varied as life itself. Scarcely a day goes by but that each of us does not investigate, study, and question some aspect of our environment to acquire facts which may help to solve problems that face us. Since most personal problems have been solved before we might find answers to such problems if we read the right source or ask the right people. But the serious problems of society are difficult to solve as there are no sources or authorities who can provide us with a solution; the growing complexity of our civilization means that in the social sciences, and especially in education, we find that difficult new problems develop more rapidly than the old ones are solved. Since a problem is a doubtful case or question difficult for solution or settlement, it is necessary to understand the relevant facts in order to solve the problem. No reduction in vagueness can be made until the problem has been carefully defined and broken down into specific questions or sub-problems. In all aspects of life – social economic, educational, political, and business — there is increasing emphasis upon research to give man the factual data he needs to solve individual and social problems.

Research has other uses than solving problems. Man wants factual information to help him satisfy his curiosity and to learn the direction he is going, how far he has progressed, and to learn the direction he is going, how far he has progressed, and how his progress compares with that of his fellows. Important as these types of research may be, we may concentrate on research as a method of solving problems.

3. Meaning of Research

Man uses various tools for the solution of his problems, some of which have been handed down to him from the past. In the use of some of these tools he may not question how the basic information was acquired or whether it has been verified, for example man may passively accept custom or tradition, the dictates of various authorities, his own limited experience, or syllogistic reasoning from propositions appearing to be self-evident. Then finally he may base solution for his problem upon the findings of scientific inquiry, a synonym for research.

3.1 *Definition*

Research is a careful inquiry or examination to discover new information or relationships and to expand and verify existing knowledge. It is the Manipulation of things, concepts, or symbols for the purpose of generalizing and to extend, correct, or verify knowledge, whether that knowledge aids in the construction of a theory or in the practice of an art. The mechanic or physician is a research worker only when he attempts to generalize about all automobiles or all patients in a given class.[1] Certain writers on the topic have emphasized one or more characteristics of research that others have minimized, but the general nature of the activity is not in dispute.

Progress in research has been accelerated by the discovery and development of methodological procedures making the process more rigorous, discriminating and dependable. The new electronic dataprocessing machines collate data and detect relationships so rapidly that it is possible to carry on investigations that would have been too costly and too much time consuming, a few years ago. Methodological developments have been enhanced by researchers' dedicated belief that unbiased study of all relevant facts is the best way to solve many problems. It must therefore be admitted that the word, "Research" is abused in common speech in that it frequently is used to mean "looking up" something in a standard reference book and not the acquisition of new knowledge.

4. **Library Research**

Library research may be briefly described as a kind that is conducted primarily through the use of written materials most commonly located in large libraries. It is concerned with the seeking out of significant facts and interpretations from the past and from the extensive data and statistical information about contemporary life which are frequently found in government documents, professional journals and similar sources. Studies concerned with the evolution of theories and research into possible cause and effect relationships are likely to rely heavily on the use of library material.

Library research that is worthy of the name necessitates generalizations and conclusions not previously appreciated. Education being the principal tool for development of human resources has a direct contribution towards achievement of economic goals and aspirations of the country. This is more so in the field of technical education, since major emphasis in this area is equipping the manpower with requisite skills with the objects of maximizing man's contribution to the production of goods and services the community needs. The techniques and processes of production of goods and services do not make demand only on technical skills, but on a cluster of skills a significant part of which is related to the total humanistic growth of the man.

Within the library profession concern is expressed (as also in other professions) about keeping members up-to-date, about bridging the gap between research and development and everyday practice, and about the problem of developing competence to cope with fairly rapid technological changes. Moreover in professions which have (or are aware of the need for) a strong orientation, there is a growing sensitivity to the needs of user groups, but the appropriate skills are not always on hand to analyse and respond to these needs. Continuing professional education is the solution frequently proposed for such problems.[2]

The chief ways for any professional to keep up-to-date is by reading the literature and one might expect a librarian who qualified ten years previously to glance through number of periodicals regularly, to keep up with reviews and use them to select a few books each year relevant to his or her particular job, or which might widen the outlook from a particular post to throw light on general developments in the profession. A recent British Library Association survey shows that 33% of public librarians and 26% of the academic librarians had read no books on librarianship in the previous year. Regular readers of book reviews amounted to 14% of public librarians and 37% of academic librarians.

5. Quality Improvement Programmes

The Ministry of Education and Social Welfare, Government of India, launched the Quality Improvement Programme (QIP) in the year 1970 as a means of upgrading the expertise and capabilities of the teachers of the Engineering College and polytechnics in our country. The short-term courses (QIP) are also conducted during summer/winter vacations every year in various fields of Engineering, Technology, Teaching Methodology and Management of Technical Education through the following agencies :

(1) Indian Society for Technical Education
(2) IIT, Bombay, Delhi, Kanpur, Kharagpur, Madras
(3) Indian Institute of Science, Bangalore
(4) Technical Teachers Training Institute, Bhopal, Calcutta, Chandigarh, Madras and Allahabad polytechnics
(5) University of Roorkee

During the Sixth Five Year Plans considerable outlay has been provided for these short-course programmes in order that as many faculties of the Engineering Colleges and the polytechnics in the country as possible are benefited in terms of increased expertise, both in academic areas and in educational technology. In order that there is a wide awareness of the programmes conducted by the various agencies so that both the participant-teacher and their sponsoring institutions are able to make a judicious choice and coordinated approach. Participants other than the teaching faculty of technical institutions can also be admitted to the short course programmes to a limited extent, if vacancies exist. Such participants could be from industries, government departments and similar organizations and the entire cost of their travel, boarding and lodging, cost of books etc. will be borne by their/sponsoring organizations or themselves.

It is high time that Indian Library Association may also arrange to start similar QIP for librarians where by working librarians in the Central/provincial/autonomous/private organizations may study for Master in Library Science (Courses) in Universities which are offering the courses and further the few universities which are offering Ph.D. facilities in Library Science.

The "Report of Working Group on Technical Education" (page 114 Para 2.4.2 Library Facilities) published by the Government of India, Ministry of Education and Social Welfare (1978) says:

(i) *Organizational Efficiency*: The library is the heart of any educational institution. It provides the materials necessary to support and supplement the teaching-learning programmes. While the size, scope and character of a library are important, its proper organization is of even greater importance. With the vast amount of published literature available today and the newer methods of information retrieval it is of utmost importance that libraries and the library staff be well qualified and libraries well organized. There is considerable scope for improvement in this. The committee recommends that educational institutions be urged to improve the efficiency of their services. If need be the scale of pay of librarian could be upgraded, with a corresponding raise in the minimum qualifications required, so that better and more efficient library services would result.

(ii) *Other Services:* Other services which have an important bearing on the quality of education are audio-visual aids and reprographic aids. To start with these services could be organized in the library. The Committee recommends that adequate support should be given to institutions to organize Audio-visual Services and Reprographic Services as a part of their library facilities.

6. Learning Resource Centres

Although Learning Resource Centres are new to this country, they are being experimented upon in other countries as a means of improving the teaching-learning process, especially when a very large number of students is involved. Such Centres assist in course development, production of instructional materials, design of new instructional facilities, instructional research, etc., and serve all the academic departments of an institution. The committee recommends that such learning Resource Centres be started in one or two selected institutions on an experimental basis.

7. Conclusion

In view of the foregoing it is really now high time that our Library Associations in consultation with the Ministry of Education (Government of India) and the Association of Indian Universities, New Delhi, if need be may provide Masters degree courses for top tier working librarians and information scientists in our country, since many universities/IIT's are well equiped with computer centres which provide facilities for their libraries. This will also go a long way so that the librarians may get their position on a par with the teaching faculty in colleges and institutions for higher learning.

REFERENCES

1 *Encyclopedia of Soical Sciences*, Vol 1-13. New York, Macmillan, 1934, pp. 330-334.

2 OPEN UNIVERSITY: *Report of the Committee on Continuing Education* O U 1976 (Venables Report).

3 BOARD OF APPRENTICESHIP TRAINING (Western Region), Bombay: Apprenticeship Facilities Available for Graduates .& Technicians (Diploma Holders) in Engineering/Technology Under Apprentices (Amendment) Act 1973 in Western Region. p. 1.

4 INDIAN SOCIETY FOR TECHNICAL EDUCATION ITI Campus, New Delhi: Quality Improvement Programme, Sponsored by Government of India, Ministry of Education & Social Welfare: *Programme Brochure for Short-term Courses for the year* 1978-79. pp. 5-6.

5 Library Publications, Raipur, (*Library & Librarian* Vol 2, December 1977, p. 37).

6 INDIA, Ministry of Education & Social Welfare, New Delhi: *Report of Working Group on Technical Education*, Jan 1978: p. 114.

E 1

Library Automation— A New Dimension in Arabian Gulf Librarianship

Zahiruddin Khurshid

1. Manpower Situation

The tremendous increase in the petrodollar income brought a turning point in the economic condition of the Arabian Gulf region. The development plans of the Gulf States allocated very large sums of money to the socio-economic sector. "The education budgets are second to defence budgets in many cases, and if not for the Arab-Israeli conflict, education budgets would have been higher. The slogan adopted by the Kuwait Government, "everything for education and education for all", typifies what many of these countries feel."[1] Libraries of all types received enormous support from the government to develop their collections and services toward international library standards. Consultants and library experts from the United States and Europe were hired to prepare plans for improving library resources and services. University and special libraries received much more attention because of their expected role in promoting the national educational, scientific and research activities. The shortage of skilled manpower has been an acute problem in all the States of the region. The abundance of money could not solve this problem. Each agency, governmental and non-governmental, has to be run by someone, and these "someones" are difficult to find. While Namlah[2] describes in these words the manpower situation in Saudi Arabia, it also reflects the overall situation of the Gulf region. In addition to importing commodities, they also acquire manpower, both skilled and unskilled in millions from all around the world. On an average, libraries in the region have more than 50% foreign staff on their payrolls. The dependence of libraries on foreign staff to this extent may have repercussions in the long run, but their short-term advantages are more than worth the amount spent on hiring them.

2. **Application of Modern Technologies**

Libraries in the region began to apply modern technologies to improve services in support of teaching, learning and research in the early 1970s. Some academic and special libraries initiated communication links with Western data bases including Lockheed's DIALOG and SDC's ORBIT for online searching. Notable among them are the King Fahd University of Petroleum and Minerals (KFUPM) (formerly University of Petroleum and Minerals – UPM) library, the National Scientific and Technical Inforamtion Centre (NSTIC) of the Kuwait Institute for Scientific Research (KISR).[3] Today the number of libraries with online searching facilities have increased substantially.

The KFUPM library and NSTIC continued their efforts during the past decade of 1970s to further improve the library services by making use of the computer facilities of their respective institutions. The development in these two libraries inspired many academic and special libraries in the region to apply modern technologies to provide better services to their patrons. The objective of this paper is to review the state-of-the-art automation in libraries of the Gulf States.

3. **Kuwait Scenario**

In Kuwait NSTIC was the first library to start an automation programme in 1975. Mohamed Zehery has identified two stages of automation at NSTIC. "The first stage when NSTIC used the government computer centre at the Ministry of Planning via a telephone line and a remote printer. At that time computer programmes were developed in house and systems were designed and developed in batch mode environment. The second stage started when KISR acquired an IBM 4341 in 1981, thus allowing NSTIC to develop its project and programmes in an online realtime mode.[4]

3.1 *Bibliographical Services*

The first computer generated periodicals list was completed in 1975. Preparation of the list was part of a 'Bibliographic control program' undertaken by the Automated Information Systems (AIS) Group of

NSTIC[5]. "The programme was later expanded to the regional level representing library holding from Saudi Arabia, Iraq, United Arab Emirates as well as those of the major libraries in Kuwait. The data base for the Regional Union List of Scientific and Technical Periodicals in the Gulf Region includes over 9,000 periodicals in selected special libraries and academic libraries of the region. The union list is published biannually. Another union list of Arabic periodicals in 15 libraries of Kuwait is also produced annually.

A progrmme which was started in 1977 to produce an automated book catalogue for the NSTIC collection was later extended to prepare a union catalogue for special libraries in Kuwait. The data-base thus developed represents over 65,000 titles available in science and technology areas in 15 special libraries of Kuwait.

3.2 *Circulation Services*

The AIS Group next developed an in-house circulation control system based on two main files, the "Circulation Transaction File" and the "Borrowers File". The system was designed to produce overdue notices, borrowers lists and some management statistics reports.[6] Since there was no bibliographic file available, each time the book was checked out the control number, title, call number, borrower number and the transaction date were entered manually.

3.3 *Stairs*

In 1981 NSTIC acquired the Storage Information Retrieval System (STAIRS) It operates as an interactive programme under VM/SP with CMS (Conversational Monitor System) and offers both data-base creation and maintenance services. NSTIC adopted STAIRS to serve as the main component in an integrate data-base approach to automation of NSTIC functions. The Centre started loading LC MARC records to provide on-line access to its library holdings of non-Arabic materials. Terminals are provided on various locations both within and outside the library. The problem of providing access to the library's holdings of Arabic materials has also been solved by developing an Arabic version of STAIRS. All the original codes and tables in English have been translated and bilingual IBM 3278/2 terminals are provided to retrieve the Arabic script catalogue records. An Arabic synonyms, table has been developed for the Arabic version of STAIRS which allows the user to retrieve all variant forms of a word by entering a single-word search term.

The AIS Group at NSTIC is now preparing programmes to implement STAIRS in automating other library functions such as acquisitions and serials control.

3.4 *University of Kuwait: Automation System in Library*

Also in Kuwait, the University of Kuwait is currently doing a feasibility study of acquiring an intrgrated library automation system. As part of the study a team from the University of Kuwait consisting of two persons from the library and computer centre recently visited some libraries in Saudi Arabia including the UPM Library in Dhahran. At UPM they spent two days observing various functions of DOBIS/LIBIS in operation. They seemed motivated for acquiring the same system at the University of Kuwait.

4. **Saudi Arabia Scenario**

The pioneer effort towards library automation in Saudi Arabia was made in 1975 when the KFUPM library administration sent a librarian, Terence Walton to the University of Dortmund, West Germany, to evaluate DOBIS with a view to acquiring it for the KFUPM Library. The KFUPM library at that time was too small to support a large and sophisticated system as DOBIS, but the rationale mentioned by the then library administration was that "UPM could serve the role of a national library for Saudi Arabia, and indeed for the Gulf area, in the area of bibliographic control, interlibrary loan, etc.".[7]

4.1 *Automation Programme Shelved*

As a result of change in the library administration in 1976, the automation project was shelved for some time. The Director of Library, Michael Moran felt that "an online interactive system is beyond the needs of the UPM at this time".[8]

4.2 *Automation Programme Revived*

The issue of library automation at KFUPM was revived again in 1979 when a Task Force on Library Automation (TFLA) was appointed to investigate and provide a plan for library automation.[9] After a careful investigation DOBIS/LIBIS, which was evaluated earlier in 1975, was selected for the KFUPM library for the following reasons:[10]

1 It was well suited to our needs.
2 It was the least expensive system.
3 Vendor (IBM) support is available locally.

A licensing agreement between IBM and KFUPM was signed in 1980 and the system was installed in 1981.

4.3 *Software*

DOBIS/LIBIS is a software package developed for the University of Dortmund in West Germany and Catholic University of Leuven in Belgium respectively. The system's cataloguing, database maintenance, and online searching modules are derived from the Dortmunder Bibliotheksystem (DOBIS); and circulation, acquisitions, background processing, and batch output capabilities were initially developed for the Leuvens Integral Bibliothek System (LIBS).[11] The "periodical control" module as part of the DOBIS/LIBS software package was incorporate in release 3 of DOBIS and was distributed to users in April 1983.[12]

4.4 *Chronology of Events*

Chronology of major events in library automation at KFUPM is as follows :

March 1981	DOBIS/LIBIS base system installed
February 1982	Online cataloging of new materials and retrospective conversion of the card catalogue started.
December 1982	Four colour terminals provided for public search of the online catalogue.
July 1983	Online circulation started.
January 1985	Periodical control including check-in of periodicals issues began.
December 1985	Card catalogue frozen with the completion of the retrospective conversion project.
July 1986	Online acquisitions started.

4.5 *Arabized Version of DOBIS*

The KFUPM library automation project has been completed with the exception of the in progress Arabized version of DOBIS. This programme will enable us to create the Arabic script catalogue records online. The Arabic script records will be kept in the local file with the facility to access them by as many access points as are available in the non-Arabic script catalogue. The programme has been successfully tested and will be moved into the production system in early 1987.

4.6 *Libraries of KSU and IPA*

Two other libraries of King Saud University (KSU) and the Institute of Public Administration (IPA) followed KFUPM in acquiring DOBIS/LIBIS. Originally KSU was considering OCLC and Frederick Kilgour was even invited to visit King Saud University for consulting in the fall of 1982, which did not materialize. The attention was later focused on DOBIS/LIBIS, and finally the system was installed in 1983.

4.61 *KSU Library*: The KSU library is the largest university library in the Kingdom with 350,000 titles in 650,000 volumes. Cataloguing of new materials online started in 1983. For the retrospective conversion of its card catalogue several vendors were contacted including OCLC five hundred randomly selected titles were sent to these vendors to find out which of these vendors could provide a better hit rate. OCLC was found to have a 95% hit rate. A contract was, therefore, negotiated with OCLC for the retrospective conversion of the non-Arabic records.

King Saud University claims to be the first library to have prepared an Arabized version of DOBIS. They have completed translation of DOBIS code tables and maps and have recently started translating various screen information. Their database is the largest in the Middle-East and includes about 1.3 million records.[13]

4.62 *IPA Library*: The Institute of Public Administration (IPA) Library was the third library in the Kingdom to install DOBIS/LIBIS. The collection of the IPA Library consists mostly of government documents and technical reports. Because of the special nature of its collection the Library follows local rather than international cataloguing practices for processing. The implementation plan of DOBIS/LIBIS suffered a setback from the very beginning and the library is finding it difficult to continue with its automation programme.

4.7 *Other Libraries*

4.71 *ARAMCO Library* : In 1985, the Arabian American Oil Company (ARAMCO) signed a contract with IBM to install DOBIS/LIBIS at its Central Headquarters Library in Dhahran. In addition to a technical library, ARAMCO also has a Recreation Library. The collection of both the libraries are entirely different. The techncial library's collection is about 40,000 volumes and includes monographs, maps, reports and AV materials, mostly in pure and applied sciences. On the other hand the Recreation Library has about 120,000 volumes of fictional, juvenile and recreational materials. Currently, ARAMCO is building up an initial database to start the retrospective conversion of the card catalogue. Sixty thousand MARC records have already been acquired from Blackwell North America (BNA), a major book supplier for ARAMCO.

4.72 *The Recreation Library*: The Recreation Library has recently started converting catalogue records by matching the shelf list record with the online record. The "hit" rate is about 80 per cent. Printing of bar-code labels representing the numeric copy number assigned by the computer to each volume/item, and their scanning by a laser scanner has been tested successfully. Bar-coding of each item will make it possible to check-in and-out materials online.

4.73 *Umm al-Qura University Library*: Another library that has purchased, but not yet installed, DOBIS/LIBIS is the Umm al-Qura University Library in Makkah. They have a number of problems which are delaying installation, including the lack of an implementation plan, lack of programmers and the lack of coordination between the library and computer centre. A test system of DOBIS was made available to the library staff for about three months. During this short period a few of the technical services staff made use of the system for practising, searching and cataloguing subsystems. Eighty per cent of the library collection is in Arabic which require them to first develop the Arabized version of DOBIS. Starting a system for 20% of the collection is not what they want. With all these problems there is no indication that DOBIS/LIBIS would be installed at Umm al-Qura University in the near future.

4.74 *The Library of Ministry of Finance and National Economy*: Two libraries in the Kingdom with the automated systems other than DOBIS/LIBIS are the libraries of Ministry of Finance and National Economy and the King Faisal Centre for Islamic Studies and Research.

The Library of the Ministry of Finance and National Economy is using VTLS (Virginia Tech Library System). The library has access to the OCLC database for searching and cataloguing, but the systems availability is very limited because of the time diference between Saudi Arabia and the United States. For Arabic materials the King Adbulaziz City for Science and Technology (KACST) develop software, ARABWRITE, is being used.

4.75 *The Library of the King Faisal Centre for Research and Islamic Studies*: The King Faisal Centre for Research and Islamic Studies Library using MINISIS system, which also has the capability of handling Arabic script records. The Centre has developed a database on King Faisal, Saudi Arabia, Islam, Arab and Muslim world and other subjects of interest to the Centre.

5. Sultanate of Oman Scenario

5.1 *Sultan Qaboos University Library*

The Sultan Qaboos University opened in the Fall of 1986 as Oman's first Institution of higher education. The university project started in November 1980 and a library consultant was hired in 1982 to prepare a plan for a comprehensive library that will be fully automated.[14] DOBIS/LIBIS was chosen in 1985 to start an integrated library automation system. IBM completed installation of the system in November 1986 and a combined testing and training programme is already underway.

6. Bahrain, Qatar, United Arab Emirates Scenario

Some of the special and academic libraries of the other three Gulf States, Bahrain, Qatar and the United Arab Emirates, have hired the services of foreign librarians and consultants to plan for library automation, but, there is no evidence that any of the libraries in the three States have implemented any major automated system yet.

6.1 *Bahrain*

In Bahrain, the Gulf Polytechnic is developing its own microcomputer-based system for cataloguing, catalogue search and circulation control. They will not use MARC or any other communication format to build up the database. A librarian from the Gulf Polytechnic visited the KFUPM library to observe DOBIS/LIBIS in operation to benefit from the KFUPM experience in developing their own system.

6.2 *United Arab Emirates*

In the United Arab Emirates, the Dubai Municipality which already has Hewlett-Packard computers is looking for a system that runs on HP. A librarian from the Dubai Municipality participated in the recently concluded KFUPM Library sponsored short course on Computer applications to Modern Library Management. He observed DOBIS/LIBIS in operation and gathered some information that will help them in seeking a suitable system. Because of the already available HP computers the DOBIS/LIBIS or any other system which does not operate on HP computers will not be considered.

6.3 *Qatar*

In Qatar, libraries of the University of Qatar and the Gulf Organization of Industrial Consultants (GOIC) have already established communication links with the Western databases for online searching. The University of Qatar hired the services of consultants in 1984 to advise them on upgrading the collection and improving services. They are now planning for library automation with the possibility of acquiring the MINISIS system.

6.31 *GOIC Library*: The GOIC is making use of its computer (PDP-11/70) facilities to carry out a number of activities related to collection and maintenance of information. The Industrial Data Bank Department – a vital wing of the GOIC – has developed several data bases on Gulf industries, technology, socio-economics, etc.[15]

7. **Conclusion**

In recent years, there has been a growing awareness among libraries of the Arabian Gulf region to review their needs and potentials for the automation of their operations. So much so that libraries that have not yet streamlined their manual operations, and have a serious shortage of qualified and trained librarians, are also acquiring computers and inviting experts to plan automation programmes for them. In reality, however, there are only a very small number of libraries able to complete automation projects. A lot of effort in terms of money and manpower are being wasted by each library taking its own course towards library automation. Most of the problems common to libraries in the region, such as a shortage of professional librarians, non-standard procedures and policies, depleting library budgets, problem of converting the Arabic script records to machine-readable form, require them to work together not only to solve these problems, but to save time and money by avoiding duplication of effort. But, unfortunately no significant cooperative effort has so far been made in the region to solve these common problems. One single problem of treating Arabic as a dialogue language in a computerized system has been tackled differently by three different institutions in Saudi Arabia alone. In addition some more libraries are attempting to develop their own systems.

7.1 *Study on Library Automation*

In Saudi Arabia during the past five years the Council of Deans of Library Affairs has been trying to unify efforts of the university libraries in the kingdom on several important issues. The council in its meeting at King Abdulaziz university in Jeddah in 1983, requested the Saudi Arabian National Centre for Science and Technology SANCST (now King Abdulaziz City for Science and Technology – KACST) to conduct a study of the present state of library automation and the implications it holds for university libraries in the kingdom.[16] The importance of this project lies in the fact that while SANCST did not recommend any particular system for Saudi Arabia, it evaluated eight automated systems against local requirements and ranked them according to their capabilities of meeting local requirements. The decision was left to libraries to choose the one system which suits them best. The positive effect of this survey is becoming clear now with libraries singling out DOBIS/LIBIS as the most suitable system for Saudi Arabia. The cooperative effort should not end here. There is a long way between selecting a system and successfully implementing it in all library operations. KACST could take further steps towards combining the efforts of university libraries in developing programmes for the system to handle Arabic scripts records, exchange of MARC records and programmes on local enhancements. Above all KACST could also coordinate libraries with DOBIS/LIBIS system to form a network in Saudi Arabia. DOBIS/LIBIS has a network capability. Instead of libraries developing their own databases and thus duplicating efforts, they could develop a central data base and share their bibliographic records with other libraries in the network for searching, cataloguing, ordering, interlibrary loan and other activities. Each library in the network can also maintain a local file representing it own holdings. The importance of network in the Gulf region is second to none. On an average 75% of the libraries collection is in Arabic. These require original cataloguing which is more difficult than the cataloguing of non-Arabic materials because of the lack of bibliographic standards. The Library of Congress provides cataloguing data for a very small percentage of Arabic materials, and that too in the transliterated form which is not acceptable to libraries in the Arab world. In the present situation, an Arabic title if available in 10 libraries of Saudi Arabia, is being catalogued 10 times. While in the network situation the book will be catalogued once and to the same catalogue record location information for other libraries would be added. Or, the participating libraries will copy the record and transfer it to their local file with or without modifications. This will not only save labour, it will also help libraries to maintain consistency in bibliographic records. Libraries in the United States are achieving tremendous advantages by joining major networks such as OCLC, RLIN, WLN, etc. The Gulf libraries need to follow them and develop networks on both local and regional levels.

REFERENCES

1 AMAN, Mohammad M and Khalifa Sha'ban: Library and Information Services in Arab Countries. (In: *Librarianship in the Muslim World.* edited by Anis Khurshid and Malahat Kaleem Sherwani. Karachi; Islamic Library Information Centre, University of Karachi, 1985. p 3).

2 NAMLAH, Ali I: Manpower Deficiency in Saudi Arabia: Its Effect on the Library and Information Profession. (*International Library Review*, 14, 1982, p 19).

3 KHURSHID, Zahiruddin: Application of Modern Technologies in Arab Libraries. (*Libri*, 33 June 1983, p 107).

4 ZEHERY, Mohamed H: National Scientific and Technical Information Centre: A Case for the Development of Special Librarianship and Information Systems and Services in Kuwait. (A paper presented to the Conference on "Library Development in the Middle East," Bahrain, December 5-6, 1982). p 12.

5 KHALID, Farooq A: Automation in NSTIC. (In: *Proceedings of the Symposium of New Technology in Libraries: Prospects and Problems for Libraries in the Gulf States*, Dhahran, April 26-28 1982. Dhahran; University of Petroleum & Minerals, 1982, p 29).

6 KHALID, Farooq A: Report on the Development of Arabic STAIRS. (Internal

memorandum), 1982, p 1.

7 MORAN, Michael: This Question of Automation (*UPM Library Scene*, 3 March 1978, p 9).

8 *Ibid.*, Michael: This Question of Automation (*UPM Library Scene*, 3 March 1978, p 9).

9 ASHOOR, Mohammed Saleh: Planning for Library Automation at the University of Petroleum and Minerals. (*Journal of Information Science*, 5,1983, p 193).

10 GADO, Salah Hussein: DOBIS/LIBIS at UPM: A Successful Experience in the Library Automation. (In: *Proceedings of the Symposium on New Technology in Libraries: Prospects and Problems for Libraries in the Gulf States*, Dhahran, 26-28 April 1982. Dhahran; University of Pertroleum and Minerals, 1982, p 66).

11 SAFFADY, William: Dortmund and Leuven Library Systems (DOBIS/LIBIS) (*Computer Equipment Review*. 7 Jan-June 1985, p 39).

12 KHURSHID, Zahiruddin : Automated Serials Control at the University of Petroleum & Minerals using DOBIS/LIBIS periodicals Module. (*Serials Review*) 12, Spring 1986, p 50).

13 "King Saud University translated the library automation system." (In Arabic) (Okaz, 28 Sept 1986).

14 VARNET, Harvey: Sultan Qaboos University in Oman. (*College and Research Libraries News*, 45 April 1984, p 176).

15 HUSSAIN, M Talib: GOIC Library Services: Problems and Projections (*UPM Library Scene*, 5 March 1980, p 13).

16 SAUDI ARABIAN NATIONAL CENTRE FOR SCIENCE AND TECHNOLOGY: *Alternatives in Library Automation: System Evaluation.* Riyadh; SANCST, 1984 (unpaged).

F 1

On-Line Data Base Technology: A Trend Setter for a Library System

Harish Chandra

0. Introduction

In recent years data base technology has become one of the most rapidly growing areas of Computer and Information Science. The data base is basically a computer based recordkeeping system that records and maintains the user information. According to James Martin, "Data base is a collection of inter-related data stored together without harmful or unnecessary redundancy to serve multiple applications".

1. Objectives of Data Base Technology

There are a number of objectives of data base technology. Some of them are as follows :

(1) to make an integrated collection of data available to a wide variety of users;
(2) to provide for quality and integrity of the data base;
(3) to ensure retention of privacy through security measures within the system;
(4) to allow centralized control of data base, which is necessary for efficient data administration.

1.1 *Advantages*

A data base may be designed for batch processing and on-line processing. On-line processing is a dynamic inter-active process which has the following advantages :

(1) On-line processing is much faster than batch processing;
(2) On-line processing requires less time;
(3) Large data can be accessed in no time;
(4) On-line processing has better precision
(5) On-line processing manipulates database efficiently and effectively;
(6) On-line processing provides greater number of access points.

2. On-line Data Base

The on-line processing concept has given rise to the concept of on-line data base. An on-line data base is one which can be directly accessed by a user from a terminal which is usually a visual display service. The observable equipment consists of a keyboard through which instructions are given, a visual display unit on which the information which is being retrieved is displayed, and a printer, allowing the facility to print information after it has been displayed. On-line data base is an effective and natural way to meet the on-line revolution in the Libraries where Librarians and Information Scientists collect, retrieve and disseminate information. On-line data base offers various means of escape from the numerous constraints of a batch system.

Major objectives of an on-line data base is to make critical information more readily available to the people who will use it. The data base is kept on-line and is available all the time. Examples of such data base systems are in airline reservation, banking, etc. The capability for on-line access to the data base enhances the value of data in two ways. First, it makes possible the implementation of many applications that requires the rapidity of access to a shared data that is not possible with batch system. Secondly, if permits interaction between human and the DBMS.

3. Components of On-line Data Base

An on-line data base has basically four components :

3.1 *User*

User includes application programmes, responsible for writing application programmes that use the data base, and users accessing the data base from a terminal and Data base administrator.

3.2 *Data*

Data are the stored information. Data are either integrated or shared. By integrated we mean that the data base may be thought of as unification of several distinct data files. By shared we mean that individual pieces of data in the data base may be shared among different users, in the sense that each of these users may have access to the same piece of data.

3.3 *Hardware*

The data base resides on hardware that consists of the computer, disks, drums and tape devices.

3.4 *Software*

This is called Data Base Management Systems. All requests from users processed to the data base are handled by DBMS.

4. **Types of On-line Data Base** (OLDB)

On-line data bases may be grouped as under :

—Bibliographical
—Relational
—Distributed
—Discipline Oriented
—Mission Oriented
—Problem Oriented
—Multi-disciplinary
—Inter-disciplinary

5. **Characteristics of OLDB**

Some of the striking features of OLDB are as follows :

1. Many users can access and update a large data base in real time

2. Users can access the data base in a random manner
3. Better representation of the user-needs
4. It allows user interfaces
5. Responsive to change in applications requirements
6. It reduces data redundancy
7. It provides effective searching and immediate response.

6. Data Base Management System

DBMS is a software system that creates, maintains and manipulates the data base, and permits the execution of Computer programmes to access information contained in the data base. The DBMS consists of the following components :

1. Source data
2. A stored data
3. A database administrator (DBA)
4. A data model
5. A subdata model
6. A user
7. User profiles

6.1 *Functions of DBMS*

There are a number of DBMS available like TOTAL, ADABAS, dBase II & III. The DBMS performs the following functions :

1. Providing for mass storage of relevant data
2. Eliminating redundant data
3. Creating a new data base
4. Adding the data to the data base
5. Editing the data in the data base
6. Sorting the data
7. Searching for particular item in data base
8. Reporting output from the data base
9. Providing recovery services in case of failure
10. Making the latest modifications to the data base available immediately
11. Protecting the data from physical harm and unauthorized access

12. Providing rapid generation of reports for management.

7. Library Applications

On-line data base technology can be applied in libraries like in other areas. There is ample scope for on-line database technology applications in library operations. Librarians can spare their precious time if they introduce this advance technology. The challenges and problems caused by information explosion and its overload can be solved easily by introducing on-line database technology. An overview of an on-line library data base is given in Figure 1.

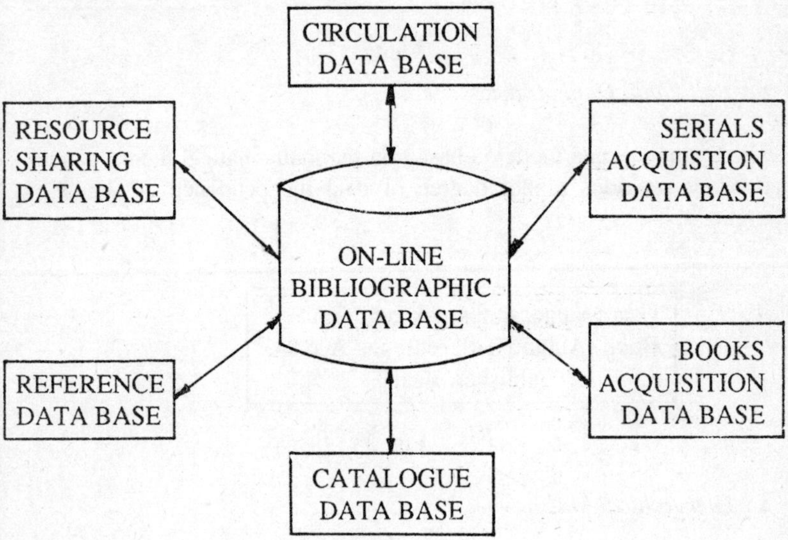

Fig. 1

Data models which are also called schemes play an important role in the database technology. There are three types of data models which may be useful in designing on-line library data base. The data models are as follows :

8. Network Model

A network data model is a more general model than a hierarchical model. The network model is able to depict the real-world situations efficiently and effectively as shown in Figure 2.

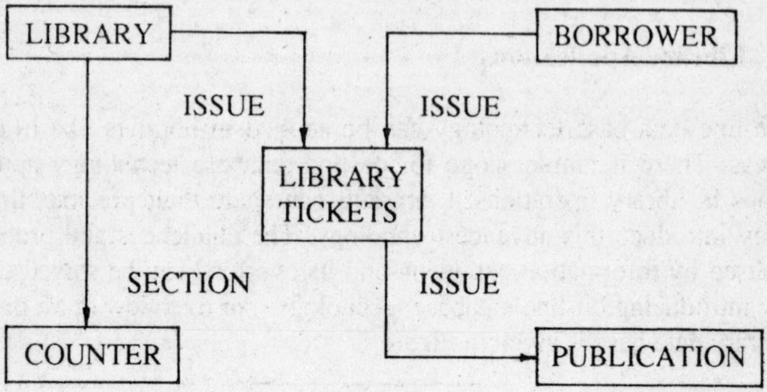

Fig. 2

8.1 *Relational Data Model*

The relational data model is based on the mathematical theory of relations. It provides higher degree of data independence as shown in Figure 3.

User (Name, status, sex, address)
Book (Author, Title, call no., Acc. no.
Publisher, Year)

Fig. 3

8.2 *Hierarchical Model*

In this model hierarchy is visualized up to the last ladder. It depends on every entry being subject to a higher one, up to the top. It is explained in Figure 4.

9. Conclusion

The on-line database technology is a boon to Librarians and Information Scientists. The application of this technology can revolutionize the methods and ways in which Librarians and Information Scientists collect, retrieve and disseminate information. Intensive data models visualizing real world's situations of separate Library operations like circulation, book acquisition, serials acquisition, readers services, location and reservation of books, inter-library loan, etc., may be designed. John Sandy says that on-line information retrieval will be indispensable to productive research scientists who must seek to understand and adopt this technology.

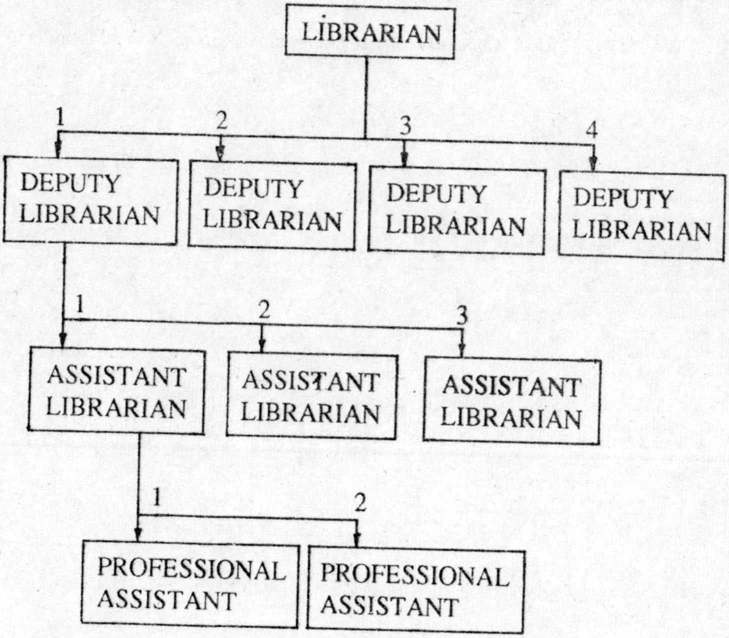

Fig. 4

REFERENCES

1 ATRE, S: *Database : Structural Techniques for Design, Performance and Management*. New York, 1980.

2 BURNS, Allen: *New Information Technology*. N Y, ELLIS, 1984.

3 BURCH, J G: *Information Systems : Theory and Practice*. New York; John Wiley, 1979. p. 122

4 COHEN, L J: *Database Management Systems*. Willesley. Q.E.D. Information Science 1978.

5 DATE, C J: *Introduction to Database Systems*. New Delhi, Narosa 1985.

6 GOLDSTEM, R L: Database Technology and Management. N Y, John Wiley, 1985.

7 MARTIN, James: *Computer Database Organization*. New Delhi, Prentice-Hall. 1984, p 22.

8 MURDICK, R G: *Information Systems for Modern Management*. New Delhi; Prentice-Hall, p. 143.

9 ROSS, R G: *Computerised Data Base Systems*. Computers and people. Jan 1976, pp. 28-30.

10 SANDY, John: On-line Database Vital for Scientific Research. (*Science*, 126:4553, June 1982).

11 WATSON, K H J: *Computer Based Information System*. N Y, Macmillan, 1984.

F 2

Computer-based Library Systems

B Vijaya Lakshmi

0. Introduction

Computers are used in libraries to assist in a number of library routines necessary for efficient day-to-day functioning. These library tasks fall into the area of "house-keeping" and consist of procedures for acquisition, cataloguing, circulation control and serial control. Computers are also used for formatting and generation of indices.

1. Computer-based Library Systems

Computer-based library systems were developed in the early sixties, when libraries in the USA and UK began experimenting with using computers in information processing. These were in the main punched card data processing systems. With improvements in computer technology and libraries becoming more acquainted with computers, we find that in the late sixties the computer came to be viewed as a tool for aiding routine procedures and activities. Most of these systems were developed locally in academic, special and public libraries.

The 1970s saw the development of the cooperative systems phase, when resource sharing and library networks came to be established, and many mechanized cooperative projects such as the BLMPC (Birmingham Libraries Cooperative Mechanization Project, UK) the OCLC (Ohio College Library Centre) were started. In the eighties of course this trend towards computerized library and information network has gained impetus with the highly effective and speedy communications technology coupled with sophisticated computer hardware and software developments.

1.1 *Advantages of Computer-based Library Systems*

(1) *Speed*: The computer can processes information much faster than human beings, and this permits better work flow through the library.
(2) *Accuracy*: The degree of precision and accuracy in processing information is high however it is dependent on the accuracy of information fed into the system. (There is a computer proverb that reads "garbage in garbage out".)
(3) *Costs*: Operating costs can be reduced if the system is well designed and well managed.
(4) Library workloads can be reduced, as the computer can do vast amounts of work and processing in keeping with the large amount of information being published.
(5) Improved services to users.
(6) Easier.
(7) Access to external data bases.

1.2 *Disadvantages*

There are also arguments against computer-based systems in libraries on the grounds that many of the so-called advantages of using computers may be only fallacies. Some of the points argued against are :

(1) Using computers does not make everything so simple or effortless.
(2) Computers are costly.
(3) They do not save time.
(4) Implementing systems on new computers is difficult.
(5) Better service is not achieved.
(6) Integrating systems into a network is difficult.

Perhaps there is also somewhere a hidden fear that computers may replace librarians, or prove them to be incompetent.

2. **Observations**

However it is perhaps ultimately a question of using the capabilities of the computer and electronic data processing to help librarians and information scientists in their work. The computer is an example of man's ingenuity and intelligence, and a computer system can only be as good or as bad as the persons who design, implement and operate the system.

3. Housekeeping Activities

Housekeeping procedures in a library are those routines or tasks that are required for everyday management and functioning of the library. They are broadly:

(1) Acquisitions
(2) Circulation control
(3) Cataloguing
(4) Serials control.

3.1 *Acquisitions*

Acquisitions and ordering systems in libraries cover the selection, ordering and accessioning of items into the library's collection. Computers are used (1) to send order slips and "chasers" for unacknowledged or overdue orders to the booksellers, (2) to produce lists of books on order, (3) to keep accounts of money spent, and (4) to produce accession lists of recently acquired books.

The detailed input to an acquisition system covers :

(1) New orders
(2) Amendments to existing orders
(3) Booksellers' reports
(4) Acknowledgments of receipt of items in the library.

Selection of new books can be done from commercially available services which disseminate information about forthcoming documents, or directly from MARC tapes, or any local inputs.

Two files are maintained in a computer-based acquisition system. One is the main file containing records of all current orders. The second is a file with the names and addresses of booksellers used by the library. A code number for each bookseller links the two files, so that bookseller information is not repeated in the order file.

The system prints out the orders addressing the appropriate supplier. Printing of orders can also be done on special pre-printed stationery that can be sent directly to the bookseller.

By checking with the date of entering the order record into the file, "chasers" can be sent to the booksellers, if no information regarding the order has been received within a predetermined time.

When the item is received in the library the order record with the bibliographic details becomes the basis of the catalogue record. The edited record is merely added to the catalogue file in an integrated system.

3.11 *Other Processes*: Other processes that can be performed by a computerized acquisitions system are :

(1) Listing items on order, by author, department or subject
(2) New accessions listing
(3) Notifying individuals who have recommended a particular book about the receipt of that book
(4) Control of accounts
(5) Production of relevant statistics to help management decisions.

3.2 *Circulation Control*

This is one-library service that is most amenable to computerization. The advantages are especially seen in the amount of time saved in issue and discharge routines, and the avoidance of bottlenecks which are the bane of any library. In very large libraries, users may be asked to fill up slips in duplicate at the circulation desk, and later at the end of the day these slips can be entered into the computer. Or a terminal at the circulation counter, with an operator entering the data directly is another way of doing it. Broadly, circulation systems using computers have the details of the book issued and the person borrowing it entered on files. Dates of return are on the basis of the period of loan (one week, a fortnight, etc.). Daily check of the files will identify what books are due or overdue and notices can be typed and sent to the users who have borrowed them. Provision for reservation data will make it possible to pick out those books for which there is a request and a user can be asked to return that particular book.

The circulation process in a computerized system depends on giving unique identification codes to books and to users. An accession number, or a call number can be used as this unique identification key for a book. Users can given individual identity codes.

3.21 *System Developed:* The system developed at the ENVIS Centre, INCOR is based on the use of such unique identification codes. It is a system operating with relational file structure. The files are divided into fields with relevant data, each with one key field, which can be referenced by any field in the other files.

There are in this system three main files. The first is the library catalogue, or a file containing bibliographic details of the books in the library. Each book has its unique document-ID which is the key field. The second file is the user file, containing the name and address of each user of the library, and a unique user-ID. The third file is the circulation file, in which are entered the document-ID, (of the book borrowed) the user-ID date of issue, and "reserved by" field to be used when necessary). The document-ID field is referenced by the document-ID of the catalogue file while defining the data base. The user-ID of the circulation file is referenced similarly to the user-ID of the user file.

As and when a book is issued, the details of document-ID user-ID and data of issue are entered in the circulation file. Depending on the system of issue (issue only on certain days, daily, etc.), the file can be run to give the names of users who may not have returned books in time. The system with the help of the key fields matches the user-ID from the circulation file against user-ID from user file, and document-ID from the circulation file against document-ID from the catalogue. This gives details of the user and the books borrowed. If it has been reserved by a particular user, the user-ID code in the "reserved by" field is matched to the user-ID of the user file to get the details of the user. The current date is checked against the date of issue plus the time allowed to the borrowers (say 15 days). If the current date exceeds this then a letter is issued to the particular user asking him to return the book as it is overdue or reserved by someone else.

Simple searches can be done by screen searching, by the end user or data entry personnel. For complicated searches, however, one can use SQL/DML (Structured Query Language/Data Manipulation Language) to formulate a query as shown below:

Query:

```
Select author, title, user-name, user-address, reserved-by
from catalogue, user-file, circulation-file
```

Where

documented-id of circulation = document-id of catalogue
& user-id of circulation = user-id of user-file
& reserved-by of circulation = user-id of user-file
& today > issue-date + 15

The results of the query can be formatted into a letter to a user asking him to return a particular book which might have been reserved by some other user.

Conceptual Framework of a Circulation System

Catalogue File

Document ID	Author	Title	Place of Publication	Publisher	Year
CS45	Kent, M	Remote Sensing	New York	McGraw-Hill	1984
DI102	Lancaster, F.W.	Information Retrieval	New York	John Wiley	1980

User File

User-ID	User Name	Address
GE 1	Dr. V.Venkateswara Rao	Centre for Water Resources
RS 3	Dr. Y.V.N. Krishna Murthy	Centre for Remote Sensing

Circulation File

User-ID	Document-ID	Date of Issue	Reserved by
GE 1	CS 45	1-11-85	RS 3
RS 3	DI 102	17-11-85	

3.3 *Cataloguing*

Cataloguing includes the job of describing, recording and displaying details of the holdings of the library. Computers are used to aid in the production, maintenance and updating of catalogues. The quality of the catalogue depends ultimately on the cataloguer. In other words initial input data are still the cataloguer's work.

Bibliographic details are gathered from relevant sources, or from the acquisitions system. Usually there is one main or master file for the holdings of the library, and a temporary file for cumulating the additional records, because printing the master file is done only once in a way.

After initial input of the records, the computer can perform simple tests on the record structure, and errors can be located and checked. Again if a basic record structure of a package format as that of the CDS/ISIS is used (as is now being done at the centre), entry of data becomes a very simple process. The computer can be asked to generate added entries if required, which can later be sorted into the main file. Separate listings for author, subjects and key points of access can be created. A postings file and an inverted index help the computer search and display records relevant to a specific query.

3.4 Serials Control

Serials control through the use of the computer is perhaps one of the most complicated tasks of housekeeping. This is perhaps because of the literally unpredictable nature of serial publications. Some of the functions of the serials control system that can be handled by the computer are :

(1) Listing of serials holdings.
(2) Accessioning of serials (which includes selection, ordering, checking-in, renewal of subscriptions, sending notices when issues are not received).

(a) Listing of serials holdings is basically producing a catalogue of serials. However, with serials there are problems relating to change in title, periodicity, etc. A listing system will depend on the bibliographic record for each serial being available in machine readable form. From a master file of such serials records, individual listings can be made based on title, subject, publishers/suppliers, etc. Union lists of serials holdings by librarians within a geographic region can also be produced by computer.

(b) Accessioning of serials must take into account receipt of issues, and periodicity of the serial, likely date of receipt in order to be able to send claims notices to suppliers for items not received, and to update the holdings file. To predict the arrival of periodical parts each record must contain information about the publication pattern of the serial. This relates to the number of volumes per calendar year, number of parts per volume, supplements, if any, the pattern of numbering parts, and the frequency publication. Algorithms can be written with reference to the real calendar, which use information on the details given above, to predict the arrival of each issue. Prediction cards can then be generated, and by checking them periodically "chaser" notices can be sent to the suppliers when an issue is overdue.

Details of the suppliers and the price per volume are necessary for the system to handle subscription, renewals and accounting functions.

4. Information Search and Retrieval

The search process on a computerized database has many advantages over search from a catalogue by manual methods, in terms of speed and accuracy. Any library or information centre can create first a set of machine readable records of its holdings, based on a structured format, or using a data base package like the CDS/ISIS which is described later.

Users can search the data base through key terms of author, subject or title, which are formulated into a search expression using Boolean operators (logical connections AND, NOT, OR). The computer will display relevant terms/records, that match the terms of the user's request. Current Awareness Listings and Selective Dissemination of Information (SDI) Retrospective searches are services where the computer capabilities can be used very effectively.

Index generation is another area where computers are generally of use. Computers can be used to format the entries in a permuted index, and also to generate the entries for an index. Key words can be derived from the bibliographic description, or assigned to describe the document (subject keys) and then put into the required format. KWIC indices for instance can be produced from titles of documents, with keyword and context generation performed by the computer. Stop lists or puffword lists prevent words like "a", "the", "of", etc., from being used as the key terms. Fully automatic indexing can also be done through statistical analysis and word frequency counts with weighting, provided the text is in machine readable form.

REFERENCES

1 JAMES, A Senn : *Analysis and Design of Information Systems*. New York; McGraw-Hill, 1985.

2 KIMBER, R T : *Automation in Libraries*. New York, Pergamon Press, 1974.

3 SALTON, Gerald and MICHEAL, McGill : *Introduction to Modern Information Retrieval*, London McGraw-Hill International Book Co., 1983.

4 TEDD, L, A : *Introduction to Computer-Based Library Systems*, 1977.

F 3

Introducing Computers

P Mohan Krishna

0. Introduction

As we move into the 21st century, we must ask ourselves, how well or ill, we, as librarians and information scientists, and equipped to meet the challenges that it brings. The growth of information has been so rapid and so extensive that users are puzzled when confronted with the problems of selection and access.

To cope with this deluge of information, a vast array of technological devices have been called into action. A whole new area of information technology has been developed which assists librarians and information workers in reaching the correct information, in any of a variety of repackaged forms, to the user, when he requires it. The automating of library routines and services has become a common feature, especially in the West, and reliance on the computer, the electronic wizard that can tackle any job, is complete.

We in India are lagging behind in making effective use of technology in our libraries and information centres. It is time we look to the future, and see how we can derive the benefits of the "black box" in rendering services to our users. Computers are not competition to human beings, but they can be used with success in performing a variety of everyday jobs, as well as being a powerful aid in information processing and dissemination.

But first let us try to understand what the computer is and what it does, and how best we can harness its capabilities to our advantage. What follows is a brief overview of and introduction to these electronic machines?

1. Computer

The computer is an electronic device which can manipulate data by a set of instructions, and which can store the data in its memory for any amount of time, to be retrieved with high speed when required. Computer history can be divided in terms of generations.

2. Computer Generations

2.1 *ABC*

Modern computers originated in December 1939, when Dr John Vincent Atanasoff, Professor of Mathematics at Iowa State College, developed a working model of the first electronic computer. Using vacuum tubes for the internal "thinking" circuitry and capacitors for main storage, the ABC (Atanasoff-Berry Computer) model had the characteristics and makeup of today's electronic computer. The ABC was the first true computer, although it is not popularly recognized as such.

2.2 *ENIAC*

While the ABC was being developed, John Mauchly of the University of Pennsylvania visited Atanasoff. Using Atanasoff's basic principles, he and J. Presper Eckert of the Moore School of Engineering (University of Pennsylvania) began working on an electronic computer. In 1946, they built the ENIAC.

The ENIAC differed from many pervious devices. For example, two years earlier (1944), Aiken of Harvard had developed the MARK I, under an IBM grant. Yet unlike the MARK I, which used electromechanical relay switches, the ENIAC was completely electronic. The ENIAC had no moving parts. It contained nearly 19,000 tubes for the electronic pulse-switching functions. It performed 5,000 additions in one second which outperformed electromechanical devices 300 to 1. It was programmable and had the capability to store problem calculations. The primary limitations of the ENIAC, however, were its size and batch processing drawbacks. It occupied 1,500 square feet of floor space and processed only one programme or problem at a time.

2.3 *UNIVAC*

After their success with the ENIAC in 1946, Eckert and Mauchly left the University of Pennsylvania to design commercial computers under the name Eckert-Mauchly Computer Corporation. In 1949, the company and the ENIAC patent were acquired by Remington Rand Corporation which developed the UNIVAC Computer.

2.4 *The First Generation (1951-1958)*

The introduction of the UNIVAC (Universal Automatic Computer I) by Remington Rand Corporation in 1951 marked the advent of the first generation of computers. Also initiating this generation were the IBM 650 and the Burroughs 220. The sales figure for the IBM 650, originally set at 50, rose to 2,000. Its popularity set the tone for IBM's steady domination of the market from that point on.

This generation utilized the vacuum tube as a means of storing data in memory. The addition of memory made the punched card systems and the calculators virtually obsolete. The wire board was replaced by computer programmes written in a new language for processing. Computers of the first generation :

(1) reduced processing time by a factor of ten,
(2) were bulky and somewhat inflexible,
(3) demanded strict observance of air-conditioning requirements,
(4) were relatively unreliable due to electric current fluctuations and tube failure (in the IBM computer, the tubes burned out at the rate of one tube a day),
(5) contained limited and primitive memory (main storage was made of magnetic drum that stored approximately 16,000 characters),
(6) leaned toward batch applications (the entire computer was dedicated to a specific application or a programme until completed), and
(7) required programmes written for a specific computer (programmes could not be run on another computer model).

When the first generation computer became available, no educational programme precisely met the requirements of the new technology. The user organization was ill-prepared to implement the new system. A new breed of technicians appeared. They were the programmers, the computer operators, and the systems analysts. To determine qualifications, aptitude tests had to be administered by the manufacturer. He also evaluated the user's EDP staff, exerting a direct influence on hiring decisions.

2.5 *The Second (Transistorized) Generation (1959–1964)*

Transistorized circuits formed the basis for the second generation of computers in 1959. Typical second generation computers were the IBM 1401 and 7000 series, Control Data 3600, and Burroughs 5500. The IBM 1401 was the most popular computer by far. By the end of this generation of computers in 1964, there were more IBM 1401s than all other computers in operation.

The new transistor technology made the previous generation obsolete. The large-scale computers were marked by large memory banks, by faster milli-second processing speed and by more reliable operations. (The time required for a computer to do a calculation is measured by a special unit of time-a milli-second which is one-thousandth of a second. In contrast, a microsecond is one-millionth of a second. Third and fourth generation computers calculate at the nanosecond (one billionth of a second) speed. An idea of the smallness of a nanosecond can be seen from the fact that there are as many nanoseconds in one second as there are seconds in thirty years.) Other primary characteristics were :

(1) The use of the transistor reduced the physical size of the computer. A model of transistor circuit cord for computer is given in Figure 2.

(2) Main memory capacity was improved by the use of magnetic cores. Large systems could store up to 1 million characters compared to the 16,000 character capacity of earlier computers.

(3) Reliability improved through built-in error detection and correction features.

(4) The transistor and magnetic core reduced the storage cost per character from $ 2.50 to $ 0.85.

(5) Versatility improved by accommodating multiple users to access the computer concurrently.

(6) Data storage was improved through the introduction of the disk file. Data could now be written and read simultaneously and directly without having to go through the bulky tape

files. Disk systems were capable of storing millions of characters. Data and programmes from any disk could be retrieved within fractions of a second.

(7) Programmes were written in symbolic language. Although it required special translating programmes, it relieved the programmer of the details required in first generation computer programmes.

(8) High-level machine-independent languages (FORTRAN, COBOL, and the like) began to appear. It made the programmer's life easier. He or she no longer had to have detailed knowledge of the computer.

The new languages, however, brought inefficiencies, which had an advers effect on the escalating cost of computing. Data processing and personnel costs increased in direct proportion to the increased cost of computer systems. As computers became more sophisticated during this generation further job classifications had to be made. The traditional programmers became a systems programmers. Systems managers began to appear, to work with the operating systems that controlled the computer. (An Operating System is a set of programmes of software designed to control the computer and monitor its operations).

2.51 *Software*: Up to this point, computer manufacturers were developing high-level languages and software to accommodate the data processing specialist rather than the end user. While this strategy promoted a centralized facility, disregard for the real needs of the user prompted the end of the "main-frame" era and the dawn of the mini-computer in the late 1960s.

2.6 *The Third Generation (1964-1971)*

Typical of the so-called third generation computers introduced after 1964 were the IBM System 360, the Honeywell 200, the RCA Spectra 70 series, and National Cash Register Century series. The transistor was replaced by solid state technology and monolithic integrated circuits. The main features of third generation computers were as follows :

(1) Operating Systems handled several jobs at the same time. Most applications could also be run in real time.

(2) Time sharing systems emerged. Several users could use the computer facility at the same time.

(3) Standardization developed among different computer models and applications oriented languages such as COBOL, FORTRAN and the rest.

(4) While computation output per dollar was increased, main memory costs dropped approximately to $ 0.25 per character.

(5) Minicomputers increased in popularity and provided a vehicle for redistributing computer power to the user, when needed.

(6) A wide range of input-output and direct-access devices (such as disk storage) sprang up, including special magnetic-ink readers and graph plotters.

(7) Reliability and processing speed were improved. Internal computer errors were reduced and nanosecond speed became a reality.

A significant contribution of third generation computers was the remote (intelligent) terminal to permit geographically dispersed users to communicate with a central computer. Unlike the batch processing computer that handled one application at a time, the third generation computer handled many programmes and responded to inquiries without delay. The on-line (direct), real-time (immediate) computer mode became a routine environment with most large systems.

In retrospect, the gains are remarkable. The ENIAC exhibited processing speed 10,000 times faster than earlier computing methods. Twentyfive years later, through three successive generations, data processing speed increased nearly 10,000 times or roughly 100,000 times over the speed of the ENIAC.

Although these figures are approximate, they give us an idea about the direction and the rate of development in data processing.

2.7 *The Fourth Generation (1971–?)*

In 1971, a new line of controversial fourth generation computers was introduced. Although they offer users significant improvements over the third generation, they are considered more evolutionary then revolutionary. Typical computers are the IBM 370, Burroughs 700, and Honeywell 6000 series. Regardless of their brand name, their general features can be summarized as follows :

(1) The miniaturization of circuits reduced them to the size of a pinhead.
(2) Breakdown diagnosis and error detection techniques increased. Most models have built-in automatic features that reprocess and error and record the occurrence in a log for analysis by the systems engineer.
(3) Multiprogramming increased. Multiprogramming is the concurrent execution of two or more programmes by a computer.
(4) The CPU can operate in more than one mode to improve the system's overall performance.
(5) Main memory cost was further reduced to $ 0.05 per character.
(6) Improvements in operating systems made virtual storage possible. This feature allows secondary storage devices (disks, tapes, etc.) to be treated as an expanded part of the computers' main memory, so that it gives the appearance of one macromemory unit.
(7) The implementation of special software for managing data bases gave rise to what is called "data base management systems".

With fourth generation computers, the user can now access files directly, schedule various production and other problems, and acquire authorized data when needed. They constitute a step toward a truly user-oriented, interactive computer system.

One significant outcome of the evolutionary computers of the 1970s is the effort to pack tremendous data processing power into the minicomputers at a relatively low cost.

In line with decentralization trend is the emerging concept called distributed data processing (DDP). Such a system redistributed computer power back to the user, making authorized data immediately available. It also enables the people-oriented computer to assume a new position as a managerial tool rather than as a dehumanizing centralized controller of operations. Distributed data processing is not the same as dispersed data processing. In distributed data processing, dispersed computers are interconnected to each other and to a central computer facility, allowing each end user to function as a part of a total system. In contrast, dispersed data processing represents semi-autonomous mini or microprocessors that are located at sites other than that of the central computer system. Little or no staff is committed on a full-time basis to data processing. Furthermore, few data processing professionals are required by the end-user organization.

The organization's computer data are accessed on-line by terminals or by minicomputers. The terminals are distributed at the user's sites but tied into the computer through telephone lines. Distributed data processing's effectiveness rests on the fact that it shifts responsibility for data availability and data base to the user. It returns system control to the user and eliminates the need for the traditional centralized computer facility, even though the DDP system may have a central site.

3. Types of Computers

We can classify computers basically as : (1) Analog computers for scientific purposes, (2) Digital computers used for general purposes, (3) Hybrid computers which can be used for both purposes.

3.1 *Analog Computers*

The name "analog" comes from the word "analogous", meaning "similar". The thermometer, for instance, records various mercury levels based on changes in temperature. In other words, changes in temperature are shown by analogous changes in the level of mercury. The same principle is used by the analog computer to perform arithmetic functions. It converts data into voltages and computes by measuring the changes in voltages. Thus, as a measuring device, it represents values by continuously varying physical data such as the amount of pressure, voltage, or electric current. Computations are performed by combining these quantities.

Analog computers are commonly used in process measurements in industries, such as chemical and electric power plants, and petroleum refineries. Their primary advantage is their prompt response to the handling of data generated by an ongoing physical process. The obvious drawback is the accuracy factor. Compared to the digital computer, an analog computer produces systematic errors which occasionally cause slight deviation from the true value. The input is usually set upon the machine by a plug board. Since there is usually no provision for storing results internally, the output is sent directly to a curve plotter.

3.2 *Digital Computers*

In a digital computer, all arithmetic computations depend ultimately on counting. Unlike the analog computer, which receives data in a continuous form, the digital computer handles numbers in discreate from. It is capable of reading numbers in degrees of accuracy far greater than those reached by the analog computer. In addition to arithmetic operations, it edits input data, and prints out the results of its processing at high sop speed. Although the analog computer has similar characteristics, the method of accomplishing them is very different and cumbersome for business applications.

In summary, analog computers are ideal for scientific and engineering problems, when physical measurements are manipulated as data for arithmetic operations and when a high degree of accuracy is not critical. In contrast, digital computers are used in handling business applications, when repetitive routine arithmetic operations are involved and when 100% accuracy is demanded.

3.3 *Hybrid Computers*

Although both analog and digital computers are extensively used and widely accepted in various industries, manufacturers have attempted to design a computer that combines the best features of both types. This special purpose machine, called a Hybrid computer, combines the measuring capabilities of an analog computer and the logical and control capabilities of the digital computer. It offers an efficient and economical method of working out special types of problems in science and various areas of engineering. Among the applications are space vehicle simulations and the training of space pilots, analysis of signals received from special sensors attached to humans and animals in laboratories, and the solving of differential equations for chemical reactors.

4. Categories of Computers

We can also classify computers into five categories according to their speed, word length and memory.

4.1 *Microcomputers or Microprocessors*

These have Microprocessor CPU and Semiconductor memory.

Semiconductor Memory	664-128 K
Word Length	8 bits - 16 bits
Speed	250 microseconds/instructions

Ex: Apple, Micorsense and IBM PC and its compatibles

4.2 *Minicomputers*

These are faster than Micros.

Semiconductor Memory	1 mb to 4 mb
Word Length	8 bits - 16 bits
Speed	Mips (Million instructions/second)

Ex: HP-3000, PDP-8, Omega 58000

4.3 *Mainframe*

Semiconductor Memory	1 mb to 16 mb.
Word Length	32 - 48, 64 Speed
Speed	10 mips

Ex: Cyber 170, IBM 360/370

4.4 *Supercomputer*

Semiconductor Memory	
Word length	56, 80 bits
Speed	50 Mips

5. Computer Configuration

The main components of a computer system are: (1) Hardware, (2) Software, and (3) Peopleware. Components of a computer system are also explained in Figure 1.

5.1 *Hardware*

The physical units making up a computer system including electric and electronic equipment are called hardware.

5.2 *Software*

A generic term for those components of a computer system that are intangible rather than physical. All the programmes come under software.

5.3 *Peopleware*

Persons who are involved with computer systems, like programmers, systems engineers, etc.

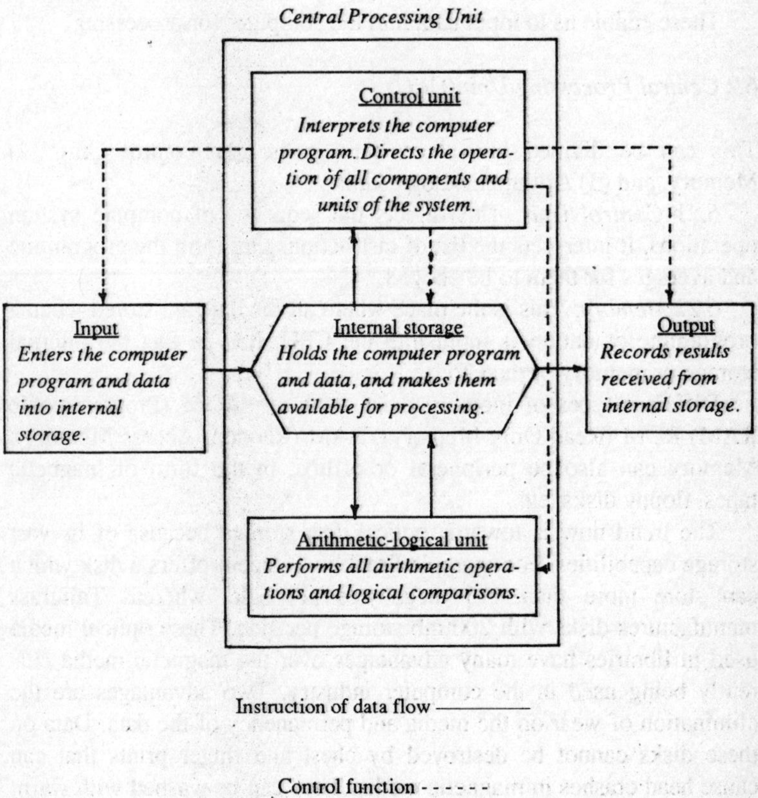

Fig. 1: *Components of a Computer System*

6. Hardware

Hardware can be divided into three components : (1) Input, (2) Central processing unit, and (3) Output.

6.1 *Input*

This constitutes the various data input and storage devices. Some of them are (i) Punched Cards, (ii) Punched Tape, (iii) Magnetic Tape, (iv) Magnetic Ink Character Readers, (v) Key Board, (vi) Voice Recognizers, (vii) Optical Character Recognizers, (viii) Digitizer, (ix) Computer Readable Microfilm, and (x) Optical Disk, etc.

These enable us to input data into the computer for processing.

6.2 *Central Processing Unit (CPU)*

This can be divided into three main parts: (1) Control Unit, (2) Memory, and (3) Arithmetic-Logic Unit.

6.21 *Control Unit*: This directs the sequence of compute system operations. It interprets the list of instructions that form the programme and averages for them to be obeyed.

6.22 *Memory*: This is the place where all the data are stored when a programme or datum is input into the CPU. It is in fact the internal storage or memory of the CPU.

Different types of memory exist, such as PROM (Programmable RAM) ROM (Read Only Memory), RAM (Random Access Memory). Memory can also be peripheral or offline, in the form of magnetic tapes, floppy disks, etc.

The trend now is towards optical disk storage because of its vast storage capabilities. For example Franklin Telecom offers a disk which can store more than 115 megabytes per side, whereas Tallgrass manufactures disks with 200 mb storage per side. These optical media used in libraries have many advantages over the magnetic media currently being used in the computer industry. Two advantages are the elimination of wear on the media and permanency of the data. Data on these disks cannot be destroyed by chest and finger prints that can cause head crashes in magnetic media. They can be washed with warm water and mild soap if there is any decrease in response time. These disks do not warp as floppy disks can. Neither are they affected by climatic conditions. Maintenance costs are therefore very low.

6.221 *Other Types of Memory*: Other types of memory now appearing on the scene are described below :

6.2211 *Bubble Memory*: This is a revolutionary alternative to the core memory. Since no wires are used as in core memories Bubble Memory would be easier to produce and miniaturize. It thus offers hope for greater reliability and longer life. Other advantages are that:

> It has an error rate of less than 1 in 100 trillion bits and the capacity to retain stored data for a 100 years. There is a hundred-fold improvement in access time. The operating cost is much less than that for any other memory. The Bubble Memories have very high density. A square inch garnet with 3-micron bubbles can store three million bits of data. The same size garnet with 0.4 micron bubbles is capable of storing 100 million bits of data.

Other memories like the Josephson Circuit, Tunable Dye Laser Memory, Photodigital Memory, Holographic Memory have also been developed.

6.23 *Arithmetic-Logic Unit*: Execution of most operations within the computer takes place in the arithmetic-logic unit. Consider a typical example: suppose two numbers located in the main memory are to be added. They are brought into arithmetic unit where the actual addition is carried out. The sum may then be stored in the memory. Similarly, any other arithmetic or logic operation (for example, multiplication, division, comparison of numbers) is done by bringing the required operands into the ALU.

7. **Output Devices**

Output devices display the results of data which are manipulated.

7.1 *Cathode Ray Tube Terminal*: Cathode ray tube terminals are those where we can see the data on a visual display unit.

7.2 *Daisy Wheel Printer*:

Daisy wheel printers can print the characters using a serial impact printer with a print element composed of a series of spokes radiating from a hub. Each spoke contains a single character. Its speed varies from 30-100 characters/second.

7.3 *Dotmatrix*

The dotmatrix printer uses a print head containing banks of fine wires at high speeds against an inked ribbon. Wires are arranged in a matrix as 5X7, 7X9, 9X9, or 12X9. It can print 30-90 characters/second.

7.4 *Band Printer*

The band printer is the most popular line printer using fully formed character technology. It prints at a speed of 150-4000 lines/minute.

7.5 *Chain/Drum Printer*

In this device individual characters are formed as slugs linked together to form a chain. The chain is pulled across the paper and a hammer strikes when the correct character is in the proper position on a line. It can print 300 to 1500 lines/minute.

7.6 *Inkjet*

This is a non-impact printing method whereby a stream of ink is sprayed on to the paper forming the characters. Its speed is 72-95,000 lines/mintue.

7.7 *Thermal*

In a thermal printer the print head moves across specially treated heat sensitive paper at a speed of 30-120 CPS.

7.8 *Electro Sensitive*

This device uses specially prepared paper made with a metallic coating over a black background. Voltages are applied to a mooring print head which burns off the metallic coating, leaving the black background as the character. Its speed is 600 CPS to 6,600 CPS.

7.9 *Electrostatic*

This method of printing also uses a specially coated paper that is passed over an assembly of matrix elements or styli. These deposit on electrical charge in the form of dots, which form the character outline on the paper. The paper is then passed through a toner so that the electrically charged dots attract ink particles which create the character image speed of 300-18,000 lines/mintues.

7.10 *Laser/Xerographic*

This is a highly advanced technique introduced in the 1980s. It uses a rotating polygon mirror to deflect a modulated fiberoptic light beam or laser beam onto a photosensitive surface of a drum or belt. This forms a latent image which attracts a toner to the exposed areas. The toner is then electro-statically transferred to the paper and fused to form the final printed image. The speed is 10 pages/minute to 215 pages/minute. It is very costly, often costlier than super minicomputers.

7.11 *Plotter*

These use different coloured pens and produce various graphic outputs. However they are slow. Recenlty a laser scanner/writer system has been developed which provides for resolution of 100 to 2,000 lines per inch, with a 2,563 range of colours from three primary colours. However this is not economically feasible right now.

7.12 *COM (Computer Output Microfilm)*

This refers to techniques, devices and systems used in the recording of computer output on microfilm. This can be done by a COM reader which microfilms an elctro-optical display of data processing of the exposed microfilm can be an integrated part of the COM recording. Nowadays this is gaining popularity due to its advantages in terms of space saving, economy of multiplication, economy of distribution and rate of output.

8. **Software**

Software includes all the programmes that a computer system uses for its regular operation and for solving users' problems. Software can be divided into system software, and application or user software.

8.1 *System Software*

The computer manufacturer is responsible for this type of software. These are for the regular operation of the system and allow the user to have an interface with the system. This software consists of (1) Machine Language, (2) Assembly Language, (3) Translators and (4) Operating System.

8.11 *Machine Language*: The basic language that can be directly understood by the machine is machine language in which data are represented by a listing of binary patterns. The binary patterns of machine language programme are represented in both octal and hexadecimal notations.

8.12 *Assembly Language*: A machine language programme for a specific computer can be executed on that computer without the aid of other programmes. However, since programming in machine language is a cumbersome process, programmes are usually written in a language that has a more symbolic and stylized form. The simplest is assembly language. However its scope is very limited.

8.13 *Translators*: A programme written in any language other than machine language is called a "source programme". Source programmes are translated into machine language by system programmes called "translators". In the case of assembly languages, these translators are called "assemblers". When the source programme is in a high-level language the translator is called a "compiler". The output of the language the translation process is called an "object programme".

8.14 *Operating System*: This is a special type of software which provides an essential "logical- to-physical" interface between the user and the physical machine. Besides these softwares many utilities like editors, calendars, calculators, data bases, dictionaries, etc., may be provided by the manufacturers.

8.2 *User Software*

This is also known as "application software". This is generally developed by the users themselves for their individual and specific requirements. They are written generally in high level languages like "COBOL", "FORTRAN", "C", etc.

Software packages for specific problems are also available from commercial software vendors. These do not require much expertise in handling. Apart from packages for educational or managerial purposes, a large number of recreational software are also available, that match the skill of the user against that of the computer.

REFERENCES

1 AWAD, E M: *Business Data Processing*. New Jersey; Prentice-Hall, 1980.

2 DAVIS, G B: *Computers and Information Processing*, Tokyo McGraw-Hill Kogakusha Ltd., 1977.

3 DESMARIAS, Norman: Laser Libraries (Byte: *The Small Systems Journal*, Vol 11 (5), 1986, pp. 235-249).

4 KENT, Allen and GALVIN, T J Ed.: *Information Technology: Crictical Choices for Library Decision-Makers*, 1982.

5 PHILIPPAKIS, S A and KAZMIER Leonard: *Information Systems Through COBOL*. McGraw-Hill International Book Company, 1978.

6 TEDD, L A: *Introduction to Computer-Base Library Systems*, 1977.

G 1

Use of Personal Computers in Library and Information Systems

S S Murthy and V K Rangra

0. Introduction

Information explosion, a phenomenon of the past few decades, resulted in the exponential growth of printed matter, which created for the libraries the problems of bibliographical control, storage and dissemination of information. This adversely affected service to the users who had by now become more conscious and appreciative of the value of information. A number of new systems, techniques and strategies were developed to find out solution to these problems.

1. Library in a Desk

A few areas of science and technology such as computer, telecommunication, photography, printing, which have potential application to information processing, were carved out to form a separate discipline called information technology. This discipline has made many strides and revolutionized the state-of-art.

A new concept of paperless information society was put forward by FW Lancaster, according to which by the year 2000, paper as a medium of communication and record will cease to exist and will be replaced by electronic medium[1]. Earlier in 1972, Robert Landau had conceptualized a "Library in a Desk" which comprised a computer terminal connectable to any on-line retrieval system through a telephone line, and a microfilm reader for temporary storage and viewing. The use of computer for information processing, storage, retrieval, dissemination and performance of a number of library operations has made it possible to realize this concept, particularly so, on the emergence of microprocessor-bases small sized computers popularly known as tabletop models or personal computers.

2. Rise of Personal Computer (PC)

Within a span of about 40 years, since the first computer ENIAC appeared on the scene, the computer has considerably shrunk in size. This has been made possible by the chip technology wherein hundreds of thousands of transistors can be put on a single chip of size 5 sq mm (1 mm thick) by a process called VLSI (very large scale integration). For example CPU of HP-9000 microcomputer has a single chip containing 450,000 transistors.[2] A modern microcomputer is thousands time smaller than its ancestors.[3] By bringing enormous computer power at drastically reduced cost, the modern microcomputer competes with earlier mainframe computer. It can be put on desk in homes, schools and offices and can be used by layman. Because of its small size and easy-to-operate mechanism (user-friendly system), it is called personal computer (PC). It was in 1980 that Apple Computer Company started the PC revolution in the United States and the British maverick Clive Sinclair began the "Home Computer" revolution.[4] The first largescale production of PCs was started in 1981 by IBM, the pioneer in this field, with only 17,500 pieces and by 1985 this figure rose to 2,072,000.[5]

3. Characteristics of PC

A PC usually meets the following requirements:[2]

(i) The cost of the system is normally about Rs. 50,000. The cost is further decreasing due to hard competition among the manufacturers.
(ii) The system is designed to accept secondary memory devices.
(iii) It provides user interaction with the system.
(iv) The system has facility to use one or more of the programming languages such as ADA, BASIC, COBOL, FORTRAN, PASCAL.
(v) It is designed to solve wide variety of problems and not for a single application
(vi) It is easily available through normal trade channels.

4. Constituents of a PC System

CPU (Central Processing Unit)
Memory (main/core)
Floppy Disk Drive
Hard Disk Drive
Keyboard Terminal
Monitor/VDU (Visual Display Unit)
Printer
Operating Systems
Compilers (for programming languages)
MODEM (for communication)

The significant feature of a PC is not so much its physical features as the characteristics of its operating system. In a PC emphasis is laid on making it a more user-friendly system even at the cost of its computing power. The modern trend in microprocessor technology is to have larger word-length and higher circuit speeds. These assets give advantage of greater speed, memory access and accuracy. The larger word capability is reflected in the larger number of bits of the chip or microprocessor. Thus PCs are available as 8-bit, 16-bit and now 32-bit systems.

5. Choice of a PC

The main criteria in the choice of a PC is the services it is expected to provide and ease of its operation. As the prices of PCs are falling, one should not be tempted to wait for further fall as the price of a PC system is expected to stabilize at around $1,500. Future PCs are likely to offer more improved features such as increased memory, reduced sizes, increased processor power, improved printers, more powerful programming languages, improved user access (keyboard supplemented or replaced by touch screen and voice systems) are greater flexibility.

Due to a rapid change in the semiconductor technology, the PCs may rapidly become obsolete. The new system should be able to support the old software although total compatibility may not be possible. Software of a PC is an important factor in its choice as it is very expensive and for most of the users, development of software may not be possible. There should be option for off-the-shelf software so that a buyer can buy what he needs. For this purposes the user should gain some experience with the available programmes before making the purchase. All business oriented PCs offer text-editing for word processing, which should also be taken note of. System configuration should be examined to assess the proper combination of hardware and software for current and projected requirements. Computer word-length as reflected in the number of bits of the chip (whether it is 8, 16 or 32 bit) is an important point in the choice.

Memory capacity in the form of floppy disk and hard disk drive is an important consideration. Choice of printer is another criteria, i.e. whether it is thermal or dot matrix printer. These days laser-printer is available which gives a high quality print. Although PCs are meant for individual users and serve as stand-alone work stations but their ability to receive and transit data to other computer system is an important requirement to acquire networking capability[2].

6. PC Industry in India

The Government of India under its computer policy is giving all possible incentives and encouragements in the production of PCs in the country. The credit for introducing PC in India goes to Minicomp Pvt Ltd who marketed it in the mid 1984 with a price tag of Rs.1.2 lakhs[4]. There are about 30 manufacturing companies in India which at present are mostly importing "Kits" from UA, Japan, Taiwan and South Korea and then assembling them here. These assembled PCs are usually made IBM compatible. Installed capacity of PC manufacturers in India is shown in the table below:[6]

	Manufacturer	Installed Capacity	Total Manufactured Items (%)
(i)	Sterling Electronics Pvt Ltd	1800	18.1
(ii)	Hindustan Computers Ltd (HCL)	1800	18.1
(iii)	Usha Microprocess Controls Ltd	1550	15.6
(iv)	Wipro Information Technology Ltd	1400	14
(v)	Minicomp Pvt Ltd	1300	13.1
(vi)	Others	2100	21.1

Some of the PC makes available in India are :

Busybee (HCL), Siva (Sterling), Eagle (Usha) Neptune (Minicomp), Zenith (Zenith), Wipro (Wipro), Uptron S-1600 (Uptron), Tandy 1000 (DCM). These are usually available in two versions XT (extended technology) and AT (advanced technology).

Indian manufacturers produced some 8,000 home computers system in 1985 as against only 1,200 in 1984. This figure is expected to reach 20,000 by 1986.[7]

7. Application of PCs in Library and Information Systems

The PCs are used in the libraries and information centres for a variety of tasks, ranging from usual housekeeping library operations to on-line search. In a survey carried out in the U.K. by the Forum for Information Resources in Libraries (FIRM) in association with the Library Association Library, the use of microcomputers (PCs) in the libraries in the U.K. (covered under the survey) is as under[8]:

Use Type	*Frequency*
Housekeeping	36
Indexing	27
On-line Access	19
Terminal	12
Prestel	11
Public Use	6
Other	4
Ordering	2

Besides applications in library and information work, the microcomputers (PCs) have also been found useful for writing of papers. A study of 60 university professors using microcomputers in their work showed that 67% believed that microcomputers enabled them to write more; while 53% said that they improved the quality of their writing. An indication of the trend is that about half of the American doctoral dissertations will be written on computer and a similar proportion of scientific and technical journal articles.[9]

8. Use of PCs in DESIDOC

PCs were acquired and put to use in DESIDOC in 1985-86, although the computerization work started much earlier on the mainframe computer PRIME-750. The PC systems are available in DESIDOC, in addition to the use of the mainframe system (PRIME-750) are given in the appendix.

8.1 *Services/Operations on PCs*

The following services or operations are conducted on these PCs:

8.11 *Information Storage and Retrieval*

— SDI
— Bibliographies (Monthly/Weekly Alert) with Indexes
— Database creation and updation
— Access Vocabulary of standard terms used for information storage and retrieval
— Key Word Out of Context (KWOC) of standard terms used in the data base.

8.12 *Library Operations*

(a) Classified Accession List with Indexes

— Printing of various catalogues
— Author
— Title
— Series
— Book label details

(b) Circulation Control

— Reminders for return of documents
— Reservation of documents
— On-line Query regarding a particular document through
Accession Number
Author
Title
Member/Borrower
Subject Identifier
Call Number

(c) Serial Control

— List of current periodicals
— Reminders for missing issues
— Holdings details
— Vendor wise lists
— Document-typewise lists
— Supply orders

(d) Acquisition Control (under development)

— Reminders for non-receipt of books, reports, etc.
— Information of requisition on arrival of book(s)
— Financial control.

9. Conclusion

The computerization of library and information systems has become a necessity for improving efficiency in services. It cannot be avoided, and cannot be delayed and longer. The question of computerization is note "whether" but "when" and "how". PCs, because of their within-the-reach price range and satisfactory performance can prove to be an asset to the small and medium sized libraries and information centres. The new entrants in this field should take full advantage of the PCs and other current information technologies. These technologies and their application to L&I fields must be discussed in the annual meetings of the professional associations like SIS, IASLIC ILA, GILA (Now called AGLIS – Association of Government Librarians and Information Specialists). This will provide a forum for discussion and exchange of ideas on computerization and utilization of other information technologies among the professionals.

REFERENCES

1 LANCASTER, F W: *Towards Paperless Information System.* Academic Press, 1978.

2 TOONG, H D and GUPTA, A: Personal Computers. (In: *Information Technology Revolution*, Edited by Tom Forester, Basil Blackwell, 1985, pp. 169-181).

3 TOONG and GUPTA, A: Shrinking Chips and Humourless Micros. (*Computers Today*, Oct 1986, p 381).

4 RAJU, Chellum: Where Computers Dare. *Times of India* (Sunday), 16 Nov, 1986).

5 RAJU, Chellum: Growth of IBM PCs. *(Computers Today*, Oct 1986, p. 6).

6 RAJU, Chellum: PC Prices — Aftermath. *(Computers Today*, Oct 1986, pp. 4-6).

7 MATHUR, R S: Computers making humans obsolete. (*Hindustan Times*, 18 Oct, 1986).

8 BATT, C: Microcomputers in UK Public Libraries: A Review of Current Trends (*Programme*, 19 (1), Jan 1985, pp. 39-47).

9 CASE, D: Personal Computer: Missing Link to the Electronic Journal ? (*JASIS*, 36 (5), Sept 1985, pp. 309-313).

APPENDIX

List of Computer Systems Available at DESIDOC

1.	IDM S/40-II	Two
	CPU	64 KB, 8-Bit
	2% Floppy Disk Drive	800 KB (unformatted) 5 1/4" DSDD
	Dot Matrix Printer	180 Cps
	Software Supported	BASIC, COBOL, d Base-II Electronic Spreadsheet, FORTRAN, PASCAL Prime Interface, Wordstar
2.	EAGLE PC/XT PLUS	Two
	CPU	640 KB, 16-Bit
	1% Winchester Disk	20 MB
	Additional Floppy Disk	20 MB
	Dot Matrix Printer	300 cps
	Daisy Wheel LQ Printer	36 cps
	Software Supported	BASIC COBOL, d BASE-II, FORTRAN, LOTUS 1-2-3, PASCAL, Wordstar
3.	SIVA PC/AT	One
	CPU	3 MB, 16-Bit
	1% Floppy Disk Drive	1.2 MB
	1% Winchester Disk	30 MB
	Colour Monitor	
	Laser Beam Printer	
	Colour Plotter	
	Software Supported	BASIC, d Base-III, 'C', LOTUS 1-2-3, Wordstar 2000, AUTOCAD, SIDEKIK, STORYTELLR, CROSSTALK

4	MACINTOSH PLUS SYSTEM	One
	CPU	1 MB 32-bit Microprocessor
	1% Floppy (3 1/2") Disk Drive	820 KB
	Hard Disk Drive	20 MB
	Laser Printer	
	Software Supported	PAGEMAKER, MACWRITE, MACPAINT, CL 1CKARI EFFECTS MACDRAW MICROSOFT WORD
5.	NEPTURE PC/AT	Eight
	CPU	1 MB, 16-Bit
	1% Floppy Disk Drive	1-2 MB
	1% Winchester Disk Drive	30 MB
	Colour Monitor	
	Dot Matrix Printer	Two, 160 CPS
	Software Supported	BASIC, d Base-III, LOTUS 1-2-3, Wordstar-2000, CROSSTALK

G 2

Trends in Information Technology

Arun K Sinha

0. Introduction

The ways of communicating available information from various sources to potential users are among the major challenges of our times. The term "information technology" in the English language, "*informatique*" in French and "*informatika*" in Russian encompasses the notion of information handling. For many it represents the ever-increasing array of tools with which information is stored, retrieved, processed and disseminated. Others use the term to describe not only the hardware and software involved but also the management techniques used to handle and process information, their applications, etc. In our context we will restrict its applicability to information science and accordingly we will try to find out the trend in this field which helps in the present context to achieve our professional role and the future technology which will shape our profession.

The words "Information Science" have been used and are being used to refer to a branch of library science dealing with automatic retrieval of information. Information science activities cover the entire continuum of information transfer, i.e. the flow and handling of information from the writing of literature by an author through its editing, printing, publishing and distribution by the publisher; through indexing, abstracting and dissemination in reference periodicals; through acquisition, organization, storage and dissemination in an information centre and, finally, through its use by another author (citation) in the production of new literature. Throughout the ages the representation of information has been a basic human requirement and from time to time various means have been used along with devices for storing, transmitting and processing information and interfacing it with users. Information technology can be viewed as a technical support evolved over the years to handle information processing and communication.

1. Information Technology

In the context of information technology, information can be described as knowledge in any form in which it can be transferred. In other words, information can assume any format and mode. As long as the basic requirement that a message is passed through an identifiable channel is fulfilled the use of the term is justified. And information technology is a application and commodity support through which or by means of which information is transferred, recorded, edited, stored, manipulated or disseminated. It will be worthwhile to consider some of the definitions of information technology to find out the concerns and emphasis stated therein.

2. Definitions

(1) Information technology means the collection, storage, processing dissemination and use of information. It is not confined to hardware and software but acknowledges the importance of man and the goals he sets for this technology, the volumes employed in making these choices, the assessment criterion used to decide whether he is controlling the technology and he is being enriched by it. (Quoted in *Information Technology Serving Society*), edited by Chartrand and Morentz. Pergamon, 1979, p. 121).

(2) The scientific, technological and engineering disciplines and the management techniques used in information handling and processing; their applications. Computers and their interaction with men and machines; and associated social, economic and cultural matters. (*Report on Information Technology*, H M Stationery Office, 1980).

(3) Information technology connotes an assemblage of technologies. They particularly cover the computer's capability to store and process information. Known as information processing and telecommunication technology it is capable of transmitting information to distances.

Zorkoczy has discussed information technology from four different viewpoints, viz., of society, economics, technology and the individual first and says that common element of information technology is the concept and volume of information. Further he mentions the four features which affect the quality of information. These are :

(1) Accuracy
(2) Content (the breadth/scope)
(3) Recency (uptodateness); and
(4) Frequency of presentation.

Among these content ranks first followed by accuracy and recency.

3. Historical Background

During the 1950s and 1960s the term "information explosion" was coined to refer to the vast increase in the information being generated in science, technology and other subject fields. Royal Society discussed the implications of information explosion at the first international conference on the subject held in London in 1948. At that time it was already clear that the publishing rate was increasing exponentially and that specialization in individual sciences and interdisciplinary research were generating multiple uses for the same information. Although information storage and retrieval technology saw their beginning in the world of science they soon spread to other areas. Recognition of information explosion and of the urgent need to employ means to cope with it was a major force, in the introduction of technology into information work. Today we speak of the "information revolution" to describe ongoing changes in the handling of the increasing volume of information. The revolutionary aspect is the result of fairly recent advances (mid 1970s to date) in computing used in support of information handling activities.

4. Components of Information Technologies

Some of the products and systems which form the "technology" component of information technology and are relevant in our context are as follows :

(1) Computers:

Microcomputers
Wordprocessors

(2) Telecommunications
(3) Storage technologies
(4) Data bases
(5) Information systems
(6) Microforms or Micrographics
(7) Expert systems
(8) Videotex and teletext, etc.

4.1 *Computers*

The computer is a general device for automatically processing information. The revolutionary concept of the programmable universal computer goes back to the Charles Babbage, a 19th century English inventor and mathematician, but its full realization had to wait for the invention of electronic switching circuitry and the vital concept of the Stored Programme due to Van Neumann in 1946. Computer technology has undergone tremendous change both in its hardware and processing capabilities which in computer terms is known as First Generation Computer, Second Generation Computer, Third and Fourth Generation Computer, and now Japan claims to have developed the Fifth Generation Computer.

The basic elements in a design of a computer are : a *programme* of instructions specifying the operations to be carried out; *input* devices such as keyboards, magnetic tape readers, light pens sensors, by means of which the programme together with the other information on which it is to work can be fed into the machine; *memory devices* to receive and store the information; a *Central Processing Unit* (CPU) to carry out the instructions; and *output devices* such as printers, TV screens actuators, to pass on the results to where they are required.

In the computer instructions and data are put on the same footing as *bits* of information. Devices for storing information are classified as primary or secondary storage. Primary memory devices are LSI devices, i.e., *memory chips*, which are regarded as integral part of the computer. Secondary devices are external components consisting of magnetic discs of either the rigid or "floppy" types, and magnetic tapes.

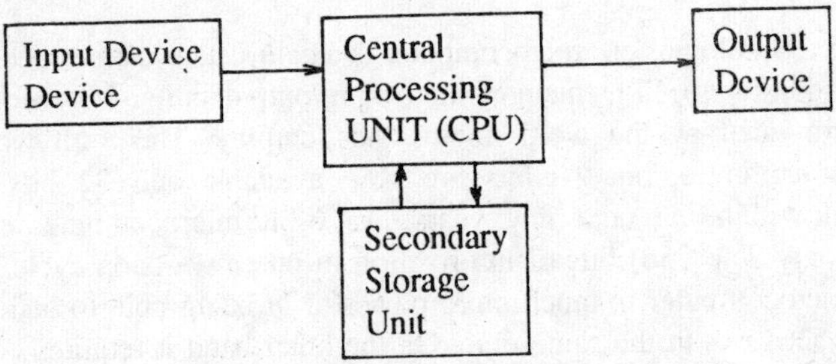

Fig. 1: *Components of Comuter System*

Primary memory has to date been more limited in capacity than secondary but its advantage is that the time required to access information is faster, being a fraction of a millionth of a second. Primary memory is thus used for holding information that requires fast access or frequent access and in particular instructions currently being executed.

Further, memory chips may be read-only memory (ROM) containing information that may not be altered and cannot be erased. Random access memory (RAM) contains information that may be overwritten. Other types of devices are programmable read-only memory (PROM) which can be once only programmed by the user, and erasable programmable read-only memory (EPROM) which can be rewritten and modified by the user at will. ROM chips are commercially available with a capacity of up to 64,000 bits of information. Also chips with capacity of 1,28,000 are now emerging.

Secondary memory systems provide virtually unlimited capacity but with slower access time. While magnetic based systems are currently in use other systems are being developed which will provide storage that will be several orders of magnitude more compact, faster and cheaper. These include magnetic bubble memories with no moving parts and laser-based optical systems. Such developments will provide even brief-case computers with virtually unlimited memory and that will increase enormously their capabilities.

In the field of information science this technology has been applied to exercise computer's ability to perform such processes as automatic indexing automatic abstrating, machine translation, automatic searching, automatic dissemination and automatic question-answering. It is also playing a significant role in automating library operations.

4.11 *Microcomputers*: The microcomputer, a complete computer on a single chip, is behind many of the recent changes in information-handling technologies. A microcomputer is a complete system processing, in addition to CPU memory and input/output units. Microcomputers are rated by the word-lengths they employ. The 8-bit word length is common, but 16 bits are now available and 32 bits is projected within the next few years. An 8-bit microcomputer can process only 2^8 (=256) bits of information in one instruction cycle. A 16-bit microcomputer is much more powerful in being able to handle 2^{16} (=65,536) bits in the same time. On the other hand it requires correspondingly a much greater number of components per chip.

Microcomputers can perform many of the information handling functions traditionally run on larger computers such as circulation control, acquisitions, catalogue and production, information storage and retrieval, etc. In addition, the introduction of microcomputers for information handling has resulted in the development of a number of innovative applications.

Although microcomputers are increasingly being employed in libraries, documentation and information centres most of the existing software packages have been developed for small-scale or specialized applications; only a very limited number of generalized packages making use of the potential of larger micros have been written. The majority of the existing software packages are bound to specific makes of hardware which is a major constraint for potential users. Among the large number of available packages the following are worth mentioning.

4.111 *Minisis*: MINISIS stands for Interactive Minicomputer System for Information Retrieval and Library Management. MINISIS is a generalized information management system designed to perform a variety of tasks for libraries and information centres and can be used on the *Hewlett-Packard* 3000 series of minicomputers. MINISIS gets its name from ISIS (Integrated Set of Information System), a software package developed by International Labour Organization (ILO). It was further developed by International Development Research Centre, Ottawa, Canada specifically to meet the need for a low-cost, turn-key hardware/software package permitting on-line data entry and interactive retrieval. It performs essentially the same function as ISIS, but does not require a large frame computer. Although it was developed primarily for use in bibliographic information systems it is flexible enough for many types of applications.

4.112 *Sci-Mate*: Sci-Mate developed by the Institute for Scientific Information, Philadelphia, is a software for microcomputers designed specifically for manu-driven searching of a wide variety of on-line data bases and for the management of textual information. Sci-Mate's manu-driven command system guides the user through searches on DIALOG, ISI, BRS, SDC and MEDLINE data bases, making the search process simpler while retaining the original search capabilities of the host system. With permission from the data bases produce or vendor bibliographic information retrieval with the Universal Online Searcher can be captured in the user's Science Mate Personal Data Manager.

With the Sci-Mate Personal Data Manager users can create their own data bases. The data bases can contain any kind of textual information entered from the keyboard, or can include hits retrieval online with the Universal online searcher and transferred automatically to the Personal Data Manager.

Sci-Mate software on floppy disks is currently available for IBM PC, Vector 3 and 4, Apple II, TRS-80 Model II microcomputers and all other CP/M-80 systems with standard 8" drives.

4.113 *The IV+V System Software Package*: It has been developed by the Institute for Machine Documentation (IMD) Graz., Austria and called IV+V system (*I*nformation *v*er mittlung und*v*eravbeitung)

The IV+V system is conceived as a generalized data base management system intended for both bibliographic and factual information management. It is designed as an implementation of the relational data base model. Basic system functions are : data entry/data editing, data base creation and maintenance retrieval and output. The system also includes a screen processor which permits user developed screens and user controlled screen sequencing for specific applications and task scheduler, which provides operating system control of tasks. The software is written in UCSD Pascal. This system is under active consideration of Unesco for using as portable software package for information handling and they are preparing a demonstration data base on its own microcomputer using IV+V and implementing the common Communication Format.

4.12 *Wordprocessors*: Wordprocessors represent one aspect of the microelectronics revolution. Much of the microcomputer work in information handling was initiated in the 1970s by extending the application of previously acquired wordprocessing equipment to simple text storage and retrieval. Wordprocessors can be considered as special purpose microcomputers dedicated to a single function – the processing text. JB Whitehead has described the development of wordprocessing systems and their application to information handling. He listed the areas where wordprocessors can be of benefit to the library and information system. The areas are :

—library catalogues (access by author, title or subject and automatic generation of book lists by author, subject, date of acquisition, etc.);
—order processing (constant check available of items outstanding and the production of standard letters on request, showing progress on orders);
—abstracting and indexing bulletins (input of bibliographic information which can be stored, sorted and printed in any sequence);
—online searching (internal and external database access using word processors as computer terminals, the ability to store and edit input as required);
—communications (wordprocessor-to-wordprocessor communication providing electronic mail facilities and offsite access to data store);
—borrower records (global search and select up-date facilities will provide uptodate record of all loans and borrowers); and
—periodical acquisition (constant check on periodical acquisition and location of each issue on circulation).

A dedicated wordprocessor consists of a TV-like viewing screen along with a keyboard similar to that of a typewriter, a programmable microcomputer and magnetic "floppy" disk, together with a high speed printing unit. Regardless of their design, capabilities or configuration, all wordprocessor systems incorporate five basic components, namely, a processor (CPU) with operating logic, a keyboard, a display screen or panel, same type of removable storage media and a printer.

When the text is entered on the keyboard, signals travel to the CPU. Depending on the instructions, each letter can be printed directly on the printer, stored in the CPU memory or written on the removable storage media (usually a disk). Subsequent instructions can modify this text according to requirements.

The generation, storage, transmission and retrieval of textual information in electronic form is seen as the key application of microelectronics in the commercial sector.

It is possible to programme some word processors to store information and to retrieve it in any specified format – a facility which can aid the production of indices and abstract bulletins. For example, bibliographic details of articles can be fed into the store of the word processor, plus any key terms needed for identification purposes. The system can then be programmed to print out the file in any sequence (e.g. by subject, author, title, etc.).

4.2 *Telecommunications*

Telecommunications are at the heart of many applications of information technology. The development of telecommunications technology is in a sense a symbol of man's impatience arising from his need to communicate rapidly over the great distances. The main purpose of telecommunication is to transmit representations of information (signals) between remote locations. Most of the telecommunication systems in operation today employ electrical or electromagnetic media (including light waves) as carriers of signals. The media are harnessed to provide worldwide telecommunication networks.

The growth and utility of computerized systems for information dissemination, library retrieval and other related applications have been and will continue to be heavily influenced by communication technology. As the computing and communications technology have evolved together over the past decade, a variety of improvements have been evolved together and a variety of improvements have been introduced in communications to facilitate development of data-oriented systems.

4.21 *Types*: Communications technologies are of three basic types : transmission, switching and terminal technologies. Transmission is concerned with the means of transmitting the signals over distance; switching is concerned with the user devices for initiating and receiving signals. At each source terminal, the originating information must be converted to a form suitable for transmission to the remote point. The signals must travel through whatever transmission media are in the path of information flow, so that, when they reach a destination terminal, it is possible to recover the form of information sent with same reasonable precision.

4.22 *Functional Elements*: Functional elements of a typical communication system have been shown in Figure 2 given below. The message from the source of information may be a human voice, musical tones, a classroom scene, a paper document, a roll of microfilm not to mention dozens of other possibilities, including machine stored data.

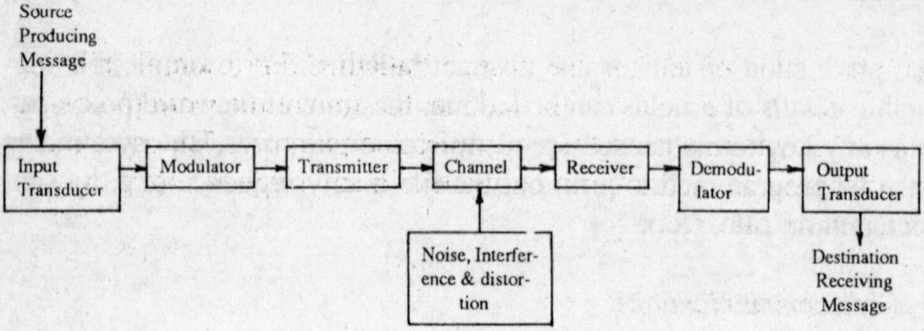

Fig. 2: *A Typical Communication System*

The first step in the transmission of the message is its conversion to an electrical form, that is, in the form of a continuously varying electrical signal, since, in general, a message product by source is not electrical. This conversion is accomplished by means of an input transducer, a general term which could be taken to mean, for example, a microphone (for voice) a TV Camera (for scenes) or a facsimiles scanner (for paper documents). In this process an electrical signal from the input transducer is sent to its output counterpart which converts the signal "message" form, that is, as a voice out of a telephone receiver, a picture on a TV monitor and so on.

4.23 *Network*: Also to some extent the microprocessor counteracts the rapid growth of computer communications networks. The central idea of networking is to share both functions and data. As small computer systems have become more powerful and compact, they have also become more independent in function. The general trend, therefore, is towards data sharing across network and away network designs based on shared functions.

4.24 *Applications*: On the other hand, certain applications of microprocessors have opened whole new vistas for the transfer of information by telecommunications. The developments in microelectronics have led to home microcomputers and television-based information terminals. Such trends towards inexpensive machines with communications, storage and processing capacity require a reassessment of the economics, convenience, movement and storage of information. A balance needs to be established between convenience and economics in determining the amount and kinds of information to be stored and processed locally in microcomputers and the amount and kinds to be accessed through telecommunications links.

Recently, there has been considerable activity in evaluating the potential for document delivery systems based on satellite communications. When linked with other telecommunication technologies, such as cable and facsimile transmission, satellites have considerable potential for application in the information field. Application include remote brow-sing using slow-scan television, searching of automated catalogues, searching of bibliographic and numeric data bases, SDI (Selective Dissemination of Information) services, document delivery via facsimile transmitters, distribution of cataloguing information, teleconferencing etc.

4.25 *Telecommunication Experiment in India*: In India, an experiment was conducted to demonstrate the use of satellite communications for bibliographic information retrieval. The experiment was called "PECON on-line demonstration project linking to world sources of information; a Unesco/Unisist project with participation of the European Space Agency" was organized by the Department of Science and Technology in collaboration with Posts and Telegraphs Department, Overseas Communication Service, Tata Institute of Fundamental Research, Bhabha Atomic Research Centre and Indian National Scientific Documentation Centre. The demonstration was held at the TIFR from September 20-25, 1976. The P & T Department had laid special data circuits suitable for transmission at a terminal at TIFR was connected to the computer in ESRIN, Frascati viz OCS, Bombay and Rome. Satellite facilities were used for data transmission from OCS, Bombay, to Rome. The ESRIN Centre having more than 10 data base and over 7-5 million references was made available for retrieval purposes. Some 800 scientists and engineers, librarians and information scientists use experiment for their specific information queries.

4.26 *Other Developments*: The recent advances in this field are utilization of *Optical fibre* and *laser beams* as transmission media. In the optical fibre communication, glass fibres are used to convey pulses of light energy packets as signals. This media offers very wide bandwidth and thus high transmission rates and low losses. A single hair-thin optical fibre measuring 0.125 mm in diameter can transmit 10,000 telephone circuits or several hundred TV channels. Also the laser beams having a high frequency can transmit 1,00,000 times more information than a microwave.

The recent developments in telecommunication has resulted in the following systems/services :

Recent Telecommunications Developments	Resulting Systems/Services
Co-axial cables	Videotext
Optical fibres	Teletext
Radio propagation	C A T V
Satellite transmission	Electronic Directory
Digital techniques	Electronic Mail
Communications	Teleconferencing
Packet-switching	Document preparation & transfer
Data rates	Euronet
Facsimile transmission	Database handling
Intelligent nodes	Volume Added Networks/ Local Area Networks

4.3 *Storage Technologies*

The advances in storage technologies have a significant effect in information handling. The technology of digital storage is one of the most rapidly changing sectors of microelectronics. Over the last decades, operating speed and reliability have been increased by at least an order of magnitude at the same time as physical size, power consumption and cost per unit of storage have been reduced by factors of up to 1,000. Similar improvements are predicted for the next decade before physical limitations are encountered. The storage technologies include the following :

(A) Magnetic Storage

- A.1 Tape/Disk Storage
- A.2 Floppy Disks
- A.3 Winchester & Removable Hard Disks

(B) Optical Storage

- B.1 Optical Digital Disks
- B.2 Digitally Encoded Optical Video Disk
- B.3 Digitally Encoded Compact Disks
- B.4 Erasable Optical Storage

4.31 *Magnetic Disk*: Magnetic disk storage is the predominant technology for computer information storage. The fundamentals physical elements are the magnetic surface and the read/write head(s). The tape and read/write head(s) suffer wearout. Hence Disk/Drum (rotating) have random accessibility. Many improvements have been made in the disk/drum and also operational aspects of magnetic disk technology.

4.32 *Floppy Disk*: Floppy disk or flexible disk has been adopted in microcomputers. The floppy disk is either a 5-1/4 inch or 8 inch platter that can be recorded on one side or both sides. The read/write heads on a floppy disk actually contact the surface of the disk, so that wear has always been a problem. Floppy has today one megabyte and access time is about 100 milliseconds. Technological improvements have brought in higher densities longer life new materials, faster access time improvements.

4.33 *Microfloppy*: Microfloppies have less than 4 inches format. The Sony microfloppies range from 3 inches to 3.8 inches. It incorporates a hard plastic jackets. It is likely to have 1.6 MB equal to that of 8 inches floppies. The smaller microfloppies have improved bit densities and can rotate at a higher speed (up to 600 rpm) than their bigger brethren.

4.34 *Winchester Disk*: Winchester Disk drives consists of hermetically sealed entire disk peak and heads in a single, non-separable enclousre. In each such unit, head to surface gaps are down to tenth of microms, allowing ever greater storage densities. Such disks are cost beneficial. Mini Winchesters are of 5-1/4 inches while large ones are 14 inches. Mini Winchesters range from 5 to over 300 MB. They are less flexible for handling than microfloppies. In recent years Winchester disk cartrigdes have been developed which are removable. They are in the range of 3.9 inches (100 mm) disk drums with capacities from 6.38 to 38.2 MB including a removable disk.

4.35 *Optical Storage Devices*: Large-scale mass storage of information for both micros as well as maxis is the optical disk technology. They are of three types : (i) Optical Digital Disk (ODD); (ii) the digital encoding of information of optical videodisks (DE/OVD) and (iii) the storage of digital information on the digital audio compact disc (DE/CD). Apart from disk format, there are other categories of optical recordings such as microforms, aperture cards, ultrafiche, ultrastrip and video disk.

Holography is another optical system. It is the process recording and reconstructing a wave front of light patterns. A hologram is the record resulting from the holographic process. Holography is like photography but in this an image recorded on film offers many advantages including three dimensionality that traditional photography cannot.

4.4 *Data Bases*

Information services devoted to specialist fields and professional interests are one of the fastest growing areas of information technology. Their expansion mirrors the growth in the amount of published items — books, periodicals, reports catalogues, audio and visual materials, patents, designs, computer programmes — the records of human intellectual activity. Indeed it has been estimated that the sum total of human knowledge is currently doubling every five years.

Such an exponential increase in potentially useful information would be impossible to handle without some new tools for its storage and retrieval. Libraries, the conventional storehouse of knowledge, are running out of space and financial resources in trying to keep up with the output of recorded information. It has become virtually impossible for any particular library to possess every published item of information. Instead libraries and entrepreneurial information services increasingly specialize on particular topics. Moreover, more and more of the information is being placed in *computerized data bases.* Specialist computerized data bases are now available in different subject areas and in different countries. Access to them may be gained through computer terminals which either display the required information on their screen or can be used to request a printed version. The terminals may be located anywhere that has a telecommunication link with the computer.

4.41 *Data Base and its Operations*: A data base may be defined as a non-redundant, multi-useable, independent and physically available set of data elements. From this definition we can infer that :

(a) Each data element is stored once and only once, in a record;
(b) Any number of users can have access to a data element, any number of times;
(c) Data elements in the data base are independent from data representation, devices, descriptions, programmes, or special structures of the data;
(d) A data base is a physically available object.

Bibliographical data these are stored more or permanently in a computer readable file are termed as a bibliographical data base. The software that allows one or many persons to use and/or modify these data are a data base management system (DBMS).

The on-line data bases most often used by information professionals were developed originally to generate printed indexes to scientific and technical literature, and contained bibliographic information (author, title, publisher, date, subject terms, etc.). Soon after, abstracts were added to the bibliographic record to enhance the descriptions of the literature. Until very recently these bibliographic data bases containing abstracts were the predominant type of data bases accessed by the library community (both in on-line and printed format). Advances in data-base technology and the emergence of data-base management systems have resulted in the growth of numbers of commercially available numeric (financial, Economic, statistical, etc.) data bases.

Possible future developments include the extension of existing bibliographic data bases to include the full text of documents rather than abstracts (this already exists when texts are relatively short as in newspaper articles, or highly structured as in legal documents). The storage problems previously restricting the length of a bibliographic record can be overcome by utilizing the optical disk technologies.

4.5 *Information System*

The term "Information System" now-a-days is used to denote computer based services which provide information in response to specific requests from users. There are two types of input to such a system : the data which they store in anticipation of requests, and the requests themselves. The data may be stored as reference to documents, microforms or computer coded text, graphics, etc. The service may be available on a local basis or via a telecommunication network.

The main purpose of an information service is to satisfy users' information need. The way in which these needs are expressed largely determines the principles of operation of particular information system.

Computer-based information systems differ from one another in a number of important respects :

(a) the range of subjects or documents covered;
(b) the assumptions made about the users of the service;
(c) the input-output interface;

(d) the equipment used to store the data;
(e) the programmes which assist in the input, indexing, store, identification and output of data.

Example : Euronet - Diane

Euronet is a data network inaugurated in 1979 by telecommunication authorities of the member countries of the European Economic Community. It is used to provide users in those countries with access to the information system Diane (Direct Information Access Network in Europe).

The information available through the network is aimed at researchers, scientists, engineers, managers, the legal and medical professions. The subject coverage is correspondingly broad embracing bibliographical data in these areas (publications, documents, etc.) reference and handbook material (catalogues, directories, statistics, etc.,) patents, compilations, etc.

There are many information systems both of the national and international level which aim at providing information service in the area of their concern, viz. : INIS, AGRIS, etc.

4.6 *Micrographics or Microforms*

Like computer technology micrographics is one of the fastest technologies today. It is a powerful microforce for Records Management and Information Control. It encompasses techniques and methods for compacting storage of voluminous information records for *high speed searching* and *timely retrieval.*

Today it is possible to interface micrographics with computers, word processors, Laser-Graphics, etc., for developing integrated information handling systems.

Micrographics in its simplest meaning is miniature reproduction of familiar objects. The micro images must have quality standards for faithfulness to the original in geometry, detail, clarity, reproducibility in its own kind (film to film) and its enlargements or reduction (film to paper-hard copy).

Micrography is the term covering:

(a) The *input process* which includes preparation of the

document/drawing, microfilm, processing and duplication.

(b) The *output process* which includes reading and printing, indexing and retrieval.

(c) The *equipment* which includes camera, processor, duplicator, reader/enlarger printer, and storing facility.

Microimages can be recorded in various microforms.

Microfilm: The most commonly microform is 16 mm or 35 mm roll microfilm which is usually retained in lengths up to 69 m on spools 10 cm in diameter. Magazines or cassettes are mainly used in 16 mm system requiring frequent high-speed reference to information.

Aperture card with pouches for 35 or 16 mm: The aperture card is a data processing 80 column punched card containing one or more holes specially designed to accept 16 mm or 35 mm microimages. Its main application area is in *engineering drawing microfilm systems* where one 35 mm microimage occupies one frame in the aperture card.

Microfiche: Microfiche of size 15 cm X 10 cm are used in micropublishing systems where it is necessary to distribute a large number of copies such as in the dissemination of information to libraries, engineering units or industrial firms. A sheet microform of size 15 cm X 10 cm or 80 column punched card size contains between 60 (20 : 1 reduction) and 200 (40 : 1 reduction) microimages. The internationally accepted microfiche format contains 98 frames.

Ultrafiche: The ultrafiche with microimages at a reduction ratio of 150 : 1 accommodates approximately 3000 images on one A6 size microfiche.

4.61 *Computer Output Microfilm (COM)*: COM is the conversion of computer output information on magnetic tape to microfilm in a readable form at magnetic tape speeds (300 pages a minute). It is sophisticated mechanical means of storing and retrieval information. In this process data on a magnetic tape from the computer are translated into readable text produced on a cathode-ray tube and printed on film. This film is viewed at terminals or it is used to produce hard copies.

4.7 *Expert Systems*

Expert systems represent one of the most advanced facets of information technology. Basically expert systems are software packages aimed at providing expert "consultancy" advice and assistance with problem solving in specialist fields of knowledge. In fact expert systems are intelligent computer applications that use data, a knowledge base, and a control mechanism to solve problems of sufficient difficulty that significant human expertise is necessary for their solution. Expert systems represent an attempt to harness, as an intellectual tool, those features of the computer where it excels in the handling of data :

(a) its ability for storing a very large amount of data;
(b) the retention of these data for an arbitrarily long time in a prescribed form;
(c) its ability for making precise calculations and exhaustive searches of stored data at high speed.

Expert systems use *artificial intelligence* (artificial intelligence may be broadly defined as the area that seeks to make computers do things that requires intelligence and skill) problem solving and knowledge representation technique to combine human expert methods of conceptualizing and reasoning about the problem area. As a result it is expected that such systems can reach an level of performance comparable to that of a human expert in a specialized problem area.

4.71 *Implication for Information Science*: Over the last few decades topics such as inference making, knowledge creation and machine translation have been discussed in library science field. However some AI (Artificial Intelligence) concepts which have significance in a reference retrieval system are pattern recognition (the content analysis operation of comparing requests and documents are related to pattern recognition). Knowledge representation, problem solving techniques (including heuristics), learning and expert systems.

Recently the direct application of expert systems to information work has been primarily in the area of *on-line* bibliographic data base searching. The developments in this field of on-line searching will make it possible that future users will be able to conduct comprehensive and successful online literature searches without the aid of librarian or information specialist.

4.8 *Videotex and Teletext*

As we have seen now the age of electronic information storage and retrieval has begun. Videotex and Teletext are two important developments among the new information storage and display technology.

Basically videotex and viewdata are interactive (two-way) systems for transmitting text or graphics stored in computer data bases via the telephone network for display on a television screen. A variety of videotex systems exist but they all operate in basically the same way. To access those messages transmitted via the telephone network, users must have special decoders built in or attached to their television sets. To connect to the central data base the user must first dial the appropriate telephone number and place the receiver in a modern or acoustic coupler. When the connection has been accomplished successfully, an index page appears on the television screen and users begin to search for the information they require by pressing numbered keys on their hand-held control panel (the key pad). Instructions appear on the screen telling the user which keys to press for particular types of data.

The central videotex data base may contain an utmost unlimited amount of information provided by sources. The data are stored in "frames" or screenfuls and can be updated instantly. Several frames of information on the same topic comprise a "page" and may be access sequentially. To retrieve information from the data base the user employ a "tree structure" search method starting with broad subject headings and narrowing down their choices until they arrive at the frame of information they require. Such systems as currently designed are fairly limited in capability and have no cross referencing.

Teletext is a non-interactive (one way) form of videotex, that is, a method of transmitting text or graphics stored in a computer data base, as a part of broadcast transmissions, for display on a television screen. Again, it is intended for wide public use carrying information of broad public interest. Teletext was first developed by B.B.C. in 1972.

Videotex and teletext systems have a similiar structure. The main components of videotex and teletext systems are shown in the following diagram :

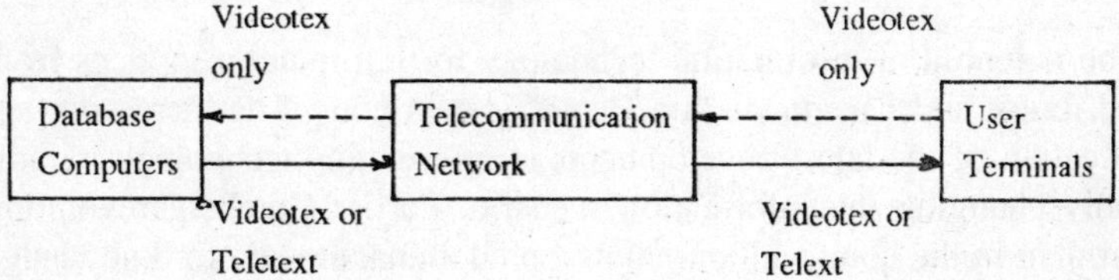

Fig. 3:

The hardware of each consists of a central data base computer (or several such computers) linked to a large number of television displays via a telecommunication network. The software for both includes a database storage and retrieval programme operating on an organized set of fextual and/or graphic data. The data are organized as "frames" each containing a screenful of alphabetic, numeric and graphic symbols. The human element also tends to divide into the same groups for both systems.

Videotex and teletext differ in the way they transmit the data and also in the way the user controls what data are to be displayed.

Teletext's chief virtue is its ability to be updated continuously for large viewing audiences. It can provide users with the most current information on a range of subjects and is easily accessible. Because it is broadcast rather than based on the telephone, teletext is also less expensive than videotex, which requires users to pay for the telephone service and for each individual frame accessed.

Teletext has its disadvantages because of its limited database size. To access information user have to wait until the specific page they are seeking cycle by, giving the decoder time to read, decode and display the data. The wait time becomes excessive when the data base exceeds 100 pages or so. Thus, teletext is severely limited in the amount of information it can carry efficiently.

Some of the examples of videotex and teletext systems developed in various countries are :

—Prestel (British Videotex System)
—Antiope (French Videotex and Teletext Standards)
—Telidou (Canadian Videotex and Teletext Standard)
—Captain (Japanese Videotex System)

5. Conclusion

The potential of information technology for information services from a Library and Documentation Centre is enormous. The increasing application of the latest developments in information technology is radically changing the information scenario. Earlier Guteberg revolution brought in the book and journal as a predominant media for knowledge communication. Today electronic storage and telecommunication media are a playing important role in the transmission of information. It has been predicted that by the year 2000 fomal communication in science and technology will be almost exclusively electronic, and that a substantial move to machine-aided informal communication will also have occurred.

Gopinath has mentioned the impact of this ever-renewing information technology on communication media and information as under :

Work	Technology	
	Old	New
1. Communication	Personal Travels, Postal Communication	Teleconferencing, Teletext, Satellite Transmission
2. Inputting text (Primary format)	Oral Representations, Writing and Typing	Word Processing, Optical Scanning through Computers
3. Multiplications	Printing and Near-printing Process	Computer Visuals, Display Terminals, Video Disks and Cassettes, Computerized Photoprinting
4. Storage	Book Shelves, Pamphlet Cabinet, Microform Storage Disks.	Computer-based Digital & Analogue Storage, Disks, Tapes and Drum Storages.
5. Information Retrieval	Browsing through the surrogates in a catalogue and through the shelves	Browsing through online terminals, Computerized database softwares

Neelameghan has mentioned that information technology application in library, information and documentation work can be grouped into following operations and products :

(1) Catalogue and catalogue production
(2) Indexing and production of indices
(3) Union catalogue generation
(4) Lists and bibliographies
(5) Directory preparation
(6) Thesaurus construction
(7) Local data base creation
(8) Online access to remote data bases
(9) Use of external data bases on local computers
(10) Circulation control
(11) Document Acquisition

(12) Serials control
(13) Computer-assisted Information
(14) Data communication and networking
(15) Management Information services, Computing, tabulation, simulation, graphics, statistics, reports,

The electronic media can store very large quantities of information in very compact forms and enable retrieval much faster. Also the storage cost per unit is far less. Personal computers, telecommunication facilities, emergence of videotex technology, teleconferencing are definitely to bring about a sea change in the function of Library and Information centres of the future. Electronic filing system and Computer Assisted Retrieval (CAR) are gaining ground. To sum up information technology and continuous advancement in this field will shape the future information retrieval processes and they can't be any escape from it.

REFERENCES

1 AVRAM, H: UNIMARC Version of MINISIS. *IFLA Journal*, 11 (2), 1985; pp. 120-123.

2 BOSS, R W: *Library Manager's Guide to Automation*. Ed 2. N, Y; knowledge Industry, 1984.

3 BURNS Christopher: Information Storage and Display. (*Journal of American Society for Information Science*, 32 (2) 1981 pp. 141-147).

4 CLARK, A and CROWIN, B: Expert systems and Library/Information Work. (*Journal of Librarianship* 15 (4), 1983. pp. 277-292).

5 GOPINATH, M A. Impact of Information Technology on Information Retrieval Systems and Libraries. [In : *Current Trends in Information Sources and Communication Media, DRTC Refresher Seminar*, 15 (1984), Chap L].

6 GRIFFITH, Jose-Marie: Main Trends in Information Technology. (*UNESCO Journal of Information Science. Library Science & Archives Administration*, 4 (4), 1982 , pp. 230-238).

7 KAMATH, V A: *Evolution of Information Technology* : *An Overview*. Bombay; Micrographic Congress of India, 1983 (Mimeograph).

8 KAMATH, V A: Micrographics Technology — An Overview. [In : *Micrographics for Information Management Souvenir*. MCI — 84 Convention & Exposition. Delhi; Micrographic Congress of India, 1984].

9 LINE, Maurice B: Some Possible Future Effects of Information Technology. [*IFLA Journal* 10 (1), 1984.]

10 LOHNER, W and KOCH, W: Portable Software Packages for Microcomputers. [*IFLA Journal*, 11 (2) 1985, pp. 124 - 128].

11 MALWAD, N M: Current Trends in Information Handling and the Role of Modern Communication Technology. [*International Information Communication and Education*, 1(2) 1982 pp. 203-223].

12 NEELAMEGHAN, A: Integrated Systems Design for Library and Information Systems. [In : Parthasarthy, S, ed. *Seminar On Library Automation and Information Retrieval, Challenges and Opportunities*, 7-9 Oct 1985, ed by S Parthasarthy, I I S, Banglore].

13 NOLAN, Richard J: *Information for Industrial Development* UNIDO/IS. 415., 1983.

14 THOMA, George R: Transmission of Information, [*Journal of the American Society for Information Science*, 32 (2), 1981, pp. 131-140].

15 WHITEHEAD, J, B: Developments in the Wordprocessing Systems and their Application in Information Needs. [*Aslib Proceedings*, 36, 1980, pp. 118-133].

16 YAGHMAI, N S and MAXIN, J A: Expert Systems : A Tutorial. [*Journal of American Society for Information Science*, 35 (5), 1984, pp. 297-305].

17 ZORKOCZY, Peter: *Information Technology : An Introduction*. N Y; Knowledge Industry, 1983.

H 1

Special Aspects of INIS Operations in Japan

Yukio Ebinuma

0. Introduction

The acronym INIS stands for International Nuclear Information System. INIS has been operated by the International Atomic Energy Agency (IAEA) since 1970, in collaboration with its Member States and cooperating international organizations. Its main purpose is to provide a comprehensive abstracting service in English for nuclear literature using modern computer.

Japan Atomic Energy Research Institute (JAERI) has been taking an active part in this information system as the INIS National Centre for Japan since the beginning of INIS. Contribution of the Centre to input to INIS accounts for 5% of the whole INIS data base containing over one million records and increases to 6 % in the recent years. Concerning the use of INIS data base. One batch mode and two on-line information retrieval systems have been operating for scientists and engineers in this country. Annual use of them reaches 10,000 access times for retrospective search (RS) and 500 profiles are in service monthly for Selective Dissemination of Information (SDI). In the course of this realization, the Centre had to over come many difficulties caused by the main reasons of the non-English-speaking nation and domestic position of JAERI. These special aspects are described on both input to INIS and use of INIS data base.

1. Internal Committees for INIS Operations

(1) Since the JAERI was designated the INIS National Centre for Japan by the Government Authority, "Advisory Committee for INIS Operations" was set up in JAERI in October 1970. It is to make necessary comments for determination of

management policies on INIS operations by the President of JAERI. Members of the Committee are composed of about 20 highly experienced and knowledgeable experts from universities, industries and institutions in the fields of both documentation and nuclear science. The Committee has made a number of valuable comments on improvement of the whole INIS operation. These comments have been proposed at the INIS Advisory Committees and INIS Liaison Officer Meetings sponsored by the INIS Headquarters in Vienna and by correspondence to the INIS Technical Notes issued by the Headquarters.

(2) Three ad-hoc sub-committees were also set up under the Advisory Committee by 1973, in order to establish practical structures for both input to INIS and utilization of the INIS products.

"Technical sub-committee for input to INIS" consists of about 10 experts from Information Centres in various fields concerned to the INIS subject scope and coverage. It has been contributing to smoothening of input business to INIS at our Department by clarification of the INIS reference manuals and input rules, comments on improvement of these tools to Vienna and application of these to our input processing.

"Technical sub-committee for use of INIS data base" consists of about 10 experts on machine information processing. It has given many technical advices on development of INIS retrieval systems, analysis of retrieval results and networking of copy services of primary documents.

"Special sub-committee for dissemination of nuclear information" consists of about 20 scientists and engineers who are regular members of the Atomic Energy Society of Japan. It aims to comment from the viewpoint of users on the way that information services should be and to assist the services from the viewpoint of academic societies. It has contributed to investigation of use patterns of nuclear documents and information by members of the society, to construction of effective INIS retrieval systems and to promotion of keywords assignment to articles in academic journals.

2. Reference Tools for Input Processing

(1) It was necessary for us to become familiar with the various

INIS rules and standards at the beginning of input processing to INIS. Since most of the persons to take part in this work were not skilful in English, main INIS Reference Manuals were translated into Japanese. These Japanese versions were greatly effective to understand the rules and standards more precisely than by the original versions in English. The Japanese versions were used frequently for discussion with staff of the cooperative Information Centers. Each of these versions has been revised immediately after publication of a revised edition of the original in Vienna.

(2) In addition to these versions, supplementary manuals were provided in Japanese, as a result of discussions on application of the INIS rules and standards to input processing of Japanese literature.

(1) *Internal Criteria for Coverage and Selection of Japanese Literature.*

Selection of documents to report to INIS is left to each INIS National Center within the INIS subject scope and coverage. This internal criteria were prepared to keep uniformity of document selection at the Information Centers concerned. Principle of the selection is based on whether a document has suitable information for world-wide circulation or not, within the INIS subject scope and coverage. Let me here quote and example from the criteria. Although the translations from Japanese into English are included in input to INIS, the translations from English into Japanese are excluded from input to INIS. Because the latter translations are published for readers in Japan and are not fit for international dissemination.

(2) *Manual for Romanization of Japanese Authorities*

There are many organizations and journals which have no proper names in English. We must transliterate these Japanese names into alphabet in English. This manual was made for preparation of files for personal authors, corporate entries, affiliations and journal titles.

(3) *Manual for Bibliographic Descriptions of Japanese Literature*

This manual was made to describe bibliographic data on worksheets as precise as possible, in accordance with the INIS Descriptive Cataloguing Rules. It includes many examples of descriptions by a journal article, technical report, patent and other types of records.

(4) *Supplementary Manual for Indexing*

This manual was made on the basis of experience in indexing and machine retrieval. It suggests over-indexing rather than under-indexing but forbids extra over-indexing. This comes from the fact that subject specialists of our Department are capable of correcting over-indexing more easily than under-indexing on the one hand and under-indexing leads to loss of relevant documents in retrieval on the other.

(5) Three kinds of authority files have been prepared and updated currently. These files at present include 7,000 personal author names, 2,000 journal titles and 800 affiliations.

A Japanese name is generally composed of only two kinds of names, that is, a surname (family name) and a forename (given name). About 80% of nuclear documents written by personal authors and originating in Japan contain a full surname and forename romanized. However, about 10% contain not a full name romanized but surname and only one initial of forename in Roman. The remaining 10% do not contain any romanized name. In other words, the 10% contain only proper names described with Kanji (Chinese characters).

We need a romanized full name of a personal author for input to INIS. In the case of the 20% mentioned above, our cataloguer ascertains a romanized full name by various lists of members of academic societies or requests an author to inform us directly on how to spell his full name in Roman. There are, of course, some personal authors whose romanized full names are unknown for non-response. In this manner, romanized full names have been cumulated. Such procedures also have been applied to other kinds of files.

Some staff members of our Department investigated on descriptions of Japanese personal author names on the INIS data base. Results of the investigation are as follows : 92% of items from Japan have full forename with surname and the remaining 8% have one initial of forename with surname. However, 99% of the items from other INIS National Centers have only one initial of forename with surname, though 45% of the items have full forename on original papers.

Another investigation was made on the Personal Auther Index P-Z, one of the cumulative indexes to INIS atomindex in 1981. Titles of 14 papers appear under the very same entry "Sato, K." on page 224. Judging from the titles and affiliations, "Sato, K." represents 10 personal authors who are quite different from each other. All of these entries are included in the inputs from countries other than Japan. On the other hand, there are seven entries of "Sato" with the same initial "K" but different forenames on the same page. You can distinguish seven different persons by description of these forenames in full. These entries are included in the inputs from Japan.

3. Decentralized Input Processing System

The INIS subject scope and coverage are extensively broad. It is impossible for our Department to collect all of primary document sources originating in Japan and falling within the INIS. Because the activities for document collection are restricted within the range of research and development at JAERI, which includes reactor engineering and radiation chemistry in principal but excludes nuclear medicine, basic science and so on. It is further difficult to perform all of such special works as cataloguing, abstracting, indexing in English and machine processing by staff of our Department from the viewpoint of manpower. For these reasons, it has been a consistent policy on the INIS operations to obtain cooperation of other organizations as much as possible.

Concerning the scanning, our Department takes charge of main journals of 300 titles, technical reports and other types including conference proceedings and books, International Medical Information Center, medical and biological journals of 400 titles, Japan Information Centre for Science and Technology, peripheral journals of 300 titles and Japan patent Information Organization, nuclear application patents. In order to avoid duplication of the scanning, a list of journals to allot is prepared and distributed to these Centers by our department. This list, of course, is renewed once a year in view of the number of papers selected for input and of discontinuance or of new publication of a journal which falls within the INIS subject scope and coverage. Work at each Centre consists of scanning, classifying, cataloguing, abstracting and indexing. These efforts are completed on a worksheet. These worksheets are sent to our Department semi-monthly and are checked manually by specialists of the Department to keep quality and accuracy of inputs. Filling of blank entries and/or correction of errors are performed carefully on categories, abstracts, descriptors, subject headings and catalogues.

4. **Use of INIS Data Base**

4.1 *Multi-Channels of the Use*

We prepare three service channels for information retrieval using INIS data base in Japan. The first channel is the JAERI in-house INIS retrieval service for staff of JAERI. Information contained in the data base is stored in a large computer which is operated by the computing center of JAERI located at Tokai-mura. For batch service, searchers of our Department make Boolean query formulas upon request from end-users. The number of RS service is a very small. This is due to the existence of inhouse INIS on-line service. In fact, the number of RS service on the batch mode had amounted to more than 200 profiles a year, before the beginning of the on-line service from 1981. SDI service is carried out on a monthly basis using the latest data base sent from Vienna once a month. The on-line service is used very well. One of the reasons is that end users are able to access to the INIS data base from its about 250 terminals which are connected to the computer at Tokai-mura by lease lines from Tokyo head office and four research establishments of JAERI. All of these services mentioned above are offered free of charge to the staff of JAERI.

The second and the third are retrieval services for domestic people except for the staff of JAERI. These services are executed in cooperation with other Information Centres because it is very difficult for JAERI to carry out these services to other organizations at cost. The Information Centre of the Atomic Energy Mutual Aid Association has been taking charge of batch service since 1978, using the computer of JAERI. Charges are 20,000 Yen for RS 24,000 Yen for standard SDI and 36,000 Yen for request SDI. JICST takes charge of on-line service from January 1984. JICST manages a domestic on-line information retrieval service network named "JOIS" (JICST On-line Information System). Our Department offers a copy set of INIS MT to JICST. End-users are able to access to the data base through the JOIS from everywhere in Japan. A connection fee to data base is 200 Yen a minute.

4.2 *Use Patterns*

Users of the JAERI in-house INIS on-line service are divided into two groups; the first group consists of trained users of our Department and the second group, untrained users of scientists and engineers of JAERI. The trained users of the first group use the service system very often for their retrieval service and various investigations of both document sources and the data base.

The untrained users of the second group attended a training course of two hours on how to use the service system which were held several times by the department at the beginning of the service. They generally prefer so high a precision that they make rather tight queries with simple Boolean logic in many cases. If they find some relevant documents to their search topics, most of them are satisfied with the retrieval results operated by themselves. And, they don't intend to challenge again to get more relevant documents.

It is quite natural that 90% of the users use mainly the keyword of the trained users, professional searchers use keyword only or a combination of keyword and subject category in most queries, when they are requested to search for subject topics by end-users.

Of the trained users, referencers use all of the search tags by various combinations. They often face the cases that they are unable to access to a source of document asked to copy its full text by end-users. It is due to imperfection or error of bibliographic descriptions which are written on request form for document copy by the end-users. These cases reach 15% of the number of copy requests. The referencers try to find the document source by making different combinations of the search tags on terminal from the descriptions written on the request form. Of 15%, 10% are confirmed but the remaining 5% are not found even by the service system as well as other reference tools.

The untrained users of the second group take pleasure in using keyword and author name. Most of them don't like to study to use such special tools as the INIS Subject Categories, the INIS Authority for Report Number Prefixes and the INIS Authority List for Journal Titles, in addition to the INIS Thesaurus.

5. Conclusion

The present important problem is to improve the timeliness between input date and publication date. This will be realized specially by establishing a direct on-line input system through communication lines by the use of mini-computers between each Centre and ours and by increasing the number of abstracts-in-English to be written by original authors in journals of many academic societies. We also study an automatic query formulation scheme for untrained users of the INIS on-line retrieval system. We shall continue to make our efforts for further development of INIS.

H 2

Role of Commercial Data Bases in Information Retrieval Systems — A Case Study with C A Search Data Base using CAN/SDI Package

S Kasiviswanadham

0. Introduction

This paper aims at discussing various aspects of commercial data bases to be used in the libraries and information centres for information retrieval services. The sources of these data bases and the tape services offered by multinational or national information systems have been dealt with. The various aspects of computer, such as hardware and associated software and processing these data bases either off-line or on-line have been described. In the batch mode process, the various operational aspects of SDI service rendered from INSDOC Regional Centre, Madras, from Chemical Abstracts tapes have been explained through a Flow Chart (Figure 1).

1. Commercial Data Bases and Their Growth

For the purpose of information storage and retrieval, a data base means a bibliographic data base in machine readable form usually available in tapes. The data contains bibliographical details (citations/abstracts or even full text of documents). The data stored in these data bases are identical to the hard copy version of various abstracting and indexing services.

The growth rate of these commercial data bases can be understood by the fact that DIOLOG II in the USA offers now six full text data bases, such as Drug Information Full Text and Harvard Business Review. It offers more than 50,000 password holders, access to more than 200 data bases containing 100 million records on-line and available in over 80 countries. The citations are culled from more than 60,000 journals. Currently an estimated 2,500 data bases are available.

1.1 *Some of the Data Bases are:*

Sl. No.	Name of the Data Base	Organising Agency	Approx.No. of record	Field
a.	COMPENDEX	Engg. Index Corpn, USA	1.3 Million	Engg.
b.	CA SEARCH	Chem. Abstract Service, USA	6.4 Million	Chem. & Chem. Engg.
c.	METADEX	American Society of Metals	5.6 Million	Metallurgy
d.	NTIS	Nat. Tech. Infn. Service, USA	1.1 Million	Science & Tech.
e.	SCI Search	Instt. of Science, USA	5.6 Million	Science & Engg

1.2 *Commercial Data Bases and Information Systems*

The importance of commercial data bases in the computer based information systems has been realized by major libraries/information centres. Realizing the importance in the library applications, and more particularly in Information Storage and Retrieval, multinational Information Systems and National Information Systems with the support of agencies such as IAEA, FLO, UNESCO, FALO, WIPO and UNIDO come into existence. These national as well as international information systems are mainly discipline-oriented systems. For examples INIS, AGRIS, ISDS, EXCERPTA MEDICA, MEDLINE, CAS and INSPEC.

Also information systems are formed by groups of countries. A few example of such systems are: Space Documentation Centre (SDC) of European Space Agency (ESA), European Nuclear Documentation Service (ENDS) of European Atomic Energy Community (EURATOM).

Also network information systems have come into existence, making on-line access to remote data bases (i.e. data bases situated very far from the searcher/user of the system) feasible with the help of data communication networks.

The services from the data base tapes can be had either from the data base producers or vendors. However, services from data bases, such as NTIS, can be obtained only from vendors. Hence, service from vendors, such as SDC, USA and BRC, USA, is essential with reference to specific data bases.

1.3 *Commerical Data Bases and Sources*

The sources for commercial data bases are :

(a) Information networks – multinational or national
(b) Commercial Agencies
(c) Private Agencies

The data bases produced by multinational or national information networks cannot be purchased, leased or hired.

The only way of availing the tape service from these data bases is to actively participate in the network system. Examples of these data bases are : (1) AGRIS, (2) INIS and (3) MEDLARS.

1.4 *Commercial Data Bases and Hardware Requirements*

Commercial data bases can be processed with any main frame computer system such as IBM 360/370. The hardware requirements may be two to three tape drives and one disk drive with on-line printer/terminal. The system should possess direct access devices such as (a) Magnetic Drum, (b) Magnetic Card, (c) Fixed Disk Store and (d) Exchangeable Disk Store. The feasibililty of processing the commercial data bases with the mini and micro-processor based computers may have to be observed. The experience of the Department of Library Science, Brigham University, for on-line search may be taken into consideration. "According to T S Rajagopalan, Scientist-in-Charge, INSDOC, New Delhi-9, locally made microprocessor systems would practically solve the hardware requirements. There are at least 20 or more well-established vendors in the country at present Some of the brands are already tried and tested for library applications. It is also claimed that they are compatible with the IBM-PC Series and the system may need Rs. 3 to 4 lakhs for installation."

1.5 *Commercial Data Bases and Software*

The operational aspects of any computer-based information system are mainly dependent on the availability of the existing software. The development of software is very costly and time consuming and efforts must be made to utilize the existing packages.

Generally the associated software is available with the database producers or vendors. The package has to be slightly modified depending on the computer system for installation. Also the packages has to be modified when the formats of the tapes are changed. For example, the reformatting programme of the CA Condensates tapes of CAN/SDI package installed at the Computer Centre, IIT, Madras, has been modified for converting CA search data base into NRC MARC II format.

In the context of an institution providing information retrieval service with a single data base and to limited users and having the availability of computer facility, it may be advisable to develop its own software. But, for national or international services, it is economical to use the software which deals with an environment suitable for multiple data bases such as CAN/SDI, TEXTPAC, VEERA II, GETEL, ISIS, and STAIRS. With the promotional efforts of UNESCO, CDS/ISIS microversion and IV + V are becoming available now almost free of cost. MINISIS package can be run on HP 3000 system.

2. Commercial Data Bases and Processing

2.1 *Off-line Processing*

These commercial data bases can be processed either off-line or on-line. In batch process, the user has to wait for his answer and the response time may be in the order of hours and days. Many organizations developed off-line Information Systems for their use and some commercial organizations such as CAN/SDI have designed systems and the associated software is available with them.

2.11 *Indian Scene*: In India, the Indian Institute of Science, Bangalore, offers off-line SDI service from INSPEC and BIOSIS.

The Indian National Scientific Documentation Centre (INSDOC), Madras Regional Centre, is providing SDI Service from Chemical Abstracts Search tapes by using the IBM 370/155 computer located at IIT, Madras.

2.2 *The Operational Details of Batch mode Process : A Case Study*

As part of Current Awareness Service, Selective Dissemination of

Information, in short SDI, from Chemical Abstracts Search Data Base tapes is being rendered from the INSDOC Regional Centre, CSIR Complex, Madras. The work flow of this batch mode operation is illustrated in the Flow Chart (Fig.1). Provision has also been made for generating the data base. The system uses CAN/SDI package and the computer jobs are run at the Computer Centre of IIT, Madras, on IBM 370/155. The system requires a core memory of 512k bytes. It can run under OS/MFT/MVT or OS/VS, OS/TSS compilers on IBM 360/370 computer systems. The peripheral configuration for the package is minimum three tape drives for 800/1600 bpi, a disk drive, a card-reader punch, and an on-line printer.

The entire operation is in five phases, namely:

(i) Profile generating/updating
(ii) Data base conversion
(iii) Searching data base with user profiles
(iv) Sorting the searched answers
(v) Supplying computer list of bulletins at regular intervals.

2.21 *Profiling*: This has been represented in the first phase of the Flow Chart (Fig. 1).

"The user profile is a list of terms representing the user's interest in the language of the data base and a statement of the logical conditions required for a match. In a computer search, anything that is machine readable can be considered as a profile term and it consists of a word or a word fragment from a title or abstract, keyword, subject index term, journal coden, author's names, parts of the bibliography, and so on. The task of the profile construction is to choose those terms most likely to appear in the records of the data base."

Construction of a profile is more a technique than mere an arrangement of key words vertically and horizontally. It depends not only on the knowledge of the data base but also on the ability to define the subject matter in terms of the contents of the data base.

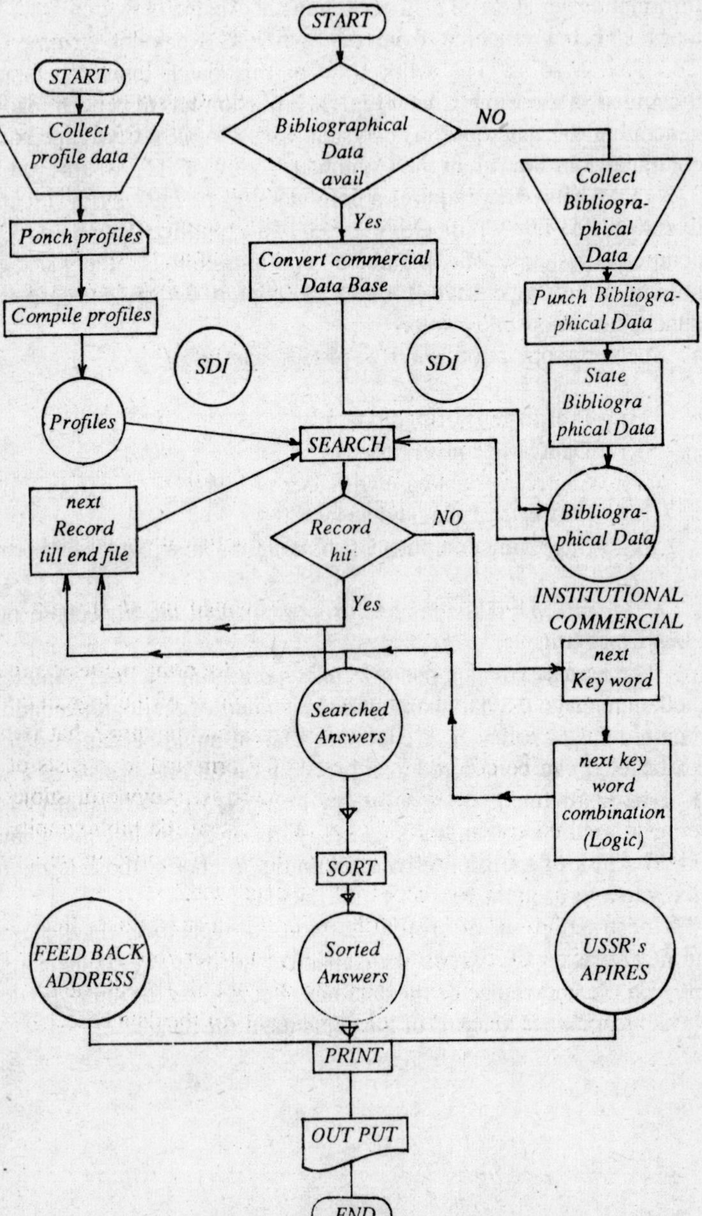

Fig. 1: *Flow Chart Explaining Various Aspects of SDI Service at INSDOC Regional Centre, Madras*

Profiling requires the following operations :

(a) Analysing the topics
(b) Gathering profile terms
(c) Drawing concept maps
(d) Coding profile terms
(e) Formulating search expressions
(f) Punching - preparation of profile decks
(g) Compilation of profiles.

The compiled profile programme creates the user profile master file on a magnetic tape. This as well as the database tapes are input to the search operation.

2.22 *Database Conversion*: This has been dealt with in the second phase of the Flow Chart (Fig. 1). INSDOC Regional Centre, Madras, provides SDI service from the commercially obtained Chemical Abstracts Search Tapes.

CA Search is a weekly computer readable service which is obtained from the American Chemical Society, Ohio. It provides references to Chemistry and Chemical Engineering related documents abstracted in Chemical Abstracts and includes the control, Bibliographic, and Index Data Segments for all documents in all 80 sections. The odd numbered issues contain references on biochemistry and organic chemistry. The even numbered issues cover analytical, physical, macromolecular, and applied chemistry and chemical engineering. Over 15,000 journals and patents issued by 26 countries, new books, conference proceedings, and Government reports are regularly monitored.

The tape format is in a variable length blocked form. The maximum record length is 3,516 bytes, the maximum block size is 3,520 bytes. Tapes are 9-track unlabelled. The CA search tape is in SDF (Standard Distribution Format).

The conversion programme has been written in PL[1] language. The progamme first reads the SDF record and checks the copyright. The programme calls the external routine USASCII to translate ASCII characters into EBCIDIC. The programme checks (CAN) citation abstracts number unlike (TAN) temporary abstracts number in CA Condensate tapes. The conversion programme for reformatting CAC has been modified in order to reformat CA Search.

The controlling data element in the CA Condensate data base and CA search Data Base are different.

2.23 *Searching*: The third phase in the Flow Chart (Fig. 1) explains the search procedure. The user's queries in the form of search expressions will search the data base and these search results are stored on to a magnetic tape. The search logic has been obtained through Boolean logic "AND" (+), "OR" (/), and AND NOT (–) symbols.

The converted database tape and the profile tape are being used as input to the search programme.

The search programme reads the compiled profiles and matches them against the records on the NRC MARC data set. The programme is very sensitive to the format of the compiled profiles data set and the format of the NRC MARC data set. The programme is coded is OS 360/F level assembler language for efficient operation.

The search will be made from all the access points in the data record, namely author, title classification code, type of the document, language corporate author, coden, etc. The searched answer tape is input for sorting the searched answers.

2.24 *Sort*: The search programme gives all the hits on a file called SDI ANS. This file is sorted by passing on the required parameters to the IBM utility programme called SORT available in all OS.

2.25 *Print*: The print programme does the last job of SDI system, that is printing on hard copy. It puts each record in a predetermined format and the print out is in double punched card format. Each record is printed on both sides of the hard copy, i.e., left side and right side. The left side part is for users and the right side for feedback which consists one extra feedback questionnaire line "Is the citation useful" with options YES/NO/CANNOT TELL COMMENT. Each reference is consecutively numbered.

2.26 *Advantages of the System*:

- (i) It minimizes time spent in locating and scanning the current literature;
- (ii) It extends coverage to publications not readily available;
- (iii) It produces highly personalized bibliographies needed by individual workers;
- (vi) It permits the expansion and narrowing of literature requirements, if any;
- (v) User can build his own personalized information file or references for current and future use;
- (vi) User is having literature from range of access points, for example, key words, title words, author's organizations,

classification code, etc.

3. Commercial Data Bases and On-line Processing

There are different types of on-line systems. There are as follow:

(i) On-line inquiry systems
(ii) On-line updating systems
(iii) On-line time sharing systems
(iv) On-line interactive systems.

The user may have access to files from direct access devices such as magnetic disk and may obtain instantaneous response to his query.

In this system, access to remote data bases, i.e., database situated very far from the searcher/user, is feasible due to suitable communication links between the terminal (used for searching) and the data bases being available. In fact, data communication networks such as Tymnet and Telenet connecting various data bases and user terminals in the USA and UK and some other countries have already been set up and are in use.

In the Indian context, this can be performed by INDONET of Computer Maintenance Corporation and NICNET of the National Informatics Centre.

3.1 *On-line Search — Indian Scene*: In India, in National Aeronautical Laboratory (NAL), Bangalore, a project is in progress to set up high-speed terminals known as MIKROTEL package with effective support of scientific user organizations in Bangalore, Defence Research and Development Organization, CSIR, and UNESCO experimentally for six months envisaging the establishment of a 2400bps Post and Telegraphs Microwave link from Bangalore to Bombay and of an Overseas Communication Service and ITALCABLE satellite link through INTELSAT from Bombay to Frasacati, Rome. DESIDOC (Defence Scientific Documentation Centre) has now a hookup with DIOLOG costing about $70 per query.

4. Commercial Data Base(s) vs Data Base Generation

The role of commerical data bases for information retrieval service is significant. But, generation of data base has become necessary in a library/information centre where the size of the data is small and specific, and the information needs of their users are specific in well-defined areas.

For example, Environmental Information System Centre, Madras. The centre is one of the first nine centres (later one more centre was added) selected by the Government of India, Department of Environment, for Information Retrieval Services in the areas, namely, (1) Ecotoxicology, (2) Biodegradation of Wastes, (3) Environmental Impact Assessment, and (4) Environmental Systems Analysis. The centre is part of the Centre for Environmental Studies of the Anna University, Madras. The Centre creates awareness and provides information retrieval services in the said areas.

4.1 *Environmental Abstracts*:

The Centre for Information dissemination brings out once in six months a publication called "Environmental Abstracts" in four parts in the abovedefined areas and also once in a year a publication called "Environmental Data Base Survey" which consists bibliographical details of primary sources available in 12 major libraries situated in the city of Madras and from its own collection in the abovementioned areas. It is also having a good report collection.

4.2 *Current Awareness Service*

As part of Current Awareness Service, the Centre also brings out a publication called "Current Literature Listing" in the abovereferred areas.

The Centre proposes to computerize its information system since it is having access to an IBM 360 and a prime computer situated in Anna University, Madras, and access to a terminal is also feasible.

The important element in the proposed Information Retrieval System is to generate its own data base according to a standard format such as MARC II. However, the format proposed by the International Standards Organization is suited not only for bibliographic exchange but can also be used for data bases oriented to content-oriented search techniques (ISO 2709-1973).

4.3 *Software*

The next important element in the proposed computer system would be the software in terms of the computer in use.

In this regard, it is worth considering the experiences of the Department of Library Science, Brigham University, for the proposed Computer System.

To summarize Keith H Stirlling ("Micro-based emulator for on-line search services")[8]

> "A programme, Dialtwig, written in IBM PASCAL and operating IBMPC, is used to many features of the dialogue system. Structured search assignments are given to the students. These assignments are performed on an information science data base obtained from the School of Library Science (Berkeley) and on a Data-base (SLIS) Reporting Students Research Reports. In addition, other data bases are being created locally or downloaded from ERIC."

It also states that information storage and retrieval service can be rendered through IBMPC microcomputers. It states that originally 64k memory IBMPC be purchased with an expansion board. An additional 192k of memory can be added. It can have one disk drive, 10 megabytes and two or three floppy drives. Special programming techniques, usually at the assembly language level, do permit efficient utilization of memory the 64k.

If the proposed system uses an IBM 360 , software packages such as CAN/SDI and TEXTPAC can be used for processing the data base generated at the institution level. But the format of the data base should be in accordance with the package such as NRC MARC II or TEXTPAC format as the case may be. In the case of a Prime Computer, the package has to be altered or software has to be develped.

It is ideal for this Centre to have a micro-computer compatible to IBMPC. If it can process the computer jobs through micro-computer, the software for information storage and retrieval service can be obtained from the manufacturers of the system or has to be developed.

5. **Conclusion**

The importance of commerical data bases in computer-based information retrieval systems for information retrieval services either from commercial data bases or from data bases generated at institutional level are preferred in view of world-wide information explosion, degree of specialization in search, and heavy increase in the price of the hard copy versions of the commercial data bases.

REFERENCES

1 KASIVISWANADHAM, S: Role of Standardization in Computerised SDI. DOC. S4/D1 (paper presented at Sixteenth ISI Convention, Bhopal, 1973).

2 KASIVISWANADHAM, S: Automation in Libraries and Information Retrieval Units (paper presented at the National Seminar on "Automation in Libraries" at Rani Durgavati Vishwavidyslaya Library, Jabalpur, July 1985).

3 KASIVISWANADHAM, S and RAIZADA, A S: Chem SDI profiling. [*Annals of Library Science*, 23(3), 1976].

4 SATAYANARAYANA, R: Computer Based Information Systems and Services (paper submitted for UNESCO Training course in Information Handling — Sept 10-22, 1979, INSDOC, New Delhi).

5 DADD SUE, A: Building an On-line Bibliographic/MARC Resource Data Base. [*Journal of Library Automation*), 12(1), 1979].

6 CHRISTOFFERSON: Automation at University of Georgia Library. [*Journal of Documentation*) 12(1), 1979].

7 KAMATH, V A: Global Information Systems (paper submitted for UNESCO Training Course in Information Handling — Sept 10 - 22, 1979, INSDOC, New Delhi).

8 STIRLING Keith H: Microbased Emulator for On-line Search. [*Drexel Library Quarterly*, 20(4), 1984].

9 RAJAGOPALAN, T S: Computer Applications in Library Work [paper presented at the Seminar on 'Library Automation', The Madras Library Association, Madras, June 19-20, 1985].

10 MURTY, S S: On-line Access to Foreign/International Libraries. (paper presented at the National Seminar on 'Automation in Libraries', Rani Durgavati Vishwavidyalaya Library, Jabalpur, July, 1985).

H 3

On-line Information Networks

B Vijaya Lakshmi

0. Introduction

Science and Technology are concerned with the creation and application of knowledge through research and development. Research and publication of the results of research are inextricably linked together, and so we find that the size or quantity of information and knowledge is in a state of constant flux and growth. The very growth of knowledge again is dependent in information as in fact is the resultant overall development and progress which is the mark of an information-based society. Information is an intangible commodity recognized today as a valuable national resource. Nations must depend on all such available resources, both their own and those of other nations, in order to improve their scientific, technological, educational and social environments.

It is here that the principles of resource sharing and networks have an important role to play. Developments in communication technologies and computer equipment have made it possible to have immediate access to far-flung items of information through large-scale network systems. The computer industry has shown unprecedented growth, and from being highly localized units contained within the glass walls of a single room, computers have developed over the past 20 years into mass produced, super powerful units with chips no bigger than a thumb nail. Equally rapid have been the developments in sophisticated communications technology and the establishing of worldwide satellite links and networks.

The merging of these two powerful instruments has brought about vast changes in computer systems and the way they can be used by interconnection. This is the concept of computer networks which means an interconnected collection of autonomous computers. The computers are said to be interconnected, if they are capable of exchanging information, through connection media ranging from copper wire to lasers microwaves or satellites.

1. Network Goals

Centralized computer systems are giving way to networks because of the need to extract, access and correlate information produced in isolation and to render it available to all. This is true whether one is talking of information and data pertinent to a single company whose factories and offices are distributed at any place; or whether in a wider context one thinks of a person needing access to information but located at a far-off place. Interconnection via computers solves the "tyranny of geography". Again distributing computing power enables data analyses at the point of capture, and only summaries or synopses of such analyses need be sent periodically to the main computer centre in a network, thereby reducing communication costs.

Computer networks provide a unique communication medium among widely separated people. Two or more people who live and work distances apart can write a report, with the text kept online so that all authors have access to the current version. This speeds up the communication process and has far-reaching impact on the "invisible college" and "paper less information system" concepts. Teleconferencing is another major trend coming in with participants from various continents "talking" to each other through push-button contact. Attendees can also switch off when they get bored.

For librarians and information scientists computer networks enable the accessing online, of large data bases, thus providing researchers and scientists and immediate link with information resources.

2. Types of Networks

Computer networks may be broadly categorized as follows :

(1) *Public data communication network* – Customers connect their hosts and terminals together via the public telephone and telegraph networks on lease.

(2) *Private data processing network* – users connect their hosts and terminals together via a network which is owned by the users themselves.

(3) *Public data processing network* – vendors connect their hosts and terminals together via a network such as INDONET, TYMNET etc.

3. On-line Systems

On-line processing implies that a user is in contact with the computers through some direct mode of linkage. It gives the user the feeling of talking or interacting with the computers as if he were the sole user. However more than one person can "talk" to the computer in a time-sharing mode, though users do not notice this, as the computer is so fast.

On-line retrieval systems provide access in a conversational mode to hundreds of data bases through telecommunication networks. Both numeric and non-numeric data bases, containing non-bibliographic data or bibliographic records are available for search through a number of networks.

The main components of on-line systems are computers that operate in a time-shared mode, and terminals linked through communication channels and other equipment, from where access to the main data bases can be made. The overall networks configuration in an interactive online system is shown in Fig. 1. The mode of satellite link-up is shown in Figure 2.

3.1 *Advantages of On-line Systems*

(1) Interactive database access overcomes an organization's need to possess information (subscriptions to journals, etc.) and converts it into the need to have access to information.
(2) A very vast amount of information is available for search from the data bases, both retrospective searching as well as current literature searches for SDI.
(3) Search profiles and strategy can be created and refined more quickly and easily online in terms of logic, terminology and truncation forms, and through various selection parameters of language, year, etc.
(4) Search is very fast and accurate.
(5) On-line and off-line printing is possible.

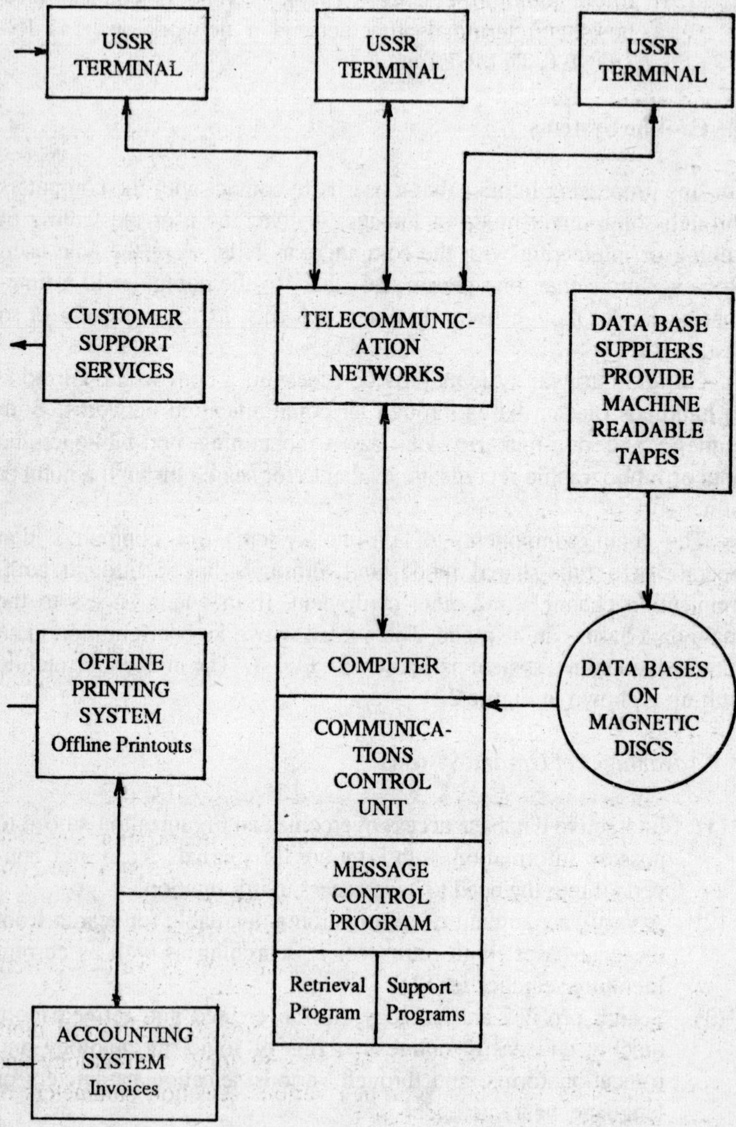

Fig. 1: *Network Configuration in an Interactive On-line System*

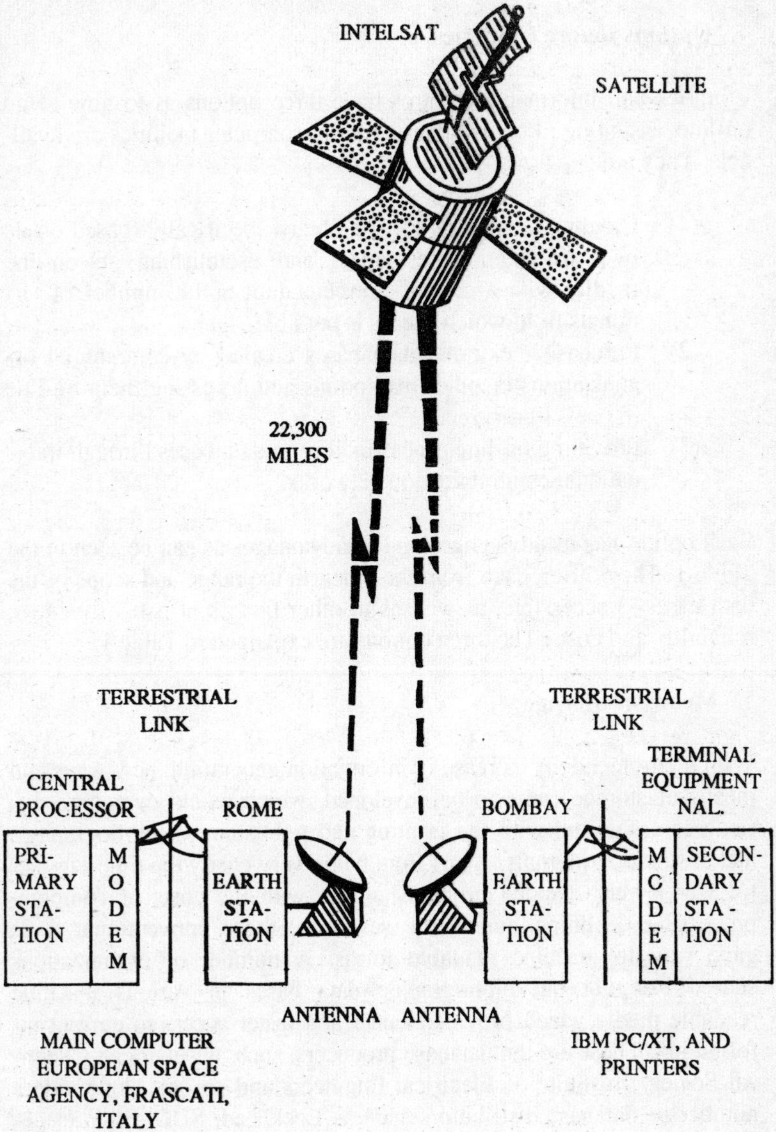

Fig. 2: *Mode of Satellite Link-up*

4. Options Before Libraries

Libraries and information centres have three options as to how to go on-line, assuming of course that the basic computer facilities are available. They are :

(1) Creating data bases for the library specifically (based on its own information resources) and establishing an on-line facility with a central computer unit and a number of terminals from which access is possible.
(2) Purchasing external data bases created by commercial organizations or other institutions and accessing them on-line in one's library.
(3) Providing on-line access facility to data bases through international communication networks.

Each option has its advantages and disadvantages as can be seen in the Table 1. They differ, each from the other, in the range and scope of the data bases(s) accessible, as well as in other factors of exhaustiveness, reliability and costs. The three options are explained in Table 1.

5. Means of Storage

With the tremendous increase in information generation, new ways and means of storage came to be developed, which would overcome difficulties associated with the printing and publishing of bibliographies and abstracting journals. Apart from being very costly the time-lag factor was a very decided problem and so with the costs of computer processing declining during the seventies, these conventional tools gave way to machine readable forms. A number of organizations started bringing out bibliographic data bases in various machine readable media which provided easier and faster access to current information. These are the database producers, such as American Chemical Society, Institute of Electrical Engineers and so on. Along side a number of database distributors such as Lockheed, SDC, ESA, established themselves as commercial organizations who built up a large collection or stock of these database in various subject fields and through data network providers such as TYMNET, TELENET, ESANET, provided on-line access to the data-bases. Any organization/library/information centre can on payment enter into a contract with the database distributors and access any of the data bases with them to provide information to their clientele or users. This framework of on-line access system is seen in Fig. 3.

TABLE 1: ***Providing On-line Information Services : The Options***

OPTION I	*OPTION II*	*OPTION III*
Creating your own data bases and make them accessible on-line	Purchase of external data bases and make them accessible on-line	Provide on-line access facility to inernational networks/data bases
ADVANTAGES	*ADVANTAGES*	*ADVANTAGES*
1. Local facility	1. Local facility	1. Less initial investment on hardware; software
2. Easy access	2. Easy access	2. Large No. of databases
3. Better control	3. Better control	3. Retrospective & Inter-disciplinary searches
4. Suited to your needs	4. Better control	4. On-Line document order
		5. SDI and other services
		6. Interconnection through Local Networks (e.g. INDONET)
		7. Convert the need to possess information into access to information
DISADVANTAGES	*DISADVANTAGES*	*DISADVANTAGES*
1. Very expensive (at least RS 300 per record)	1. Very expensive	1. Normal tele-communication Links unreliable
2. Time-consuming	2. Only current files can be obtained	2. Need for dedicated line (expensive)
3. Limited scope	3. Retrospective searches not possible	3. Payment of "connect-hour charges"
	4. Inter-disciplinary searches not possible	

In on-line systems, computers operate through control programmes which.

(1) interface with many communication lines,
(2) interpret and execute search formulations and commands interactively with the user,
(3) format, sequence and transmit the related output records,
(4) do this for many users simultaneously while keeping detailed accounting records of these activities,
(5) operate concurrently with some background jobs such as file conversion, statistical analysis and new programme development work.

On-line systems need extensive communication capability and support to allow use by a large number of users, dispersed over wide areas. National and International data bases can be accessed through :

(a) the telex networks
(b) the automatic telephone network, or
(c) a special or dedicated data network

(1) DATABASE PRODUCERS
e.g. American Chemical Society
Inst of Electrical Engineers

(2) DATABASE DISTRIBUTORS
(Value-added System)
e.g. LOCKHEED/DIALOG
SDC/ORBIT
EURONET/DIANE
ESA/IRS

(3) DATA NETWORK PROVIDERS
e.g. TYMNET
TELENET USA
UNINET
EPSS UK
TRANSPAC France
ESANET ESA/IRS

(4) INFORMATION INTERMEDIARIES
(5) INFORMATION USERS

Fig. 3: *Components of an On-line Access System*

The speed of transmission of data using these different types of media varies from one to the other (Table 2). In an on-line information retrieval system, a user therefore can sit at a remote computer terminal, which is connected to the host computer by telephone/telecommunications or a data communications network. The user has access to a vast range of data bases from a number of on-line services. It is estimated that more than 3,000 data bases containing over millions of records are currently available for on-line search and retrieval through networks, that permit sharing and remote use of hardware, software and information.

6. Steps in an On-line Search

(1) Connecting the user terminal to the network (for example by dialling the nearest entry point of the network through modem or multiplex devices).

(2) Identification of terminal type.

(3) Identification of the search service one wants (ex. DIALOG, or ORBIT or ESA/IRS).

(4) Linking, through the network, of the user to the search services computer facilities.

(5) User identification (through unique identification code and password which enables the user to start the search, i.e. login procedure.

(6) *Choosing a Data Base*: (that is selection of the data base, one wants to search — incidentally the charges for search are dependent on the data base)

(7) Searching the data base. The steps in a sample search from DIALOG can be seen below :

BEGIN 10 (Where 10 indicates the data base code, (in this case AGRICOLA)

SELECT CROPS (Where crops is a keyterm)

TYPE 4/2/1-15 (where 4 indicates the search set number, 2 is the format type number, i.e. full bibliographic description without abstract 1-15 the first 15 records that are to be displayed on-line)

PRINT 4/2/1-15 (printing the above search result off-line)

(8) *Ending the Search*: "Log off" is the command used (in

DIALOG) to end the search and sever the connection. Before disconnecting the search service facility will generally display information about the costs of the search.

TABLE 2: *Speed Variation of Transmission of Data using Different Types of Media*

Transmission speed in baud*	No. of Characters/Sec.**	Transit Network	Type of Terminal
50 bauds	50 Chars /second	Telex Network	Telex
110 baud to 300 baud	10 chars to 30 chars per second	Automatic Telephone Network/ Specialised network	Visual Display Unit terminal + printer or Teleprinter or micro-computer
1200 baud	120 chars second	Automatic telephone network or specialised data network	VDU terminal + printer; Teleprinter; Micro-computer
Higher speeds 2400, 4800 and 9600 bauds	240, 480, 960 characters/ second	Specialised data network or dedicated line point to point	VDU terminal + printer; Microcomputer

* One baud is equivalent in general to one bit (or basic unit of information) per second.

** In telex a character five bits long is employed while in other methods a character of eight bits is generally used when two or three control bits per character are accounted for it is a good approximation to calculate the character rate by dividing the baud rate by 10.

7. Networks in India

Communication networks that how exist in the west include Government-sponsored networks (e.g. ESANET of the European Space Agency) and commercial networks such as TYMNET, TELENET, TRANSPAC, ITAPAC and so on. In India, the CMC limited have set up INDONET, which is a national computer network with mainframe computers being set up at Bombay, Calcutta, Delhi, Hyderabad, Madras, Bangalore and Pune with distributed data processing facility. Data bases available at any of these INDONET nodes can be accessed on-line from remote terminals. International data bases from Lockheed/DIALOG, SDC/ORBIT, ESA, can also be accessed through an international Gateway located at Videsh Samachar Nigam (Overseas Communication Service). The Gateway will link up the TYMNET and TELENET networks in the USA and ESANET in Italy, and later to other countries. Through the establishing of such connecting channels researchers in India will have immediate on-line access to data banks and data bases abroad. Information flow is expected to be initially at a rate of 2400 bps and grow to 9600 bps later.

7.1 *NICNET*

This is a computer network set up by the National Informatics Centre (NIC), Government of India, to provide information services to Government Ministries and Departments. The main computer in this network is a CYBER CDC 170/730, set up in 1980, connected with 60 interactive terminals. In addition there are 12 mini computer terminals. The systems is a dual processor system, with a processing power of about 3 million instructions per second per processor. The links to the computer are through land-leased lines from the Posts and Telegraphs Department and VHF, and it operates at a speed of 2,400 bps. More than 150 data bases have been created so far by NIC. Ultimately all State capitals and also all districts are to be linked to this network.

8. **On-line Search Services**

8.1 *DIALOG*

The DIALOG Information Retrieval Service was established in 1972 from DIALOG Information Services Incorporation, a subsidiary of Lockheed Corporation at Palo Alto, California, USA. It is an on-line service with a coverage of about 250 data bases on practically every subject field and contains over 119 million records. Records are units of information ranging from a citation with bibliographic information and an abstract of an article in a journal or a conference paper, to a directory type listing of specific manufacturing plants, or in certain cases actual data/factual information.

DIALOG data bases offer subject coverage in science business, technology, chemistry, law, medicine, engineering, economics, social sciences current events and many more areas.

The DIALOG Information Retrieval Service which is the largest data base operator in the world provides online access through providing an interactive search mode. A user can enter into the system if he has the necessary computer facility and hookup through a unique password.

The DIALOG service can be used through data communication networks such as TYMNET, TELNET or UNINET or DIALOG's private telecommunication network DIALNET. Users can also dial directly to the DIALOG computer centre in Palo Alto, California or use international telex service, or TWX. With the appropriate DIALOG compatible computer terminal and linked via modems or multiplex to telecommunication channels through the main facility, it is possible for users (individuals or organisations) to search for required information. Standard search commands of the capability are typed at the user's terminal after connection has been established through a special and unique password. Logical combinations, and thesaurus terms allow for making specific searches with requests for citations with or without abstracts. Users can also order complete texts of documents needed. Off-line networks of citations are also available. An SDI service facility is also offered and users merely use a search logic relevant to their needs and ask that it be stored. This allows the user to have a search run automatically, each time a selected file is updated. The user receives periodically a printout matching the search profile.

9. European Space Agency : Information Retrieval Service

The European Space Agency has been offering an on-line information retrieval service (ESA/IRS) since 1973 through several telecommunication networks like TYMSHARE, TRANSPAC, TYMNET, etc. Leased data lines provide on-line access to the ESA network from Rabat (Morocco) and Beijing (China). It covers about 70 data bases and data banks containing around 35 million references in a wide range of subject fields. Both bibliographic information and data are available from these data bases and data banks. Data banks like LEDA give details of remotely sensed satellite imagery (details such as geographical location, land coverage, etc.). SATELDATA and SPACECOMPS give information on satellite equipment and space craft equipment, their specifications, properties, codes, etc. AEROSPA DAILY, on the other hand, is the on-line equivalent of a printed newspaper and carries the full text of published articles. ESA/IRS is the world's third largest database operator and has its main computer facility, a large IBM (with 6 MB main memory, and more than two trillion bits of disk space) at Frascati, Rome in Italy.

The ESA data bases/data banks are accessed using the software package developed by the ESA, namely, "ESAQUEST".

The ESA/IRS is another example of an on-line network that provides information with speed and accuracy. Again by using search logic users can get just the specific information they want. Search can be refined by using logical combinations, or by giving parameters of language, year, etc. Since the references can be seen immediately on the display screen of the user's terminal, the user can decide what is actually relevant to him. Printouts can also be obtained. Response is immediate and so there is a great advantage over off-line or batch processed systems.

ESA/IRS also offers access via its computer to other on-line network services as for instance EURONET'S DIANE.

REFERENCES

1 LYNCH, M F: *Computer-based Information Services in Science and Technology: Principles and Techniques*. Hertfordshire, Peter Peregrinus Ltd. 1974.

2 SALTON, Gerald and McGill, Michael J: *Introduction to Modern Information Retrieval*, London McGraw-Hill International Book Co. 1983.

3. TANENBAUM, Andrew S: *Computer Networks*. New Jersey, Prentice-Hall, Inc. 1981.

4. VAN DER LAAN, A and WINTERS, A A *Ed*: Use of Information in a changing World *(Proceedings of the 42nd FID Congress held in the Hague*, Netherlands, 24-27 September, 1984, North-Holland, 1984).

the rest [illegible] of published [illegible] and [illegible]. ESA/IRS is the world's third largest [illegible] operator and has its main computer facility, a large IBM [illegible] [illegible] main memory and more than two million bits of disk storage, at Frascati, Rome in Italy.

The ESA data base [illegible] either [illegible] searched using the software package developed by the ESA, namely, 'ESA/QUEST'.

The ESA/IRS is another example of an online network that provides information with speed and accuracy. [illegible] by using search logic, users can [illegible] specify exactly what they want. Search can be refined by using logical combinations, or by giving parameters of [illegible]. Since the references can be seen immediately on [illegible] screen of the user's terminal, the user can decide what is actually relevant to him. Printouts can also be obtained. [illegible] there is a great deal of [illegible] offline or [illegible] printouts.

ESA/IRS also offers access via its computer to other online [illegible] services at [illegible] DIALOG [illegible] DIANE.

REFERENCES

1. LYNCH [illegible]. Computer-based Information Services [illegible]. [illegible] 1974.
2. SALTON (Gerard) and [illegible]. Introduction to modern information retrieval. [illegible], McGraw-Hill International Book Co. 1983.
3. TANENBAUM [illegible]. Computer Networks. New Jersey, Prentice Hall, [illegible] 1981.
4. [illegible] and [illegible]. [illegible]. 1984.

H 4

INFOTERRA: International Referral System for Sources of Environmental Information

B. John

0. Introduction

In the world of increasing interdependancy and complexity due to urbanization and industrialization there are many problems which are coming different sources. Some of the problems are results of change in the organization and some due to the needs for change induced by the challenges of society. All the challenges contribute to the uncertainty of the future.

1. Role of Information

Information plays a crucial role in providing solutions for all the problems in modern society. Sectoral activities such as industry, agriculture, transportation and rural development require accurate and timely information for the achievement of their goals. Other activities such as those aimed at technical innovation, education, or planning and decision-making cannot be carried out without relevant information.

No nation can individually seek all requisite solutions to the complex scientific, technological and social problems that are rapidly emerging and multiplying today. A global cooperative endeavour is the only logical response to the issues challenging humanity. It is for this reason that nations seek to share knowledge and experience relating to their problems and their common goals.

The role of information in development was emphasized in the seventh special session of the UN General Assembly by the unanimous adoption of resolution 3362 (S/VII): "Developed and developing countries should cooperate in the establishment, strengthening and development of the scientific and technological infrastructures of the developing countries.

2. Special Role of Information in Environmentally Sound Development

Development in the present decade and beyond will increasingly be concerned with environmental factors. Various environmental problems are of critical importance to all countries in their efforts to satisfy the basic requirements of their people, to use rationally and effectively their resources, to develop their economies, and to improve the quality of life of their people. Desertification, soil loss and degradation, deforestation, flooding and siltation, pollution, resource depletion, noise and congestion, changes in climate, inadequate shelter and water supply; environment related diseases are some of the environmental problems confronting the human race.

Environmentally sound development is needed so that the quality of the human environment is maintained and enhanced as a vital component of human health and well-being. It is also needed so that natural resources are rationally used and managed as a means of enhancing development, and for providing a base for a sustainable development in the future.

The approaches to be developed, the types of solutions to be sought, and the kinds of techniques to be applied will vary with time and from country to country. They will be influenced by the goals of the society and patterns of development, the state of the environment and the means and resources available. They will depend on the quality and relevance of the information consulted.

The knowledge needed for achieving environmentally sound development is interdisciplinary and cross-sectorial. It is complex and wide-ranging in scope and rapidly changing, and is often unknown to those who need it, accumulated in a vast store of development experience all over the world.

To facilitate rapid access to such information, a net-work INFOTERRA — the International Referral System for Sources of Environmental Information — has been established by the United Nations Environment Programme (UNEP) for the exchange of environmental information. INFOTERRA is a referral system which directs the user to the actual sources of information.

3. Background and Design

INFOTERRA was established to facilitate the exchange of environmental information within and between nations. It is a component of Earthwatch, UNEP's programme for the critical assessment of the global environment. The system was established in response to recommendation 101 of the United Nations Conference on the Human Environment, which was held in Stockholm in June 1972. INFOTERRA became operational with the active participation of a dozen countries, most of them developed in 1977. Today, however, the primary impetus for the further development of INFOTERRA comes from the developing world.

INFOTERRA activities are financed at the global levels by UNEP and at the national level by each partner country.

Governments of the partner countries of INFOTERRA indicated that they wished to maintain some degree of control over the flow of information, however, the system has been opened to wider use.

INFOTERRA is a decentralized network of environmental information systems, its operation relies on a grid of focal points.

4. INFOTERRA Today

At present INFOTERRA consists of the programme activity centre at UNEP headquarters in Nairobi and National focal points in 110 countries. There are, in addition, one "point of contact" (a possible future focal point), three organizational participants (the International Institute for Applied Systems Analysis, the International Union for the Conservation of Nature and Natural Resources, and the Commonwealth Secretariat), two sectoral focal points (the Industry and Environment Office of UNEP and the Marine Environmental Data Information System of IOC) and regional focal point (the International Centre for Scientific and Technical Information).

4.1 *National Focal Points*

A national focal point is designed by the government of a member State following approaches from UNEP. It is generally established in a governmental agency, usually with an environmental responsibility. Its principle tasks at present are to compile and maintain a list of sources of environmental information in its natural territory, for inclusion in the INFOTERRA Directory, and to provide enquiries or request with a list of sources derived from the international directory, which are likely to have information relevant to their enquiry.

4.2 *Regional Focal Points*

Regional focal points designated by an inter-governmental agreement coordinate some or all of the INFOTERRA activities within the group of countries.

4.3 *Sectoral Focal Points*

Sectoral focal points are designated by UNEP in cooperation with an appropriate organization that has the infrastructure to operate an environmental service in that sector.

5. INFOTERRA Programme Activity Centre

This centre acts as a focal point for international agencies and government organizations not otherwise able to participate in INFOTERRA.

The decentralized structure of INFOTERRA has been chosen for good reasons. It is the least costly way of gathering information on sources, it provides the speedy response by the widely dispersed community of sources and it brings the information machinery as close as possible to the users.

INFOTERRA is based on the concept of referral. All INFOTERRA focal points are equipped to refer an inquirer to the sources best able to provide the information sought.

INFOTERRA has been designed to fulfil certain basic criteria. In particular, it is expected to :

(1) Strengthen national information flows, to provide the best support systems for environmental decision-making,
(2) Be flexible to allow the system to adopt to national requirements as well as to changes over time,
(3) Be simple, to permit the system to be brought as close as possible to the user,
(4) Make maximum use of existing and planned information systems, to avoid unnecessary duplication and waste of resources to permit the use of standardized approaches

wherever possible,

(5) Operate with limited resources both at UNEP and at the national level, and

(6) Be a catalyst, to sensitize people, who participate in and use INFOTERRA to the role of information systems in decision-making and of environmental factors in development planning.

The subject coverage of INFOTERRA is very broad, it covers all problems that they consider "environmental". The terminology used by INFOTERRA for storage and retrieval of sources of information is developed specifically for INFOTERRA, with specific uses in mind. The terminology is quite broad and describes environmental and developmental concerns in approximately 1,000 attributes.

6. Summary

INFOTERRA has focal points in 110 countries and has registered some 8,500 sources of information in 79 countries. It is under used at present, because it has been in operation for too short a time to allow the development of a sufficient awareness of its services. However, there is evidence that the referral mechanism works sufficiently well to be a valuable tool of international information exchange, and that if development of the INFOTERRA system continues, its rate of use should increase substantially.

REFERENCES

1 KHOSLA, A: INFOTERRA: An International Information Network. (In: *Proceeding of the Seminar on International Cooperative Information Systems*, Vienna, 9-13th July 1986).

2 MARTYN, JOHN: *Report on the Evaluation of INFOTERRA*, 1981.

H 5

Data Base Management Systems

A R D Prasad

1. Understanding Data Base

A data base can be defined as a collection of data designed to be used by different programme level. It can be viewed as a collection of interrelated data stored together with controlled redundancy to serve one or more applications in an optimal fashion; the data are stored so that they are independent of programmes which use the data; a common and controlled approach is used in adding new data and modifying and retrieving existing data within the data base. A system is said to contain a collection of data bases if each of these is entirely separate in structure.

1.1 *Origins of Data Base*

SM Dean traces the origin of data bases from the invention of the punched card by Dr Herman Hollerith of the US Bureau of Census in the 1880s. Further he describes the evolution towards data bases through the first electronic computer, ENIAC in 1946, the use of magnetic tape system in the UNIVAC-1 computer in 1951 and the introduction of magnetic disk in the mid 1960s. The 1960s also saw the emergence of the Management Information System (MIS) concept. One of the outstanding products of that time was the Integrated Data Store (IDS) introduced by General Electronic (now owned by Honeywell) in 1965. As the name suggests IDS was used to create large integrated files that can be shared by a number of applications. It was considered as the forerunner of modern data base systems. Its pioneer, Charles W Bachman, subsequently played a very active role in the development of the CODASYL data base proposal which incorporated many of the IDS features. It was only in the 1970's that data base systems gained fame and more popularity and the CODASYL set up a Data Base Task Group (DBTG) to provide a common frame work to all the data base designs. IBM has also been keen on data base systems. Most of its research in this area is concentrated on the relational model unlike the CODASYL, which emphasizes the network model.

1.2 *Advantages of a Data Base System*

C J Date point out the following advantages :

(1) Redundancy can be reduced;
(2) Inconsistency can be avoided to some extent;
(3) Standards can be enforced;
(4) Security restrictions can be applied;
(5) Integrity can be maintained; and
(6) Conflicting requirements can be balanced.

2. The CDS/ISIS Package

The acronym CDS/ISIS stands for Computerized Documentation System/Integrated Set of Information Systems. This software package belongs to the ISIS family, which was originally developed by the International Labour Organization (ILO). Another software package belonging to the ISIS family is the MINISIS developed by the International Development Research Centre (IDRC), Canada. CDS/ISIS runs on IBM 370, RIAD and AMDAHL mainframe computers. Recently UNESCO has developed a mini-micro version of CDS/ISIS, and is distributing the package free of cost. The Mini-Micro version 1.0 runs on IBM PCs and its compatibles.

The MINISIS package developed by IDRC runs on the Hewlett-Packard HP 3000 range of mini computers and is also distributed to libraries and information centres free of cost. Data base systems of the ISIS family have certain common features such as – similar data base structure, record structure (having leader, directory, variable length data), similar data structure (having variable length fields and subfields). All the packages are characterized by generalized data definition, on-line data entry, enquiry, modification and deletion. All are compatible with the ISO 2709 format for bibliographic information interchange. However there is a basic difference between the mini-micro version 1.0 of the CDS/ISIS and the MINISIS — the former being a hierarchical data base and the latter a relational one.

Although CDS/ISIS is widely used for bibliographic data bases, it is a generalized data base for information storage and retrieval of non-numeric data. The same set of programmes can be used to organize an unlimited number of data bases each of which may consist of a wide variety of data. It can be used to generate catalogues, accession registers, bibliographies, institutional directories, directories of specialists, directories of equipment, etc.

2.1 *Required Configuration*

The CDS/ISIS Mini-micro version 1.0 runs on all IBM PC and PC compatible machines with 640k RAM. Although for demonstration purposes, it can be run without a hard disk and with two floppy drives, it is advisable to have at least 10 MB hard disks for storing large and multiple data bases. However each data base can have a maximum of 30,000 records which is the limitation of the PC operating system.

2.2 *Functional Capabilities of CDS/ISIS*

CDS/ISIS allows its users to :

—define data bases containing the required data elements,
—enter new records to a given data base,
—modify, correct or delete existing records,
—automatically build and maintain fast access files to each data base,
—retrieve records by their contents through a sophisticated search language,
—sort the records in any sequence desired,
—display the records or portions,
—display the records in any sequence desired,
—print out full catalogues and/or indices from any given data base.

To perform the above tasks, six programmes are provided. They can be classified into two types, viz., (i) user programmes and (ii) system programmes.

2.21 *User Programmes*: Following are the user programmes :

—ISIS performs all the tasks related to data base maintenance and

retrieval,
—ISISPRT provides printed outputs such as catalogues and indexes,
—ISISINV provides inverted file maintenance and utility functions.

2.22 *System Programmes*: These are designed for the data base administrator (application programmer to create new data bases and perform various system tasks.

—ISISDEF which provides for defining new data bases and modifying existing data base definitions.
—ISISUTL providing miscellaneous systems utility functions.
—ISISXCH providing facilities for interchanging data with other systems as well as Master File utility programmes.

2.3 *Four Levels of Interaction*

Conceptually the interface with a data base can be viewed at four levels :

—development and maintenance level
—application programmers level
—data entry level
—end-user level

The first level task with regard to CDS/ISIS is the concern of UNESCO to keep the set of data base programmes regularly updated and to create newer versions with more and more facilities. For example, the present version allows Boolean operators but does not allow user's to use '>' and '<' operations. However in future they may be provided. All the features that are written in italics in the Reference Manual can only be used in the future versions but not the present version.

The second level is the task of the information personnel who are using the CDS/ISIS package. These tasks consist of defining the data base, creating inverted files, painting the work sheets, preparing the command lists to print the output in a desired format.

The third level is dealt with the data entry people, who enter the data into the data base following the worksheet. This level does not require any programming skills as the CDS/ISIS package is completely menu driven, i.e., the set of commands to be used at various stages appear in the form of prompts.

The end-user, that is, the library user comes in at the next level. The CDS/ISIS package is developed to be user-friendly. The knowledge required by the user to have interface with the system is minimal. No programming skills are required. However he has to know how to translate his needs into a search expression using Boolean logic. In other words of all the available six programmes, the data entry personnel and the users need to know only a part of the ISIS programme.

3. Commercial Data Bases and CDS/ISIS

3.1 *Fixed Field Length vs Variable Field Length*

The CDS/ISIS is basically a bibliographic data base where the record and field lengths are variable, whereas in data bases like UNIFY, dBaseII, dBaseIII, the field lengths are fixed, and this may ultimately lead to the wastage of storage space with blanks. The fields in a typical bibliographic data base vary greatly in content depending on the document for which an item is being prepared.

For example, the Common Communication Format (CCF) suggests a total number of around 250 fields to cover all varieties of documents. But most documents may require at most 30-35 fields.

In addition the user of the system has to allot the maximum possible length to a field. For example, it is advisable to declare the title field length as 300 alphanumeric characters. But in many cases it may not exceed 50 characters. In commercial data bases like UNIFY and dBase, as the field length is 300 characters, it occupies all the 300 characters, irrespective of the actual data length, leaving as many as 250 characters blank. However in data bases like CDS/ISIS, MINISIS where the record and field lengths are variable this problem of wastage does not arise.

3.2 *Repeatability*

One of the distinguishing features of CDS/ISIS is its provision for repeatable fields. This typically is a problem for libraries that use dBase and other data bases. For example, in the case of the author's field where the number of authors vary one has to enter all the authors' names in one field or has to declare a number of fields to accommodate all the authors. Whereas in CDS/ISIS we can declare authors, place of publication fields, as repeatable fields.

4. Using CDS/ISIS

CDS/ISIS can be used to create catalogues, accession registers, directories, etc. For the purpose of entering bibliographic information, the ENVIS Centre is following the CCF (Common Communication Format). As the CCF deals with bibliographic information only, for directories and accession register information, ENVIS Centre is using tags that in no way disturb the CCF standard.

Coming to the actual use of CDS/ISIS it is advisable to start interfacing the package with a sample diskette, where a data base is already created with sample data. In this context the first programme that is to be used is the programme called ISIS. As the user gives the command ISIS it displays a menu and the user can have his own choice of further steps. However, when the system asks for the data base name one has to enter CDS and type return. It is always good to have a look at all the programmes, viz. ISIS, ISISDEF, ISISPRT, ISISINU, ISISUTL, ISISXCH and how they are/can be used with the sample data base 'CDS'.

However to create a data base that suits individual libraries or information centres, one has to start from scratch. Following is the suggested course of compiling a data base.

4.1 *ISISDEF*

This programme is meant for defining new data bases or for modifying the existing data base definitions. Data base definition includes creating field definition tables, data entry worksheets, field selection tables, and display formats.

Field Definition Table includes the tags that are to be assigned to a field, such as field name, length of the field, type of the field, whether it is repeatable, whether it has a set pattern, or whether it has sub-fields. For the purpose of assigning tags to different fields, the ENVIS Centre is using the CCF. A typical entry is

Once the user visualizes and enters the possible required fields and their parameters, the next task is to design the worksheet layout. These worksheets can be used later by data entry personnel to enter or modify data using the ISIS programme.

TAG	Name of the field	Length	Type	Repeatable	Delimiter/Pattern
200	title	300	x		
300	author	100	x	r	nr

The symbol ^n indicates the subfield delimiter for name subfield, whole ^r is used for role.

CDS/ISIS uses a powerful search programme where a user can search with Boolean logic and the search response time is almost instantaneous. But for the search to be conducted, the data base application programme has to define FST (Field Select Tables) for the purpose of inverting the fields. The ISISINV uses FST, and stores in the inverted file, and produces the dictionary of searchable terms and associated record postings for the data base.

The last step in using the ISISDEF programme is to design the display format keeping in view the requirement of the library. One can design any number of formats. One can design the format for all the three levels as suggested by the AACR2 or design it in such a way, that the displayed records are in conformity with a know abstracting or indexing journal.

4.2 *ISIS*

This programme is basically meant for the data entry personnel and for the end user of the data base.

Once a data base is created using the ISISDEF programme, it will be ready for entering the actual data using the worksheets that were designed in ISISDEF programme. For this purpose CDS/ISIS provides a field editor, commands of which are displayed at the bottom of the screen, and the knowledge required on the part of the data entry personnel is minimal.

In addition to the data entry, the ISIS programme can be used for browsing the master file, searching the data base using the search language which is based on Boolean logic and for saving the search results for printing using ISISPRT programme.

4.3 *ISISPRT*

This programme is meant for formatting and printing the contents of the data base and results (records) saved in searching. The ISISPRT programme specifies titles of printouts and includes running title, linewidth, column width, number of columns indention, page numbering etc. In addition, it provides a powerful sort facility, where by, users can sort the records by a maximum of four fields. The greatest advantage in this facility is that bibliographies can be printed with the text in classified order or by author, and if an author writes two or more articles they can further be sorted by year of publication or by the title.

5. **Other Programmes**

The ISISINV programme may be used to create, update, backup, or print the inverted file of the data base. Inversion technique which is basically a powerful search technique is used to retrieve records.

An entry in an inverted file is as follows :

S.No	Frequency	KeyTerm	Disk Area	Mfn/Tag/Firstword/First Occurrence
3	2	Automation	2/71	85/ 200/ 1/ 1

The ISISXCH programme facilitates exchange and helps loading external data into the existing data base. That is, in a way it can be used for bibliographic information/data exchange. In addition ISISXCH programme can be used to import exchange. In addition ISISXCH programme can be used to import files that are in conformity with the ISO standard 2709 format. The file that is to be input can be either loaded in a new data base or can be merged with the existing data base. Although ISISXCH can be used for backup and restore operations, it is advised to use the MS-DOS backup commands for the purpose.

ISISUTL programme facilitates a few system utilities in order to perform the following tasks :

—create or edit system menus and worksheets

—print menus and worksheets

—redefines screen attributes
—print system message files

6. Conclusion

CDS/ISIS is a powerful data base system package available to all non-profit organizations. With NISSAT showing keen interest in promoting this package in Indian libraries and information systems, the CDS/ISIS package is gaining wide use. The greatest advantage with this package lies in its performance in IBM PC Compatible machines which are relatively less costly and are becoming commonplace in every organization. However the package needs to be improved further; future versions of ISIS may be even more powerful. It is expeceted that there would be many improvements with regared to ISIS's print and search language.

REFERENCES

1 DATE, C J: *Introduction to Data base Systems*. Ed 3. New Delhi, Narosa Publishing House, 1975.

2 DEEN, S M: *Fundamentals of Data Base Systems*, New Jersey; Hayden Book Co.

3 LANCASTER, F W and SMITH, L C: *Compatibility Issues Affecting Information Systems and Services*. PGI-83/WS/23, PGI and UNISIST, Unesco, Paris, 1983.

4 MARTIN, J: *Principles of Data-Base Managment*, New Delhi, Prentice-Hall of India, 1982.

5 UNESCO, CCF: *Common Communication Format*, PGI-84/WS/4, PGI and UNISIST, Paris, 1984.

6 UNESCO, *CDS/ISIS: Mini-micro Version*, Division of the Unesco Library Archives and Documentation Services, Paris, 1985.

H 6

Comparative Study of Published Papers in Pure Sciences, Humanities and Social Sciences : Citation Analysis

A K Kundu

1. Nature of Articles

When we do a comparative study of the 153 Articles of *Annals of Library Science and Documentation* (1955–75) which has citations and their pattern and type as support to the text and compare it with other scientific, i.e. Pure and applied science papers we see that Social Sciences and Humanities and other non-scientific papers cite less densely.

2. Limitations in Citations

Due to an enormous growth in pure science literature scientists are publishing short communications. This economies both in terms of space and time considerably. This is proved from the short communications accounting for 30% of the total articles. Short communications are more selective in citing references. The major source of information are journals (90%). The ranking list of journals could guide to select the journals to the following limitations :

(1) Source journals and period of study being limited, it will have its own weaknesses in generating the findings;
(2) The citations are chosen by the scientists who judge its relevancy, which may not be free from sociological and psychological aspects of individual authors;
(3) Availability of references and its language may affect the trend of citation;

(4) National bias may be a factor in selecting the citations; and
(5) This is partial picture as the references cited may not be exhaustive.

3. Pattern of Research

As the maximum researches are being carried out in the field of pure and applied sciences, it is obvious that the literature growth is a corollary to research growth. As the tendency of research has been shifted from solo research to team research the researches are carried out at a rapid speed. So the document growth is also at the same speed and in increased quantum. These days no research is accepted as valid unless it is supported by relevant literature.

3.1 Research in Social Sciences and Humanities

Moreover the scientific researches can be repeated in the controlled conditions in the laboratory and the truth can be verified and tested whenever it is required. But for Social Sciences and Humanities this testing under the controlled condition is not possible and one will have to wait for the observable factors which are never repetitive in nature. It consumes enormous time and energy to complete an experiment. As the truth cannot be tested every now and then the validity always remains challengeable. And in support of the facts appropriate documents cannot be cited as they too will be of the same nature. That is the reason, they will have to depend more on the respective documents than the latest documents. The literature growth is quite slow so the citations are not thickly populated like science and technology literature.

4. Citations in Scientific Papers

Bertram[1] suggested that the amount of citations varies significantly with sections of scientific papers as a characteristic that it will have many sections, namely:

1. Introduction
2. Hypothesis
3. Methodology
4. Presentation of result

5. Conclusions, etc.

So as sections grow, the number of citations also increase in support of the validity of the statements and processes. So it is said that the number of citations will increase proportionally to furnish a link between the present and the prior works. It will be with the context of the paper.

5. Citations in Library Science Articles

In *Annals of Library Science and Documentation* it is observed that out of 153 articles only two have cited more than 50 citations, four articles have cited within 40-50, seven articles within 30-40, 10 articles within 20-30, 40 articles within 10-20 and rest of articles had cited less than 10 citations. If seen minutely, out of those articles, 10 articles had cited only one citation, 22 articles within 2-5 and the rest 57 cited within 6-9 citations. The details are tabulated in Tables 1 and 2.

TABLE 1: *Density of Citations in Articles*

Sl. No.	No. of Citations	No. of Articles	Percentage
1.	50 and more	2	1.3
2.	40-50	5	3.3
3.	30-40	7	4.6
4.	20-30	10	6.6
5.	10-20	40	26.4
6.	Less than 10	89	57.8
Total	1550	153	

TABLE 2: *Distribution of Citations Less Than 10 in 89 Articles*

Sl. No.	No. of Citations		No. of Articles		Percentage
1.	1.0	-	10	-	
2.	2.5	-	22	-	57.8
3.	6.9	-	59	-	

It was revealed that 153 articles contained 1,550 citations. The average citation per article was about 10, tabulated in Table 3. After further analysis it comes to about 7.65 citations per paper.

TABLE 3: *Source Paper and Citations and Overall Percentage*

(a)	(b)	(c)	(d)	(e)	(f)
Main paper with citation	Main paper without citations	Total No. of citations	Average citation per paper (c/a)	Overall citation as whole article (a + b)	Average citation per article [(d + e)/2]
153	149	1550	10.1	5-13	7.65

The above table represents a diagrammatic sketch of total citation structure in *Annals of Library Science and Documentation.*

There were 153 main papers with citations and 149 papers without any citations. Total citations were 1,550 and the average citations were about 10.1. If we take the overall citations of 302 articles, they were about 5-13.

6. Comparison with Science and Technology

When compared with science and technology it is low. It had been reported by Eugene Garfield that there were some articles in *Science* and *Nature* that contained 175-200 citations. Average citations in the scientific papers reported by American scientists field of physics and chemistry were 30. In the field of biological and medical sciences it was 25 in the USA. But in the field of library science (*Annals of Library Science and Documentation*), when we compare, it is 10 per article during 1955–75 for 153 articles with citations. But during that period 302 articles appeared and 149 were without citations (Table 3). If further analysed, it was found to be 7.65 citations which means 8 citations per article. After eliminating the trash it would not be more than six citations per article.

Garfield[2] pointed out that citation frequency is a measure of research activity or of communication about research activity in itself. The number of citations of a main work is no measure of significance. Like one scale on a monogram it must be used along with other scales to obtain anything useful or meaningful particularly if the objective of the evaluation is in any way qualitative.

West Brook[3] studied the use of citation in identifying the significance of research — an essay in what now-a-days is often called the sociology of science. He also said that it will also indicate the field of work in which an institution is doing maximum work.

Citations not only provided a new noble way of approaching the literature but it afforded the possibility of using the assembled data in order to leave something about the literature itself. How it was connected and how it was being used by the population of authors.

Much of the Information Science Literature is not very scholarly. At least one-third of the papers have no references. Half of them have only four references at the most, two-thirds have eight or fewer references. Some have been shown in the Table 1 — about 89 articles with less than 10 citations. It is very clear that 1-3% of the total articles have cited 50 citations, 3.3% within 40-50, 4.6% within 30-40, 6.6% within 20-30, 26.4% within 10-20 and the rest 57.8% below 10 citations.

Price[4], stated that Index for the Physical Science journals studied is higher than that calculated for the Social Sciences. Based on the difference in utilization of recent works. Price presents the hypothesis that the growth of literature in the two disciplines, i.e., science and social sciences, is different. He stated Physical Sciences grow from skin, that is, make heavier use of the work being done at the research front, while the social sciences tend to make heavier use of the older and archival materials, thus growing from within.

7. **Low Utilization of Citations in Social Sciences**

In particular the lower utilization of the recent citations by the social scientists may be shown to reflect the great time required for scientific work. Subsequent publication of social science research contribution is opposite to one from physical sciences.

It has been calculated by Garvey[5] that for a physical scientist the median time from conception of research to publication is 26 months. For social scientists the median time is 32 months. That means that citations forming the basis of research are 26 to 32 months old at the time of publication.

8. **Evaluation of Result**

The scientific experiments can be repeated now and then under controlled conditions till a desired result is obtained, but that is not possible with social sciences and humanities as the research is carried out under natural environments and has a direct impact on the rate of citations.

It is suggested that the authors should write articles empirically and to support the statements the citations are to be provided to establish the link between the past and present research work with the context of the paper.

REFERENCES

1 BERTRAM, H: Trends of Citation, (*Science* 66, 1927, pp. 290-92).

2 GARFIELD, E: Citation Indexing for studying science. (*Nature* 227, 1971, pp. 669-71).

3 WEST BROOK J H: Identifying Significant Research. (*Science* 132, 1960, pp. 1229-34).

4 PRICE, D J de Sola: Citation Measure of Hard Science, Soft Science, Technology, and Non-Science. (In *Communication Among Scientists and Engineers*, by C E Nelson and D K Pollack, Lexington, 1970, pp. 1-22).

5 GARVEY, W D, et al.: Communication in the Physical and Social Science. (*Science* 170, 1970, pp. 1166-73).

H 7

Access to Information: The Growth and Development of Information Systems in Social Sciences and the Pioneering Work of Kaula

S Fazle Rab

0. Introduction

"Information" and "Communication" are two important terms which are used these days very frequently, commonly or sometimes interchangeably. A volume of literature has been produced to express their meaning, scope, importance and role in this modern age which is itself characterized as an "Informationage". Information is described as "Knowledge concerning some particular fact, subject, data and event in any communicable form" whereas "communication" is a process through which information is conveyed or disseminated among the members of society through a common system of symbols". Information is generated at various levels by different groups of persons such as inventors, scientists, technologists, social scientists, legislators, leaders, change agents, etc. In order to make optimum use of such knowledge or information various methods are used to disseminate it with a greater speed and clarity among the members of the society. That is why throughout the history human beings have sought to improve their ability to receive and assimilate information about their surroundings and at the same time to increase the speed, clarity and variety of their methods for transmission of information.[1] Besides there has been a constant need for information for human beings to interact with each other at various levels for their growth, progress and development.

1. Information Society

The massive growth of Information at all levels has gradually led to the transformation of the "Industrial Society" an "Information Society." Today all nations, regardless of the level of development, are already in the midst of information age internationally if not globally. The various terminologies like "Information Overload", "Information Crisis", "Information Dissemination", "Information Flow", "Information Systems", and "Information Network", etc., are being frequently used as the attributes of an information society. Hence, the essence of the information age is the massive increase in all of the following :

(i) the generation of information in a variety of forms,

(ii) the speed to send as well as to receive information from any point on earth,

(iii) the volume of information that can be transmitted from one point to another,

(iv) the ability to select the desired information from huge data bases for decision making,

(v) the dependence on artificial intelligence to conceptualize problems and their possible solutions in ways beyond human capabilities.

(vi) the growth of specialization in collecting, storing, processing and transmitting information,

(vii) the development of information trade and industry,

(viii) the relative importance of information versus labour, energy in the production of goods and services,

(ix) the quantitative and qualitative change in information handling for the rapid transnationalization of industrial and financial business.

(x) the growth of computer-based telecommunication networks through satellites.

1.1 *The Role of Information*

Today information is considered as an essential phenomenon for the around development of our society. It provides tremendous opportunities to accelerate the pace of development both at national and international levels. Economists treat it "as critical a resource to man as food, water, light and heat. . . . ". According to Howken[2] information is substituted to some degree for time, labour and energy in the production of goods and services. Noted economist and Nobel Laureate Keneth Arrow has proposed a new hypothesis that the rich get higher returns from investment particularly in terms of capital gains because of the access to information. He further says that increasing "uncertainty" in all spheres of human activities has enhanced dependence on information for decision-making.[3] It is true that information plays a very important role in overall development of a nation. Especially in a welfare state the success of its benefit system largely depends upon the flow of information. As the rational utilization of natural and human resources, scientific and technological development as well as agricultural and industrial progress and the advance of culture and social welfare demand increasingly efficient data handling and access to the most diversified and comprehensive information.[4] Thus the quality of information flow determines the level of development as well as the quality of our societies.

2. New International Economic Order vs New International Information Order

Shortly after the idea of a new international economic order was made popular among the developing countries in the early seventies it was also realized that it could be possible if the existing pattern of information system is replaced by a new international information order. As the very purpose of a "new international economic order" is not only to make "the best use of things and sharing them out fairly, but to develop all men and women, and every aspect of the individual, in a comprehensive cultural process, deeply permeated with values, and embracing the national environment, social relationships, education and welfare. It is also concerned with providing a basis for the development of the international community itself".[5] As a matter of fact it was felt that for overall development of international community one-way flow of information, "which provides an inadequate, inaccurate and tendentious picture of the overall social trends and process in the developing countries",[6] should be replaced and efforts should be made for the development and strengthening of a new international information order. In the early and mid-seventies the growing awareness for the utility of information pertaining to all spheres of human activities necessitated the idea of establishing a new international information and communication order which was officially launched with the fifth conference of Heads of State or Government of the Non-Aligned countries (Colombo, 1976) and the 19th General Conference of UNESCO (Nairobi, 1976). In the same year another Unesco sponsored conference held at San Jose (Costa Rica) resolved that "the development of communication and information system is one of the essential requirements for the achievement of integral economic, social and cultural development at both national and regional levels" and that the principle of the "free flow of information will not be applicable unless all our countries have equal access to all the sources of information and take part on an equal footing in the control over and use of international channels of dissemination".[7] Since then there has been a growing awareness about the role of information in achieving a new international economic order especially in view of the development of information technologies which is rightly called "the command and control system" because access to such technologies has made a tremendous impact on the capacity of collecting, processing, retrieving and disseminating information for greater involvement of an entire population in the decision-making process regarding all important economic, political, social and cultural issues. As a result the need of establishment, promotion and strengthening of infrastructure of information at all levels — regional, national and international — is now considered a priority task for promoting greater access to all kinds of information.

3. Information System

The need to store, process and transmit information has necessitated the growth and development of an information system in different fields of knowledge. A system is a set of interdependent parts that work together, as a whole, towards a goal or goals, in which the performance of the whole is greater than the simple sum of the performance of its parts.[8] The very objective of an information system is to build up an infrastructure comprising different components or sub-systems to promote flow of information from source to user when he needs it. In view of the increasing demand for information all nations are striving to build up a national information system linking with existing domestic and international networks. Especially the growth of information technologies has made a tremendous impact on the development of such information systems at national, regional and international levels. For instance within the framework of "inter-governmental" and "Inter-regional" international organizations, such as UN, UNESCO, ILO, FAO, OECD, FID, CAB, etc., a number of information systems have been designed and developed to promote and exchange information in the field of social science among the member countries. The *Directory of the United Nations Information System* (2nd ed.) has listed 335 information systems and data bases of 35 UN organizations which aim at the collection, dissemination or analysis of information or the creation of records or publications, etc.[9] In 1977, UNESCO, in a world-wide survey, identified 179 selected information systems which increased to 230 in 1980.[10] It indicates that there is a growing awareness among the nations of the world for the establishment and building up of infrastructures for naitonal information systems in the respective countries.

3.1 *Information System in Social Sciences*

The growing importance, exposure and understanding of social science knowledge is no longer limited to academic purposes alone but it has broadened the scope of its use by different types of users including bureaucrats, social workers, legislators, policy-makers, administrators, consultants, practitioners, etc. Hence, the conventional role of social scientists is entirely changed and they are now called upon to assist in different areas of activities like business enterprises, health care units, governmental bureaux, etc. They have further expanded their activities in different institutions of medicine, agriculture and engineering. As a matter of fact over the last three decades social science knowledge has witnessed a number of significant changes in terms also of storage, retrieval and dissemination across the national boundaries.

4. UNESCO Activities

The development of information system in social sciences is a recent phenomenon as compared to science and technology. Though the first attempt to design and develop a system for the retrieval and dissemination of social science information was made as early as 1895 by two eminent social scientists, namely, Paul Otlet and Henri La Fontaine the modern concept of information system was developed in the 1950 when with the support of UNESCO a non-governmental organization ICSSID (International Committee for Social Information and Documentation) was set up to make proposals and plans for formulating a broad information policy pertaining to social sciences. UNESCO sponsored activities have been very much instrumental in the development of international information systems in the field of social sciences. As early as 1970 a plan for an Information System was designed to introduce DARE (Data Retrieval System for Social Sciences) for processing data at Unesco Social Science Documentation Centre (SSDC), Paris.[11] The very objective of DARE is to provide a computerized information management system to store, process and disseminate information among the members regarding Unesco's social science programmes with special reference to studies on socio-economic development, social science policy, transnational corporations, the problems of human environment, population, youth, human rights and peace problems, the impact of science and technology on society and the teaching of social sciences. It has three major sub-systems : (i) indexing; (ii) updating; and (iii) retrieval. It handles with interlinking files of about 8,018 records pertaining to major areas of social sciences. This system provides a number of information services including searches of the current file, SDI service, statistical analyses of the data base, magnetic tapes, on-line access, print-outs (directories, inventories, lists bibliographies) reference publications, progress reports, etc. It also makes publications such as (a) World Register of Ongoing Research Information; (b) World Social Science Information Services; (c) World List of Social Science Periodicals; (d) World Directory of Social Science Institutions; (e) Selective Inventory of information Services, etc.

4.1 *UNISIST*

In view of the vital role of information in development a long term inter-governmental programme widely known as UNISIST was initiated in 1973 with a view to designing a "general conceptual framework for information system development in the fields of science and technology within the United Nations System to facilitate the world's information resources, particularly for the developing countries, and to create the necessary conditions for information system inter-connection and capability". But its scope was further extended in 1976 to include social sciences, archives and records management, documentation, and library science. In this way within this framework, UNISIST programme activities have been extended "to promote information transfer in all fields of knowledge servicing social and economic development".[12] In 1979 the second UNISIST conference (on Inter-Governmental Conference on Scientific and Technological Information for Development, UNISIST II) stressed the need of modern technology and its application to information system. The UNISIST covers the following areas of information management:

(i) Information Policy and Planning;
(ii) Norms and Standards for information;
(iii) Information infrastructure; and
(iv) Training and education of information specialists.

4.2 *IEEN*

Another Information System known as IEEN (International Environmental Educational Networks) was launched under the UNESCO/ UNEP in 1980 to promote exchange of information and experience in the field of environmental education. The main components of this systems are data files on institutions, specialists, programmes and activities in environmental education, identification and analysis of periodicals and bibliographical materials, study of subject classification and use of descriptors for information processing and retrieval. It operates through computer and makes the provisions of searches of the current file, SDI services, statistical analyses of the data bases. This system is an integral part of a larger information system.

5. **Other International Agencies**

Besides UNESCO's information programme, other international agencies also took initiative for the development of information systems in different fields of social science. A brief description of such information systems will enable us to understand to what extent information can play a key role in the fields of social sciences at various levels of development.

5.1 *UNIDO*

The United Nations Industrial Development Organization (UNIDO) came into existence in 1963 to promote the development of information services to industry and in assisting developing countries to build up their capabilities in industrial information. It has brought out more than 37 "Guides to Information Sources". It also publishes *Industrial Development Abstracts* four to six times a year. A computerized information system known as INDIS covers the publications of UNIDO.

5.2 *INFOTERRA*

Another information system known as INFOTERRA (International Referral System of UNEP) was developed at UNEP Secretariat, Nairobi, on the recommendation of the UN conference on the Human Environment held in Helsinki in 1972. But it became operational in 1977 and since then it has been functioning as a decentralized network of environmental Information systems operating through (a) National focal points designated by governments; (b) Regional focal points designated by inter-governmental; (c) Sectoral focal points designated by UNEP. According to 1980 estimate 109 member States are participating in the system which is storing over 8,000 sources of environmental information.

5.3 *CED*

The Commission of European Communities (CED) initiated a broad range of mission-oriented information services in the field of iron and steel, coal, nuclear energy, etc. Similarly, the European Economic Community established CID (Centre for Industrial Development) to provide necessary information for industrial development.

5.4 *DEVSIS*

Development Science Information System (DEVSIS) was launched in 1974 by the International Development Research Centre (IDRC), Canada, in collaboration with OECD, UNESCO, UNDP, ILO and United Nations Department for International Economic and Social Affairs. It was modelled, on other international systems such as INIS and AGRIS and developed as a network of national and regional centres using standard methodology to feed in information and providing services to users, together with an international centre responsible for constituting the common data base, maintaining the system and training staff for the participating centres. DEVSIS is regarded as a sectoral application of the UNISIST Programme, with which it maintains close links. It intends to cover conventional literature on all aspects of economic and social development. It is expected to include two data bases, a bibliographic data base using USIS format and software and with in-depth indexes for the documents and a referral data base containing the description of information and data sources on economic and social development. The system would serve development specialists in national and international administration, research and educational institutions, and economic organizations. It is planned to publish the bibliographic file twice monthly as a Bulletin (DEVINDEX) or on magnetic tape, and the file of sources (DEVPROFILE) every three months.[13] In 1970 the International Cooperation in the field of Transport Economics Documentation (ICTED) was established in Paris on the initiative of the European conference of Minister of Transport to make access to a wide range of information in the field of economics, political science, sociology, transport, economics, transport policy, transport sociology, transport planning and management.

5.5 *IINDR*

Under the auspices of OECD (Organization for Economic Cooperation and Development) an important information system known as IINDR (International Information Network for Development Research) was initiated in 1977 at Paris to promote information on development research primarily in the field of social sciences and other inter-disciplinary areas among OECD member countries plus non-member countries in Africa Asia and the Pacific and Latin America.

5.6 *WRU*

The Work Research Unit Information System (WRU) was established in 1976 at London. It provides information on any research relating to employment work, and work environment, including industrial psychology, quality of working life, etc. In Germany, the Information Centre for Social Sciences was created in 1968 to exchange information among German-speaking countries — Federal Republic of Germany, Australia and Switzerland. It provides information about the research activities of the various organizations which are members of the working group for Social Sciences Research Documentation and also about 12 other organizations with interests in social sciences. It has also created three additional reference files at the Information Centre to facilitate exchange of information in the field of social sciences : (1) SOLIS (Sociological Literature Information System) containing 5,000 abstracts of the sociological literature, (2) PROFIS (Programme Information System) containing over 800 social sciences application data processing systems in the Federal Republic of Germany and (3) DANIS (Reference Information System for Social Science Data) containing 1,000 records referring to various social science information systems.

5.7 *EUDISED*

The European Documentation and Information System for Education (EUDISED) initiated its information service in 1968 covering 14 countries including Austria, Belgium, Denmark, the Federal Republic of Germany, Finland, France, Ireland, Italy, the Netherlands, Norway, Spain, Sweden, Switzerland and the UK. It is affiliated to the Council of Europe and the Council for Cultural Cooperation, France.

5.8 *ECSSIO/WG-II*

Similarly, in 1980, the European Centre for Research and Documentation on Social Sciences, Vienna (Austria), started a pilot information programme know as ECSSIO/WGII (European Cooperation on Social Science Information and Documentation project on the exchange of Ongoing Research Information, Working Group II) covering different fields of social science including anthropology, demography, economics, education, political science, psychology, sociology, law and geography.

6. **Information Activity in USSR**

In USSR, within the framework of the presidium of the USSR Academy of Sciences, the section of the social sciences has developed an information system to promote social science knowledge. This section consists of four divisions : History Division, Economics Division, Philosophy and Law Division, and Literature and Language Division, with a total of 28 institutes under them. The section presides over 50 research councils specializing in key problems of modern social scientists. Social science research is also being conducted in 19 institutes and independent departments within the framework of the Academy's Siberian Division and Ural and Far Eastern Science Centres and branch divisions located in various parts of the Russian Federation. As a result there is a rapid development of information systems to cater to the needs of social scientists in the USSR. The world known VINITI (All Union Institute of Scientific and Technical Information) acts as a powerful information network for collecting and disseminating current information on various aspects including techno-economic nature. Recently another organization INION (the Institute for Information in Social Sciences) has been set up to organize, control, retrieve and disseminate information dealing with social sciences whether issued at home or abroad.

7. Regional Agencies

7.1 *APINESS*

In May 1986, a new information system known as APINESS (Asia Pacific Information Network in Social Sciences) was launched in Bangkok at an experts meeting convened by UNESCO and the Association of Asian Social Science Research Councils (AASSREC). For the time being the APINESS secretariat is located at the Regional Unit for Social and Human Sciences, Unesco, Bangkok.

The following will be the guiding principles for the proposed network :

- (i) that the network should help in development of infrastructures at the national level;
- (ii) that it should promote an inter-institutional arrangement rather than act as a supranational centre and thus National Contact Point (NCP) of each participating country should have its own circle of interactions guided by the commonality of interests and pattern of priorities.
- (iii) that it should promote a system of linkages — national, regional and international;
- (iv) that each country should decide its own priorities for development of information infrastructures; and
- (v) that it should promote a system of the financial resources which should be raised from member countries as well as

from those agencies and organizations — national, regional, international which are interested in networking programmes.[14]

7.2 *EURONET and Others*

On the other hand there are various information systems which cover a wide range of subjects including social sciences. For example EURONET, an on-line information network, was established by the Council of the European Communities in 1975 to provide direct access to scientific, technical and socio-economic data to the users anywhere in the community. It was open to public in 1979 and now it has around 100 data bases covering a wide range of fields from medicine to agriculture, available on-line to users. TYMNET is also a computerized telecommunication network which is managed by a company of the same name. It started functioning from 1971 and covers a wide range of fields such as agriculture, education, medicine, chemistry, social sciences, etc. Similarly, there are other organizations such as Canadian Plains Research Centre Information System, Information Exchange Centre for Federal Supported Research in Universities, Canada, Information System for the Results of Scientific and Technological Research, Czechoslovakia, Danish On-going Research Information System (DORIS), Denmark, Current Research Information Service, Information and Documentation Systems, France, Agriculture Research Management Information System (ARMIS), Ireland, Information System of Scientific Works, Research Development, Poland, Current Research Information System (UCRIS), Energy Research Information System (ERIS), Research and Development Information System (RDIS), USA, National System and Fund of Information for Development (NASFID), Bolivia, Brazilian Current Agricultural Research Information System (BRACARIS), Brazil, National Information System, Colombia, Costa Rican On-going Research Information System (CRORIS), Costa Rica Information System for Research and Development, Venezuela, etc. All these information systems, interdisciplinary in nature, play a very important role in the dissemination and exchange of information on different fields of human activities. Some of them are linked with international systems and networks such as AGRIS, INIS, MEDLARS, DEVSIS, ISIS, etc.

8. Social Science Information System in India

Like other developing countries India has witnessed a massive growth of information in different fields of social sciences. But, unfortunately, a major portion of such information remains underutilized or sometimes unutilized. It has been observed that on many occasions socio-economic and political decisions are made before information is collected, processed and disseminated for decision-making. This is because of the absence of an information system in the field of social sciences. It is, therefore, desirable that a well designed information system integrating different components of information sources should be built up at the national level to ensure flow of information from source to user.

9. Pioneering Work of Prof Kaula

Documentation of Labour was first started in November 1951 by the Ministry of Labour and Employment, Government of India, New Delhi. On the appointment of P N Kaula as its Librarian in June 1951 with training in documentation, as the first M.Lib.Sc. product of Delhi University, its library became the first in the Government of India to start systematic documentation work. On his own initiative, the librarian started listing the articles pertaining to labour problems. The list was prepared on fortnightly basis.

In 1957, the list of all the previous five years were cumulated with an index to make reference to the materials of all the previous years easy. Thereafter an annual volume made of the entries of the 12 monthly lists of each year maintained also in cards regularly brought out at the end of the calendar year, with a cumulated index.

The schedule of Labour Economics of the Colon Classification was redesigned for the documentation work. The outline of the redesigned schedule was published in *Depth Classification Reference Service and Reference Material* published by the Indian Library Association.

10. Initiation of Documentation Series

From 1957, the Library of the Ministry started Bibliographical and Documentation Series. *A Bibliography of the Labour Literature* 1951 — 57 was compiled in a short period of three months and released for the Asian Regional Conference of the International Labour

Organization (ILO) held at New Delhi in November 1957. This micro-bibliography has since been kept up to date by issuing half-yearly supplements. Bibliographies-cum-documentation on several other topics were also compiled and published. Including the above mentioned one, these are :

1 Labour Literature : A Classified Bibliography 1951–57, 1957
2 Select Bibliography on Labour Problems, 1958
3 Bibliography on Current Labour Problems, 1958
4 Labour Literature : A Classified Bibliography, V 2, 1958
5 Bibliography on Wages, 1958
6 Bibliography on Labour Relations, 1959
7 Bibliography on Workers' Education, 1959
8 Nanda and Abid Ali on Labour Problems, 1959
9 Trade Unionism : A Bibliography, 1959
10 Labour Literature : A Classified Bibliography, V 3, 1959
11 Labour Literature : A Classified Bibliography V 4, 1960.

The entries in the bibliographies are minutely classified according to the Colon Classification, *Labour Literature : A Classified Bibliography* was received as the first classified subject bibliography in India. The schedules of the subject pertaining to each bibliography were expanded and redesigned. The *Bibliography on Wages* was hailed as a fine specimen of a classified bibliography-cum-documentation.

10.1 *First Classified Index to a Learned Periodical*

The Library prepared and published a minutely Cumulative Index with an alphabetical index of itself to all the volumes of the *Indian Labour Gazette* begun in 1922 and now called *Labour Journal*. This is virtually a documentation list in this field of knowledge. This Index is perhaps unique in the history of documentation in our country as it is the first cumulative index of a classified kind to a learned periodical.

11. Documentation of Labour Awards

Industrial awards form an important source of information in assessing the employer-employee relations as settled by adjudication from time to time. In India there have been Labour Appellate Tribunals with a three-tier machinery as provided by the Industrial Disputes

(Amendment and Miscellaneous Provisions) Act, 1956. These are Labour Courts, Industrial Tribunals, and the National Tribunals. Besides these, the High Courts and Supreme Court also admit labour dispute cases and announce their awards.

It was, therefore, decided by the Librarian (P N Kaula) to document Labour Awards from January 1958 and issue a separate documentation list on a monthly basis. The 12 Lists issued during the year 1958 containing 897 entries. A consolidated Index was issued for the Annual Volume containing the 12 lists. The Index to the Awards, apart from being the first classified documentation list in India, has certain peculiarities.

12. Reaction to the Pioneering Work

The documentation/information work at the Ministry of Labour brought mixed reaction. While it became a trail blazer in starting documentation/information activity in Government of India libraries and had received appreciation from various quarters including ILO, there was an adverse reaction from some of the professional colleagues. Dr S R Ranganathan has recorded this attitude of the Professionals in Documentation.

13. Attitude of Librarians to Documentation

The Librarian of the Ministry of Labour, P N Kaula, unfortunately for him, started publishing a Documentation List periodically. His Minister, who was a voracious reader, appreciated this, and often sent for the Librarian and got the benefit of his documentation service. This latter event reached the notice of the librarians of the other Ministries. This made some of them use their new status to go to the room of the Under Secretary of the Ministry of Labour, spend an hour or two in chatting and ejecting some venom into his mind against the Librarian of that Ministry. But that Librarian was not second to anybody else in putting in Under Secretary in good humour. However, the documentation list proved to be a real red-rag to the other librarians. The Librarian of the Ministry of Labour was regularly sending copies of his documentation list to the Chief Officers in the other Ministries. This made some of the Officers ask their respective librarians to give similar service. This was too much to bear after having become a gazetted officer.

Result: The Librarian of the Ministry of Labour was boycotted. No other Librarian of the Secretariat would speak to him.

14. Reaction on the Librarian of the Ministry of Labour.

The Librarian of the Ministry of Labour did not mind this. He was capable of doing tit for tat. But through God's grace, he abstained from doing so. On the other hand, the extra time gained by the excommunication was turned on the intensification of his library service — in reclassifying the documents, in building up a depth version of Colon Classification for this purpose, and in giving intensive training to his staff in documentation work and service. He also produced special documentation lists on special occasions such as the Regional Conference of the International Labour Organization held at Delhi.[15]

15. Concept of Social Science Documentation Centre

The first library seminar on Social Science Research and Libraries was held at New Delhi in 1959 under the auspices of the Indian School of International Studies in cooperation with the Indian Council of World Affairs Library. It discussed a number of papers and considered Social Science Documentation necessary. In fact, one of the papers by P N Kaula, "Documentation and the Social Sciences", had proposed for the first time the setting up for Social Sciences. It adopted a number of resolutions to be implemented by respective authorities. Based on the paper of Prof Kaula it resolved to urge upon the Government to "establish an Indian National Documentation Centre for Social Sciences". Thus the genesis of the establishment of National Social Science Documentation Centre set up by the Indian Council of Social Science Research in 1970 had been in the resolution adopted 11 years earlier in the Seminar on Social Science Research and Libraries based on the paper presented by Kaula. But despite the thinking and executive actions of the Government at different stages, endorsing the fact that information is a vital resource worthy of care, harnessing and management, positive guidelines from the Government for a harmonious development of a versatile integrated information system for the country, encompassing the information requirements of all sections of society, are still lacking.[16] This is because of the lack of national information policy which is considered essential for a nation to promote and exchange information through a well-designed integrated information system based on appropriate laws and regulations. Unfortunately the Indian Government has not yet framed a broad-based National Information Policy to ensure flow of information through the integrated information system and network. However, credit goes to Pandit Jawaharlal Nehru under whose leadership the Science Policy Resolution of 1958 was adopted which later on paved the way for the establishment of a National Information System for Science and Technology (NISSAT) and the National Informatics Centre (NIC). But no such efforts have been made in the field of Social Sciences at the Government level. However, a proposed Five Year Plan of Rs 5.43 crores for the establishment of National Information System in Social Sciences (NISSS) is under active consideration of the ICSSR. It has the provision of establishing a Central Secretariat, strengthening of NSSDC (National Social Science Documentation Centre) and NSSDA (National Social Science Data Archive), setting up six regional and eight sectoral centres.[17] If this plan is finalized and implemented it will certainly make a great headway in the development of national social science information systems in India.

16. **Developments in Information Activities**

Though in the past few years a number of documentation centres have been developed to promote information services in different fields of Social Science such as NASSDOC, NIRD, SENDOC, these centres have not yet been transformed into international information system like AGRIS, DARE, DEVSIS, etc. In 1982, the UNESCO Regional Cooperative Programme in Social Sciences for Development, Training, Research and Documentation in Social Sciences in Asia and the Pacific, held in Delhi, also strongly recommended the setting up of national social science documentation and data archival centres and to establish a regional network of such centres to promote exchange of data and information.[18]

REFERENCES

1 International Commission for the Study of Communication Problem : *Many Vocies, One World.* Paris, Unesco, 1984. pp. 23.

2 Quoted by the Don A Dillman: Social Impact of Information Technology in Rural North America. (*Rural Sociology*, Vol 50 (1), 1985, pp. 6-7).

3 *Indian Express* (Delhi Ed), 26 Nov. 1986.
4 UNESCO: *Informatics: A Vital Power in Development.* Paris, Unesco, 1980, pp. 11.
5 *UNESCO: Moving Toward Change (Some Thoughts on the New International Economic Order).* Paris, Unesco, 1985, pp. 19.
6 PAVLIC, Breda et al : *New International Economic Order: Links Between Economic and Communications.* Paris, Unesco, 1985, pp. 15.
7 *Ibid.*, p. 16.
8 CHURCHMAN, C W: *System Approach.* New York, Delacorate Press, 1968.
9 LAZAR, Peter : International Information System. (*International Information, Communication and Education*, Vol 2(2), 1988, p. 37).
10 SMITHSONIAN SCIENCE INFORMATION EXCHANGE Inc., Ed : *Information Service on Research in Progress: A world-wide Inventory.* Paris, Unesco, 1982.
11 VASARHELYI, Paul Dare : *Unesco Computerized Data Retrieval System for Documentation in the Social and Human Sciences.* Paris, Unesco, 1972.
12 UNESCO: *Informatics.* op. cit., p. 40.
13 GUINCHAT, CLAIRE et al: *General Introduction to the Techniques of Information and Documentation Work.* Paris, Unesco, 1983, p. 275.
14 *APINES News Letter*, No.1, Nov. 1986, p. 3.
15 RANGANATHAN, S R: *Documentation-Genesis and Development.* Bombay, Asia, 1973, p. 125-26.
16 RAJAGOPALAN, T S et al: National Information Policy for India (In: B M Gupta, et al, *Eds: Handbook of Libraries, Archives and Information Centres in India* : New Delhi, Information Industry Publication, 1986, p. 190).
17 AGRAWAL, S P: National Information System in Social Sciences. (In: B M Gupta, et al, *Eds.: Handbook of Libraries, Archives and Information Centres in India.* New Delhi, Information Industry Publications, 1986, p. 180).
18 *Ibid.*, p. 190.

J 1

Dr S R Ranganathan and American Librarianship

M B Konnur

0. Introduction

When one considers Dr S R Ranganathan, the Father of Library Science in India, in the context of American librarianship, one has to keep in mind that unlike in the UK and in the USA, Ranganathan became known rather late, i.e., during 1950s, though his *Colon Classification* and *Classified Catalogue Code* were reviewed by a couple of American Writers even before 1950. Although Ranganathan touched all aspects of librarianship, it was in the field of philosophy of librarianship, (through his Five Laws of Library Science), classification and cataloguing that his work was recognized in the USA and had some impact on it. How Ranganathan's work in these areas has influenced the American librarianship and how he is acknowledged, honoured and respected in the USA, is shown in the following pages.

1. Five Laws of Library Science

In the field of philosophy of librarianship, it is true that *Five Laws of Library Science* is Ranganathan's most acceptable work. There are a few American writers like Pauline Atherton, Eugene Garfield, F W Lancaster, Michael Gorman, and Jesse Shera, who consider the *Laws* as an important contribution of Ranganathan. The very fact that Atherton chose to present an Amercian view on these laws.[1] In the Sarada Ranganathan Lecture Series reveals the importance she attaches to these laws. Garfield[2] observes that the importance of these laws lies primarily in their emphasis on service to individual reader. Lancaster[3] goes a step further and demonstrates the relevance of these laws to the evaluation of library services and how these laws can guide decisions on what needs to be evaluated, by what criteria and by what methods. In modern times, too, whenever American people speak of library mechanization, MARC records, on-line automated circulation, cataloguing, etc., they are doing nothing other than agreeing with Shera[4] who found in these laws "a philosophy of librarianship that harmonizes with the American concept of service". Atherton appropriately thinks that if Ranganathan had done nothing more than publish Five *Laws of Library Science*, he would have to be seriously considered for a Library Hall of Fame.[5] One has, therefore, to accept Gorman's view that if for nothing else, Ranganathan deserves to be long remembered for his *Five Laws of Library Science* as these are the best summary of what libraries are or should be about.[6]

2. Colon Classification

As a system of classification, it is true that Colon Classification did not influence American people for various reasons. However, the method of "Facet Analysis", developed fully by Ranganathan, was well received in the USA and its importance is increasing in information retrieval in this age of electronic technology as has been shown by Jesse Shera and James Perry[7] by pointing out that it (facet analysis) has opened the door for the introduction of electronic technology, popularly known as machine searching, for those who are seriously concerned with the retrieval of information. So also Vickery[8] points out that, "if we turn to the latest and best American textbook, Lancaster's *Vocabulary control for information retrieval*, we will find the term "facet" cropping up every dozen pages". Certainly, the method of "facet analysis" has not out-dated become after Ranganathan"s death in 1972 but is relevant even in modern librarianship.

3. Cataloguing

In the area of cataloguing, one may find little influence of Ranganathan on the cataloguing practices in the USA, the reason being that the dictionary catalogue is considered the most appropriate choice in the USA, whereas Ranganathan was a staunch supporter of classified catalogue. However, the concept of Pre-Natal Classification and Cataloguing can be claimed as Ranganathan's direct contribution to American librarianship. It was on this principle of Pre-Natal Cataloguing that, in June 1958, the Library of Congress introduced the Cataloguing as Source Project. It was a one-year project in which 158 publishers and 230 libraries participated. In July 1971, the Library of Congress started the Cataloguing-in-publication project which had its roots in Ranganathan's Pre-Natal Cataloguing. Indeed, Pre-Natal Cataloguing was Ranganathan's gift to American librarianship.

4. American Acknowledgment to Ranganathan

Various honours bestowed upon Ranganathan in the USA clearly show how much he is acknowledged, respected and honoured there. The greatest tribute to Ranganathan came from the American Library Association on his seventy-first birthday. A.L.A[9] wrote thus " . . . Most of us are not your disciples, all of us are your students, . . . we are proud to be in your debt". In 1964, Ranganathan was awarded an honorary Degree of D.Litt. by the Pittsburgh University. One has to take into account the fact that only four people (including Ranganathan) were awarded the D.Litt. Degree in 1964 by the Pittsburgh University. The other three recipients were Shanon, the father of information theory; weaver, the man who first saw the possibility and worked out some of the early details of machine translation; and Quincy Mumford, the Librarian of Congress. This was a great honour given to Ranganathan by the Pittsburgh University. In 1970, Ranganathan was presented the Margaret Mann Citation. That was the first time that the Citation was presented to a person from outside the United States. Both these honours conferred on Ranganathan clearly show the American acknowledgment of his contribution.

Recently, Eugene Garfield has clearly mentioned that "we at ISI have fulfilled some ideas that are implicit, if not articulated, in Ranganathan's work. And I am happy to acknowledge the debt that all workers in classification and indexing owe this revolutionary thinker. . . . We acknowledged Ranganathan's contributions several years ago when we included his portrait in the mural at ISI entitled "Cathedral of Man" The American acknowledgment of Ranga-nathan's contribution can best be summed up in the words of Atherton[10] who writes,

> In time and space his work out-distances most;
> In personality he has no living equal;
> In energy he knows no limit, working past the point of exhaustion

for most;
In matter, the scales would indicate great weight."

5. Conclusion

In concluding the above account of Dr S R Ranganathan and American Librarianship, it can be said that Ranganathan was passionately concerned about library science not only in India, but in the entire world. He saw it as a vital tool for the development of mankind.

To quote Ranganathan's[11] words:

"Thus by the promotion of international cooperation in library science, the library profession will make its own contribution to the ultimate benefit of :

(1) the development of each of the nations of the world towards its own fullness at its own speed and along its own lines;
(2) the development of an atmosphere of peaceful co-existence among nations;
(3) the evolution of One-World.

May every Human Group become Happy!"[12]

REFERENCES

1 ATHERTON, Pauline A: *Putting Knowledge to Work : An American View of Ranganathan's Five Laws of Library Science*. Delhi; Vikas Publishing House 1973. P. 158.

2 GARFIELD, Eugene: Tribute to S R Ranganathan, the Father of Indian Library Science. (In: *trends in International Librarianship : S R Ranganathan Festschrift to Mark the Platinum Jubilee of the Madras University Library*, edited by P A Mohanrajan, New Delhi; Allied Publishers, 1984. p. 263-79).

3 LANCASTER, F W: and MEYROTRA, Rashmi: Five Laws of Library Science as a guide to the evaluation of library services. (In: *perspectives in Library and Information Science* Vol, 1, edited by S N Agrawal et al., Lucknow; Print House. 1982. p. 26-39).

4 SHERA, Jesse: S R Ranganathan : One American View. (*Wilson Library Bulletin*, 37, (1963), pp. 581-82).

5 ATHERTON, Pauline A: Dr S R Ranganathan. (*Library Resources and Technical Serivces*, 14, (1970), pp. 582-84).

6 GORMAN, Michael: Let us Now Praise - A Reflective Look at Six Persons Who Greatly Influenced the Art of Cataloguing. (*American Libraries*, 11, (1980), pp. 201-03).

7 SHERA, Jesse and PERRY, James W: Changing Concepts of Classification : Philosophical and Educational Implications. (In: *Library Science Today*

(Ranganathan Festschrift) Vol 1, edited by P N Kaula. Bombay: Asia Publishing House, 1965. pp. 37-48).

8 VICKERY, B C: Ranganathan's Contribution to Indexing . (In: *S R Ranganathan,* 1892—1972, edited by Edward Dudley. London: The Library Association, 1974. pp. 9-11).

9 Cited by K Guru Dutt in "The Inwardness of Dr Ranganathan. (*Herald of Library Science*, 12, (1973), 117-22).

10 GARFIELD : Eugene op cit.

11 ATHERTON Pauline A: op cit.

12 RANGANATHAN S R: *Heading and Canons : Comparative Study of Five Catalogue Codes*. Madras, S Viswanathan, 1965, p. 281).

J 2

International Librarianship and Kaula

Peter Lazar

1. On the Notion of International Librarianship

The notion of "international librarianship" seems to be ambiguous. It may refer to library activities of international organizations: the librarian of an international organization or institution may be considered as international librarian, and the activities he or she is exercising fall clearly into the sphere of international librarianship.

Another aspect of the term "international librarianship" concerns international relations which play an important role in library work, especially in the work of special, academic and research libraries. Such type of libraries have to promote actively the international flow of books and other documents as well as information incorporated in these information sources. They have to face problems arising out of the barriers to international exchange of knowledge and experience such as, for instance, the language barrier, or the technological barrier, the letter manifesting the differences between countries in the level of the information and communication technologies available and adopted.

In addition, international relations play a substantial role in the exchange of knowledge and experience in our specific field, librarianship.

In the following I shall try to outline one of the main characteristic problems of international librarianship in the broad sense, namely, the relation between librarianship and information science (in the following: LIS). This relationship poses an international problem on which many eminent librarians and information specialists have presented their views. Prof P N Kaula has reviewed several times this question and expressed his thoughts on this subject. I would like to summarize my own views on this most interesting and highly important question, important from the view of both theory and practice.

It should be clear that I am using the term "librarianship" in the title of this paper and on several other places in the text as an abbreviated term for LIS.

2. On Prof P N Kaula

The subject in the title of this paper is rather well known, it is some sort of a "common place" subject, whereas the personality of Prof Kaula is, on the contrary, one of the most interesting representatives of the species "librarian" and the subspecies "Indian librarian". He is unique.

I feel highly honoured for having been invited to contribute to the Sixty-first Birthday Felicitation Volume, entitled "Dimensions of Library and Information Science", devoted to Prof Kaula.

2.1 *At the International Scene*

I am following with attention and appreciating highly the extensive activities of Prof Kaula in international librarianship for about 20 years. We have met several times during my activities in India as a Unesco advisor for the development of INSDOC and the national information system for science and technology. In addition, I had the chance to exchange views with Prof Kaula at the UNESCO Headquarters in Paris and in various international conferences and symposia organized by the International Federation for Information and Documentation (FID).

I had the honour in 1974 and in 1980 to receive Prof Kaula as our guest at the Hungarian Central Technical Library and Information Centre in Budapest, organizing his lectures on classification systems and other questions of LIS addressed to Hungarian librarians and information specialists, and organize his visits to other libraries, information centres, educational and training institutions in Hungary.

2.2 *Kaula Award*

Last not least, I had the great privilege to receive the Prof Kaula Award for 1978 and to participate, on the invitation of Prof Kaula, in the activities of the Department of LIS of the Banaras Hindu University, Varanasi, as Visiting Professor.

2.3 *Banner Carrier of Indian Librarianship*

Prof Kaula is widely known and appreciated in the international community of librarians and information specialists. Most of his professional activities are closely related to international librarianship. As Professor of Library Science, later that of Library and Information Science (LIS), he took utmost care to open up the international world of LIS to Indian students and to transfer to them the essence of valuable knowledge and useful methods and experience gained outside India. On the other hand, he did not fail to seize any opportunity to communicate the achievements of Indian LIS to specialists abroad, following thus the example of his veneered teacher, Dr S R Ranganathan.

2.4 *A Journalist*

Prof Kaula is the editor of excellent library journals such as the traditional *Herald of Library Science* and the recently founded International *Information, Communication and Education*. Both journals carry contributions of authors from several countries. Their international scope is further reinforced by their extensive sections of foreign news items especially characteristic for the *Herald of Library Science*.

2.5 *Recipient of International Awards*

Prof Kaula is the recipient of several awards and citations from various learned institutions from all over the world.

2.6 *On Library Science Education*

Although one can hardly find a chapter in LIS which did not receive full attention by Prof Kaula, the education and training of librarians and information specialists is one of his favourite subjects. He has presented many papers on this subject at several international conferences and meetings. A paper submitted to the Workshop of the FID Education and Training Committee (FID/ET) held in Copenhagen, Denmark, 13-15 August 1980, includes considerations concerning the requirements of the education and training of both librarians and information specialists and gives an outlook for curricula development in both directions.[1] Another paper presented at the FID/ET Workshop in Kowloon, Hong Kong, 6-9 September 1982, provides a very detailed comparative picture and a wealth of data on training facilities and courses existing in Asian countries.[2] Most recently Prof Kaula submitted an excellent paper to the FID/ET Pre-Congress Seminar held in Ottawa, Canada, September 1986, the text of which will be published by FID.[3]

2.7 *IATLIS*

In the early 70's Prof Kaula advanced the idea of establishing an international organization of teachers of library science. Unfortunately, circumstances were at that time, and still are, not favourable for the foundation of a new international organization in the field of LIS. But the Indian Association of Teachers of Library and Information Science (IATLIS) nevertheless came into being due to the efforts of Prof Kaula.

2.8 *Information Science*

Prof Kaula's personality and professional activity are largely characterized by his open-mindedness, his progressive attitude, his sense for innovation. He felt the need to extend his teaching activities from library science to LIS, he fully understood the role of the growing trend of mechanization and automatization of information and communication work for LIS. His recent paper on the changing field and role of information is one proof of my assertion.

When dealing with the relation between library and information work, between librarianship and information science, I shall refer on some places to the thoughts of Prof Kaula.[4]

I am aware of the fact that Prof Kaula's activities in international librarianship are much broader in comparison to what I have mentioned in this chapter. My indications concerning Prof Kaula's contributions to International Librarianship may nevertheless provide a rough survey of his activities and interests on the one hand and the intellectual background for the specific problem I intend to deal within the following, on the other.

3. **Librarianship and Information Science**

3.1 *The Evolution of Modern Librarianship*

Libraries are cultural institutions the origin of which dates back several thousand years when human beings started to put in writing data, events, ideas. Libraries accompanied the social evolution of mankind, took on various forms, keep records on a variety of materials and information carriers, preserving thus knowledge and experience collected by the human race during its history.

Modern librarianship developed in the past 100-150 years, according to the needs of modern society. Libraries proved to be important means for cultural and social development and the general education of the members of society.

The first industrial revolution and the *parallel* social development induced a considerable increase of the volume of printed literature, both special humanistic, which helped on its own part to promote the development of society in various aspects.

Libraries evolved as systematic depositories and collections of printed works. Librarians were first custodians of the collected treasures of human wit. This basic, and still valid, task was supplemented in the last century with library services developed on the basis of the pioneering work of Dewey, Cutter, Brown and many other librarians in several countries. Viable cataloguing and classification systems and rules came into being and use by the end of the last century, answering the growing need for systematizing and ordering the rapidly increasing mass of books and periodicals. National and subnational library associations were founded, library journals appeared in greater and greater number. In 1927 the International Federation of Library Associations [now International Federation of Library Associations and Institutions, (IFLA)] was founded.

During the 20th century the book and the journal volume ceased to be the only objects of library activities. Several other forms of printed sources emerged, or their volume and importance grew very rapidly, such as scientific and technical reports, patent specifications, standards, conference proceedings, etc. In addition, new information media invaded the libraries, such as the different forms of film (Microfilm, microfiche, diapositive, etc.), photographs, drawings and other illustrations, later various types of audio and audio-visual materials and media, and, last not least, magnetic and electronic media.

The library had to adapt itself to all these changes but the task of the librarian remained principally the same: to collect, process and stock information sources in order to be able to offer suitable library services to the readers or, using a broader term, library users.

3.2 *The Evolution of Modern Information Work*

When the development of scientific research and the volume of scientific literature has reached a certain level, the differentiation within the research staff has resulted in the creation of a new specific function: the provision of information. Modern information activities originated within the scientific community in order to cover the information needs of scientists. The social need for such a development manifested itself in the foundation in 1895 of the International Institute of Bibliography which was transformed in 1931 into the International Institute of Documentation and became in 1937 the International Federation for Documentation.[5] After 50 years FID's name has been recently changed to the International Federation for Information and Documentation while maintaining FID as its abbreviation.

The rapid spread of the notion and the ideas of documentation, the quick development of FID and its national and institutional members, the emergence of other national and international bodies and institutions for information can hardly be believed to build on hazard. The development of documentation, later called information, or documentation and information, the emergence of information science and practice, the appearance of information centres and similar institutions was the result of a very pressing societal need which had to be answered by the development of information services forming a substantial part of the scientific superstructure.

Thus we find both on the international level and on the national level parallel organizations of librarians and information specialists, parallel sets of libraries and information centres, parallel structures of library and information services.

4. **Prof Kaula's Views on the Subject**

Prof Kaula has contributed several papers and notes to various aspects of the history and development of LIS both in India and on the international scene. I would like to lay emphasis on the international aspects of his work, on the development of LIS, libraries and information centres as international phenomenon.

The international character of this subject is based upon the similarity of the moving forces in all countries, forces which cause the social need for the development of these institutions and induce the establishment and growth of libraries and information centres needed for building up the services as needed. In addition to this common background, the international exchange and flow of information sources among libraries and information centres is another aspect of internationalism within this subject.

I would like to draw the attention to the excellent paper of Prof Kaula on the actual changes in information activities mentioned in chapter 2.[4] This paper provides a very progressive view on LIS and library and information activities. The subject of the paper is exposed in the introductory chapter with great skill and high preciosity :

> We have moved from a concept called 'library' where the emphasis has been on book study, to 'documentation' where the emphasis is on an item of information. The change has been significant, and today in the fields of education and research, economics and sociology, science and technology, humanities and environmental psychology, information is sought, exploited, assessed, synthesised, interpreted and analysed to give the desired results for the development of mankind. It is therefore, important that a re-analysis of information activities be made to show us how to move forward effectively.[4]

The paper consist of chapters on the changing concepts of documentation and information, the information revolution or the information explosion, the use of documents, the modes of formation of subjects, documentation activity in India (INSDOC, NISSAT, Social Sciences, expansion of research activities), information and communication, role in communication network and, finally, the changing role of libraries.

I gladly associate myself with most of the views expressed by Prof Kaula in his paper in *International and Institutional Organisation*.[4] The majority of his conclusions are sound and valid not only for India, but also in a wider international context.

4.1 *Evaluation of the Effect of New Information and Communication Technologies*

Prof Kaula is correctly considering the effects of the application of new technologies to library and information work. I fully support his opinion which says, in essence, that the role of new technologies consists mainly in promoting and assisting library and information work, not supplanting them, as several information specialists and sociologists have already predicted since 10-15 years.

We have to understand that new information and communication technologies, especially electronic technologies, will have a deep and lasting effect not only on LIS but as well on society in general. Electronic technology will clearly invade all parts and aspects of everyday life, similarly as electrical technology has contributed to the transformation of society and the day-by-day life of mankind about 100 years ago.

But the development mentioned by Prof Kaula as the "electronic revolution" will not necessarily lead to the extinction of libraries and information centres. Prof Kaula's critical evaluation of Prof Lancaster's prevision of the decline of traditional libraries with the rapid growth of information sources in electronic form is fully acceptable. I also have doubts about the timeliness of such previsions, unless we are ready to transcend the limit between rational argumentation and mythical prophesy.

After the failure of M McLuhan to foretell correctly the fate of the printed media, or in short: the disappearance of the book, one has to be very carefull when estimating the future, especially as regards basic trends concerning the information recording, preserving and utilizing methods of mankind.

4.2 *The Role and Place of Information in Society*

Prof Kaula mentions in his paper[4] in the context of the communication and information revolution that

> "In the United States, half the work force is employed in the information industry-processing information, communicating information, researching information, organising information, developing and administering information (p. 6).[4]

When appreciating such statements, which may be encountered in various information sources from the USA, one has to be aware of the fact that the term "information" used in the quoted passage largely exceeds the limits of the notion of information as we are used to when speaking if library and information work.

This surprisingly high share of information in the manpowers and in other economic phenomenaon in the USA as well, is calculated on the assumption that there exists a primary and a secondary information sector in the American economy. The primary sector includes for instance the knowledge production and inventive industries, education, communication media, insurance, finance and advertising industries, postal service, etc. As to the secondary information sector, the following occupations have been allocated, among others, 50% to the information sector and 50% to the service sector: physicians, designers, managers, foremen, inspectors, miscellanous clerical workers, etc.[6]

The theoretical basis of such calculations is given by the comprehension of the omnipresence and the enormous social impact of the phenomenon "information" which carries different meanings and forms in mathematics (see for instance the information theory), biology, natural and social sciences, and in the social behaviour of men.

Information was, of course, together with matter and energy, omnipresent in the world since ever. The gradual detection and exploration of its forms and their social impact has paved the way for the growing recognition of its role. As a result, we now understand that every act we implement, every decision we take is based upon information, quite independent of the fact whether we are aware of its role or not.

It would be fallacious to assimilate the restricted meaning of information, as the library and information profession is using it, with the general notion of information, to expect a role and an impact of the former one on society similar to that of information in its broadest sense. On the other hand, the importance and the specific role and impact of library and information services must not be lost out of sight, even if it produces only a part of the impact which may be attributed to information in general.

4.3 *The Dichotomy between Librarianship and Information Science*

All the aforementioned problems possess an international character and are not limited to this or that country. Similarly, it is a problem all over the world how to define the "relationship between librarianship, and documentation, and information science, and the role of the librarians, documentalist, and information specialist (p. 6)."[4]

Prof Kaula's mode of posing the problems caused by the changes in the information activities imply that the library, based upon a new concept, will be able to cover all the information demand described in the introduction to his paper (quoted in chapter 3.3). Before turning to his last chapter on the changing role of library, Prof Kaula summarizes his view on the parallel existence of and the relations between libraries and information work:

> In India, there has been no dichotomy between librarianship, documentation, or information science. This is because there is a single pattern of training for all those professionals who might be called upon to work in either of these areas. The dichotomy that has taken place in the UK, USA and other developed countries has to be stopped so that our efforts in serving our people with information do not militate against one another. But a *modus operandi* must be found (p. 6)."[4]

Let us, first of all, clarify what the term "dichotomy" may really mean. According to the Webster's Third New International Dictionary[7] "dichotomy" may mean:

(a) division into two parts classes, or groups, especially into two groups mutually exclusive or opposed by contradiction; or
(b) division into two: a splitting into two parts or groups: differentiation into two contrasted or sharply opposed groups; or
(c) bifurcation: separation or branching into two parts, areas, aspects, or connected segments.

When confronting these possible termini with each other and with reality, we may ascertain, first of all, that in our case only the third explanation of the term "dichotomy", namely, bifurcation, may be accepted as valid. I am convinced that librarianship and information science are neither "two groups mutually exclusive or opposed by contradiction", nor "two contrasted or sharply opposed groups". They are in fact separate groups, but distinguished by what arguments?

4.4 *The Bifurcation of Librarianship*

In order to find an answer to this question one has to look more precisely into the term "librarianship".

The tacit assumption of Prof Kaula voiced in his introduction to in his paper[4] (quoted above), namely that librarianship will be able, according to a new concept, to fulfil all functions of information science, and that libraries, as indicated at the end of his paper (pp. 6-7),[4] will be able to provide both library and information services as needed by society, is overstating the case of libraries. Unfortunately, libraries are in general not able to fulfil such tremendous task. One has to differentiate libraries very sharply according to their immediate purpose and their direct users.

Out of the vast group of libraries the special libraries (including academic and research libraries) are those which can be regarded as information centres, they are specialized in a field or subfield of science, technology, social sciences, humanities, or any other specific human activity; they are serving a specific clientele, mostly within the same organization; they have on their staff specialists in the field to be served; and, most importantly, they are able to provide not only bibliographic information but various types of consolidated, analyzed, evaluated, assessed information, ready-geared for immediate use. In short, they are professional partners of their users.

Public libraries (school libraries and other types of similar general libraries) are not equipped to fulfil the functions of special libraries or information centres. They provide information (for instance, information on local data or events), but this type of information is usually completely different from the type of information requested from special libraries and information centres by their users.

Librarianship and information science are two different fields which overlap. Special libraries can be considered as information centres, governed by the rules of information science, whereas librarianship embraces besides public libraries special libraries as well.

Librarianship is a complex entity, consisting of two big subgroups, the public libraries on the one hand the special libraries, on the other. The functions, the users, the services of these two groups are basically different. It is most deplorable that this bifurcation of the vast field of librarianship is not fully understood and appreciated in many countries.

The most unfortunate consequence of this obstinate maintenance of the fallacy of homogeneity of librarianship is the lack of bifurcation in the education and training of librarians. In most countries, and I venture to add, in the majority of developing countries, education and training is organized for librarians in general, this means practically public librarians. Education and training of special librarians is either non-existing at all, or limited to special courses.

5. Dichotomy in India

Is it likely that "In India, there has been no dichotomy between librarianship, documentation, and information science"? While asserting this fact, Prof Kaula is describing in detail documentation activity in India (pp. 4-6),[4] mentioning for instance INSDOC, its genesis and development. It is a well known fact that INSDOC started its activities in 1952 as a pure information centre, without any library basis. In the first period of its existence one of its major problems was the lack of library background. This problem was later solved gradually by the establishment and development of the National Science Library in the frame of INSDOC, an example for the symbiosis of an information centre and a special library.

About the same time as INSDOC, the Delhi Public Library was established as a grandious pilot project to serve as an example for other developing countries and metropolis. The parallel existence and the differing activities of INSDOC and the Delhi Public Library prove also my assertion of the bifurcation of librarianship and information science, and, in addition, the bifurcation within librarianship between public libraries and special libraries.

The same conclusion, namely the existence of the different "worlds" of public libraries on the one hand and special libraries and information centres, on the other, can be reached by studying in depth the activities of these different types of institutions, deferring as to their purpose, functions, user communities, services.

Similarly to most industrialized countries, a Society for Information Science has been founded in India which is providing an active forum for information specialists (including special librarians) since its establishment in the late '70s, supplementing thus the valuable activities of the Indian Library Association and other library associations in existence on the national, regional or local level in India.

6. Library and Information Development as a Function of Social Development

Similar examples can be cited from other developing and industrialized countries. It is important to note that the differentiation between librarianship and information science and within librarianship is highly dependent on the general level of development of the country.

Until the level of activities in research in general, in science and technology is low, there is no significant social pressure for the establishment and functioning of special libraries and information centres. University libraries are usually the first institutions to emerge in the vast field of LIS, followed by administrative libraries in several branches of the executive. The setting up of a national library or a national information centre is usually a difficult and complicated procedure involving considerable intellectual, organizational and financial efforts.

The establishment of a network of special libraries and information centres and a network of public libraries goes in parallel with the development of the information needs of science, technology, economics, culture, etc. and the availability of the relevant financial means. Last not least, the problem of education and training of librarians and information specialists must be solved, otherwise the whole infrastructure of libraries and information centres will not be able to function.

The described developmental process is a weary one, its speed depends on the speed of the social development of the country.

7. Conclusions

(1) The process of change in library and information activities is an obvious trend in international LIS, as described so aptly by Prof Kaula.

(2) This process is very closely interconnected with the scientific, technical, economic, cultural and social development of society, the library and information infrastructure is arising and growing according to the needs of society, but the library and information infrastructure helps, on the other hand, to clarify information needs, develop and stabilize information awareness, provide a most important intellectual basis for the development of society.

(3) This process is accompanied by the growing differentiation of the institutions involved, the user groups to be served, the information and communication technology to be used, the information services demanded and offered.

(4) Libraries are forming *two groups* which differ basically, in spite of rather formal resemblances, as to their functions, user communities, organizational setup and services

provided.

(5) The bifurcation of the totality of libraries into the groups of special libraries and public libraries is an international pheno-menon which is rapidly progressing with social development.

(6) The function of special libraries and information centres consists of providing problem-oriented professional information for decision making according to the laws and usage in information science. The function of the public libraries is rather an educative one, extended to providing practical information for day-by-day use by the community served.

(7) The relationship between librarianship and information science must, therefore, be considered separately for the group of special libraries and that of public libraries. Special libraries and information centres *complement* each other. Special libraries and information centres on the one hand and public libraries, on the other, are basically different institutions, *related* only by technicalities in the collection and processing of information sources, and *unrelated* as to their basic function, user communities, services.

REFERENCES

1 KAULA, P N: An Evaluation of Education and Training for Library and Information Services in Developing Countries. (In: *Current Issues and Trends in Education and Training for Information Work in Developing and Developed Countries*: Papers presented at the FID Education and Training Committee Workshop, Copenhagen, Denmark, 13-15 August. FID, The Hague, 1981. pp. 95-105). FID Publication 595.

2 KAULA, P N: Situation of Library and Information Science Education in Asia. (In: *Education and Training in Developed and Developing Countries: With particular Attention to the Asian Region*: Papers presented at the FID/ET Workshop, Kowloon, Hong Kong, 6-9 September 1982. FID, The Hague, 1983. pp. 135-155). FID Publication 625.

3 KAULA, P N: Education for Information/Manpower Development in Developing Countries: Paper presented at the FID/ET Pre-Congress Seminar, Montreal, Canada, September 1986. FID, The Hague, 1987.

4 KAULA, P N: The Process of Change in Information Activities. (In: *International Forum on Information and Documentation* [IFID], Vol 9, N 4, October 1984, pp 3-7).

5 RAYWARD, W B: *The Universe of Information. The Work of Paul Otlet for*

Documentation and International Organization. VINITI; Moscow, 1975. FID Publication 520.

6 PORAT, M U: *Information Economy: Definition and Measurement*. Washington, US Department of Commerce, Office of Telecommunication, 1977. OT Special Publication 77-12 (1).

7 *Webster's Third New International Dictionary of the English Language*. Merriam: Massachusetts, USA, Springfield 1974.

J 3

Impact on International Documentation : Contribution of Professor Kaula

Emilia Curras

1. Precise and to the Point in Discussion

When I first met Professor Kaula, several years ago, what really impressed me was the force of his personality. The occasion was in autumn, during a meeting of the FID Committee for Education and Training, FID/ET, in one of its now traditional seminars. Professor Kaula, ever correct and well-mannered, spoke on several occasions during the discussions following the talks. I immediately noticed that his participation was precise and to the point. Neither did he stray from the subject nor was he seeking public attention when he asked permission to speak. He merely wanted to clarify a certain concept or to ask about something that had remained unclear. His contributions to the discussion were, of course, designed to approach problems related to developing countries and in particular India.

2. Personality with Equanimity and Intelligence

After the session, I felt I wanted to know more about this person of strong character who, at the same time, reflected equanimity and intelligence. I was given the chance almost immediately — during the ever too short lunch break. We sat down together and began to talk. Our language in common was of course English, he with his charming Indian accent and myself, with my unmistakable Spanish accent. Our conversation was both fluent and pleasant, about . . . the sea and fish. We barely touched professional questions, because it is better to take a break from those long sessions at Seminars and Congresses that require one to pay close attention to matters of great professional interest.

3. A Complete Hand

On the following day we had further opportunity for conversation and this was when I learnt that Professor Kaula had founded several journals and was Editor-in-Chief. I also discovered that he was a university professor and a highly active member of several professional societies. He spoke of his experiences and his projects. I also realized that he had tremendous will-power, an excellent memory and intelligence that helped him to face up to problems and situations that he would be able to solve. Professor Kaula was a complete hand, as those of us from Madrid would say.

4. Articles in Journal

In the two years between a Pre-Congress Seminar of the FID/ET Committee and the next, we kept up a certain amount of correspondence regarding professional questions, the exchange of syllabuses and of other documents. It was at that time that he asked me to send him an article for publication in a recently created journal. A journal like others before it that had resulted from initiatives taken by Professor Kaula. The name of the journal was *International Information, Communication and Education* (INICAE). I had a manuscript on my desk which was to be sent to a Conference in Bulgaria. I changed my mind and sent it to India with the following title: "The information staff: A factor in the Management of the Chemical Industry". Some other articles of mine have since then been published in the same Journal.

5. Viewpoints on Documentation/Information

Later FID Congresses and FID/ET Committee Meetings have given me the chance of further meetings with Professor Kaula, in which we have exchanged opinions and work programmes. We likewise asked each other for advise. Professor Kaula's comments were always right and impartial. I shall always remember a long conversation we had in the hague on matters and approaches of the theoretical basis of information science. I also remember that we ended up by agreeing on the criterion regarding the philosophical-scientific bases that should be applied. Such comparison of opinions clearly serve to enrich one's own view points.

6. Meeting at Montreal

Over the past few years, my correspondence with Professor Kaula has been frequent and has served to reaffirm my opinion of him. When I was given the responsibility of organizing the Pre-Congress Seminar of the FID/ET Committee, which was to be held in Montreal, in September 1986, I did not hesitate to help, in my modest way, so that my good friend could attend, despite financial difficulties. With or without my intervention Professor Kaula managed to attend the Congress in Montreal. Once again there was opportunity for exchanging experiences. At present a visiting professor at Lucknow he has had further interesting experiences of which I never tire to hear. His manner of talking is fluent and kind, in correct and educated English, always with his strong accent. When in Montreal, Professor Kaula was kind enough to interview me and to publish this in his journal *Herald of Library Science*. I thank him greatly for this opportunity to recount certain experiences and to express my opinion on my work and my professional life. At times it is necessary to move away from oneself in order to become known. Once again, my thanks to Professor Kaula.

7. Admiration Expressed

As soon as I heard of the homage to be paid to Professor Kaula, on the occasion of his 61st birthday, I immediately wanted to contribute with this short paper to express my admiration for him. This is the least I could do !

As neither of us is lazy about writing, I hope not to lose contact with my friend and colleague. We are separated by many kilometres and our chances of meeting are perhaps not that frequent. It is not the distance that separates, rather it is the money employed in reducing the distance. Let us hope that meetings can be arranged either in Spain or in India. No matter what, we should not lose contact with such an upright, just and intelligent person, who is so well qualified professionally and is so honest. Correct in every respect, colleagues such as Professor Kaula enrich the profession of information scientist and make one feel proud to be a member.

J 4

Soviet Libraries: Perspectives and Reflections

G A Grikhanov

1. The XXVII Congress of CPSU

The XXVII Congress of the CPSU became an important landmark in the history of the Soviet Union as it defined new tasks of our country for the long perspective. The most important of these tasks are reorganization of the people's economy system and the acceleration of the socio-economic development of the Soviet society. The Congress examined and approved the new edition of the CPSU Programme and "the Main Directions of Economic and Social Development of the USSR for 1986–1990 and the Period up to 2000".

1.1 *The Decisions of the Congress*

The XXVII Congress decisions were unanimously approved by the people, and now the Soviet librarians consider their main goals, firstly, to propagate and interpret these decisions, secondly, to actively contribute to their realization through more efficient provision for the users' demands.

Our Party Congress put the tasks of raising the level of meeting the people's spiritual and material needs, of providing better conditions for developing every man's capabilities. The main directions of economic development of the USSR read as follows:

> To improve library service to the population. To meet fully the demands of population in periodical publications, social and political, scientific and technical, recreational, educational, and children's literature.

The library workers are called for disclosing the available

resources, for improving the librarianship management, for increasing the book stocks use-efficiency, for improving the working forms and methods.

1.2 *Directions for Librarians*

The librarians of our country must make their work creative and thus actively contribute to putting into practice the XXVII Congress of the CPSU decisions. The librarians of our country will do their best to achieve the fullest use of our rich book stocks for the benefit of our economic development and the Soviet citizens' spiritual perfection.

2. International Culture of the Soviet Society

The USSR is a multinational State — more than 100 peoples and nationalities live in this country. Soviet power won in 1917, and this victory radically changed the historical destinies, economic conditions and cultural development of the people populating our country. Creation of the really popular multinational culture which received international recognition became a historic event of our State system.

The unified international culture of the Soviet people expresses the common ideals of all working people. It absorbs all general and significant facets of the original traditions of the national cultures. The Soviet culture is socialist in its content and multifaceted in its national forms; it became a great power in ideological and moral consolidation of various nations and populations of the Soviet Union.

The Soviet culture has achieved such level and significance as a result of many years of hard and purposeful work of the Communist Party, the Soviet Government and all the people after the cultural revolution in our country that was started by the Great October victory.

2.1 *Cultural Revolution through Libraries*

Vladimir Ilyich Lenin grounded and fully explained the very meaning of the "cultural revolution" nation; he considered the cultural revolution as part and parcel of the socialist reorganization in the country. In the course of the cultural revolution it was necessary to solve the problem that was not only massive but absolutely new also — neither State nor society ever faced such a problem, i.e., to eliminate illiteracy; to give the cultural achievement to multimillion masses of the working people; to open to every person, irrespective of his social and national background, all historical knowledge, all spiritual riches acquired by mankind. Such problems could not be solved without books, newspapers and libraries.

Yet books were inaccessible for the larger part of the country's population: illiteracy had reached nearly 70% in the country before the October Revolution and in some national republics such as Uzbekistan and Kazakhstan illiteracy had reached even 98 per cent. It was absolutely necessary to involve libraries into the active literacy campaign; so the Soviet Government paid special attention to library development and, primarily, in the agricultural areas, in the national republics, in the Far North regions.

2.2 *Literacy Activities*

Active literacy activities of the State as well as raising of the educational level of the people were prerequisites for the increase of the number of readers at the libraries. Only in the 20-year period (1920–1940) 50 million people became literate and among them mainly peasants. And by 1939, over 81% of the population were literate.

2.3 *Publication of Newspapers and Journals*

Over 40 nationalities even had no written language of their own. Today newspapers and magazines are published in 55 languages of the USSR including 18 languages of the peoples that had no written language before the October Revolution.

2.4 *Growth of Educational Institutions*

There was not a single higher or secondary special educational institution at the territories of many today's Union Republics (Uzbekistan, Kazakhstan, Turkmenistan, Kirghizia, and Tajikistan). Now these Republics have about 120 higher educational institutions with over 6,00,000 students. These Republics have grown their own national intelligentsia, their own science and culture. The best literary works of the national culture became the common property of the peoples of our country.

2.5 *Impact of Socialism*

In the course of the cultural revolution the gulf that lay between culture and people was eliminated. Socialism opened for the broad masses a possibility to use all spiritual wealth, as well as scientific, cultural and artistic riches. Dozens of people of our country brought about such a revolution in their life in such a short period of time that unthinkable in ages. Striving for culture has become an organic trait of the Soviet way of life.

3. Results of Cultural Revolution

The results of the cultural revolution might be judged and seen from the example of Kirghizia. Before the revolution there was only one literate person per 500 Kirghizes. Today illiteracy is practically eliminated in this Republic; there are more students per cent 10,000 of population in Krighizia than in the USA or in France.

3.1 *Country of Total Literacy*

Now the USSR is a country of total literacy. The whole literacy programme was performed in stages — first, the programme of universal compulsory elementary education; and during the past 10 years, universal compulsory high education. Literacy programme is a rather complex process that takes much time and requires serious and considerable efforts.

The colossal work in eliminating illiteracy brought the desired result only thanks to the fact that the Communist Party and the Soviet Government headed and led the programme of planned building of the library network; and this network was build as close as possible to the working and living sites of the population. V I Lenin said:

> It is not sufficient to eliminate illiteracy; it is necessary to construct Soviet economy at the same time; and here only literacy is not sufficient. We need an enormous raise of culture. It is necessary that a man should use his ability to read and write in practice, that he should have what to read, that he should have newspapers and propaganda booklets, that these reading materials should be correctly distributed and reached the people. (*Complete Works*, Vol. 44, p. 170).

4. Programme of Library Construction in the USSR and its Accomplishment

The very first days of the Soviet State were marked by great attention that was paid to library development. It was V I Lenin who worked out the theoretical foundations and directions of the practical activities in creating the Soviet library system. These foundations and directions stipulated for the national character of librarianship, general availability of libraries, planned organization of the unified library network. Wide circulation of books among readers directly depended on their number and their intensity of reading — today these are the main criteria of the work efficiency of every public library and the library system as a whole.

4.1 *Lenin on Librarianship*

Beginning from November 1917 the Soviet Government adopted many decisions on librarianship. It was in November that V I Lenin wrote the letter "*On the Tasks of the Public Library in Petrograd*" the text of which is well known to each Soviet librarian. This letter was followed by the governmental decisions signed by V I Lenin: "*On Organization of librarianship*" (June 1918), "*On Safekeeping of Libraries and Book Depositories of the RSFSR*" (July 1918), "*On Centralization of Library Organization in the RSFSR*" (November 1920), etc. . . .

4.2 *Programme of Library Development*

The detailed programme of library development proclaimed general availability of all libraries, laid down plans of creating a library network that would fully meet the demands of all readers. The State took upon itself the most important functions of the librarianship development — financial provision of libraries, training and advances training of qualified personnel, library literature acquisition. Special attention was paid to the quality of book stocks. All precious books kept in old libraries were registered. There were published the best works of the world literature. The programme envisaged the community-wide participation in the library work.

The Communist Party and the Soviet Government always paid attention to development of the library network, to the problems of stock acquisition, as well as to their better use. Thousands of libraries were given well — accommodated premises, the necessary equipment, qualified personnel.

Organization of a ramified network of general available *free* libraries — it is a clear example and achievement of the cultural construction in the USSR. Libraries of different types and kinds are equally distributed on the territories of all Union Republics. In fact, there is no town, settlement, village, aul, kishlak in the country that do not know library books.

5. Librarianship in the USSR Today

At the present time 3,30,000 libraries belonging to various departments possessing about 5 milliard books and other printed works; and they serve over 220 million of readers. Each reader of the public library read on an average 24 books annually.

5.1 *Nation of Readers*

Libraries are the main source of acquiring literature for reading, self-education, teaching, or research work. Libraries organize the public usage of the large book wealth of the country; they actively propagate political, natural, scientific, and fiction literature. Exceptionally important role belongs to the libraries in the upbringing of the growing generation. Sociological researches show that 95% of the Soviet people constantly read books, newspapers, magazines; 50% of adults and 95% of adults and 95% of youth and students are permanent library users. In some regions of our country over 75% of the population are library users.

5.2 *Library Network*

During past years our country has taken a number of significant steps in perfecting the library service organization. Some changes were introduced into the organizational principles of the library network; noticeable changes were achieved in the work coordination of libraries belonging to various departments.

Reorganization of the library network has been practically completed: small libraries were joined into centralized library systems. Today the network of State public libraries comes to 4,000 centralized systems; and the largest of these systems embraces up to 60 branch libraries. There are more than 1,000 trade unions centralized systems. Interdepartmental centralized systems are in the process of creation. The work experience and the experiments carried out today show that in perspective we shall form unified powerful library territorial complexes that will include all libraries located on a given territory. Such complexes will give possibility to considerably improve the stocks use, bibliographic service, to provide all enterprises and institutions, all population of a given territory with books and information.

In future the public libraries network will develop but rather insignificantly and mainly in the urban areas. The process of regulating is closely connected with the problem of planned development of both newly opened libraries and unification and extension of libraries in towns and villages.

5.3 *Increasing Role of Libraries*

The social role of libraries increases every year as well as their ties with the party, State, and social bodies. The work of libraries is reflected in the plans of the working collectives' social development. The libraries actively propagate the advanced know-how and the scientific and technical knowledge. The traditional working forms are being improved. The informational activity of both special and public libraries is sharply increasing. Now it is common practice of the Soviet libraries to organize information days, open book reviews at the industrial enterprises and research institutions, the system of selective dissemination of information, wide use of the radio, TV, periodicals and press for the literature propaganda. The interrelations between libraries and organs of scientific-technological information have been considerably strengthened in recent years. The work on mechanization and automation of library and bibliographic processes, the creation of union catalogues for home and foreign publications were activated. The volume of microfilming and xerox copying increased. Many libraries got new premises, and many libraries in large cities, regions and Republics received new special buildings.

The USSR is a country of readers. The Soviet people's deep interest in books and reading are satisfied through hundreds of thousands of libraries of various kinds and specializations; and these libraries are equally distributed over the country's territory. In their everyday activities the Soviet libraries are guided by the decisions of the XXVII Congress of the CPSU, the decrees of the Plenums of the Central Committee of the CPSU, the provisions of the Status of Librarianship in the USSR which, in particular reads as follows:

> The libraries should provide full and effective use of their stocks with the view of further economic, socio-political and spiritual progress of the Soviet society, and education of citizens in the spirits of the norms and principles of developed socialism.

6. Target achieved under Hard Conditions

The things that were done by our country are quite possible and achievable for any other country in the world. For this goal we had to work hard during several decades. Under extremely hard conditions when our country was the only State in the world that had chosen the path of independent socialist construction — under these conditions we had to fight against military intervention, against fascism. From a backward illiterate country before the October Revolution, the USSR has become a great industrial power with advanced science, technology, and cultural base. And the librarians of the Soviet Union are happy to contribute to successes and development of other peoples' culture; they are ready to share their rich experience.

REFERENCES

1 *Large Soviet Encyclopedia*, Vol 24, Part 2, pp 139, 142, 144, 145, 403.
2 *Pravda*, May 5, 1986.
3 *The USSR: 100 Questions and Answers*, Moscow, 1978, p 107.
4 *Actual Questions of the Library Work*. 1985, Moscow: Kniga, 1986, pp 3, 7.
5 *Bibliotekar*, 1986, N 2, p 3.

J 5

Prof Kaula's Achievement and Impact on Cuba

Salomon M Dorf Rudich

0. Introduction

I had the honour to meet Prof P N Kaula during his stay at Havana, Cuba, in 1967 as Unesco expert taking part in the international organization's UNDP Project Cub-2 to be implemented at the Faculty of Technology of the University of Havana, and I have had the privilege of his guidance in the field of Library Science and Documentation and of his personal friendship since then.

I wrote to Prof Kaula by the end of 1966, inquiring about the *Herald of Library Science*, which I had a keen interest to receive but faced the problem of foreign currency control, Prof Kaula very kindly replied that I would receive his journal, and that he was coming to Cuba soon on a Unesco mission. He also inquired about the climate and other features of Havana and we corresponded by mail and telegraph until his arrival at Havana about mid-February 1967.

1. Arrival in Havana and Meeting

The Unesco Regional Office for the Western Hemisphere is located at Havana precisely, and most conveniently for me — only six blocks, i.e. 600 metres approximately from where my home at that time was and even on the same street it was known there. I inquired several times by phone at this office about the exact date of arrival of Prof Kaula and one day about noon I was told that he had arrived in the morning but unfortunately had been taken ill suddendly on his arrival at Havana Airport and had been transferred to a hospital. Next day in the morning news came about Prof Kaula's health having improved and in fact sometime in the early afternoon I was told that I could see him that day as he was already feeling quite well. He was staying at the Hotel

Nacional also only six blocks away. In the evening at about 8 o'clock (accompanied by my father, since I had not been feeling exceedingly well at that time). I arrived at the Hotel Nacional which by the way is a place with some history, as a day-long battle had taken place there in 1933 between a group of Army officials expelled from the Army after the rebellion of the non-commissioned officers shortly after the overthrow of a dictatorship which had ruled for several years. It is placed on a rock of some height and was formerly at the seaside, i.e., before some terrain was recovered from the sea and a rapid transit avenue paved which passed in front of it.

According to security regulations for hotels where foreign visitors or residents are lodging, we could not go up to see Prof Kaula and so I told him over the inter-communicator. However, the employee at the desk said after short reflection that since Prof Kaula was not quite well, we could go up.

When we stepped out of the lift we saw a tall, Latin American looking distinguished gentleman approaching the lift, and evidently it was Prof Kaula on his way down to meet us. So I boldly asked, "Professor Kaula", and after a reply in the affirmative, I introduced my father and myself, and Prof Kaula invited us to his room.

2. Mission, Discussions and Affection

After the courtesies of hospitality on Prof Kaula's side we began a conversation on library science and documentation and everything else which lasted until midnight (4-1/2 hours). He explained to me his mission in Cuba, i.e., to plan the new Library of the Faculty of Technology of the University of Havana (the faculty had moved to a new site not very long ago then and parts of the buildings were still under construction) and to train the personnel of this library for their work as well as for training others. I told him about my work at the Medical Publications Department of the Scientific Council at the Ministry of Health and later as Medical Adviser to the National Information Centre for the Medical Sciences into which the abovementioned department had been expanded. I expressed to Prof Kaula the need our Centre had of his advice and guidance and he agreed to visit it if this should be allowed by the Director of the Project. He also invited me to join the course on Library Science and Documentation he was to give at the Faculty of Technology. When my father and I left, I felt that not only had I met a great teacher but that I had also acquired a good *friend-cum-adviser*.

2.1 *On Mother's Day*

Some time later after he had shifted to his temporary home in a fashionable suburb of Havana, near the site of the Faculty of Technology, my parents and I visited him and it happened to be on the second Sunday of May 1967, which in the West is Mother's Day; and he told us that since he couldn't see his mother that day, he was very happy to receive my mother at his home. We were all very much moved specially my mother, and from that day on we became all very close to Prof Kaula and later also to his family when they arrived in Havana. We often visited his hospitable home and he and his family were also our guests more than once. We also received Prof Kaula at the National Information Centre for the Medical Sciences.

3. Advice on Medical Information Centre

Shortly after our first visit at Prof Kaula's home, he was invited by the Director of the National Information Centres for the Medical Sciences. At the meeting attended by Prof Kaula, the Director, his Deputy and myself, we discussed the main aspects of the work performed at the centre and I also had the honour of acting as his guide around the different departments of the center. He visited our centres on several other occasions at our invitation and on each visit, as on the first, we all learnt much from him on different aspects of library science and documentation. I shall return to the valuable assistance he granted to this centre later on.

4. At the Faculty of Technology: Lectures and Training Programme

In August 1967, Prof Kaula gave special lectures on "Foundations of Classification" at the Faculty of special group including the librarians and technicians from the Faculty and from other institutions, Prof Kaula's Cuban counterpart (a Professor of that Faculty), a distinguished Professor of Mathematics also from the Faculty, and the humble writer of these lines. I had the honour to translate part of Prof Kaula's lecture into Spanish when the official translator showed signs of vocal fatigue. Those lectures were each followed with a question and answer period, and lasted *over four hours each day*.

4.1 *Feat of Scholarship and Learning*

At the end of the month, the training programme on Library Science and Documentation began in seven phases worked out by Prof Kaula, and though originally planned to be held only for the personnel of the library of the Faculty of Technology and the University of Havana, but, due to the great interest shown by librarians and documentalists from numerous institutions at Havana and elsewhere, the Director of the Library, the Dean of the Faculty and the Unesco authorities consented to throw open this training course to persons in the field from several Latin American countries. People from practically every Ministry and every important scientific or cultural institution came to hear Prof Kaula's scholarly lectures on each aspect of the subject delivered extempore and to the wonder and amazement of everyone. Unfortunately, due to transportation difficulties, some of the participants could not reach in time but there remained a sizable group of faithfuls who through rain and storm (there is no snow in Cuba but it does rain heavily in summer and autumn) came to these lectures. These were held in a new and the most modern building from 3 to 6 p.m. on Mondays, Wednesdays and Fridays, according to what is called there "tropical time", i.e., almost one hour later than official, this being the rule in all social and cultural events in Latin America, most notably so, in the tropics as the humorous expression I just mentioned shows. All the lectures were taperecorded. It is interesting to state here that Prof Kaula delivered all the lectures by himself to cover the entire training programme — *an amazing feat of his scholarship and learning.*

4.2 *Special Sessions*

Prof Kaula also conducted some practical classes first on Saturday mornings, then on Friday evenings in spite of the difficulties to which one must add that, librarians and documentalists there being overworked, it was hard for them not to rest after Friday afternoons. I could not attend these classes in my case for religious reasons, the Jewish religion forbidding travel from Friday evening to Saturday evening except for safeguarding life or health. Because of all the mentioned circumstances, I suggested to Prof Kaula that these sessions be held on a weekday and to make it easier, before the ordinary lectures. This was accepted by Prof Kaula and several of the participants. However, the nature of these special sessions changed to focus on theoretical and practical aspects of classification mainly, as another idea presented by Prof Kaula had in the meanwhile begun to shape up and materialize, namely, that of establishing a Classification Study Circle which later broadened its scope to include other aspects of library science and therefore changed its name accordingly (to Library Science Study Circle). I shall address myself to this subject in detail later on.

4.3 *New Approaches Hitherto Unknown*

The course on Library Science and Documentation delivered by Prof Kaula was highly interesting and Prof Kaula captured the full attention of those present at the lectures throughout, even the most arid parts of the programme. The most important aspect of this course was that Prof Kaula presented an approach to classification and cataloguing unknown to all of us since the study of the former had been limited, in the successive curricula of the School for Librarians of the University of Havana and in any other training, given by the Cuban Association of Librarians (then already dissolved as practically all professional organizations in the country due to the social and political changes that had intervened) or by the National Library of Cuba or other institutions managing DDC (Dewey Decimal Classification) and lately UDC (Universal Decimal Classification); and because cataloguing had been limited to teach to follow the (now old) *A L A cataloguing/Rules* with no theories ever mentioned to exist. Prof Kaula was absolutely frank in his critical appraisal of the situation as given during his lecutres and in his reconversations with smaller groups such as that meeting with him at the National Information Centre for the Medical Sciences or the one attending the special sessions mentioned. His lectures and remarks, therefore, were a real eye-opener for people working in the field of library science and documentation in Cuba and elsewhere. The course lasted till the end of November 1967.

5. **Classification Study Circle**

The circle used to meet at first at the Faculty of Technology under the guidance of Prof Kaula, until the end of November, later on at the National Information Centre for the Medical Sciences and still later on at my residence. When due to the already mentioned difficulties in transportation and overwork, it became impossible to continue the meetings, we still had "bilateral" encounters and consultation over the telephone, pratically until my departure from Cuba. The circle included besides, people from the Faculty of Technology and also from the abovementioned centre, the Institute for Scientific and Technical Documentation and Information, (IDICT, which is the Cuban National Member of FID), and the Centre for Tele-communications of the Ministry of communications (Posts), Analytico-Synthetical Classification of Medicine (ASCOM).

6. Design of Special Classification System

Another important achievement of Prof Kaula's visit to Havana was the devising of a special classification scheme for a selection of the periodical holdings of the National Information Centre for the Medical Sciences. To this end, a student of Medicine of graduate in a year and I received additional special training and guidance at Prof Kaula's hospitable home, on Sunday mostly, so that he gave us generously of his time for rest. We had at first considered 12 categories or facets but then reverted to the classical five [P] [M] [E] [S] [T] of Ranganathan. After Prof Kaula's departure, we began the collaboration of the individual schedules. In spite of its analytico-synthetic base, we had to work out enumerative tables due to the scarce familiarity with medical terminology of the rest of our centre's personnel at that time (this in turn due to the large turnover of employees, characteristics of institutions of all kinds in Cuba since the revolution and caused on the one hand by emigration and on the frequent transfer of personnel according to a policy designed to avoid favouritism arising from acquaintance of the public with public servants of employees). After my disassociation from the centre in 1968, my colleague, the student and later M.D., continued to work at the schedule and after he received an assignment at one of the teaching hospitals of the Faculty of Medicine, of the University of Havana, work was carried on by other personnel of the centre including those who had attended the special lectures at the Faculty of Technology (*vide supra*). Prof Kaula continued even after his departure to assist us and our successors with his counsel-correspondence at the mentioned task. The result was the finalization of ASCOM (Analytico Synthetic Classification of Medicine) within the framework of UDC. This was an original and an epoch-making contribution of Prof Kaula. ASCOM was presented by the Centre to the World Congress of Medicine held at Brussells, Belgium, as a contribution and was approved as a scheme for computer application.

7. Impact of Prof Kaula's Visit

Besides the widespread direct effects of the training course given by Prof Kaula and the indirect ones achieved through the Classification (later Library Science), Study Circle, and ASCOM, undoubtedly Prof Kaula greatly influenced the way of thought about library science and documentation in Cuba by his visits to the National Library and other libraries and documentation institutes. There were several meetings at our Centre and each was extraordinarily useful. A modest farewell party at which all members of the circle were present was given at the Centre following the impressive one given to Prof Kaula at the Faculty of Technology.

7.1 *Guidance*

Prof Kaula's guidance enabled me to be of some assistance, after his departure, to the libraries and documentation services of the Faulty of Technology, National Institute for Agrarian Reform, National Institute of Neurophysiology (Academy of Sciences of Cuba), "House of the Americas" (an Inter-American Writers' Institution) and to the IDICT.

7.2 *Courses Planned*

There was a generalized feeling at Prof Kaula's departure, that a one-year course with examination and degree would be extraordinarily useful and was practically mandatory. Unfortunately this project has not materialized till now. However, the curriculum at the University of Havana has been modified leading now to the Licence in Library Science after four years and also a curriculum leading to the Licence in Information Science with the first two years in common. The former is now under planning with the assistance of Unesco.

7.3 *A Master Mind*

Finally, let me add that also here in Israel, Prof Kaula has made his presence felt by his visit to this country in August 1971 when he took part in an International Conference in Information Science at Tel Aviv chairing one of the sessions and also giving Lectures at the Hebrew University in Jerusalem and at other institutions. He is remembered as a Master-mind in Library and Information Science.

7.4 *"Till 120"*

My wish, and I am sure that of all his present and past pupils and associates, which is to say of his friends, is that he may still give many, many years of fruitful teaching, guidance and innovation to library science and documentation, "till 120" as our people say.

J 6

Libraries in Tanzania

Walter Bgoya

1. Libraries in the Public and Private Sectors

An early indication of the commitment of the Tanzania Government to universal literacy can be seen from its creation, in the early years after independence, of a system of public libraries. Libraries in Tanzania started out as the least privileged of libraries in the three East African countries. They had a bookstock of only 99,000 and seven librarians of whom only one was African against Kenya's 304,000 books, 17 librarians of whom one was African. Uganda had 200,000 books and 10 librarians of whom one was African. In the 1970s 'Tanzania (led) the way in library development particularly in the public library field and (had) a larger number of endogenous qualified librarians.'(6)

1.1 *The Act*

Tanganyika Library Services Board Act, 1963 was the legislative instrument which spearheaded the expansion of the library system. The board was empowered to "promote, establish, equip and develop libraries in Tanganyika" and while it enabled great work of expanding the library system to be done, by 1975 it was found to be inadequate and was repealed. Tanzania Library Services Board Act, 1975, extended the function of the Board and put under its jurisdiction all public libraries, "public" being defined as meaning "all types of libraries, i.e., any library to which a member of the public has or is permitted to have access . . . ". Other provisions of the Act relate to Legal Deposit, training of librarians, rural libraries, production and preservation of traditional literary works, etc.

1.2 *Network*

To date there are 88 libraries at the centre of which is the Tanzania Library Service. By any standards, the expansion of TLS and the acquisition of book stock has been remarkable especially when one takes into consideration the very difficult economic situation which the country has transversed during the past 10 years or so. By 1974, ten years after its establishment TLS had increased its book stock from 49,000 to 900,000. Apart from the National Central Library based in Dar es Salaam, which also acts as the Dar es Salaam regional library, Tanzania Library Services are organized at the regional and district levels and provide rural mobile services as well. In addition it operates a schools' mobile library service, a postal and book box service in over almost all of the mainland's 21 regions. At present there are 13 regional libraries and five district libraries with an average book stock of 35,000 for regional libraries and 15,000 for district libraries. The seating capacity of the regional and district libraries is 150 and 100 respectively.

1.3 *The Plans*

The development of libraries closely followed the periodic development plans, which started with the First Five Year Development Plan (1964–1969). It has been planned to extend library services to 15 regional headquarters at a cost of $4 16,666 ($ 166,666 for books, $ 250,000 for building) per library but only four (National Central Library, Iringa, Bukoba, Mwanza) were completed. In the Second Five Year Development Plan (1969–1974) six libraries were planned and built. In the TThird Five Year Plan (1975–1980) only three out of nine planned were built. In the Fourth Five Year Plan (1981–1985), a total of $1.7 million has been earmarked for the construction and stocking of libraries in Dodoma, Kigoma, Shinyanga, Lindi, Singida and Coast region.

At the same time, it is on plan to extend mobile services which at present cover only five regions (Moshi, Kibaha, Songea, Musoma and Sumbawanga) by providing a book van to each regional library.

2. **Rural Libraries**

The ultimate success of the library system in Tanzania will depend very much on whether it will be able to extend its services not only to the regional and district centres but to the villages where the majority of the new literates are found. The success of the literacy campaigns which lowered illiteracy in the country to less than 25 per cent was in great part a result of the villagisation programme. This brought hitherto scattered homesteads together into permanent villages and as a result made it possible for party and government to mobilise the population into literacy classes and to provide materials more easily than would have been possible otherwise.

There are a little over 8,000 villages of this kind and if the newly literates who live in the villages are not to lapse back into illiteracy, some form of library facility will have to be established in each village to serve the villagers. At present rural areas are served through use of mobile libraries and bookboxes but these vans are too few and prone to breakdowns which make the service extremely irregular. There are other problems of the rural environment which make this most necessary service also the most difficult to render.

3. **Adult Education Rural Libraries**

The Department of Adult Education of the Ministry of National Education operates, according to sources in the department, about 2,500 village libraries. These libraries are housed in offices of the ward headquarters of the ruling Party, Chama Cha Mapinduzi (CCM). Books are provided by the department of Adult Education and usually each library receives two copies of every new book which the department purchases from the publishers. The rationale behind the organization of these libraries is that since Tanzania Library Services have no resources to set up libraries below the district, and since the mobile book vans and therefore the book box exchange services are almost inoperative, their libraries are the only ones which are now serving rural literates. In addition the Party offers more security than any other alternative body and it is the one place that almost all people regularly visit for various reasons. Books are therefore easily reached by them.

In the past the Director of the Tanzania Library Services, advised against the setting up of these libraries. His opinion was that rather than spend scarce resources establishing them, it would be better to strengthen TLS and its Book Box Exchange Service. Static libraries with only a few books and no librarians cannot work and within a short period the books disappear and with no new ones replacing the old ones the likelihood is that the libraries exist only in name. On the other hand, with book boxes bringing in new books, and with exchanges of these boxes between different depots the system could be made to work more efficiently.

The TLS director's argument would only be satisfactory to the Adult Education Department if indeed they had mobile vans to visit the book box depots. But in the circumstances that prevail, where no books at all reach villages, it is difficult to convince anyone that the adult education solution is not more advantageous. It must be borne in mind too that thought the ongoing adult education programmes, the department has more people working at the village level and more closely with the Party than Tanzania Library Service.

4. University and Specialized Libraries

The University Library which was established in 1961 is the second largest and shares with Tanganyinka Library Services the honour of being legal depository for all printed matter in Tanzania. It has a book stock of well over 500,000, over 8,150 serials (1,300 titles on Science and Technology), 400 microfiches and 422 microfilms. It has a sitting capacity of nearly 800. The book stock of the libraries of the Faculties of Agriculture at Morogoro and Medicine at Muhimbili are around 30,000 and each has a sitting capacity of about 150. The library at Muhimbili has more than 200 serials and 500 microfiches mostly donated by international donors.

4.1 *School Libraries*

School libraries are an important part of the library system in Tanzania and some of them can boast of fairly large book stocks. They are also important centres for the inculcation of the value of books and development of the reading habit and it is a pity that the country's economic situation does not favour their development and growth.

Technically, each secondary school should have a library and a good many of them do indeed have them. The quality of the services and the importance attached to libraries, however, differ a great deal depending on Headmasters'/Headmistresses' interest in books and in the school library. There are no funds specifically allocated for libraries and Headmasters/Headmistresses have discretionary powers to use the per capita grant on what they think are the most important and pressing priorities.

In many of these libraries one is apt to find that the only books and periodicals are those that are donated by embassies and other organizations and these mostly irrelevant and unsuitable to the schools. In fact the uncritical acceptance of book gifts has been identified as a major problem arising from the inability of the schools to select and buy the books that they need.

4.2 *College Libraries*

A number of Teacher Training Colleges have remarkably good libraries as a result of a USAID. Project which was started in 1962. The programme was regrettably phased out in 1966 for lack of government funds but Dar es Salaam Teachers college which had been selected to form the nucleus of a system of libraries meant to support the training of teachers and train librarians, has remained a model college library. It has a book stock of 45,000 titles and has been growing ever since its inception in 1966.

4.3 *Special Libraries*

The specialised institutes such as the Institute of Finance Management, Dar es Salaam, the Institute of Development Management, in Morogoro, and others have good libraries. There are also many special libraries run by Ministries, parastatal organizations and professional centres such as the Bureau of Standards, National Scientific Research Council and so on. Tanzania Library Services has published a Directory of Technical Information Resources in Tanzania which is a guide to these libraries.

4.4 *Other Libraries*

Other libraries in Tanzania are those owned and run by international bodies stationed in Dar es Salaam notably the British Council Library (book stock about 18,000). United States Communication Agency, Goethe Institute (3,000) and the French Cultural Centre (3,500). The United Nations Information Centre has a small reference library and so do other international organizations.

4.5 *Children's Libraries*

Children's libraries form an important section of the Central Library in Dar es Salaam and of the regional libraries. We were unable to obtain the bookstock for the children's section of the Central Library but a whole floor is devoted to it and it is quite impressive. It has a seating capacity for 150 children and it is very popular with children and very well used.

In addition to reading, the children's section holds, on one afternoon in the week, a story-telling session for children of up to 10 years. It also publishes in bound mimeograph form a creative writing journal for children.

5. **The Library System**

The acquisition department of TLS at the Central Library acts on behalf of all regional and district libraries. There is also an inter-library loan system which operates in the country and in which all libraries, public, private schools, University and specialised ones participate.

On regional and international exchanges Tanzania Library Service has always maintained close links with the libraries in Kenya, Uganda, Malawi and Zambia. It also has extensive connections with libraries in the UK and the United States of America and in other countries and has regular exchanges of materials with them.

On the whole, the libraries have done a very commendable job but as pointed out earlier there are still many areas which are not served by libraries of any kind at all. It will take many years at the present rate of development for Tanzania Library Services to build regional and district libraries to cover all the country. But the plans are there as well as the will. General economic recovery would provide the resources to advance towards building, stocking, and running libraries to the benefit of the people.

6. **Tanzania Library Association (TLA)**

The Tanzania Library Association was formed in 1972 following the decisions taken by the East African Library Association to dissolve into associations of librarians of each country. It has the following objectives: (1) to unite all persons working in or interested in library work, by convening conferences and meetings for the discussion of matters affecting libraries – their regulations, management or otherwise; (2) to encourage the promotion, establishment and improvement of libraries and library services in the country; (3) to promote and encourage bibliographical study and research; (4) to improve the standard of librarianship and the status of the library profession in the country; (5) to watch any legislation affecting libraries, and to assist in the promotion of such further legislation as may be considered necessary for the regulation and management or extension of library services in the country; (6) to collect, collate and publish (as journals, transactions, bulletins), information of benefit to members of the Association, or for the promotion of the objectives of the Association; (7) to do all such lawful things as are incidental or conducive to the fulfilment of the above objectives. Membership in the Tanzania Library Association is open to all librarians in their individual capacity but membership is also open to institutions which run libraries or are sufficiently interested in the work of the libraries to seek membership and to contribute to its objectives. The Tanzania Library Service has 312 members.

K 1

Library Marketing

Janak Raj

0. Introduction

It is a fact that the concepts of selling, market, marketing belong to the fields of trading, economics, commerce, and business management. Before we venture to discuss about library marketing, it will not be out of place to first understand these concepts as they are looked at by their primary disciplines. It would enable us to know their proper connotations and potential for applications in the field of library and information science better.

1. Selling Pattern

Selling is as old as man started bartering goods, but the concept of selling has undergone a sea change during the past eight decades. Earlier, Production Department was the most cared for department and rather the prime concern of business houses and Sales Department received the least priority. Drucker in 1954 wrote that "Fifty years ago the typical attitude of the American businessman toward marketing was still: 'The Sales Department will sell whatever the plant produces'. Today it is interestingly: 'It is our job to produce what the market needs'."

This concept of selling is relevant to the librarians because while discussing the qualities of a good librarian the literature of library science since the beginning of the 20th century often quoted that "Librarian should be a good salesman". We shall examine during the discussing that follows as to how this role of salesmanship for librarians has undergone a change, if any.

1.1 *The Market*

The term 'market' is used in many ways. When the term 'market' is used to express the *exchange of goods*, the American Marketing Association (AMA) suggests the following definition:

> The aggregate of forces or conditions within which buyers and sellers make decisions that result in the transfer of goods and services.

When the term market is used to represent *a demand* for a product, the AMA suggests this definition:

> The aggregate demand of the potential buyers of a commodity or service.

Frequently the word market is used to define *a specific geographical area*. In that case, the following definition is appropriate:

> The place or area in which buyers and sellers function.

The word market may also be used as *a verb* that is to define an activity. To market is:

> To perform business activities that direct the flow of goods and *services* from the producer to the consumer or user.[2]

Thus, we find that the term 'market' stands for:

(a) exchange of goods;
(b) demand for product/services;
(c) a specific geographic area;
(d) an activity (verb).

Looking to these four aspects we find complete analogy between market and library, as library is in a specific area where an activity of exchange of documents or services between readers and staff takes place for which demand exists.

1.1.1 *Marketing*: Economic activity can be divided broadly into the following categories:

After production and before consumption takes place, the goods or services must be made available to consumers. Making the goods or services available is assumed to be the role of marketing. The AMA defines marketing as "The performance of business activities that direct the flow of goods and services from the producer to the consumer or user".[3] This function of marketing as a bridge between the above two economic activities is a limited view of the economic role of marketing.

In fact, marketing does recognize the need for such marketing functions as personal selling and advertising necessary to persuade potential buyers to purchase and physical distribution to get products into the hands of consumers. Thus, marketing is a broad based and pervasive function, affecting all aspects of the business operation. It both begins and ends with the consumer as shown below:

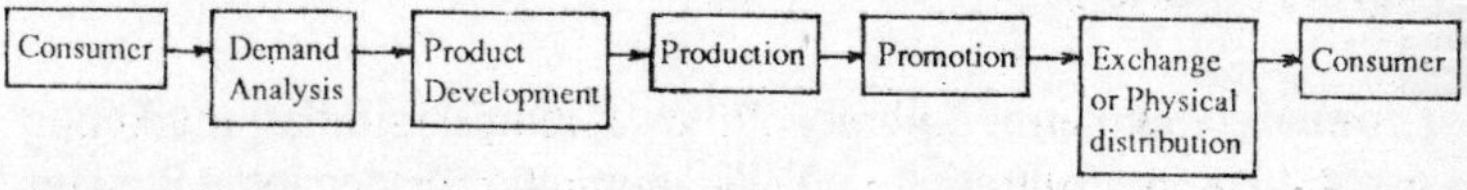

Because the basic purpose of marketing is to serve the welfare of consumer, it is essential that business operation be geared up to this end.

"The marketing concept . . . generally implies customer orientation of the total business firm. The implication of this concept is that the fundamental purpose of business activity is the satisfaction of consumer wants. It follows from this that a prerequisite to rational business activity is knowledge and understanding or consumer behaviour. The function of marketing is to study and interpret consumer needs and behaviour and to guide all business activities toward the end of consumer satisfaction."[4]

Keeping the above discussion in view the best definition of marketing that has been formulated is the following:

> Marketing is the process in a society by which the demand structure for economic goods and services is anticipated or enlarged and satisfied through the conception, promotion, exchange and physical distribution of such goods and services.[5]

1.2 *Selling* vs *Marketing*

Whereas selling focuses all attention on the interest of the seller by selling whatever is produced by a plant or firm, marketing takes into consideration the needs of the buyer through product development before actual production of a product or service is executed. This shows the voyage of the concept of selling through sales management to marketing management from early days to AD 1900. "Marketing is not only much broader than selling, it is not a specialized activity at all. It encompasses the entire business. It is the whole business seen from the point of view of its final result, that is, from the customer's point of view, said Drucker.[6]

A librarian as a good salesman was to make users use the documents whatever the library had, but now as a marketing manager he has to procure the documents users need the most and design, modify the library services as they suit users the most.

2. Library Marketing

Like business marketing, library follows almost similar marketing processes like concentration, equalization and dispersion. But for production of documents, over which libraries have little control, library also has identical channels of distribution as for marketing of commercial goods and services:

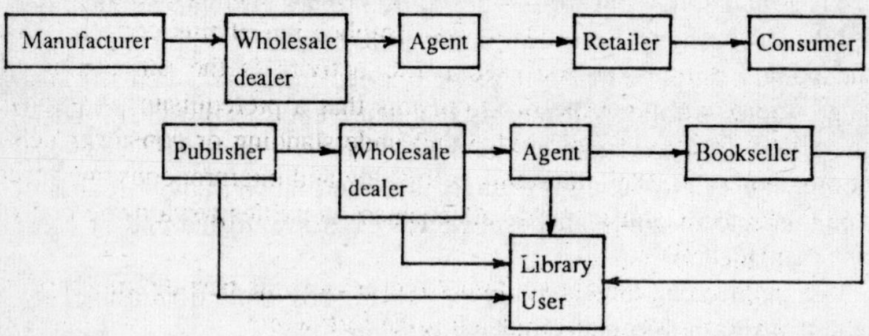

In library marketing, library and user's demands are the market, users the consumer; commodities exchanged the documents and library services; sellers the library staff; and buyers the users. Unlike business marketing, in library marketing the exchange of photocopies of documents and services may be permanent. The services like reference, translation, preparation of bibliographies CAS, SDI, interacting with data bases both off and on-line may be paid or free. In business marketing a firm besides taking care of the satisfaction of consumer also thinks in terms of earning profit. In library marketing users' satisfaction is the sole aim but has to care for the cost-effectiveness of the services rendered.

If we have a look at the functions of business marketing such as buying, selling, transportation, storage, grading, financing, risk taking, and market information, we find quite a good amount of similarity with minor modifications of functions that a library has to perform. They are almost identical with the said information services such as CAS SDI, interesting with information retrieval systems, etc.

2.1 *Histrocial Perspective/State of the Art*

In spite of such a close similarity in the processes and functions of business marketing and library marketing, the librarians did not realize till in the recent past that the sophisticated techniques of business marketing and marketing research could be made use of for the marketing of library and information services. "Nothing so well exemplifies the general absence of marketing considerations among information providing institutions as the fact that the first index entry in the Annual Review of Information Science and Technology for the heading 'Marketing' did not appear until the appearance of volume 5, in 1970."[7] "Annual cumulative volume of Library Literature for the year 1976-77 used a subject heading: "Marketing Literature" and directed to see under: "Advertising Literature" and the entries under this heading pertained to bibliographical control. Till 1976 no entry under "Marketing" was to be seen in the volume of *Library and Information Science Abstracts* (LISA). However, an entry under RBAW "Use of Marketing Techniques" is noticed in the volume for the year 1981 of LISA. (Due to non-receipt of volumes of LISA from 1977 to 1980 in Kurukshetra University Library, Kurukshetra (KULK), the fact could not be checked if some articles were reported under the subject during this period. The Indian Library Science Abstracts did not record even a single article on the subject till its volume of 1984 (the latest issue received was in May 1986 at KULK).

3. **Importance of Marketing**

"In the United States approximately 50% of each dollar spent for goods represents marketing cost and that the total expenditure for marketing probably exceeds 150 billion per year."[8] Thus the cost of getting goods from the producer to the consumer is about equal to the original cost of producing them. Library as a facilitating agency takes documents from their producers to the users and renders *product service*. As a producer of services like CAS, SDI, IRS, translation and reprographics, etc. library takes *service products* to the users. Doing so it expands on this marketing like activity. Since library is not a profiteering institution, cost-effectiveness of library marketing must be taken care of by using the techniques of market planning, strategy and research with amends suitable to the context of library marketing.

4. **Marketing Planning**

Marketing plan surveys the environment, isolates marketing opportunities and states the courses of action to be followed in taking advantage of those opportunities. A skeletal structure of a marketing plan may look as follows:

"I. Situation analysis:

(A) Demand

1. Nature of demand
2. Extent of demand

(B) Competition
(C) Environmental climate
(D) State of product life cycle
(E) Cost structure of the industry
(F) Skills of the firm
(G) Financial resources of the firm
(H) Distribution structure
(I) Legal Constraints

II. Problems and opportunities
III. Marketing strategy:

A. Objectives

(1) Target market segments
(2) Volume to be sold
(3) Profit goals

B. Marketing to mix/programme decisions

(1) Product strategy
(2) Distribution strategy
(3) Price strategy
(4) Promotion strategy

(a) Advertising
(b) Personal Selling
(c) Sales promotion".[9]

Marketing strategy which is said to be the heart of market planning is based on the situation analysis and the institution's objectives.

4.1 *Situation/Demand Analysis*

As in business marketing, library marketers have to identify users, determine their information needs and the manner in which they prefer these wants to be satisfied. Through demand analysis the users' wants are studied, measured and understood. Demand may be latent and its existence unknown. Marketing strategy can be employed to convert it into effective demand by offering a product service or service product in a manner consistent with underlying demand forces. The demand analysis should be done both prior to starting of a library or library service and off and on thereafter too.

Library use and user studies do give clue to the nature of information demands of users, besides other factors which are chosen for study. For doing demand analysis internal library use can be studied by analysing internal library records, and gathering reports from the staff working in circulation, reference, and acquisition sections. For doing demand analysis through user studies various field research methods would be appropriate. "Until the 1950s, little research was done on information needs and uses. During the decade, however, people designing retrieval systems for scientific and technical information began analysing the needs and characteristics of those who used their systems. Results were summarized in bibliographical essays which appeared in the Annual Review of Information Science and Technology (ARIST) from 1966 to 1972 and again in 1974 and 1978. The studies were not as useful to system designers as was hoped, partly because they revealed such a wide range of information needs and uses".[10] while reviewing information needs and uses studies, Mary Jo Lynch[11] drew attention to the work done in the field by John Martyn, Susan Grawford, Lois Babout et al. Thomas Childers, Edward S Warner, Branda Dervin, Ching-Chih Chem, and King Research Inc. In India some need studies of users pertaining to some disciplines have been made in the past few years.

4.11 *Marketing Management Studies*: The general purpose of market measurement studies is to obtain quantitative data on potential demand. The two main types of data obtained relate to (1) Market potential and (2) Sales potential. In the context of library, in order to measure demand, we are to obtain quantitative data on (1) Library resource potential and (2) Use potential. The principal object of any library is the satisfaction of user demand. An important factor of marketing success is the knowledge of user demand. This market knowledge can be broken down into two broad areas: the habits and motivations of the user and the size of the population.

4.12 *User Behaviour and Motivation*: User behaviour and motivations are studied so that library product service or service product programmes may be devised which are consistent with that behaviour and motivations. A librarian needs answers to many questions for this. What types of document are the user choosing? What motivates the user actually to make choice ? How does he approach his information obtaining problem ? What information does he want before making a specific choice ? Why does the user select a given document or an information service in preference to another of apparently equal quality ? Will the user prefer to meet his information need from a library which is organized on traditional functional basis or which bring together all types of material at one place and arrange it on subject department basis ?

The Problems: Besides, there are two problems involved in the study of user behaviour. The first is to determine *what* that behaviour is and the second *why* users do act as they do and what influences their behaviour.

The Answers: Answer to the first problem can be sought through the study of library's circulation and use records. Additional information can be obtained through user surveys, type of document and service preference studies. For the second problem, obtaining of knowledge of user attitudes and motivations can be valuable. For instance, advertising for educating users and use promotional efforts can be more properly directed. Adverse use trends or impediments in use can be remedied, if the cause is known. The study of why behaviour means to acquire capability to predict user behaviour which is possible only through the knowledge of user motivations. Business marketing has classified consumer purchasing motives as:

Product motives
Patronage motives
Emotional motives
Rational motives

"A compilation has been made of some 600 buying motives, as revealed in marketing research studies, which have influenced consumers at some time for some products".[12]

4.2 *Librarians' Responsibility*

Librarians should also make motivations studies and list various motives of users' choice under different information seeking situations. But mere listing of motives does not completely provide answer to the "why" of user choice question. To find answer to this "why" what is, to probe more deeply into the subconscious to reveal factors influencing user choice, the techniques of psychologists should be used. In fact, to make user motivation studies, the librarians should join forces with the students of the behavioural sciences, especially sociology, anthropology and psychology.

To serve users better, it is important to study how a user approaches information seeking situation. Studies should be conducted as to what per cent of users approach the library with their planned information needs, that is, what actually they want to know and which sources will satisfy their needs. What percentage of them approach without prior planning ? What percentage of them make an impulsive or a casual choice of their reading material? How many users make prior inquiries before exercising their choice for a document for a service ? What percentage of them exercise their information choice in a state of ignorance or indifference ?

5. Marketing Strategy

The variables, the marketing manager works with in planning strategy are of two types, controllable and uncontrollable as in Figure 1.[13]

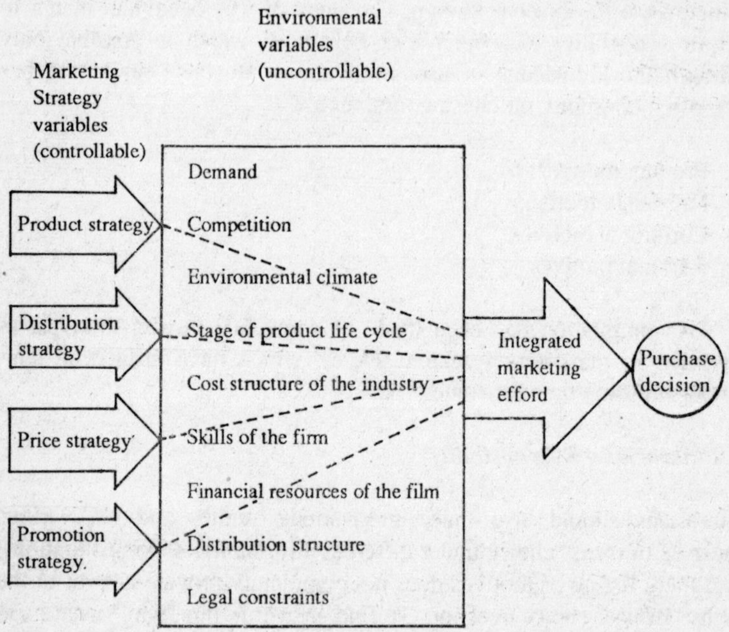

Fig. 1: *Controllable and Uncontrollable Variables in Marketing Management*

5.1 *The Marketing Manager*

The marketing manager can decide, for example, whether or not to use advertising, how much, and what kind. Similar decisions are to be made about the product line, distribution, pricing, sales promotion, and the use of personal selling. The marketing manager can weave these together into an overall marketing programme in an infinite number of ways.

5.2 *The Product Strategy*

As far as product strategy is concerned librarians have little control over the production of documents, so products differentiation as market strategy is ruled out. However, product differentiation can be made applicable in case of the library service products or commercial information services. Librarians can make use of the promotion strategies to maximize the use of the reading material and for greater satisfaction of their users. Price strategy of marketing has to be substituted by cost-effectiveness of library product service and service products.

6. **Alternative Marketing Strategy**

6.1 *Market Segmentation*

In recent years there has been increased recognition that the market is not a homogeneous mass of prospects, but rather a set of submarkets each of which may be composed of potential customers who have certain characteristics of geographic, demographic, psychographic or behavioural nature in common.

A marketing strategy that attempts to reach these submarkets has been termed a strategy of market segmentation. Market segmentation recognizes the diversity of demand and attempts to adapt to it by better meeting the needs of part of the market.

6.11 *Bases for Market Segmentation*: The variables used for market segmentation have been classified into categories such as geographic, demographic, psychographic and buyer behaviour. The categories and typical breakdowns associated with each are illustrated in Appendix I.[14]

The demographic variables include such dimensions as age, sex, family size, income, occupation, education, family life-cycle, religion, race, nationality and social class. The geographic variables are those which pertain to region, climate, size of city, town, and whether the location of the potential customer is in urban, sub-urban or rural areas.

The breakdown of the psychographic variables is like degree of compulsiveness, gregariousness, autonomy, etc.

Perhaps more useful psychological variables are those that describe the life-style of potential customers. Life-style measurement for the purpose of providing bases for market segmentation is usually accomplished by means of AIO (Activities, Interests and Opinions) rating statements.[15] Specifically life-style research is claimed at measuring people's activities, what they place importance on in their immediate surroundings; (2) their opinions in terms of their view of themselves and the world around them, and (3) some basic characteristics such as their stage in life-cycle, income, education and where they live".[16]

6.2 *Library Market Segmentation*

Among the demographic variables, age of library users, their level of education and economic status, and occupation will make a sea difference in their reading interests. Generally among the economically sound sections of the population, the rate of education is higher. Such a section has more leisure time at its disposal and more avenues to spend it as compared to the people belonging to the poor or lower income groups. Generally people in lower-middle, middle and upper income groups are the persons who are after career making, so this section of the population cares more for higher education and extra readings. Elderly people in the higher income groups may find little time for reading as compared to people of younger generation who may devote more time for recreational reading. Level of education and occupation of the users are very relevant for library marketing segmentation.

Geographically market segmentation is done on the basis whether the users reside in a thickly populated area or sparcely populated one, in rural or urban or sub-urban area. This will tell about their access to library facilities and the quantum of library facilities they require.

6.21 *The Psychographic Variable*: Geographic and demographic variables describe the users' "stage of being" (i.e. as they are). In contrast these variables that describe the users' "state of mind" can be termed psychographic. Psychographic variables may be: are the users inquisitive, curious, inquiring, temperamental, sentimental, temperate, sensitive, sensuous, adventurous, sensationalist, peace-loving, methodical, formal, idler, self-confident, impulsive, gregareous conservative, liberal, ambitious, prestige-conscious and the like. Segmentation of the users on the basis of these psychic facts will give an insight into the type of material the library should procure, the type of environment it should provide and the behaviour the users can expect from the library staff and *viceversa*.

6.22 *Users' Behaviour*: Users behaviour like library usage rate (non-user, light/medium/heavy user), readiness stage to learn about library systems "unaware, aware, interested, intending to try, etc.), and benefits sought (recreation, information, academic degree, knowledge) need study for library marketing segmentation.

The variables for the segmentation of library market may not be the same but a marked similarity between the psychographic variables of business market and library market may be found if research is done in this area. The librarians should explore this area of identifying geographic, demographic and psychographic factors for library market segmentation.

6.23 *Examples of Studies*: A good example for demographic study of underlying relationship between libraries and community is seen in the paper by Lowell A Martin.[17] Some of the prominent earlier studies which can be referred to with advantage, as examples, are by US Bureau of Education (1876),[18] Joseph L. Wheeler (1924),[19] Douglas, Waples (1931),[20] Carleton B Joeckel (1935),[21] Bernard Berlson (1949),[22] Rober D Leigh (1950),[23] Jan Hajda (1963),[24] Philips H Ennis (1965),[25] William R Monat (1967),[26] Mary Lee Bundy (1968),[27] Edward S Warner et al (1973).[28]

User studies have increase in the past one and a half decades both in India and abroad, but more user studies are needed, not going over the same broad census-type ground but focusing on sub-groups taking into consideration the psychographic, geographic and demographic variables for making segmentation studies for library markets.

6.3 *Promotion Strategy*

As business success depends upon the firm being able to sell, at a profit, the merchandise it produces, the success of a library depends upon the maximum utilization of the documents and services it offers in the most cost-effective manner. It is right that a good library plant centrally located, with proper selection and organization of its stock and necessary arrangements for the distribution of documents and services are very important. Yet these activities would be wasted to a greater extent unless the users are made to use the documents and services as a result of effective promotional programme of library use.

6.31 *Promotional Tools*: Market promotion programme is not advertisement of library and its services alone, rather it is a mix of a number of promotional tools :

- (i) Advertising (TV, radio, newspapers, magazines, mail letters, cinema slides, print materials, giveaways, etc.).
- (ii) Personal Selling (Home visits/delivery).
- (iii) Sales Promotion (quiz/declamation contest, essay competitions, premiums, combination offers).
- (iv) Display (Sign-boards, wall paintings, showcase displays: inside Library and at public places).
- (v) Shows (cultural, films, slide projections).

(vi) Exhibitions (books, paintings, photographs, coins, etc.).
(vii) User Education (lectures, demonstrations).
(viii) Book Fairs.
(ix) Visits by Opinion Leaders to Library.

6.32 *Precautions*

(a) It must be borne in mind that the same promotional tool will not suit to every segment of library market. A proper mix of these tools has to be chosen suiting to the needs of the users who may be well informed, less informed or uninformed.
(b) Stage of development of library and its service products should determine the choice of such tools. An old, well-established library or service product would not need the same amount of promotion effort as a new or less established one. At least its accent will vary.
(c) An adequate budget provision must be made for promotional work. Ratio of the budget provision to the total library budget needs to be determined through research. In business a similar amount is spent on marketing a commodity as on its production.
(d) In the excitement of promotion planning, there is a scope to over spend. A successful budgeting is to achieve the objectives at the least cost.
(e) Timings chosen during a year for such programmes should be such that suit to the convenience of the users, i.e., when they have comparatively more leisure time.
(f) Conducting of such programmes should be a continuous process and evenly spaces throughout the year. A calendar in advance should be prepared.
(g) Duration of such programmes should not be too lengthly less it should become stale and involve unnecessary expenditure.
(h) The programme should be so very properly distributed that no segment of the library market goes unattended.

7. Planning of Market Promotional Programme

The main objective of such a programme is to make a favourable attitude of the library users towards the library and create and increase demand for its product services and services products. As already said, the same tool may not suit to every segment of library market, so the user population has to be so divided that different mix of tools may be choosen for each segment.

7.1 *The Standard of Living*

If not always, by and large the standard of living is a good indicator of level of education of residents of a population pocket. Residents of a posh colony generally have a higher level of education as compared to that of a colony of lower middle income group. A public library market may be divided into three to four divisions on the basis of the economic status of various colonies. Academic and special library markets may be divided on the basis of level of education or level of information needs. Let us take six income groups in our country at the moment as below :

	Income Group	Monthly Income
(a)	Poor	Below Rs. 500
(b)	Lower	Rs. 500 to 1000
(c)	Lower Middle	Rs. 1000 to 2000
(d)	Middle	Rs. 2000 to 3000
(e)	Upper	Rs. 3000 to 5000
(f)	Higher	Rs. 5000 and above.

7.2 *The Education Factor*

On the basis of education we may have the following categories : (a) Illiterates, (b) Neo-literates, (c) Literates, (d) Educated, (e) Highly Educated, (f) Intellectuals. For each respective category, the objective for a library to be achieve may be as under :

(a) To make aware of the importance of education.
(b) To create interest to know more.
(c) To create interest in reading.
(d) To make them aware of facilities of reading.
(e) To be posted with the latest available.

(f) To be provided with the latest at their doorstep.

Thus there may be three broad objectives of promotional programme for the above six categories.

(1) For (a) and (b): To generate consciousness/awareness for education and information.
(2) For (c) and (d): To increase percentage of use.
(3) For (e) and (f): To maintain the percentage of use.

Once the library market is divided into various zones/divisions according to the information needs of users, either of the market promotional tools or a combination of more than one (para 6.3 above) to make a mix has to be judiciously chosen. It is obvious that tools like book fair, user education, sales promotion will be as useless for the illiterates or neo-literates as advertising for the highly educated and intellectuals.

7.3 *Activities*

Under each promotion tool some activities are discussed below by way of illustration. It is in no way an exhaustive list. More effective and more in number can be thought of by the working librarians according to their situations and resources. Some of the activities can be used for public libraries only, whereas others are for public, academic, and special libraries alike. The content of communication in each tool should be according to the educational level or information needs of the users.

7.31 *Advertisement*: The purpose of advertisement is to stimulate *primary demand* and then *selective demand* for a particular brand of product which in case of library is to stimulate an urge for knowing and reading and then demand for the works of a particular author, publisher, institution or on a specific subject.

To attract potential users a good guide, giving initial introduction to the library, be prepared to publicize the library and its services.

A leaflet describing newspapers and periodicals received in a public library may be distributed to all homes in the area.

Publicity information regarding library and services be included on carrier bags, art print post-cards, stickers, children's guide to the library, balloons and placards.

Literary discussions on radio stations and television be sponsored.

Slide projection in cinema halls in the area regarding library and its services can be arranged.

7.32 *Personal Selling*: Personal selling differs from advertising in that the selling message is delivered by personal contact as opposed to presentation through non-personal media, such as newspapers, TV, radio, etc. Home visits and taking along reading material to suit users; tastes will establish friendly relations and give feedback of reading needs for future visits. In the beginning reading material on popular subjects like gardening, embroidery, cooking, or interior decoration and the like may be welcome.

7.4 *Sales Promotion*

If the purpose of advertisement is to stimulate *primary demand* and then a *selective demand* sales promotion is "to help communicate an offer.[29] User promotion consists of premiums, contest, combination offers, say, "30% discount this week", "Free cup with 500g Bournvita pack", "Pay after 30 days", etc. They are also terms as "*forced methods*".

Occasional announcement of some concessions for the library users will be a beneficial step to promote use. "Fifty per cent off on overdue fine for a week", "five books against three for loan for this winter break", "20% on reprographic charges for 10 days" or some such concessions which will have the desired effect.

Literary readings at study circle meetings inside or outside library may be arranged.

Establishment of local History Corners and forming of Local History Societies will involve some citizens in library work.

Seminars about literature on some subject, say, cine lit and award for the best two papers will encourage library use.

Visit by opinion leaders to the library and talking to them about library and its services over a cup of tea be arranged once a year or two. They may be persuaded to speak a few sentences on reading or library on radio or TV.

Arranging of quiz declamation contests, essay competition are some of the forced methods to encourage use.

7.5 *Displays*

For making library more intelligible, information and use of a good library sign system with main directory and directional signs can prove very effective as suggested by Allen.[30]

Sign-boards and wall paintings, showcase displays of new arrivals or pride collection inside library and outside at public places can pay dividends.

7.6 *Shows*

- Organizing of some events for children.
- Film shows for senior citizens.

7.7 *Exhibitions*

- Sponsoring of exhibits of artists, photographers, craftsman and related programmes. It will attract new visitors and receive media coverage.
- Arranging of centenary exhibitions by allocating to various age groups of users responsibility for collecting materials regarding the various aspects of the concerned personality, event, institution, or association, etc.
- Long-term book exhibitions on places of remembrance, say, a place connected with Indian Freedom Movement.
- Topical exhibitions

7.8 *Book Fairs*

Book fairs of national, state, district, town level or books of one or more than one publisher for sale is a well-tried method.

7.9 *User Education*

User education through lectures with audio-visual aids and demonstrations according to the level of the users is a tool of recent origin.

8. Conclusion

From the above discussions it becomes amply clear that library marketing techniques have a lot of potential for their application for increasing the use of any library. Utility of application of marketing research to reduce distribution cost of library materials and services and product research of service products like Additions List, Local Documentation List, SDI, tailored services commercially available and the like for greater user satisfaction are the other areas which need to be explored.

REFERENCES

1 BRITT, S N and BOYD, H W Jr: *Marketing Mangement and Administrative Action*. Ed 2. New York; McGraw-Hill, 1968, p 4.

2 DIMOND, Jay and PRINTEL, Gerald: *Principles of Marketing*. Englewood Cliffs; Prentice-Hall. 1972, pp 3-4.

3 Ibid., p 4.

4 REWOLDT, Tewart, et al: Introduction to Marketing Management; *Text and Cases*. Ed 3. Homewood; Richard D Irwin. 1977, p 5.

5 Ibid p 5.

6 BRITT, S N: op cit., p 5.

7 WEINSTOCK, M: Marketing Scientific and Technical Service. (In: *Encyclopedia of Library and Information Science*, Edited by Allen Kent Vol 17. New York; Marcel Dekker 1976, p 186.

8 TOUSLEY, Rayburn, et al: *Principles of Marketing*. New York; Macmillan, 1962, p 6.

9 REWOLDT, Tewart H: Ibid., pp 10-11.

10 LYNCH, Mary J C: Research in Library Reference Information Service. [*Library Trends* Vol 31(3), Winter 1983, p 410].

11 Ibid., pp 310-12.

12 CLAWSON, C Joseph: Discussion. (*Cost and Profit Outlook*, May-June 1958, p 2).

13 REWOLDT, Tewart H: Ibid., p 20.

14 Ibid., p 38.

15 WELLS, William, et al : Activities, Interests and Opinions. (*Journal of Adversitising Research*, Vol 11, August 1971, pp 27-35).

16 PLUMMER, Josseph T: The Concepet and Application of Life Style Segmentation (*Journal of Marketing*, Vol 38 Jan 1974, pp 33-37).

17 MARTIN, Lowell A: Demographic Trends and Social Structure, (*Library Tends*, Vol 27(3), Winter 1978, pp 259-298).

18 U S : *Public Libraries in the United State of America*. Washington D C, USGPO, 1876.

19 WHEELER, Joseph L: *Library and the Community; Increased Book Service Through Library Publicity Based on Comparative Studies Chicago*, ALA, 1924.

20 WAPLES, Douglas: *What People Want to Read About; A Study of Group Interests and a Survery of Problems in Adult Reading*. Chicago, University of Chicago Press, 1931.

21 JOECKEL, Carleton B, Ed: *Government of the American Public Library*. Chicago; University of Chicago Press, 1935.

22 BERELSON, Bernard: *The Library's Public* (A Report of the Public Library

Inquiry). New York; Columbia University Press, 1949.

23 LEIGH, Robert D: *Public Library in the United States* (General Report of the Public Library Inquiry). New York; Columbia University Press, 1950.

24 HAJDA, Jan: American Paradox: *People and Books in a Metropolish (Ph.D) dissertation.* Chicago, University of Chicago, 1963.

25 ENNIS, Philips H: *Adult Book Reading in the United States: A Preliminary Report.* Chicago; National Opinion Research Centre, University of Chicago, 1965.

26 MONAT, William R: *Public Library and its Community: A Study of the Impact of Library Services in Five Pennsylvania Cities*, University Park, Penna, Institute of Public Administration, 1967.

27 BUNDY, Marry Lee: *Metropolitan Public Library Users: A Report of Survey of Adult Library Use in the Maryland-Baltimore Washington Metropolitan Area.* College Part University of Maryland, School of Information and Library Services, 1968.

28 WARNER, Edward: et al.; *Informatiorn Needs of Urban Residents.* Washington D C; U S Bureau of Libraries and Learning Resource, 1973.

29 RINES, Michael: Marketing Handbook. Ed 2. Hampshire, Gower, 1981. p 249.

30 ALLEN, Peter R Van: A Good Library Sign System: Is It Possible ? (*Reference Services Review*, Vol 12(2), Summer 84, pp 102-106).

APPENDIX I

Major Segmentation Variable and Their Typical Breakdowns

Variables	*Typical breakdowns*
Geographic Region	Pacific; Mountain; West North Central; West South Central; East North Central; East South Central; South Atlantic; Middle Atlantic; New England
Country size	A: B: C: D
City or S.M.S.A. size	Under 5000, 5000-19999; 20000-49999; 50000-99999; 100000-249999; 250000-499999; 500000-499999; 1000000-399999, 4000000 or over
Density	Urban; suburban; rural
Climate	Northern, Southern
Demographic Age	Under 6; 6-11; 12-17; 18-24; 35-49; 50-64; 65
Sex	Male; Female
Family size	1-2; 3-4; 5+
Family life-cycle	Young single, young, married, no children, young, married, youngest child under six; young, married, youngest child six or over; older, married, with children; older, married no children under 18; older, single; other
Income	Under $ 5,000; $ 5,000-7,999; $ 8,000-9,999 over $ 10,000
Occupation	Professional and technical; managers; officials and proprietors; clerical, sales; craftsmen, foremen; operatives; farmers, retired; students; housewives; unemployed
Education	Grade school or less; some high school; graduated high school; some college; graduated college.
Religion	Catholic; Protestant; Jewish; other
Race	White, Negro, Oriental

(Contd.)

Variables	*Typical breakdowns*
Nationality	American; British; French; German; Eastern European; Scandinavian; Italian; Spanish; Latin American; Middle Eastern; Japanese; and so on
Social class	Lower-lower; upper-lower; lower-middle; middle-middle; upper-middle; lower-upper; upper-upper.
Psychographic	
Compulsiveness	Compulsive; noncompulsive
Greagariousness	Extrovert; introvert
Autonomy	Dependent; independent
Conservatism	Conservative; liberal; radical
Authoritarianism	Authoritarian; democratic
Leadership	Leader; follower
Ambitiousness	High achiever; low achiever
Buyer Behaviour	
Usage rate	Nonuser; light user; medium user; heavy user
Readiness stage	Unaware; aware; interested; intending to try; trier; regular buyer
Benefits sought	Economy; status; dependability
End use	(Varies with the product)
Brand loyalty	None; light; strong
Marketing-factor sensitivity	Quality; price; service; advertising; sales promotion

Source: Philip Kotler. *Marketing Management: Analysis, planning and Control*. 2nd ed. 1972. p 170 (Pub: Prentice-Hall, Inc.).

K 2

Creating Corporate Identity: A Visual Approach to Marketing Library Services

Ravinder Kumar Chadha and **Jagdish Arora**

0. Introduction

At all times a library has a responsibility to exploit its resources, its stock, its staff, and its services in order to serve the users in the best possible way. With the depressing state of general economy, the declining budgets, the increasing cost of materials and services, the poor job market and the decreasing professional staff, a library can no longer afford to wait passively for people. It must set out to "persuade" its customers to "buy" what it has to offer. Otherwise it may "go out of business". It may not or probably will not disappear from the scene but its prestige, stature and financial support are likely to diminish. In order to survive and to get ahead library will need to resort to or adopt some of the aggressive, competitive and organized practices of the business world. One of these practices is that of creating a corporate image.

1. The Concept

The creation of specific identities for commercial organization is familiar to all. Corporate identity programme of major companies can be seen in any high street. This provides an easily recognizable appearance for the company, it provides a rational and consistent approach to its activities and above all an image regarding quality of its products and services. The moment we talk about "Bajaj", "Khaitan"; "Usha" group we relate these to some products and also to quality of those products to an extent. Libraries can no longer afford to ignore such image. Image about resources, services, staff behaviour has to be built up in a positive fashion. This will ultimately have a healthy effect on library usage.

2. Creating an Identity Programme

Following points have to be considered by professionals in order to improve library identity:

(a) Creating awareness about the existence of library to its target group;
(b) Developing a well-planned user communication system in terms of guiding; sign posting; staff activities services etc.; and
(c) Developing an efficient service system and build cordial relationships with the users.

2.1 *The Logo*

For developing identity programmes the foremost thing is that libraries should felt concern with begin easily recognized in the community to its target users. The best way of countering is to provide a visual image and develop good signage system for library. A library logo will make it more consistent and popular. State Bank of India can be sighted as an example. All the branches of SBI have a logo, common lettering for names with light blue colour on white background. Why do SBI make this effort. Obviously in their interest to advertise their services and service points. This way SBI branches are not difficult to locate in any vicinity.

2.2 *Illuminated Signs*

Similarly, standard signs should be used to guide readers to the library. Guiding should start from surrounding areas and, if possible, should illuminate during the night, for example, in a university library, the standard signs should be placed from university gate till its entrance to the library. Various branches of the same library system (example Delhi University Library System, Delhi Public Library System and so on) should be clearly recognizable as a part of the same system. This will not only develop a system feeling but show even a small branch library can provide a most esoteric document through being part of a larger network. A visual link, common to all libraries could show the public that these libraries work in mission and in cooperation with one another.

2.3 *Guides*

"For most library users it is a self-service process. They go to the shelves and select the documents they need." For those who cannot locate, what they wish, staff should be available to assist them. This, in essences, is what most libraries are about for most of their users. A well-planned signage system plays a significant role in explaining the collections and services of a library. Clearly visible, well designed and maintained, logically developed signage system will attract users. Signs associated with direction finding must help to explain the overall size and shape of the library and also the location of various resources within it. The system must assure the users that they have reached their desired destination. There should be detailed guides on the shelves, such as tier guides above the each bay of shelving. Tier guides should contain the name of the subject as well as the class number. The guides should be attractive, clearly visible from a reasonable distance. There should be proper end guides to inform users what is available on either side of the shelves.

2.4 *Helping Hands*

A library has to create a positive identity among its users regarding its services. The staff should be trained to adopt a friendly tone while talking to users and should be approachable for assistance of any kind. Use of badges or nameplates by library staff will help readers in seeking assistance in parts of the library where there are no information points like in the shelving area, near catalogue, near AV equipments etc. Carefully designed handouts, leaflets, posters should explain the library services, rules and regulations. These help to develop confidence in users. Instructions about how to use the various library material and equipments should be notified.

3. **Printing and Publicity Work**

3.1 *Stationery*

Corporate image of any library largely depends upon the quality of its printed material. It is the part of library that reaches out far and beyond the immediate vicinity of the building. Stationery should be thoughtfully designed and consistently used. Use of library logo and proper layout of stationery items are valuable in creating a favourable impression. Letterheads, complimentary slips, book stationery (issue/return labels, book cards, etc.), membership forms, borrowers tickets reminder cards must show a uniformity. Sizes and shapes of stationery items should be limited, preferably to standard sizes. At the same time information and language of library leaflets, posters should be planned keeping in view the level of readers who will use the same. Librarianship jargons should be completely avoided for publications.

3.2 **Publicity Material**

In addition, libraries could produce materials for sale or for distribution to it users and non-users. This can include picture cards, car stickers, diaries, calendars, carry-bags, balloons, T-shirts and other souvenirs. Such promotional material can be obtained from manufacturers themselves. These souvenirs should contain appropriate information about the library and its activities. Book-marks and posters for special purposes can be planned and used effectively.

4. **Planning for Identity Programme**

The identity programme is based on some key elements like logo, typefaces, format, colour and so on.

4.1 *Library Logo*

The logo is standardized form of the library's name. It is one of the key elements in providing the recognizability of the library. It may involve a symbol, a particular typesetting or both. Non-verbal design should be avoided, because of its abstract nature which makes it difficult to know what the symbol means. A meaning clear to a particular community may be totally obscure to others. The most important factor is the logo should be used consistently in a uniform manner for all the library activities.

4.2 *Type Faces*

It is necessary to decide what typefaces should be used in a variety of situations in order to ensure consistency. Legibility and availability of type faces should be kept in mind at the time of selection. Openness, boldness of letter, and use of serifs and sans serifs influence the aesthetics of printed material and add to the general character of the identity programme.

4.3 *Formats*

To get across the library message the corporate identity programme will make use of material in a variety of formats. Use of too many formats should be avoided or else it can lead to confusion and finally to dilution of corporate approach. To save wastage standard sizes of papers should be kept in mind while finalizing sizes for publications. Other parameters can be use of production methods, psychology of users, cost and so on. It is not the sizes which create the identity, rather it is coordination among various sizes that identifiable ranges of publications, similar in appearance, having uniformity in layouts are produced.

4.4 *Colour*

Colours attract, detract, gladden or depress the spirits. Among the four basic colour schemes, i.e., colourless (primarily black and white with natural colours), monochromatic (use of only one colour) related and contrasting are quite popular among librarians. So far as the colour schemes are concerned natural colours should be preferred. Accents can always be added from carpeting, fabrics, paintings, tapestries, etc.

5. Conclusion

If libraries are to be of any relevance in future it is necessary to give them some positive identity, which they have lacked till now. And for this purpose the corporate identity programme should be considered as an integral part of library planning. This should be given adequate resources to achieve its goals.

L 1

My Attitude Towards the Book and Its Illustrations

H C Horst Kunze

1. Interest in Books

I became a librarian, because I had discovered the book as an indispensable guide when I was young. At the age of 16 years I came across a library for the first time and in the course of long university studies I became familiar with libraries. When I was 25 years old, I knew just as little as my fellow students, how a library functions, but since the library must be a house of books — many books — for certain, I liked it from the outset.

2. Strayed into Librarianship

Truly speaking, I must confess that I was not eager to follow this for a vocation and, I had to finish my studies which had lasted seven years. On the other hand, my thirst for knowledge kept growing and I would quench it by becoming a "private scholar". I had met such men who completed the column "profession and social position respectively" of their lending forms by this cosy designation, several times. I had met private scholars already as a supplement to the author's name on title-pages. I was deeply impressed by them. Well, economic independence, i.e. to earn one's own money, had to be considered after all, and that's why I became a librarian as the presumably least evil. To relate under what difficult circumstances and under what different social conditions this had to be done at that time would be a far too long story by itself, a piece of unwritten "memories" so to say.

3. Love for Book Illustrations

It is for this reason that I should like to say just in few words about my old-age occupation, namely, about the book illustration. It was the book that inspired me to be a librarian and not an art historian. I must put is more correctly: I should like to speak about any form of illustration and decoration in the book. Or, to include at the very beginning the background of this constellation, about the symbiosis of illustration and book, of illustration and art.

4. Work on Book Illustrations

The occupation with the history of the illustrated book in Germany was suggested to me from outside, from the Insel Publishers in Leipzig, namely, the then artistic manager Joachim Walch. Actually, I appreciated this, because I was familiar with the literature: since Theodor Kutschmann's two-volume *Geschichte der deutschen Illustration* (History of the German Illustration, Goslar and Berlin, 1899) no more general work of this kind had been published. Personally, I was at once aware that I myself had recevied lasting, deep impressions from illustrated books throughout my lifetime. In retrospect, illustrations in books which had impressed upon me half a centry ago immediately appeared. They were — and still are — so lively before me, as if I had seen them only yesterday. There was my first children's book, ardently loved, often read and often cherished: Berni, a Little Boy, by Heinrich Scharrelmann with the small black-and-white lithographies by Paul Helms, which at that time really illustrated for me what I had read with difficulty: they described Berni's great and little events in the everyday life of a large town together with his mother, a washerwoman. And a short time after but already in a different light, I was able to share Robinson Crusoe's experiences made clear by Ludwing Richter in a gentle and instructive way but in the atmosphere of an infinitely distant archieplago. Later, in the years of mental awakening, I read the impressing and rousing picture novels by Frans Masereel, who crossed my way also several times as a congenial illustrator of works of world literature — Villon, Zola, Tolstoy, de Coster and Thomas Mann. Always making clear by means of pictures lasting impressions left by reading, he was an artist capable of appealing to both feeling and mind with the slightest technical expenditure and at the same item stirring up social consciousness.

Since then my understanding for pictures had matured to the point where not all interpretations by means of pictures I saw met my own ideas, but always — even to my surprise — produced impulses and prompted me to think.

4.1 *Influence of Works*

For me the background and the multiplicity of the human world of a Charles Dickens are inevitably connected with the partly kind and farcial, partly malicious and merciless figures as created by a George Cruikshank or a Phiz (Hablot K Browne) with their artistic means in accordance with the intentions of the author. They lived on in the Papers of the amiable Mister Pickwick always aspiring to do good things, they made one endure the sufferings of Oliver Twist who was the mercy of a brutal world.

5. Wood-cut Illustrations

Not slighter was the response of the acquaintance with the art of wood carving of Vladimir Favorsky, a book designer, who as one of the first who had exemplified to me the well-composed unity of the book of high artistic value long before I had comprehended in theory this correspondence of all parts of a book for the purpose of a harmonious whole and before I learned that this artist had also been an important theorist after all. In his illustrations produced with the slightest technical means, intellect and emotion meet each other wonderfully. Even the smallest woodcuts with detailed figures and objects are so impressive, because they are created entirely with a view to the atmosphere of the book. For example, as I understand it, his small size woodcuts for Shakespeare's "King Lear" or for the "Sonnets" number among the really characteristic Shakespeare illustrations.

6. Noted Illustration Works

Still later after 1945, I can say that a bookpicture experience delighted three generations alike, mine as well as those of my children and grandchildren. What I have in mind are the pictures of texts for children and for world literature which we owe to Werner Klemke, illustrations with a knack and ideas, by no means cheap jokes, illustrations reflecting liveliness and producing cheerfulness. This floating, this optimistic superiority, that is what this master has introduced into the illustration scene of these days, and to which he has even contributed by his manifold works considerably. In those difficult years of the new beginning after the Second World War this graphic enterprise was anything but obvious, it was something new. Therefore, I consider Werner Klemke's illustration work in its entirety a great, praiseworthy achievement.

On reconsidering this point I realize that in my pre-Klemke life it had again and again been the black-and-white art of wood-engraving, woodcut, or as lithography which attracted me in particular. This is perhaps not accidental at all for the lover of the black-and-white art of typography, who has conquered the world of pictures from below, what is within reach, and not from above, from the deluxe edition.

Not that I overlook the illustrations of Max Slevogt who did not create them primarily for children but for lovers of books and art, I respected them as important creations, but their overflowing vitality and impressionist their colourfulness far too richly got up aroused at the same time my suspicion, with reference to the book illustrations, and surely not painting. These expensive editions with full-page, isolated illustrations were considered "bibliophile" — so were they advertised and recorded at least for which reason they were unattainable for the majority of the people as personal property.

7. Significance of Book Illustrations

But all these are subjective experiences, individual impressions, may be they cannot be reconstructed by everybody in the same way or in a like manner. With this awareness let me further explain quite briefly in the form of these some objective circumstances to show that the book illustration has its significance — probably by undeniable facts, as it were.

The book illustration is the most democratic art form. I hate cliche expressions — much is recommended as democratic — but to make ourselves understood briefly, we cannot do without cliches sometimes. This formulation will undoubtedly imply: the illustration in the book is an encounter with art in connection with the adoption of literature. Illustration and work offer themselves for a comparison. It is art for many, also for those who so far have not yet endeavoured to recognize art immediately. The picture in the book opens the eye. By frequent repetition of looking at pictures it can become the school of seeing which enriches life.

Will you please also bear in mind the unobtrusiveness with which the book illustration approaches the text of the author: the illustrating artist's point of view is only interspersed as one of those possible, and punctually presented. In contrast to this, take the brutality with which a linguistic work of art is filmed, e.g. an important novel, and the fact that I am forced to regard the *Chartreuse de Parma* or *Anna Karenina* in accordance with the will of the director, without any initiative of my own.

8. Some More Advantages

Moreover, encounters with art in the book have the advantage of being easily practicable and repeatable *ad libitum*. They are stimulating and useful because they can provoke approval or contradiction, but they are present, within easy reach, if you have books of your own, or else available in a library.

Book illustrations have preserved much of our cultural heritage and of the foreign cultural heritage too which sometimes has been lost due to loss of the original copy.

But I see the most important role of the book illustration in the following: pictures in books have preserved both the macrocosm and the microcosm of the human life of old times and give evidence of our present world of illustrations for future generations. Since their spread they have accompanied long periods of the history of human society simply through their existence, namely, as relevant information, as committed message, as satire or as palliation of reality.

Exactly to the same effect Walter Crane once expressed himself like this: if painting is the mirror of peoples and times, the illustrated book can be called the hand mirror. It describes the life of the peoples throughout the different centuries more precisely, all little and everyday details and domestic peculiarities as well as their dreams, phantasies and ideals.

The book illustration is said to describe "more precisely", more immediately and more closely far into everyday life. Hence in greater variety and more convincingly than all the other art forms do. So far these are the objective findings with due brevity.

9. Conclusion

To conclude, in addition to all objective circumstances, important as they are for society, the illustration in the book, however is the pledge of a treasure which the individual human being susceptible to the picture (which everybody can become stores up throughout his lifetime. It urges him to do brave and just deeds for the peaceful co-existence of nations, just as it also stimulates his quiet reflection on himself and the world, a unique, most personal treasure which accompanies him all his life to pass away with him some day. But at the same moment new cycles begin, a new enrichment by pictures of young creatures — as long as books with illustrations exist. May this continue to be so for some time yet !

REFERENCES

1 Retranslation giving the general sense of a passage on p. 2 of the German translation of C. Crane, Von Der dekorativen Illustration des Buches in alter und neuer Zeit. Vortrage und Aufsatze. Aus d. Engl. v. L. u. K. Burger. 2. Aufl. — Leipzig: Seemann 1901.

2 The paper is based on the "Kaula Endowment Lecture"/delivered in Berlin on November 26, 1986.

M 1

Dewey Decimal Classification: International and Indian Aspects

John P Comaromi and **Mohinder Partap Satija**

> Dewey belongs to all; it escaped from Amherst nearly a century ago. It has crossed oceans and penetrated continents and cannot afford to be restrained as an isolationist within the heart of the Midwest.
>
> —*Joel C Downing*

1. The Opportunity for Growth

The classification system that Dewey created primordially had a simple and immediately practical aim of arranging the library of the Amherst College. The system was beautifully simple and produced magic result when applied. Moreover the scheme came at a time when it had no rival. The time was opportune as the number of libraries were growing. Then existing libraries were introducing open access which requires an arrangement helpful for browsing through the book stacks. On the dint of its intrinsic merits and egged on by circumstances the success of DDC was almost instantaneous, despite the fact that Melvil Dewey never personally did anything for its direct publicity. A few initial opponents (in fact disbelievers) of the scheme were prophetically foretold by Lloyd P Smith at the historic Philadelphia Conference (1876) that "the system of our brilliant and indefatigable Secretary (Melvil Dewey, of the then newly founded ALA) is one we shall have to come in the end". The system was increasingly adopted throughout the country; and soon thereafter its fame fanned across the borders of the United States. Rapid succession of early editions hold mirror to its increasing use: 2nd (1885), 3rd (1888), 4th, (1891), 5th (1894); and the

6th (1899) came out only 14 years after the second (1885), the edition from which the modern classification is said to begin. Arthur Fremont Rider estimates that "As far back in 1927 it was installed in 96% of all public libraries in the United States and in 89% of all its college and university libraries as well".[2] The recent (1975) Survey of the Use of DDC in North America by John P Comaromi and his team confirmed the continued popularity with as much as 85.4% high use of the scheme despite the stiff competition given by the Library of Congress Classification Scheme. Public, school and college libraries constitute the majority of its users.[3]

2. Use in UK

Surely such an efficacious tool could not remain confined to a single nation. Its use soon spanned across. Since then there has been no looking back and its use has always registered a spiking graph. The scheme was introduced in Great Britain in October 1877 at the time of another historic conference of librarians in London. (The Library Association (UK) was also founded at this occasion.) The superiority of Dewey's system over British Museum's classification was admitted by a few speakers who had used DDC and readily became its adherents. It soon became popular there too—thanks to the pioneering efforts of Louis Stanley Jast. A survey of the use of the system made by W C Berwick Sayers[4] in 1910 affirmed that more than half the classified libraries in Great Britain used the DDC. Volunteered and sponsored surveys have been undertaken from time to time. Professor W Boyd Rayward[5] on the two such surveys writes that "Surveys conducted in Great Britain in 1965 and 1972 found that a major proportion of the nation's libraries, especially public libraries, used DDC, and the number of public libraries using the classification had increased considerably in the period between the two surveys". And the extent of the use of DDC in the UK and the other countries has also been concisely described by K G B Bakewell.[6]

3. Introduced in India

In India the DDC was introduced in 1915 by a famous American librarian and writer Asa Don Dickinson (1876–1960), an inspired student of Melvil Dewey. Its use in India became widespread with the adoption of the scheme by the Imperial (now National) Library at Calcutta. Now India is the largest user of the scheme in the orient,[7] despite the fact that S R Ranganathan (1892–1972), a great Indian librarian, designed a world-famous scheme of his own. Now as per Dr P Dhyani's published doctoral thesis (1983),[8] the DDC is used in more than 50% (127/251) of the Indian libraries. This is despite the fact that the sample was based on Delhi and Rajasthan regions, whereas Delhi is a traditional stronghold of the Colon Classification. An all-India sample will produce far more rosier picture for the DDC. Story of the early spread of the system in the UK, Australia and Europe has been narrated with humane details and scientific argument by W Boyd Rayward.[9] He concludes that "the diffusion of the Decimal Classification internationally falls into two relatively distinct periods: the first, involving the Anglo-Saxon countries, began towards the end of the 19th century; the second involving Europe and other parts of the world, began after the Second World War.[10]

4. Worldwide Use

Melvil Dewey "puck-like put a girdle round the earth with his damned dots . . . and with his library methods were carried from Albany to Antipodes", to reiterate Ernest A Savage's most quoted lines.[11] In his 80th birthday letter (1931) addressed to a few select friends Melvil Dewey claimed its use by 14,000 users in 20 nations. In her worldwide survey of 1964 Sarah K Vann estimated its use in about 100 countries in all the continents. Now it is used in 135 countries of the world. Forest Press, its publisher, reports of its ever increasing foreign sales. Twentyfive per cent of the copies of DDC-16 were sold outside the USA, while in the case of DDC-17 this figure soared to 33% then highest of all the times. And in the case of DDC-18 it was approximately 40 per cent. In an analysis completed in 1987 it was estimated that 57% of the sale of the unabridged DDC-19 were made to the purchasers outside the USA. About 50,000 sets of the DDC-19 have been sold so far. Peter J Paulson, Executive Director of Forest Press, has observed that.

> In recent years overseas sales accounted for nearly half of the sales of the English-language editions of Dewey. These new figures show that our international sales are stronger than ever.[12]

4.1 *Shift to LC Halted*

The DDC at present is the most widely American scheme used abroad. It is the fourth edition (1891) that was the first edition used widely abroad. It is still attracting users mainly due to its many shining virtues. Most of the newly sprung up libraries lean upon it for arranging their collection despite the tough competition thrown by the specialized subject schemes and the ultra-modern indexing methods easily amenable to computers. The shortlived trend of the 1960s of flight from DDC to LC has practically vanished. This episode in the history of classification has reaffirmed the abiding merits of the DDC. Its strong and highly publicized criticism does not deter many of its prospective users — they are inured to it since childhood.

5. Use in Bibliographical Works

Many bibliographic services, trade bibliographies and centralized cataloguing agencies and MARC programmes use the system to organize their bibliographic wares. Prominent among such users are: *Booklist* (American Library Association); *Publisher's Weekly* (R R Bowker); *American Book Publishing Record* (R R Bowker); *Book Review Digest, British Book News* (British Council); and the annual *Indian Book in Print* 1969 –. Cataloguing-in-Publication (CIP) data of LC and the British Library also give Dewey class number. Therefore, the Dewey class numbers also appear on the MARC tapes of various national and international agencies. The LC catalogue card service and the H W Wilson catalogue cards also carry the DDC numbers. *Sear's List of Subject Headings* also give broader DDC numbers corresponding to each of the used subject heading.

A fateful and highly contagious decision of the *British National Bibliography* to use DDC 14th edition for arranging its entries strengthened its wings for soaring flights. Consequently many other national bibliographies such as *Indian National Bibliography, Australian National Bibliography, Sri Lanka National Bibliography* and the *Canadiana* used the DDC. National bibliographies of the following countries also use DDC: Iceland, Italy, Norway, Argentina, Brazil, Denmark, Ethopia, France, Greece, Iran, Ivory Coast, Turkey, Fiji, New Zealand, Papua-New Guinea, Singapore, Malaysia, Kenya, Rhodesia, Sierra Leone, South Africa, Tanzania, Zambia, Swaziland, Botswana, Nigeria, Gambia, Cyprus, Barbados, Guyana, Jamaica,

Trinidad and the Caribbean countries.[13] The story of the march of the DDC throughout the world has been told by Comaromi (1976),[14] Batty (1976)[15] and now in much detail by W Boyd Rayward (1981, 1983).[16]

5.1 *Obligation to International Community of Users*

The international usage of DDC has placed its governing bodies under an obligation to make DDC come true to the expectations of its large and varied international community of users. This task has been made enormously difficult as well as sensitive by the historical fact that the DDC when conceived in 1873 was not shaped for its international role that the circumstances have placed over it.

6. Evident American Bias

It is common knowledge that the scheme is biased towards American culture and knowledge. In today's fashion of acronyms it is described as WASPISH (White, Anglo-Saxon, Protestant) bias. This WASPISH bias is more a natural outcome than any calculated one. Some reasons are also historical. US libraries in the 19th century, unlike today, were not procuring material from the outside world. Majority of the books on American library shelves were the product of the native brains mostly on indigenous topics and problems. Since this essentially pragmatic scheme is principally based on literary warrant, so it is no wonder that the non-American subjects have not got adequate, not even due representation on the DDC schedules.

7. Unauthorized Expansions and Alterations

Once the scheme was adopted all the world over, the libraries outside America, not only in Asia and Africa, but in Europe too, began to realize the meager treatment given to the subjects of their central concern. Most of the non-western subjects have been poorly represented. Many a foreign culture and their elements get no better treatment than a mere name. And many not a mention even. Such a handicap is not peculiar to the DDC. This argument is amply illustrated by the demonstrated fact of the inadequacy of the LCC to classify Chinese material[17] and the fact that LCC is quite modified in Nigeria, where it is otherwise most popular.[18] It is therefore a built-in flaw in every classification as "No classification in any field is value free" as has been aptly said by

Eric de Grolier.[19] A J N Judge[20] further goes on to say that classification is a political act meaning that politico-cultural bias naturally creeps in while designing classification schedules. Sarah K Vann's Survey[21] amply attested that a classification reflects the culture in which it was created. Zia-ud-din Sardar,[22] the wellknown Islamic philosopher, aptly sums up the matter that "any classification of knowledge can be influenced by the political and cultural philosophy of the individual(s) who first created the scheme". Therefore the DDC, like any other such classification, creates problems for foreign users — for the simple reason that it was primordially not created for them. Such librarians though dissatisfied with the DDC do not abandon the scheme for its numerous advantages unavailable from any other such system. Nevertheless to meet their local needs many librarian outside America devised unauthorized expansions and alterations; and have amply and adequately conveyed their genuine problems. This unhealthy trend became so rampant that it was once found that there was no library outside the USA using the scheme as such. Growth of unauthorized tinkering assumed alarming dimensions. It was a matter of serious concern which threatened to jeopardize the status of the system as a standard and international classification. This crisis urged the DDC authorities to seek an early and acceptable solution to the problems. At the first instance the DDC authorities have acknowledged the difficulties of the non-American users as genuine. And secondly many steps have been taken to assurage their feelings of being ignored.

8. Methods devised to Meet Limitations

To make it a square peg in a square hole, and to gear it up to efficiently discharge its international obligations, many methods both technical and organizational have been suggested and devised. The DDC authorities have adopted a very accommodating attitude, though they themselves are constrained by many structural limitations and ideological bindings. Nevertheless, John A Humphry,[23] a former Executive Director of Forest Press, made it clear that the "Forest Press accepts the idea of international Decimal Classification and will broaden the schedules to reflect this attitude". The DDC authorities earnestly endeavour to make it equally useful to the varied users of different cultures and nations by resorting to the following methods:

1 Expansion or introduction through revisions of hitherto inade-

quately provided non-American subjects;
2 Sponsoring international surveys and seminars;
3 Official translations;
4 Officially sponsored and recognized variations even through the use of artificial notation; and
5 Involvement of experts from different cultures in preparing and revising schedules.

8.1 *Expansion of Inadequate Local Topics and Enumeration of Hitherto Unprovided Subjects*

The editors of the DDC, apprised as they are of the cultural bias in the scheme, provide for more African and Asian subjects in every revision. Some expansions and fresh additions are a part of normal revision routine. But since the 16th edition extra efforts have been made to provide for such subjects on a larger scale. The 17th edition[24] made "the first full-scale attack" on the WASPISH bias by systematically enumerating subjects exotic to Americans. It has been done without "reducing the traditional emphasis on and featuring of subjects American. . . . " It simply means that needs of the American libraries are their primary concern. Benjamin A Custer[25] made it clear in unmistakable terms: "In preparing an edition it is desirable to allow positively for the needs, both in details and in order, of countries outside the US. Where there is conflict between these needs and those of the US the Editor should give his preference to the needs of the US, but must make provisions for an alternative use by libraries outside the US in a manner appropriate to the particular problem". A cursory survey of the provision of Indic subjects, as an example, in various recent editions will illustrate our point. For example, nine subdivisions at 181.4 Indian philosophy in the 16th edition were expanded to 16 in the 17th. Similarly subdivisions of 295.4. Hinduism in the 16th edition were expanded three times in the 17th. The 19th edition incorporated more subdivisions with a major relocation of Sikh religion from 294.553 to 294.6, making it amenable to addition of a facet. Similarly, many more such provisions for other Asian and African subjects can be detailed. In this way revision process comes handy to incorporate the hitherto unprovided subjects and to gradually lessen the WASPISH bias.

8.2 *Sponsoring International Surveys and Seminars*

To get a reliable feedback and consequently make a true assessment of the needs of the users many surveys of the "use and misuse", as Custer puts it, of the DDC have been conducted throughout the world. These surveys both sponsored and volunteered among others include: Dr John P Comaromi[26] and his team in the USA and Canada (1976); Keith Davison (1966), Russell Sweeny (1973) and K G B Bakewell (1977) all in UK; and Sarah K Vann and Pauline E Seely in Asia, Africa and Middle East (1964). Smaller surveys conducted as academic exercises may be many more. Vann's (1964) survey is of special interest to us. Known as "Field survey of the Dewey Decimal Classification use abroad" (Albany, N Y: Forest Press, 1965), the survey, though conceived in 1959, could only be conducted in 1964. The purpose of the survey was "to make the classification more useful to the libraries where it has been adopted". The survey was financially sponsored by the Asia Foundation, Council of Library Resources, Inc., Forest Press, the Library of Congress and the Editorial Policy Committee of the Dewey Decimal Classification. The countries visited were: Southeast Asia, West Asia (the Middle East), and Africa included Taiwan, Hongkong, Korea, Japan, India, Pakistan, Sri Lanka, Iran Iraq, Thailand, Malaysia, Singapore, Vietnam, Indonesia and the Philippines. For this purpose, the principal investigator Sarah K Vann herself visited India. She met many libraries throughout the country; visited libraries using the DDC; attended specially convened seminars and conferences to apprise herself and discuss the problems being faced in India by the DDC users. She endeavoured to find out the extent of the use of the DDC; and how it was used and what modifications have been made or were necessary for effective use of the scheme in India. She got enthusiastic response from individuals as well as corporate bodies of librarians in India. The Indian Library Association convened an emergency meeting of its Executive Council on September 17th 1964, with Sardar Sohan Singh, then its President, in the chair. Many important decisions were taken including the one to provide Miss Vann with a bibliography of six items of adaptations and home-made extensions of the DDC in use at that time in India. A brief note was prepared to this effect mentioning especially the persistent work of S K Mukherjee and the verbal extensions made by the monthly *Indian National Bibliography* (1958+). Miss Vann was also briefed about the areas lacking details for Indian subjects. She was also invited to attend the Third All India Seminar of the Indian Association of Special Libraries and Information Centres (Iaslic) held at Lucknow in October, 1964. In the following December (1964) seminar discussions were organized at the National Library, Calcutta. Recurring motif was the inadequacy of the DDC to effectively classify Indian subjects. Miss Vann gained intimate knowledge of the problem. It was made clear that it would not be possible to incorporate the suggested even needed changes. Anyhow the DDC authorities amassed a huge fund of data for the future expansion of the relevant portion when required.[27]

Influence of Vann's survey on the succeeding editions, namely, the 17th and 18th was obvious. These expansions are not less due to the survey recommendation than the usual dose of expansions in every normal revision.

8.3 *Official Translations*

The DDC uses pure Indo-Arabic numerals as notation, which serve more or less as an international language transcending all barriers of culture; and has always been a greatly favourable factor to outspread the scheme. 510 is mathematics in China as well as in Greek irrespective of the fact what it is termed in vernacular language. On this account the DDC has been projected as an international language and for this there has been less difficulty in applying the scheme in the non-English speaking countries. Nevertheless, the DDC has been translated into various languages to remove any linguistic barrier whatsoever there exists; to make the non-English users feel one with the DDC; and above all to incorporate expansions suitable for that linguistic group. So far it has been translated into about 35 languages of the world including Afrikaans, Japanese, Korean, Thai, German, Norwegian, Hebrew, Turkish, Malayan, Vietnamese, Sinhala, Spanish (1955), French (1974), Hindi (1976) and Arabic (1985). Italian translation is in active preparation. It is worth noting that these language editions are not mere translations. Some of the subjects belonging to that culture are enormously detailed out by the decimal fraction device while the base number remains that of the basic schedule. These translations are biased or culture-oriented at best. Translations usually make use of the official policy guidelines of variations from recommended practice to provide in-depth enumeration for subjects of the culture concerned. Of this John A Humphry[28] writes that "If a needed topic cannot be accommodated in the basic edition then the appropriate foreign language editions must provide for these developments carried out frequently through translations, expansions and adaptations".

Apart from language translations there also exist some other versions in English itself to make the DDC more useful to the users outside America. Utility and popularity of the abridged DDC, now in its 11th edition, is well established. Another such work in point is the *Introduc to DDC for British Schools*, 1961,[29] a joint collaboration of the School Library Association (UK) and the Forest Press. The usefulness of the edition can be gauged from the fact that it fourth edition designated as international edition is now available. Occasionally a demand has been raised to write the "Editor's Introduction" in a simplified language for the users for whom the English is the second or only the official language.[30] May be someday this not ingenuine demand is met in some way. As another such measure Melvil Dewey's passionately loved and zealously advocated simplified spellings have been gradually reduced at the altar of internationalization in the 19th edition there is hardly any relic of them. All these translations and different versions simultaneously play a multipurpose role to make the scheme popular and useful to the library and information workers all the world over.

8.4 *Officially Recognized Variations and the Use of Artificial Notation*

Official translations and some self-made extensions also make use of the officially recommended policy of using artificial notation and mutual migration of class numbers. Use of these techniques to give prominence and make a detailed enumeration with a brief notation of some local but sparsely enumerated subjects is too well known. As per the official recommendation a class number for any topic requiring detailed enumeration can be mutually exchanged with the corresponding western subject with a long span of notation. For example, a library specializing in Urdu literature may use 810 for Urdu literature, while American literature may be transferred to 891.439 basically meant for Urdu. Similarly a library specializing in Buddhism may use 201-209, 220-280 for subdivisions of Buddhism, while Christianity may be shifted to the class number 294.3 meant for Buddhism. This technique has been used in the Hindi Dewey (1976) by P N Gour.[31] Ample space provided by this mutual migration is obvious. C D Batty[32] terms it as a "revision with a vengeance".

Alternative method is to use artificial notation to give prominence to such subjects. According to this technique a library specializing in Hindi literature may use 8HO as the base number for Hindi literature purported to be filed before 810. Similarly 4HO can be used for Hindi

Language instead of 491.43. Accordingly Hindi grammar will be 4H5 instead of 491.435: brevity in class number and space for further detailed enumeration is strikingly obvious. Dr Panday S K Sharma[33] has availed himself of this technique to expand DDC-19 for some Indian subjects. These variations though officially sanctioned are endorsed half-heartedly as a counsel of despair. It is also warned that such changes however apt and useful bring in their own problems sometimes quite bristling. Indulgence in them may sometimes make a bad position worse and put the readers in a vicious trap and throw them out of the mainstream ultimately. Anyhow, the disadvantages of such options have been fully discussed more than once in our literature.[34]

8.5 *Involvement of More Experts from Different Nations*

Recently the representation on the Editorial Policy Committee (DCEPC) has been widened to make way for British expertise. Canada already plays a sizeable role on this decision-making body. Even sometimes the Chairperson of the DCEPC is from Canada. There are Dewey Decimal Classification subcommittees in Britain and Australia to meet the DCEPC needs. These subcommittees inturn make their constant contact with the users. Surveys and opinion polls are occasionally conducted on the proposed changes. Editors and publishers of DDC also visit other countries to supervise the preparation of language editions and thrash out other problems. For example, the new Area number for -41 and its detailed subdivision of DDC-19 and the phoenix schedule for 780 music have also been prepared by the British experts. The DDC has thus opened its windows to a wide range of opinions. So far the developing nations have no representation on this committee though their views made directly or voiced through literature are fully documented and studied. It is hoped that these nations will be given due representation on the decision making body, and provided a forum to be heard and consequently make direct contribution towards the development of the scheme. This increased and varied representation paves the way for provision of neglected subjects. These organizational methods though slow are quite effective and deep rooted-spirit of institutionalism is always conservative.

These are some of the methods through which the scheme fastens its hold over the international community of users. It also checks the epidemic of unauthorized expansions to keep it intact as a standard tool for universal classification.

9. DDC and India

The DDC was introduced in India in 1915 by Asa Don Dickinson (1876–1960), a famous American Librarian, who was appointed the Librarian of Punjab University of undivided India at Lahore. He also started a junior level library training school. It was Dickinson who proved instrumental in spreading DDC throughout the Indian subcontinent. In 1931 Dickinson, when back home, wrote for a Festschrift presented to Melvil Dewey that "Fifteen years ago it was my privilege to introduce the DC to the sub-continent of India and as one of my students of 1915-16, (K M Asadullah) has recently been appointed librarian of their 'LC', the Imperial Library of Calcutta, I look forward to the adoption of the DC by many Indian libraries, as these become completely organized". His hopes proved quite true. the DDC spread throughout the country very soon, and became an integral part of the syllabi of every library school. Therefore, its use spread. Another American equally instrumental in popularizing the DDC had been William Alanson Borden (1853–1931) who like Asa Don Dickinson was a direct student of Melvil Dewey. Borden was in India from 1910–1913 to direct the library developmental work of the then princely State of Baroda. Borden being aware of the limitations of the DDC for Indian subjects suggested some way out of this impasse.

9.1 *Use in Bibliographical Works*

Though India has a world-renowned classification scheme of her own Colon Classification – the DDC is still the most widely used scheme in this country. Not only this, as revealed in Sarah K Vann's survey: "Dewey Abroad", India is the largest user of the DDC in the Orient out of the total 150 universities in India, an estimated 100 university libraries are using this scheme; in college libraries its use is sweeping and in public libraries its use is universal. It is the scheme employed by India's National Library (at Calcutta) and the *Indian National Bibliography*. Many bibliographies such as *Indian Books in Print*. Bibliographies of English Books published in India (BEPI) have now ceased to use DDC for arranging bibliographical entries. The local accession lists using the DDC are numerous. Apart from its well-adaptive and practical use, the DDC is taught in all the library schools. Detailed introduction to the principles of the scheme and all its number building techniques are an invariable part of all the 65 library schools in India offering Bachelor of Library Science, besides many junior level library science courses.

9.2 *Inadequate in Indian Subjects*

It goes without saying that the DDC scheme coming from an alien culture poses some problems on the Indian Soil for classifying Indian subjects as would any other foreign classification do. From the very beginning it was found *inadequate in respect of Indian subjects*. It is rather interesting to note that no sooner the DDC landed on the Indian subcontinent than amendments were made in it as if to acclimatize it to the Indian environment. From time to time Indian librarians have articulated their difficulties and dissatisfaction with the scheme. As back as 1935 in an All Indian Library Conference, it was decided to make the necessary adaptations in the DDC to suit Indian needs — though nothing materialized. These complaints and criticisms and adapted schedules form a good literary warrant in the form of individual articles, national conferences, amendments made and used, published or otherwise, theoretical suggestions for adaptations, practical but not published. All this ultimately culminated in a Ph.D. thesis on the topic (published in 1979) and an official Hindi edition of the DDC in 1976 published by the Forest Press, as a part of centennial celebrations of the DDC.

9.3 *Hindi Version*

The Hindi DDC is an epoch-making work. It is based on the 18th edition of the DDC lated, adopted and abridged by P N Gour who is known *inter alia* for his work in English Hindi Library Science terminology. This work has been done under the immediate guidance of late Miss Pauline A Seely. This Hindi edition has made use of the official options to enumerate fairly and prominently the India subjects with sufficient details but with brief class numbers.[35] It is not a full translation of the 18th edition but an bridgement running to 701 pages only. To solve the local problems it fills Indian subjects meanings to the class numbers meant for Americans and Christian subjects. For example, section 353 has been given the meaning "Indian Central Government", similarly Hindi literature is transposed from 891.43 to 810 giving ample space for further expansions. Indian Philosophy has been enormously expanded to three pages of schedule (pp. 171–173), with total entries numbering 64. The schedule of India Religions has been expanded to more than 10 pages (pp.185-195)-further ample expansions are obvious. The principle of literary warrant has been made use of to give brief class numbers to Indian subjects.

It is evident that the Hindi edition has removed many long-standing and often voiced complaints of the Indian librarians. It endeavours to skilfully solve some of the chronic problems. The wealth of details for Indian subjects is quite satisfactory in this adapted general scheme. In addition to the Indian subject *per se* "Relevant numbers in other subjects bearing in India have been added" (p. A.16 Hindi DDC). The printing of the translation is bilingual (Hindi-English) "to help other languages speaking librarians in India", writes P N Gour in the Preface. It is Indian as well as official — an authentic work.

9.4 *Presentation to Kaula*

We take great pleasure in presenting this flower for the colourful garland being presented to our beloved Prof P N Kaula, a very familiar figure on the International Library Scene and for whom classification theory and its teaching remains the first love.

REFERENCES

1 DOWNING, Joel C: Dewey Today: The British and European Scene. (In: *Major Classification Systems: The Dewey Centennial*, ed by K L Henderson, Ubran-Campaign, Ill; University of Illionis, 1976. p 74).

2 RIDER, Arthur Fremont: The Story of DC, 1876—1951. (In: *The Catalogue and Cataloguing*, ed by Arthur Ray Rowland, London, Crossby Lockwood. 1969, p 290).

3 COMAROMI, John P, MICHAEL, Marry Ellen, and BLOOM, Janet: *Survey of the Use of the Dewey Decimal Classificatiron in the United States and Canada*. Albany, N Y; Forest Press, 1975.

4 SAYERS, W C B: Dewey Decimal Classification After Thirty Years. (*Library Association Record*, Vol 12, 1910, p 330).

5 RAYWARD, Boyd W: Early Diffusion Abroad of the Dewey Decimal Classification: Great Britain, Australia, Europe. (In: *Melvil Dewey: The Man and the Classification*, ed by Gordon Stevenson and Judith Kramer-Greene. Albany, N Y; Forest Press, p 149).

6 BAKEWELL, K G B: Classification and Indexing Practice. London; Clive Bingley. 1977, pp 15-16, 34-36.

7 VANN, Sarah K: Dewey Abroas: The Field Survey of 1964: (*Library Resources and Technical Services* Vol 11, (Winter 1967, p 64).

8 DHYANI, Pushpa: *Classification Schemes and Indian Libraries*. New Delhi;

Metropolitan, 1983. pp 47-48.
9 RAYWARD, W Boyd: op. cit., pp 149-173.
10 *Ibid.*, p 169.
11 SAVAGE, Ernest A: *Manual of Book Classification and Display*. London; George Allen, 1949, p 67.
12 *Library Times International* Vol 3 (6), May 1987, p 91.
13 DOWNING, Joel C: Commonwealth National Bibliographies: Classification Practices. (*International Cataloguing* Vol 11 (13), July/Sept 1982, pp 26-27. (Also in *DC & 4* (3), Winter 1983, pp 17-19).
14 COMAROMI, John P: *Eighteen Editions of the Dewey Decimal Classification*. Albany, N Y; Forest Press, 1976. pp 349-351.
15 BATTY, C D: Dewey Abroad: The International Use of the Dewey Decimal Classification. (*Quarterly Journal of the Library of Congress* Vol 33, 1976, pp 300-310).
16 RAYWARD, W Boyd: op. cit., pp 149-173.
17 LEE, C F: Comparative Study of the Three Popular Chinese Book Classification Schemes. (in Chinese). (*Journal of Hong Kong Library Assoication*, Vol 9, 1985, pp 81-94).
18 ORIMOLOYE, S A: Lagos University Modifications to the Library of Congress Classification. (*Nigerian Libraries* Vol 8(1), April 1972, pp 45-50).
19 GROLIER, Eric de: Classification One Hundred Years After Dewey. (*Unesco Bulletin for Libraries*, Vol 30(6), 1976, pp 326-327).
20 JUDGE, A J N: Functional Classification. (*International Classification* Vol 11(3), 1984, p 145).
21 VANN, Sarah K: op. cit., p 67.
22 ZIA-UD-DIN, Sardar: Islam Outline of Classification Scheme. London; Clive Bingley, 1979, p 16.
23 HUMPHRY, John A: Decimal Classification and Its International Commitments. (In: *Dewey International* ed by Joel C Downing and M Yelland, London; Library Association, 1977, p 13).
24 DEWEY, Melvil: *Dewey Decimal Classification and Relative Index*. Ed 17, edited by Benjamin A Custer. Albany, N Y; Forest Press, 1965, Vol 1, p 55. (Sec 5.4).
25 CUSTER, Benjamin A: The Responsiveness of Recent Editions of the Dewey Decimal Classification to the Needs of Its Users. (In: *General Classification systems in a changing world*. The Hague; FID/CR, 1976. p 84.
26 COMAROMI, John P and Satija, M P: History of the Indianization of the Dewey Decimal Classification". [*Libri* Vol 33(1), March 1985, p 17].
27 SATIJA, M P: Internationalisations of the Dewey Decimal Classification". (*Libra* Vol 22/23, 1984/85, pp 22-23).
28 HUMPHRY, John A: op. cit., p 13.
29 SOUTH, Mary L, Ed: *Dewey Decimal Classification for School Libraries*. British and International Edition. Albany; Forest Press, 1986. ix, 179p.
30 MOSS, R: Dewey: The Neglected Introduction. (*International Classification*, Vol 8 (3), 1981, pp 139-144).
31 DEWEY, Melvil: Selective Hindi Dewey Decimal Classification; translated and adopted by Prabhu Naryan Gour. Albany, N Y: Forest Press, 1976, 701 p
32 BATTY, C D: op. cit., p 307.

33 SHARMA, PANDEY, S K: *Depth Schedule: Indian Philosophy and Religions for Dewey Decimal Classification* (19). New Delhi; Ess Ess Publications, 1986.

34 COMAROMI, John P and SATIJA, M P: *Brevity of Notation in the Dewey Decimal Classification.* New Delhi; Metropolitan, 1983, pp 59-61.

35 Momeni, Mahvash Keshmiri: *Socio-Cultural Factors Affecting the Adaptations of the Dewey Decimal Classification in the Middle East.* (Ph D Thesis, University of Maryland, 1982, Supervisor: Professor Hans Wellisch) pp 124-188.

M 2

Colon Classification on the March : An Overview of Edition 7

P Soma Raju

0. Introduction

Dr S R Ranganathan, Father of Library Science, has made very significant and far-reaching contributions in the field of library and information science. He enunciated Five Laws of Library Science (1925), whose impact is all pervasive in theory and in practice. He left no stone unturned in the field of library science and revolutionized all the existing empirical and unscientific practices and provided a scientific theoretical base to guide the work in the field. His contributions are well accepted and his novel ideas are well acclaimed throughout the world and thus he has placed India on the world map of library and information science in a prestigious position.

1. Colon Classification Through Editions

The Colon Classification was first published in 1933. S R Ranganathan has revised this scheme six times in his lifetime. In each revision, he brought out several modifications, improving the facilities in number-building provisions, without changing the basic structure of the scheme. The Seventh Edition of Colon Classification has recently been brought out (1987) by his disciple Prof M A Gopinath who is well known for his contributions in the library classification. However, the basic framework for the present revision was given by the author himself in 1971.[1]

As in the case of earlier editions, the present edition is considerably modified, by including several new subjects, specializations, facets and isolates and special components in different basic subjects, making the scheme much more comprehensive to suit the present-day classificatory needs. As the universe of knowledge is dynamically continuum, a scheme of library classification should be revised from time to time incorporating all the newly developed subjects and isolates going along with them, at array and in chain, without changing the existing sequence. Otherwise, no scheme of library classification can survive for a long time. Therefore, the present revision of colon classification is a welcome feature for classifiers, learners and also for the successful survival of the scheme.

2. General Layout of the Scheme

The General layout of the Colon Classification Ed 7 is somewhat modified and the chapter division is as follows :

Part A : Introduction
Part B : Guidance to beginner
Part C : General rules
Part D : General divisions and Common Isolates
Part E : Special Isolates (Schedule of subjects)

A good feature of the present edition is that all these chapters run in a continuous pagination which facilitates users to locate any part of the schedule without much difficulty. In addition to a brief historical development of the scheme, it provides clear definitions of various pertinent terms that come in and need to understand in the field. The rules part provides a detailed working instructions, with examples for easy understanding for the working of the scheme. In addition to general rules, specific rules and instructions are also provided at the end of the each Basic Class (BC) and common isolate tables. This is a very helpful, feature for students to understand the given provision easily while classifying documents.

3. Schedule Structure

There are some modifications in the schedule of subjects and are discussed here under different headings:

3.1 *Traditional Main Subjects*

A schedule of Traditional Main Subjects (Main Classes) is provided in

Chaper DC and it is the same as it was in CCEd 6. They are altogether 26 Main Subjects and Roman Capitals are used to represent them. Besides, Δ is also used to represent the basic class Mysticism and Spiritual Experience.

However, some of the subjects are identified as Main subjects, but due to notation limitations in the Main subjects list, they were included in the schedule of Basic subjects are "non-Main Basic Subjects". Therefore, the connotation of "Main Subject" is not limited to Traditional Main Subjects list, but it also covers some of the non-Main Basic Subjects list included in the schedule of Basic subjects.

3.2 *Subject Bundles*

Some of the subject areas are of common interest to specialists working in different subject fields. They are interested to study such a subject from their specialization point of view.

For instance, Soil Science is considered as Subject Bundle. Physical scientists are interested to study the physical aspects of soil science, and Chemists are interested to study chemical aspects of soil science, and so on. Hence different specialists are interested and involved in the study of subjects like Soil Science, Ocean Science, etc. Documents dealing with such subjects are appearing in the field. Hence, there is every need to make provision for classification of those documents. A list of subject bundles identified is provided for the first time, in the present edition in Chaper: DF. They are as follows:

AC	= Surface Science	AP	= Ocean Science
AD	= Soil Science	AP4	= Deep Sea Science
AE	= Material Science	AR	= Atmosphere Science
AM	= Earth Science	AS	= Space Science
AN	= Hydro Science	AV	= Defence Science

3.3 *The Schedule of Basic Subjects*

The schedule of basic subjects is improved to a great extent in the present edition, incorporating several new subjects, specializations, that have cropped up on the horizon of universe of knowledge in the past few decades. Besides in some of the basic classes, speciators to a specific facet and special components are provided, for the first time in the schedule. This provides more facility to construct coextensive class numbers for micro-documents. A list of newly formed subjects is given in Appendix 1.

3.4 Canonical Divisions

As in colon classification Ed.6, all canonical divisions are shown in the present edition. Similarly, in some Basic Classes like G = Biology, E = Chemistry and Y = Sociology and X = Economics, basic class is further divided into sub-classes along with related isolated and a separate facet formula is provided at the beginning of the class, as in the case of canonical classes.

3.5 *Specials and Systems*

Systems and specials are provided in the Basic class L = Medicine. But in some cases, the systems are included as agglomeration to the Basic class. For instances in C = Physics, S = Psychology T = Education and X = Economics, such agglomeration classes are found.

3.6 *Speciators and Special Components*

Another new and good feature of the present edition of CC is that speciators are enumerated in some classes immediately at the end of concerned facet : For instance :

C	= Physics	= Speciator to 1P1
BYC	= Astrophysics.	= Speciator to 1M1
SY	= Social Psychology	= Speciator to 1P1
		= Speciator to 1M1
		= Speciator to 1E1

Similarly, in some classes, special components are provided to form a compound isolates. For instance, E = Chemistry, P = Linguistics, Z = Law, etc. Wherever warranted, it is possible to form compound isolates with special components.

4. Facet Analysis

Facet analysis is one of the chief contributions of Dr S R Ranganathan. Colon classification is analytico-synthetic scheme of library classification, in which it is necessary to analyse a given title into constituent parts and synthesize them in a given fashion using appropriate connecting symbols.

According to Ranganathan, facet formula is mental process. He postulated that each facet of a subject is the manifestation of one and only one of the five fundamental categories. (PMEST). Further, he stated that these five fundamental categories fall into the following sequence, when arranged according to their decreasing concreteness with corresponding connecting digits, P; M; E. S ’T.

In the present edition, there is some modification in the manifestation of Matter facet. It has been divided further as Matter Property, Matter Method and Matter Material. Comparative positions of Fundamental categories with changes are shown below for clarity:

Fundamental categories	Connecting digits	Symbols	
		Ed.6.	Ed.7.
Time	"	T	T
Space	.	S	S
Matter	;	M	-
Matter Property	;	-	MP
Matter Method	;	-	MM
Matter Material	;	-	MMt
Personality	,	P	P

As shown above, the matter facet has been further subdivided into Matter Property [MP], Matter Method [MM], and Matter Material [MMt]. The connecting symbol to be used in this case is semicolon (;) for all the matter facets. As per the new change, there will not be any matter facet and [E cum 2P] facet in the present revised edition of Colon Classification, and this new change should invariably be followed hereafter, while classifying documents as per this schedule.

5. **Indicator Digits**

There are number of indicator digits in Colon Classification. These indicator digits play a key role in any faceted scheme of classification. Such indicator digits show the nature of facet or isolate used and the type of relationship exists among them. The ordinal values of such indicator digits have also been fixed, to facilitate the sequential arrangement of documents on the shelf, with different class numbers. In the present edition, five more indicator digits have been introduced to represent a variety of concepts in the schedule.

The new indicator digits introduced in the present edition and the purpose for which they can be used are shown in the following table:

	ID		Purpose
1.	*	Astrick	To indicate agglomeration formation and interpolation
2.	"	Double inverted comma	To indicate Common Isolate facet.
3.	&	Ampersand	To indicate Phase relation.
4.	=	Equal sign	To indicate Speciator Kind 2.
5.	+	Plus	To indicate the second and latter part of the fraction of integral number or the second part of multinomial in AD.

6. Synthesizing Provisions

Dr Ranganathan has formulated a variety of synthesizing provisions in colon classification. It gives the facility to combine different concepts, to form a compound isolate. In the present edition some new provisions and modification in the existing provisions have been made and are discussed here, under different headings:

6.1 *Time Isolates*

As regards time isolates, there is no change from its earlier edition. The connecting digit (') is also the same as it was. Time 2 isolates are also provided in the schedule. There is a little change in the combination of Time isolates. Here a compound time isolate (CTI) can be formed by combining Time 1 with Time 2 isolates with a connecting digit [hyphen (-)] as a speciator. For example:

’N72 = 1972.
’N72-u = 1972 Rainy Season
’N72-23 = 1972 New Moon days
’N72-23-u = 1972 Rainy New Moon days

6.2 *Space Isolates*

In the present edition the space isolates improved considerably, incorporating several new concepts and in some cases changed the sequence of such isolates. Such a change, in fact, is necessary because of the modifications, that have been taking place in the political divisions around the globe in the past few decades. The connecting digit is the dot (.) to attach to any host class.

Besides, a schedule of special component isolates is also provided to form a compound space isolates (CSI). These special components can be attached to any space isolate to form a compound space isolate, if warranted, to bring any specific space concept in the class number. Here an equal sign (=) is to be used as connecting digit in between them. For example :

44	= India
44=9G	= South India
44=9G=03	= Towns of South India.

6.3 *Language Isolates*

The language isolates provided in the present edition are the same as in Edition 6. However, a schedule of special components is given to form compound language isolates (CLI). With this provision, special components can be attached to any language isolate to form a specific compound language isolate, if warranted in the classification of documents. Here the equal sign (=) is to be used as a connecting digit. For example :

35	=	Telugu language
35=a	=	Variants of Telugu
35=b	=	Telugu slang
35=d	=	Telugu dialects
152	=	Hindi language
152=xJ	=	Hindi dialects
152=xJ=d4411	=	Hindi dialects in modern Tamil Nadu

6.4 *Environment Isolates*

For the first time, a schedule of "Environment divisions" is provided in

C C Ed 7. This is like any other common isolate table applicable throughout the schedule. The environment concepts, whose use is warranted, are identified in different classes and put together in the environment table separately for the first time, in this edition. Whenever, the use of such environment isolates is warranted, while classifying documents, it can be attached to any host class by prefixing the digit '9' to the given isolate. Rules and working instructions are also provided in the schedule.

6.5 *Phase Relation*

Phase relation is a special and peculiar provision given in the Colon Classification right from the beginning. With this provision, it is possible to bring in relation two Basic classes, two facets in a Basic class and two isolates in a facet. Besides, it is also possible to indicate the type of relation that exists between them in the class number.

In the present edition, a new phase called "Tool Phase" is identified and included in the already existing list. In this Tool Phase, the isolate which is used/served as tool in the exposition of another isolate is treated as phase 2, in the formation of compound isolate. That is, phase 2 is always used to expose phase 1. The connecting digits for the tool phase are z, p, e respectively for the subject, facet and isolate levels.

Moreover, the connecting symbol to be used between phase 1 and phase 2 is also changed. Now it is ampersand (&) and not zero (0) as in the case of C C Ed 6. For example:

Relation between history and politics :

V &a W = C C Ed 7
V 0a W = C C Ed 6

7. Common Isolates

There is no substantial change in the anteriorizing common isolates table (ACI) in the present edition, except that a connecting symbol double inverted comma (") is to be put before attaching to any Host Class. However, there is a scope and use need to make a provision for a variety of forms of documents that are appearing in the documentary would to day.

Whereas, in the case of Posteriorizing common isolates (PCI), there is a lot of change and improvement. Three separate schedules of PCI isolates are provided — Common Energy Isolates (CEI), Common Matter Property Isolates (CMPI) and Common Personality Isolates (CPI) — in chapters DK, DL and DM in the present edition. The connecting digits for energy, matter property and personality isolates respectively are — : ; , and they can be attached to any Host Class.

8. Shortcomings in the Schedules

In this cursory study, some of the shortcomings are identified and are noted here, with an aim to bring to the notice of the publishers to rectify them in the next print to make the schedule much more perfect and lucid. They are as follows :

(1) In Colon Classification, the facet formula is generally provided at the beginning of each Basic class, indicating the type of facets that occur in the given class. Such facility is very useful for learners to understand the structure and to identify the given isolate concepts easily in the classification of documents. However, in the present edition, such facet formula is missing in some of the Basic Classes as shown hereunder :

E = Chemistry	Y = Sociology
G = Biology	X = Economic

It is but necessary to rectify this lapse in the next print to avoid any type of confusion for learners.

(2) There appears a confusion regarding the notation provided for the following subjects and it is of immediate necessity to avoid the discrepancy for the sake of users.

HV : is used to represent three concepts in the schedule.

HV = Geophysics
HV = Hydrology
HV = Oceanology

(3) Two notations are used to indicate a Basic subject as shown hereunder and it is of immediate need to clarify the confusion arisen, for the sake of users.

GWE = Biochemistry
GX = Biochemistry

(4) In the Basic class Y = Sociology, the facets [1MP1] and [1E1] isolates seem missing in the schedule, but references have been made to such facets. Besides, the facet formula to be given at the beginning of the class is also missing. Hence, it is necessary to clarify the discrepancy for the sake of users.

(5) Similarly, in Basic class V = History, [1P2] isolates are provided in the schedule, but not shown in the facet formula given at the beginning of the Basic Class.

Therefore, it is necessary to rectify the above lapses in the next print, to make the scheme much more perfect.

9. Suggestions

Colon Classification Edition 7, is much more superior to its Edition 6, in respect of improvement of new concepts in the schedule and new synthesize provisions introduced for the construction of class numbers for multifaceted documents. Another good feature of the present edition is that elaborate rules, working instructions, with examples, are provided not only in the rules part but also throughout the schedule wherever it is found necessary. It really helps learners and users to understand a given provision easily and to use such facility without much difficulty.

However, since it is a new and modified schedule, and it is expected to be used by all library schools in India, it is of immense help to organize a workshop for all teachers who are involved in the classification teaching to make them much more familiar and fully aware of potentialities of the present edition of Colon Classification.

Similarly, there appears a scope and need to improve ACI isolates incorporating several new relevant concepts for various forms of documents that are appearing today in the documentary world.

The space isolates table has been improved considerably in the present edition. However, it is desirable to provide numbers for all capital cities of all countries in the world. For instances the present edition does not provide numbers for the following cities :

1	Afghanistan	=	Kabul
2	Greece	=	Athens
3	Italy	=	Rome
4	Nepal	=	Khatmandu
5	Australia	=	Canberra
6	Philippines	=	Manila, etc.

REFERENCES

1 RANGANATHAN S R: Colon Classification, Ed 7: A Preview. (*Library Science*, Vol 6, 1969, Paper M).

2 RANGANATHAN S R: *Colon Classification*, Ed 7: ed by M A Gopinath, Bangalore Sarada Ranganathan Endowment for Library Science, 1987.

3 SOMA RAJU, P: Area Table of Dewey Decimal Classification, Ed 18: A Detailed Study. (*Herald of Library Science* (Dewey Commemoration Number), Vol 15, (3-4), (1976) pp 248-255).

4 SOMA RAJU, P: Dewey Decimal Classification, Ed 18: Standard Subdivisions : A detailed study. (*IASLIC Bulletin*, Vol 22(2), (1976), pp 68-76. (Paper presented in 7th IASLIC National Seminar at Burdwan in December).

APPENDIX 1

List of newly formed subjects given in C C Ed 7:

1	1	Universe of Knowledge
2	3	Book Science
3	4	Mass communication
4	8	Management
5	B4	Group theory
6	B6T	Topology
7	BT	Statistical Calculus
8	BTT	Operation Research
9	BV	Cybernatics
10	BYC	Astrophysics
11	C5C	Geometrical Optics
12	C6T2	Semiconductor Physics
13	C98Z	Microphysics
14	C98	Molecular Physics
15	C9E	Particle Physics
16	CV	Space Physics
17	E4	Synthetic Chemistry
18	FV	Foundry
19	FX	Welding
20	GT	Cytology
21	GV	Microbiology
22	GWC	Biophysics
23	GX	Biochemistry
24	HV	Geophysics
25	HV	Hydrology
26	HV7	Meteorology
27	HX	Astrophysics
28	NP	Furniture
29	NE	Plastic Arts
30	NM	Inlay Arts
31	PW1	Calligraphy
32	PW6	Typewriting
33	PW7	Short Hand
34	SY	Social Psychology
35	TUS	Educational Psychology

N 1

Union Catalogue for Arab Countries: Problems and Prospects

Anis Kurshid

0. Introduction

Holding a population of about 175.8 million over an area of 13,680,463 square km, the Arab countries stand sandwitched between the continents of Asia and Africa. The largest country in the region is Sudan (2,505,813 sq. km.) while the smallest country is Bahrain (622 sq. km.). The most populous country, on the other hand, is Egypt (44 million) while the smallest population is held by Qatar (250,000).

Politically the region represents an amalgum of monarchies, federated emirates, military, socialist and representative governments. The per capita national income, according to World Bank (1984), ranges from US $ 21,920 (UAE) to US $ 260 (Somalia). The world's high-income five oil exporters also belong to this region.

The literacy rate among the Arab countries varies from 80% in Kuwait to 5% in Somalia. The literate population in 10 countries ranges from 56% (Algeria, Jordon, Lebanon, Syria, Tunisia and UAE) to 40% (Bahrain, Egypt, Libya and Qatar). Between the range of 30% and 12% fall eight countries while Somalia ranks below 10% literary rate. Arabic is the national and official language in all countries in the region except in Djibouti and Mauritania where French is the official language; Somalia uses Somali and Arabic both as official languages. French and English are second languages which are largely spoken in the region. Other languages spoken in the area are Berber, Hussaya, Kurdak, Persian etc.

The statistics for book production available for 1981-82 for 13 countries of the region, register some 11,600 books and 1960 periodicals having been published in that year.[1] The largest book producing country in the region is Egypt (6,585). The number of periodicals published from that country (194) is, however, smaller to that of Tunisia (250). The smallest number of books are published respectively from Kuwait (25) and Qatar (8).

Despite the disparity in the Arab countries, the Arabic language, which is the language of the Quran and Islam, according to Abdullah Sharif,[2] binds them together. "The educational system in all States is almost the same with all States having national plans and policies that attempt to modernize their societies." Muhammad M. Aman and Sha'ban Khalifa[3] say ". . . the education budgets are second to defence budgets in many cases and if not for the Arab-Israeli conflict, education budgets would have been higher. The slogan . . . by Kuwaiti Government 'every thing for education and education for all' typifies what many of these countries feel".

1. Library Infrastructure

The expansion of education in the Arab countries has resulted in growth of libraries as well. Consequently, not only their number has increased but their services have also improved. According to a rough estimate,[4] there are some 21,126 libraries in the region which contain a collection of about 44 million volumes. These statistics are in no way complete but they help provide useful directions on the subject.

1.1 *National Libraries*

Yet, there are about eight countries in the region [Bahrain, Djibouti, Jordan, Kuwait, Oman, Sudan, UAE and Yemen (PDR)] which do have the institutions of national libraries in their countries. Four of these countries have made *ad hoc* arrangements with other libraries/centres/departments to perform some or all of the functions of a national library. All the Arab countries except Djibouti, Oman, UAE and both Yemens publish national bibliographies duly supported by legal deposit laws, mostly at annual intervals.[5] The largest national library is that of Egypt (1,500,000 vol.) while the smallest library is that of Somalia (9,000 vol.).

1.2 *University Libraries*

All the countries in the region except Djibouti have university libraries.

The largest number of university libraries (13) is in Egypt. In all, there are about 74 university libraries in the region possessing a collection of about 110.95 million volumes. The largest individual library collection is that of the Jamiat al-Malik Saud al-Maktaba al-Markazia, Riyadh in Saudi Arabia (founded 1957; coll: 1,123,200 vol.)[6] while the smallest collection is that of the Arabia Gulf University in Bahrain (10,000 vol.). The oldest library possessing the richest Arabic manuscript collection, not only in the region but also in the entire Muslim world,[7] is the library of Al-Azhar University holding a collection of 60,000 vol. and 20,000 manuscripts. The largest number of current periodicals, subscribed by individual libraries, ranges from 11,900 by the Jamiat al-Malik Saudi al-Maktaba al-Markazia, Riyadh in Saudi Arabia to 8,200 by the Library of Universite de Tunis in Tunisia 5,000 by the University of Khartoum Library in Sudan and the American University of Beirut Library in Lebanon.[8]

Most of these libraries despite their very impressive collections suffer from some inadequacies ranging from their failure to meet the needs of large number of students using them in some cases to the lack of consistency in collection development in still others.[9] These libraries, by and large, are also deficient in up to date literature in science and technology. "There does not exist," says M M Dayab "coordinated structure which could integrate the resources and services of these universities either at the state or interestate level." Muhammad M Aman and Sha'ban Khalifa[10] do not find these libraries as an "integrated part of educational process." The shortage of qualified librarians is yet another serious problem to which they draw attention.

2. Absence of a Coordinated Structure

The absence of coordination is also very much there in other types of libraries in the region. This is equally true even in one type of libraries. Even the constituent libraries of one university are no exception, to this. The various factors which hamper wholesome development in all the Arab countries, according to Sharif,[11] among others, include lack of national planning for library and information services, absence of library standards, and important of all, the non-existence of library association in many countries.

More than half of the countries, in the region, do not have any library association. There are thus only eight countries where library associations are actively participating in their countries' developmental programmes, such as in Jordon,[12] where the Jordon Library Association, since 1959, is engaged in compilation of the country's national bibliography.

The UNESCO Regional Seminar on Bibliography, Documentation and Exchange of Publications in Arabic-speaking countries, Beirut, Dec. 8-19, 1959, also made a recommendation[13] for the formation of a well-organized library association in each country in order "to promote the library movement and raise professional standards". The Seminar also recommended establishment of a federation of these associations as a regional body. Four of the existing library associations including the Jordan Library Association were established in the post-Seminar period perhaps as a result of the above recommendation but no federation has yet come up.

3. ALESCO's Role

The founding of the Arab League Educational Cultural and Scientific Organization (ALESCSO) in 1970 and with it the establishment of the Arab League Documentation Centre (ALDOC) in 1981,[14] however, has resulted in creating growing awareness towards the need for professionalization of library services in the region as a result of its various seminars and conferences held by it from time to time. Some useful cooperation in the Arabization of International Standard Bibliographic Description (ISBD) has thus resulted.

4. Resource Sharing

The collections in the region have developed, by and large, without a national library and even without a national library association in a number of countries, and hence, no attempt to develop and plan library book stocks collectively and maximize their use effectively. The bibliographical apparatus, where it exists, largely fails to maintain up to date and comprehensive control of national publications. A common communication format is yet to develop.

However, in the process of library expansion, certain developments have taken place in the region which may profitably be used for developing a model for collective resource sharing in the Arab countries. The remarkable development in the fields of telecommunication services and telephone services in the Gulf region particularly in Saudi Arabia and Kuwait, has resulted in the establishment of a computer-to-computer network (Gulfnet) between some academic and research libraries of Saudi Arabia and Kuwait.[15] Thus, a developmental stage has been attained in the Gulf region which may help guide building up an on-line bibliographic system between other countries of the region as well.

In Kuwait alone, on the other hand, many major developments are taking place simultaneosly. The development in the field of libraries has been quite significant. The Kuwait University Library, founded in 1966, has grown quite fast both in resources and services. The library holds a collection of 384,000 volumes and subscribes to some 3,243 periodicals. The Kuwait Institute of Scientific Research (KISR) is yet another organization which is playing an important role in the free flow of information in the region. So much so that K. Shearer[16] says, "it would be enlightened public policy for Kuwait to aggressively seek to become a Centre of Arabic librarianship, publishing and information technology".

The Saudi Arabian National Centre for Science and Technology (SANCST), Riyadh, in Saudi Arabia, is yet another organization which holds out great promise. Speaking of SANCST,[17] Maurice B. Line thus says, "Saudi Arabia could take a marvellous, quite possibly unique, opportunity to plan a really effective system from scratch. . . . With its resources, Saudi Arabia could provide a first-rate service not only to institutions and users in the country but to other Arab countries in the Middle East, which are not in a good position to develop a good system for themselves." He further says, "Saudi Arabia has [thus] exceptional opportunities to innovate. . . . Saudi Arabia could, if it took a sufficiently radical approach, provide a salutary example to other countries.[18]

The establishment of the Gulf Cooperation Council (GCC) has, at long last, resulted into a computer-based bibliographical networking, called Gulfnet, among seven university and research libraries of Saudi Arabia and the KISR of Kuwait. The Sultan Qaboos University Library in Oman[19] uses DOBIS/LIBIS software package for automation of its services. The Arabian Gulf University in Bahrain, supported by GCC, also offers "On-line data retrieval services, through DIALOG."[20] The Gulf region as such provides an excellent opportunity to set out a salutary example for others to follow, as rightly pointed out by line.[21]

5. The Problems

But the situation in other countries of the region is not yet ripe for traditional cooperation much less computer-based on-line sharing of resources and services. In Egypt, which possesses the largest book collection, not only in the region (about 14.5 million volumes) but also in the entire Muslim world, minimal facilities for inter-library loan services exist. "Libraries at the same university do not share library resources and no central processing exists.[22] Sharif[23] attributes absence of cooperation among libraries in all the Arab development in the region as one of the important factors inhibiting overall library development in the Arab world. Suhait Manzoor[24] complains of uncoordinated approach in academic libraries even in Iraq where union catalogue in a number of university libraries had produced good results. He therefore urges upon the central library in each university in the country to act as a focal point in knitting together the constituent libraries into "a cohesive system, with common procedures and services".

It would thus appear that the library developments in the Arab countries are not uniform and, hence, the resulting services are uneven and their resources are not fully exploited for use within the country itself much less in the region as a whole. In the Gulf region the advent of automation has opened library resources for wider sharing but a common communication format with local adaptations is yet to be evolved.[25]

Consequent to these inadequacies, the library resources in the region, limited as they are, rendered inaccessible to users of other libraries in a country itself, much less in the region. The research being done in the region is thus supported by inadequate research materials contained in the libraries to which access becomes available on chance basis because there is no central agency charged with the responsibility of making a country's entire resources accessible both bibliographically and physically. The libraries lack any interlinking. The religion of Islam and the language of the Quran however bind the Arab countries together in the region and with it the challenges faced by the *Muslim ummah* are almost the same. The research being done to meet these challenges all over the world also suffer from the inadequate availability of the resources of the region which remain largely latent because of their bibliographic inaccessibility on a large scale. The sources that are used for these researches are those which are compiled in the United Kingdom based on the Western language literature. The *Index Islamicus* which provides access to such literature is largely West-oriented as disclosed in a study made by Abdul Sattar and Sajjad ur Rehman.[26]

The absence of the availability of accumulated literature in the region is thus the biggest problem which renders a "cohesive system" most difficult to attain in the present situation. Inter-library loan becomes impractical; any planning of library stocks is rendered difficult and, hence, collective development of library resources in each country, to begin with, is not possible. Uniform methods for bibliographical control of Arabic language materials and uniform procedures and practices in keeping with the local needs of the region, necessary for any sharing, remain unrealized.

A union catalogue provides a useful mechanism consolidation, coordination and maximization of a country's library resource to the full advantage of the country's research and progress. But such a catalogue is almost non-existent in the region.

There is, therefore, an urgent need to establish a union catalogue in each country of the region, directed to the establishment of a total system for the region which the Arab League Documentation Centre (ALDOC) proposes to create in the form of ARIS-NET.

A common communication format therefore needs to be developed as a prerequisite for the establishment of a national union catalogue in the region.

An attempt is, therefore, made in the following pages to discuss the functions, purposes, kinds, forms, organization and structure of a union catalogue and to suggest, in the end, a workable model for the establishment of a union catalogue in each country of the region.

6. Meaning and Uses of Union Catalogue

A union catalogue has been variously defined by many writers each differing with the concept of its arrangement from the other. Knud Largen[27] recommends this workable definition in one of the UNESCO handbooks thus: "A union catalogue is a catalogue listing in one sequence the holdings of two or more libraries." This definition is also acceptable to L. Brummel.[28] Silvere Willemin,[29] however, defines it "as an inventory common to several libraries and containing all or some of their publications listed in one or more orders of arrangement". This definition, according to the author, "protects the unity of union catalogue while allowing for the possibility of their future development". This term is also sometimes used for Union List of Periodicals, such as the *British Union – Catalogue of Periodicals* published by Butterworths from London.

Larsen[30] speaks of two basic and essential elements — a national library and a national bibliography — which closely linked together help make and develop a country's cultural life. A national bibliographical centre, when established to publish a country's national bibliography, parallel to the development of a national library in that country, should be required to create a union catalogue with a view to maintaining any unity of development in the cultural life of the country. For, it is a union catalogue which helps provide reach-out services of not only the national library of a country but also of many of the research and academic libraries to users throughout the country which otherwise would have remained latent, and hence research in the country would not have benefited from the resulting accumulated bookstock of the country.

The other functions[31] of such a catalogue include bibliographical research, bibliographical information and library functions, such as unification of catalogues. To these functions, Brummel[32] adds, assistance in loan; coordination in book acquisition programme; and, use as a shadow catalogue for reconstruction of lost collections.

6.1 *Types of Union Catalogues*

A union catalogue can be established at the following levels :

(1) Local, such as in cities like, Tunis in Tunisia, Cairo in Egypt, etc;
(2) Divisional/provincial/governary at larger administrative division level;
(3) National at country level; and
(4) Regional or intergovernmental level, such as for Gulf Region or French-speaking countries as a group.

The local level catalogue is generally used for inter-library loan purposes in a public library system. Because of location of participating libraries in one city, such a catalogue does not create much problems in unification. It is also less expensive to maintain. The divisional catalogue, on a small scale, represents a national catalogue but its functions very according to the organizational structure of the catalogue whether it is part of a public library system or that of a national bibliographical system. The national catalogue is generally faced with the problems of growth and handling of inputs received from the participating libraries, on a much wider scale than that in the case of other two catalogues. The increase in cost and skilled manpower is also obvious. The problems of regional and international catalogue, for that matter, are manifold because of the increase in the number of cards to be handled and varied system of library operations in countries which participate in the union catalogue.

The catalogues at these levels are further divisible into general and speical types of union catalogues. A general catalogue includes publications of all subjects together whereas a speical catalogue contains its holdings according to subjects or types of literature, such as a union catalogue limited to science and technology, or just one subject, like economics, in the case of former and, limited to foreign literature, periodicals or manuscripts, in the latter case.

6.2 *Organizational Problems*

Selection of the type of literature for inclusion in a union catalogue is a matter on which different viewpoints exist. Larsen[33] is against inclusion of the literature produced in the country and with it the inclusion of the national library on the analogy that the existence of national literature in a national library is legally assured. Hence, location of such literature in a union catalogue is not necessary, according to him. Popular public libraries are very similar in their holding and the nature and quality of literature and, hence, Brummel[34] disputes their inclusion in a union catalogue at divisional/provincial and national levels. Its inclusion at local level is, however, justifiable, according to him.

Research libraries, whether large or small, and academic libraries, however, constitute a valid group for inclusion in a union catalogue. National libraries, insofar as their collections on foreign literature and reference materials are concerned and special libraries also need inclusion in it. But the most important point that needs consideration in this connection is the willingness of the libraries, selected for inclusion in a union catalogue, for making their collections available to users outside their libraries.

In regard to choice of literature for inclusion in a union catalogue Willemin[35] cautions against over ambitious planning for inclusion of everything in a union catalogue. In this connection, he refers to a survey made by UNESCO in 1952 which revealed that more than 30 countries limited their union catalogues to foreign literature and periodicals because of the high costs of books and periodicals. This was in 1952. The prices of these materials have received tremendous hike thereafter. The decision for selection of literature for inclusion should, therefore, be made keeping in view the bibliograhical situation and the specific research and development needs of the country itself. Periodicals, however, would need listing in a separate catalogue which should be produced in printed form for wider use.

The materials which are generally excluded from a union catalogue are school textbooks, popular treatises, children's literature and pamphlets. Other materials, such as gramophone records, microforms, tape recordings, incunabula and manuscripts, should be included in separate catalogues for each category of materials.

6.3 *Date of the Material*

The history of scholastic activities and books in the region goes back to a glorious and distant past but the attempts at replenishing the lost collections and consolidating them in a usable catalogue is a development of a recent origin. The union catalogue in the region should, therefore, be limited to a workable date so that such a catalogue could be established without any further loss of time. Efforts, however, should be made to catch up with the retrospective holdings in phases. The period fixed for the inclusion of publications in the catalogue should be strictly adhered to. The plans for the inclusion of retrospective literature should also be made simultaneously to enable their inclusion in phases later.

Prior to the establishment of a union catalogue, it should be ensured that the national libraries duly exist in the countries going for union catalogues or else, the national bibliographies do publish regularly in those countries and include national literature comprehensively and fully. The national bibliographies already being published but having gaps in their printed issues should make them up immediately on a planned basis. Retrospective bibliographies should equally be brought out in phased programmes where such bibliographies have not been published or planned for publication as yet.

6.4 *Size of Union Catalogue*

A union catalogue grows very fast but the staff that is made available for maintaining such a catalogue is not generally augmented to catch up with the growth of the catalogue. The staff always comes last.

An optimum size of such a growing catalogue is hard to indentify. The catalogue should need to be split up at some stage to meet the exigency of the growth. P Bourgeois[36] suggests division of the catalogue into periods of 50 years. J H P Pafford[36] recommends its splitting into special catalogues by subjects or types. Willemin,[37] however, wants the "problem of the size of the catalogue . . . to be mastered at all costs".

7. Authority

There are various practices in vogue for the organization of a union catalogue. It is either attached to a central or national library or functions independently as a separate bibliographical institution outside a library or within a library. There are instances where it is merged with the catalogue of a central library. Such could be the case in a university where a central library files cards of the departmental or constituent libraries of the university in its main catalogue.

It would be advantageous to house a union catalogue in the country's national library at the national level and in a divisional/provincial library or a designated library at the subordinate level, if a decentralized system exists, which enables it to collaborate closely with the housing library in terms of use of the library's bibliographical tools and technical expertise. But it should be independent of the library housing it and should occupy a spacious and distinct place in that library for its services and equipments necessary for performance of its functions.

The work of the union catalogue is of specialist nature and, therefore, needs sufficient organizational, administrative and technical know-how in the managerial staff. The size of the staff will depend on the size of the catalogue itself. A workable ratio between professional and non-professional staff would be around 1 professional: 1-1/2 non-professional staff.

8. Mechanics of a Union Catalogue

There are various methods which are used for arrangement of cards in a union catalogue. Among them are :

(1) Alphabetical arrangement by author and by title in the case

of works of more than three authors and annonymous works and by geographical names in the case of corporate authorship. These files are separately arranged.

(2) Systematic arrangement by classification schemes.

(3) Berghoffer system named after C W Berghoffer of West Germany which divides the files by name, geography and title.

In the Berghoffer system the name file arranges cards alphabetically by combining surname with title. The geographical file arranges corporate entry cards under geographical names occurring in the title followed by arrangement by catchwords. In the case of annonymous classics and sacred books, the arrangement is by catchwords[38] alone. The Berghoffer system has also the support of IFLA.

A union catalogue also needs to adopt a system of numbering or symbol for its participant libraries. Here again, there are various views for adopting such a system. In any case, such a system should be easy to read and use it without reference to a key which should invariably be the prepared and kept for reference no matter what system has been chosen. Such a system, according to Brummel, should be alphabetical by the first letter, then by the second letter until the fifth letter of the name of the library.

The examples of these symbols will illustrate their varied forms from country to country in the table given on next page.

It would thus appear that in some cases identification of cities and countries form initial part of the symbols (NUC, Gulf Regional List). Others suffice from two to four letters of the name elements of the libraries. They differ in the choice of the number of letters and the way the letters representing the names of the cities/countries are prefixed. S R Ranganathan suggested symbols indicating the eastern/western or northern/southern direction of the libraries possessing the materials from the centre of the union catalogue with a view to determining the closeness of the libraries requesting them.

9. Need for a Catalogue in Arab Countries

The need for the establishment of a union catalogue in the region is undisputed. The consolidation of the region's resources, widely dispersed and largely inaccessible, will help ascertain the strengths and

Source	Name of Library	Symbol
British Union-catalogue of Periodicals (1962)	(i) Aberdeen Public Library	AP
	(ii) Univeristy Library, Aberdean	AU
National Union Catalogue (1975)	(i) British Columbia Medical Library Service, Vancouver British Columbia (Canada)	Ca BVaM
	(ii) University of Nevada, Reno Nevada (USA)	NvU
Regional Union List of Scientific and Technical Periodicals in the Gulf Area (1980)	(i) Kuwait University Central Library	KUWAIT KU
	(ii)Kuwait Institute for Scientific Research Library	KUWAIT KISR
	(iii) University of Petroleum and Minerals, Dharan	S. ARABIA U P M
South Pacific Union List of Periodicals (Univ. of the South Pacific Library Suva, Fiji (1978).	Library Services of Fiji Training Office, Suva	LSFT
World Bibliography of Translations of the Meanings of the Holy Quran, Printed Translation 1515–1980 (Istanbul: RCIHAC, 1986)	Islamia University Library, Bahawalpur, Pakistan.	IUL

weaknesses in the region's library collections and with its help develop them collectively to meet the research needs of the Arab countries. In this process it will also be possible not only to share the resources of the region between its libraries but will also help exchange of bibliographic information from country to country in the region thus providing wider access to their indigenous materials not only to the Arab world but also to the world at large. Thus the present bibliographic system that makes available Western-oriented materials to world scholarship with regard to the *Muslim ummah* and for that matter to the Arab world will be replaced by a fuller bibliographical system comprehensively covering the indigenous literature produced by the Arab countries as well which presently is not the case.

The attempts at bibliographic networking made in certain Arab countries, such as in Saudi Arabia, with the publication of a union list of Arabic-language periodicals of the university libraries in the kingdom prepared by the King Saud University, Riyadh, and, on the larger scale, with the institution of a union catalogue of books of eight libraries of Kuwait and Saudi Arabia and a union list of scientific and technical periodicals of 35 libraries of four countries (Iraq, Kuwait, Saudi Arabia and UAE) in the Gulf region are not uniform and consistent in their application of the bibliographical methods.[39] The establishment of a union catalogue will also help remove these inadequacies.

Among others, the essential requirements for a union catalogue to which attention has been drawn by Brummel[40] include uniformity of cataloging practice which is largely non-existent in the region. Most important of all, the spirit of cooperation has to be inculcated for which an effective forum needs to be created before initiation of any activity directed to create a union catalogue, to begin with in each country of the region. This forum should discuss and develop an agreed policy for participation of libraries, selection of materials for inclusion and a common communication format for insertion of bibliographical information on a catalogue card to be filed in the union catalogue

10. Suggestions for a Union Catalogue

The development necessary for a union catalogue as discussed above should be simultaneous to the establishment of a national library, where it does not exist or where its services are not performed by any other library, backed by effective copyright laws. And, publication of a current national bibliography on a regular basis with arrangements in phases for catching up retrospectively with the years for which bibliography has yet to be published should also be assured. To begin with, this bibliography should be published every year, but after its establishment on sound basis, it should be changed to a quarterly if not a monthly publication with annual cumulation.

For adopting a uniform bibliographical policy, each country should decide upon a national cataloguing policy to be strictly followed throughout the country. This policy should be directed to attain a common communication format for all countries of the Arab world, under the aegis of ALECSO. For this purpose, ALECSO should accelerate its attempts for Arabization of ISBD, classification schemes, subject headings, etc. The schemes already developed should form a nucleus for arriving at an agreed formula. These efforts should be directed to establish a national system in each country on the pattern of National Information System (NATIS) with a view to making it a compatible system within Arab countries as a constituent unit of a larger system ARIS-NET.

10.1 *Location and Management of Union Catalogue*

The union catalogue should be housed in a national library or any other library which has been designated to perform the functions of a national library. The catalogue should function as an independent department of the library housing it as is the case in Holland where it functions as an independent department of the Royal Library. It should occupy a distinct place in the library and should possess sufficient space to house the catalogue and to provide necessary services. It should also have sufficient budget separate from the library. In large countries, such as Egypt and Sudan, this catalogue should be decentralized at divisional/provincial levels and should be housed in central/larger libraries at that level to coordinate it with the national union catalogue. Such catalogues should cover materials of participation libraries in their respective areas. Funds for their maintenance at that level should be made available by the central agency. At city level, local union catalogue should be maintained as part of an integrated public library system, where such system exists, and coordinated with the national union catalogue.

A Union Catalogue Managing Committee, as suggested by Inese A Smith,[41] should be constituted at the centre to administer the catalogue and make policies for selection of libraries for participation in the union catalogue, and choice of materials for inclusion in the catalogue. The committee should also be responsible for selection and appointment of the personnel for the catalogue and arrange for their training within and outside the country. The qualification required for the Manager and technical staff should include, among others the administrative, professional and statistical skills.

10.2 *Equipments for a Union Catalogue*

Necessary equipments, such as memory typewriters and copying machines, should be readily available both at the national centre and divisional/provincial centres and even at the local centres where such centres exist. Printed manuals should be distributed widely to the centres and participating libraries for using these equipments and maintaining uniformity in production of cards. Such a manual should also include instructions for maintaining uniformity for rendering bibliographical information and using symbols, for location of libraries, on catalogue cards.

10.3 *Selection of Libraries for Inclusion in a Union Catalogue*

All the university libraries, research libraries, selected special libraries meeting the goals of the union catalogue, along with the country's national library, insofar as its holding on foreign publications is concerned, should participate in the union catalogue. The selection of these libraries should be made on the basis of their willingness to share their collections for use by outside readers. Further, these libraries should be made to adhere to the agreed principles for selection of types of material for inclusion and rendering of entries in keeping with an agreed common pattern. These participating libraries should liaise with the national or divisional/provincial library, as the case may be, through its senior members of the staff, designated for this purpose.

10.4 *Arrangement of Cards*

Each participant library should be required to send two cards for each publication to the divisional/provincial centre, in case such a centre exists, otherwise, directly to the national centre. The cards should be reviewed and edited to ensure its compatibility with the common communication format, agreed upon, before their filing and onward transmission, if the reviewing agency is not a national agency. In case of default, the discrepancy should be duly made known to those committing errors.

The arrangement of these cards should be by languages (Arabic, French and English). Each language file should be divided in three files: (1) author file; (2) geographical file for corporate entry cards and, (3) title file for annonymous and sacred books. The arrangement should be alphabetical by the first entry word combined with the first usable part of the title. The second card received from the participant library should be used for a subject-index in which all cards irrespective of their language should be interfiled with distinct guide cards designating subject headings in English language. Under each guide indicator, the cards should be filed alphabetically according to trasliterated romanized forms of entry words to enable filing of all non-Western language cards together. The transliteration scheme should be decided by the Union Catalogue Managing Committee while adopting a common communication format for the catalogue.

10.5 *Location Symbols*

The location symbols to be used by the participating libraries in their card should represent city symbol along with that of the library. These symbols should use letters in a pair for each symbol. The symbols in the case of University of Petroleum and Minerals, Dharan in Saudi Arabia, should be as follows: *Dh UP*. The first symbol represents first two letters of the city where the library is located while the second symbol comprises two letters representing the first letter each of the two name elements of the library, both in capitals as in acronym. In a Gulf regional catalogue the country symbol representing two letters of the country (Saudi Arabia) will be affixed thus, enlarging the above symbol to, "Sa DH UP". In case of the two Yemens, because of the common form of the symbol for both countries, (Yemen, AR, Yemen, DPR), according to the above pattern, a third letter (D) from the second name element should be added to make the country symbol as "YeD" for the latter. The former would suffice with "Ye".

10.6 *Printing of Union Catalogue*

The printing and wider distribution of a union catalogue at this stage is not desirable. When computer-to-computer link becomes available between libraries as is the case in most of the countries in the Gulf region, the up to date on-line access thus becoming available within and outside a country outweighs the usefulness of a printed union catalogue since the catalogue becomes outdated the moment it is finalized for the purposes of printing. All that is needed at the moment is adherence to a common communication format, in each country in the region. both in the cases of national bibliography and union catalogue so that when automation in libraries becomes a reality it won't be any problem for conversion of these records in machine-readable forms.

As already discussed the publication of a union list is less expensive and more usable than a union catalogue. Its use both for inter-library loan and planning of national acquisition and exchange programme for periodicals has been widely acknowledged. The increasing costs of periodicals and at the same time their growth make it all the more imperative for a planned policy for their acquisition, storage and dissemination even in most developed countries. This need is, therefore, quite apparent in the region. Its publication would be a step forward in planning a national policy for acquisition of periodicals in the Arab countries. Such a catalogue/list would also need a common communication format and a national agency to maintain and publish it until necessary information about them becomes accessible through on-line computer-based network. In some countries union lists of scientific and technological periodicals and Arab-language periodicals have already been prepared. In the Gulf region such a list for science and technology holdings of four countries of the region has been published. These attempts need streamlining to attain compatibility to form a usable nucleus for the ARIS-NET.

11. Conclusion

It is encouraging to note that there is growing awareness in the Arab countries for pooling and sharing their informational resources directed to sustain the national development in each country and that of the Arab world and for that matter of the *Muslim ummah* as a whole.

There is an imperative need, therefore, for a unified national information system on the pattern of NATIS designed primarily to suit the local needs of the country and the Arab region as a whole. The government in each country of the region should, therefore, provide necessary incentive and political support for the establishment of such a system and with it, a well-established union catalogue in each country of the region on the lines suggested above, to form a nucleus for the proposed regional system ARIS-NET.

The *Muslim ummah* and for that matter the Arab world needs a viable and effective information system of its own to remove completely the information poverty of the Muslim countries. For, the transfer of information form the West has resulted in socio-cultural subservience and political servility and, consequently, have been thwarting attempts at scientific and technological progress and unification of *Muslim ummah.*[42] The sooner we shake off our dependence for information transfer, the better it would be for the entire Muslim world.

REFERENCES

1 KHURSHID, Anis *et al*, Ed: *Librarianship in the Muslim World*, 1984. Karachi ISLIC, Deptt of Lib & Inf Sc, Univ of Karachi, 1985.

2 SHARIF A : Factors Which Effect the Development of Librarianship and Library Education in the Arab Countries. (*International Library Reviews*, Vol 11, April 1979, p 253).

3 AMAN Muhammed M, *et al*: Library and Information Services in Arab Countries. (In: *Librarianship in the Muslim World*, 1984, *op. cit.*, p 3).

4 ZAFAR, Syed Ahmed: University Libraries in Muslim Countries. (In: *Librarianship in the Muslim World*, 1984, *op. cit*)

5 UNESCO: Bibliographical Services Throughout the World (In: *ALA World Encyclopaedia of Library and Information Services*) ed by Robert Wedgeworth, ed Chicago; ALA, 1986).

6 ZAFAR, Syed Ahmed, *op. cit.*, p 36.

7 DYAB M M: University Libraries in Arab Countries (*International Library Review* Vol 15, Jan 1983, p 19).

8 ZAFAR, Syed Ahmed, *op. cit.*, pp 36, 37, 26.

9 DYAB, M M: *op. cit.*, pp 28-29.

10 AMAN, Mohammed M: *op. cit.*, p 4.

11 SHARIF, A *op. cit.*, pp 253-57.

12 UNESCO: Bibliographical Services Throughout the World, *op. cit.*, p 179.

13 *UNESCO: Bulletin for Libraries*, Vol 14, May-June 1960, p 123.

14 ZAHAWI, Faria: Access to Information in the Arab World, the Development of the Arab League Documentation Centre (ALDOC) and Plans of the Arab Information System Network (ARIS-NET). (Paper presented at the Congress of Muslim Librarians and Information Scientists, Kedah, Malaysia, 20-22 Oct 1986).

15 ASHOOR, M Salleh: Bibliographical Networking in the Arabian Gulf Region: Prospects and Problems for Information Exchange. (Paper presented at the Congress of Muslim Librarians and Information Scientists, Kedah, Malaysia, 20-22 Oct 1986, p 7).

16 SHEARER, K: Arabian Gulf Plans: Its Library Future (*International Library Review*, Vol 13, July 1981, p 271).

17 LINE, Maurice B: Libraries in Saudi Arabia: Some Reflections, (*International Library Review*, Vol 15, Oct 1983, p 372).

18 *Ibid.*, p 373.

19 ASHOOR, M Salleh, *op. cit.*, p 5.

20 *ALA World Encyclopaedia of Library and Information Services*, *op. cit.*, p 95.

21 LINE, Maurice B: *op. cit.*, p 373.

22 AMAN, Muhammad M *et al*: Egypt (In: *Encyclopaedia of Library and Information Services*, *op. cit.*, p 264).

23 SHARIF, A *op. cit*, p 254.

24 MANZOOR Suhail: Academic Libraries in Iraq (*International Library Review*, Vol 17, July 1985, pp 283-91).
25 ASHOOR, M Salleh, *op. cit.*, pp 9-10.
26 SATTAR, Abdus *et al.*, Coverage of Islamic Literature in Selected Indexing Services, (*International Library Review*, Vol 17, Oct. 1985, pp 357-70).
27 LARSEN, Knud *National Bibliographical Services: Their Creation and Operation.* Paris; UNESCO, 1953, p 56. (UNESCO bibliographical handbooks, 1).
28 BRUMMEL, L: Union Catalogues –– Their Problems and Organization, Paris; UNESCO [1956], p 29. (UNESCO bibliographical handbooks 6).
29 WILLEMIN, Silevere: Technique of Union Catalogues: A Practical Guide (*UNESCO Bulletin for Libraries*, Vol 20, Jan-Feb, 1966, p 3).
30 LARSEN, Knud: National Bibliographical Services [*UNESCO Bulletin for Libraries*, Vol 15, (Nov-Dec 1961), p 301].
31 WILLEMIN, Silevere *op. cit.*, pp 3-4.
32 BRUMMEL, L *op. cit.*, pp 32-34.
33 LARSEN, Knud : *op. cit.*, p 306.
34 BRUMEL L, *op. cit.*, p 37.
35 WILLEMIN, Silevere *op. cit.*, p 6.
36 *Cited in*: BRUMMEL, *op. cit.*, p 43.
37 WILLEMIN, Silevere *op. cit.*, p 10.
38 *Ibid.*, p 16.
39 -ASHOOR, M Salleh, *op. cit.*, p 9.
40 BRUMMEL, L *op. cit*, p 48.
41 SMITH Inese A: Planning and Implemenataion of a Union Catalogue of Holdings (including serials) in University Libraries in Pakistan, (In: *Project Reports prepared by participants of the Educational Seminar* for Pakistani Academic Libraries . . . Lahore . . . 20 March-7 April 1983; ed by Inese A Smith and John Feather, Loughborough, Deptt of Library & Information Studies, Loughborough Univ of Technology, 1984, p 11.
42 JALIBI Jameel: Foreword (In: *Librarianship in the Muslim World, op. cit.*, p 7).

P 1

Users' Education and Training in Scientific and Technical Libraries in India

Inder Vir Malhan

0. Introduction

For the library to act as an effective agency for the communication of timely, relevant and comprehensive information, there should be sufficient relevant collection, competent and experienced library staff, and the users should also be interested and trained in gathering information. The execution of mental abilities of a users to grasp relationships directly depends upon the availability of relevant information. However, users can perceive, interpret and draw relationships of information within the limits of their own knowledge and education. An important factor in ensuring effective use of information is, therefore, the information education and training of users, their working and reading habits, work environment, etc.

1. Complex Problem of Users' Education

To organize users' education and training programmes, is not an easy task. It is a complex problem because users' habits, motivation and facilities offered differ within an organization and from one organization to another. Their areas of specialization may change with time. Their age groups, capabilities, opportunities to display their talents and productivities also vary. Moreover, a small number of users do more reading, while a large majority of scientific and technical community is not actively engaged in the pursuit of information search, collection and use. Even the scientists who are making serious attempts in the matter of reading and gathering information cannot claim to be in touch with all the latest developments in their fields. The human capacity and time for gathering information is limited, whereas the generation of information is increasing with every increase in the number of scientists. J G Miller has studied the relationship of information overload to various forms of mental illness. He states, "Glutting a person with more information than he can process may lead to disturbance".[1] Keeping in view this contention of J G Miller, the user education and training programmes must ensure that active users of information should be able to make timely and effective use of most relevant information and passive users should be motivated and trained to make such a use. The overall productivity of scientific and technical knowledge will depend upon the availability of information and profitable use of information made by more number of users.

2. Impact of Information and Communication Technologies

Developments in information and communication technologies and their applications to libraries too demand users' education and training in making effective and economical use of such technologies. Moreover, lack of such an education and training may cause a void between the facilities available and their use. In a developing country like India, presently library staff is given priority over users in such an education and training. However, as the facilities become more common, India will require to train end-users in the operation of computer systems, educate them in the elements of systems' languages, use of logical connectors, etc.

3. Scope and Methodology

This study attempts to assess the conventional users' education and training programmes organized by the Indian scientific and technical libraries. Efforts made in India in training the users in the use of modern information and communication devices have also been assessed. A countrywide survey of major scientific and technical libraries was conducted by the author. University libraries except the agricultural university libraries are excluded from the scope of this study. This paper includes as many users' education and training programmes as the investigator is able to trace.

4. Findings of the Investigation

For research scholars at Punjab Agricultural University (PAU),

Ludhiana, education regarding the use of the library is one of the optional course requirements in research. The Haryana Agricultural University (HAU), Hissar, too runs user education programmes. The libraries of G B Pant University of Agriculture and Technology (GBPUAT), Pantnagar, and Jawahar Lal Nehru Krishi Visva Vidyalya (JNKVV), Jabalpur, also organize education and training of library use for their research scholars. The courses organized by the agricultural universities mainly include the teaching of information sources, familiarity with the services of their libraries and methods of gathering information.

The Bhabha Atomic Research Centre (BARC), Bombay, provides training in the use of its library to its trainees and also to deputed persons from other libraries. Some of the Indian Institutes of Technology (IIT) libraries give some kind of orientation course or education to their users. One of the best programmes is run by IIT, Madras. Every Thursday at 3.30 pm, an audio-visual programme is arranged by the library which introduces the users to the library, its information services and some information tools such as *Physics Abstracts, Chemical Abstracts, Engineering Index*, etc.

4.1 *Voluntary Efforts of Scientists*

User education programmes in India are also designed and organized by the voluntary efforts of some devoted scientists. Subbiah Arunachalam, editor, Publication and Information Directorate (PID) of the Council of Scientific and Industrial Research (CSIR), has helped in organizing user education programmes at Madras, Trichy, Hyderabad, Bombay and New Delhi. He designed a programme for the *Physics Abstracts* in collaboration with the library staff of IIT, Madras. Vishwanathan, a faculty member at the Department of Chemistry, IIT, Madras, has designed a programme for the *Chemical Abstracts*. Both these tape and slide programmes are being demonstrated at IIT, Madras, among others. According to Vishwanathan, "Sixty to eighty per cent of the users do not know how to make the best use of the available library and information resources. The problem is not that users do not know but that they are not even interested in knowing".

4.2 *Understanding the Need*

The Central Road Research Institute (CRRI) Library, New Delhi, imparts education to its users regarding the use of the library. The librarian of Central Scientific Instruments Organization (CSIO), Chandigarh, feels that a large number of scientists have not acquired the needed information use habits. The organization of information education and training programmes for them may not be very successful as there is lack of concern and not sufficient pressure for searching, collecting and utilizing information for research and development activities. A number of librarians of the Indian Council of Medical Research (ICMR), the Indian Council of Agricultural Research (ICAR), and CSIR research laboratories realize that their scientists do need some sort of education or training for making effective use of information services. The programmes are not run because majority of the scientists do not like to be taught by anybody.

4.3 *Programme in Textile Libraries*

A unique kind of users' education programme is run by the textile libraries in Bombay. The Silk and Art 'Silk Mills' Research Association (SASMIRA) Library, Bombay, formed a Textile Information Users Group (TIUG).

This group acts as a medium for thorough informal discussions amongst textile librarians and users of textile information. Librarians and users of a number of textile libraries are participating in this programme. Users who are not aware of certain textile information resources and services are educated in an informal way. This method of users' education has proved to be very gainful and pragmatic.

4.4 *Education Through Kits*

The Indian National Scientific Documentation Centre (INSDOC), New Delhi, has acquired some commercially available kits such as "How to use *Excerpta Medica*", "How to use *Science Citation Index*", etc. Some of the kits are being developed through INSDOC's own efforts, keeping in view the local needs. The INSDOC's Training Section conducted a two-day Workshop on User Education on Drugs and Pharmaceutical Information on February 19-20, 1982, for the benefit of a group of 25 members comprising faculty members, research scholars and students of the College of Pharmacy. The Workshop included not only formal lectures and exercises, but also a tape-slide demonstration. The INSDOC believes in the philosophy that proper information gathering habits should be developed right from the school level. This centre has developed a tape-slide programme of one hour's duration for providing library instructions to science students at school level. This tape-slide programme was demonstrated in some of the schools, at Delhi.

4.5 *Education Through Demonstration*

For the first time in Asia an on-line demonstration of interrogating a remote data base was conducted in India. The ESRIN data bases in Franscati, near Rome, were made accessible during the demonstration which was held at the Tata Institute of Fundamental Research (TIFR), Bombay, during 20-25 September, 1976. About 300 scientists, technologists, information scientists and librarians witnessed the demonstration and searched the data bases for their queries by operating the terminal at TIFR.

4.51 *DST*: The Department of Science and Technology (DST) arranged an experiment on March 10, 1980, called audio-graphic conference facility. During this experiment Indian users exchanged information with their counterparts in the USA, UK, Canada, W Germany, Spain and Norway. The National Informatics Centre (NIC), New Delhi, also conducted some experiments and provided demonstrations of online information search. In February-March 1981, European Space Agency (ESA) data bases at Franscati were used through telephone and satellite link during an experiment conducted at Hotel Ashok, New Delhi. This demonstration was organized during the Annual Convention of the Computer Society of India and various participants witnessed the methods of searching ESA data bases through on-line use. Now permanent computer terminal facilities (two IBM-PC/XT micro computers) have been set up at the National Aeronautical Laboratory (NAL), Bangalore, for making online use of ESA data bases. The NAL organises online demonstrations for the benefit of users, charging some fee. Four demonstrations each of three days' duration were organized during November-December 1986.

4.52 *Others*: Some of the libraries which have set up computer facilities familiarize their users with functioning of their computer systems, e.g. TIFR, Bombay, BARC, Bombay, Reactor Research Centre (RRC), Kalpakkam, etc. Following the meeting of Advisory Group on Biomedical Management Information and Planning set up in April 1985, ICMR has established a Centre on Biomedical Information at NIC, New Delhi, in 1985-86. Besides making available the global services such as MEDLINE to ICMR scientists, this centre will facilitate improved scientific information dissemination in biomedical field through the provision of workshops/training courses for scientists as well as librarians. M/s Informatics (India Ltd.), Bangalore, an Indian agent of Lockheed's DIALOG, is organizing on-line demonstrations for the benefit of the users of various organizations. For example, an on-line demonstration was organized by this firm at Regional Research Laboratory (RRL), Trivandrum, to access world data bases managed by Lockheed's DIALOG, using RRL's telex terminal. The RRL Hyderabad, too organized on on-line demonstration for the benefit of library staff and user scientists. The Informatics (India Ltd.) has organised about 30 such demonstrations in various organizations".[2] The student wing of the Computer Society of India has started a computer literacy campaign. It organizes computer weekends at Bombay. It also publishes a magazine entitled *Computer Education for You*, which includes the articles meant for general audience.

During seminars and conferences organized by various professional associations and societies (e.g. Society for Information Science, Micrographic Congress of India, etc.), business firms display their information products and organize demonstrations of their operations and functions. While librarians and information scientists are the major beneficiaries of such demonstrations, the local users can also witness the exhibitions of such modern information and communication devices.

5. Conclusions and Recommendations

User education programmes are essential for maximizing the use of library resources. They have not yet been developed to an appreciable extent in India. The major reason being that several libraries lack of comprehensive information resources and the necessary wherewithal for organizing users' education and training programmes. There is no use in educating the users regarding the information tools and services which the libraries are unable to provide in practice.

In spite of poor resources of several libraries, some sort of users' education and training is necessary and desirable because due to lack of library use knowledge many users even may not be able to utilize the information resources and services existing in the country.

5.1 *TIUG Programme*

Informal users' education programmes of TIUG proved to be very effective. It indicates that informal users' education and training programmes may prove to be more useful to achieve the objectives of users' education and training. Further, such programmes will ensure more closer communication between users and librarians. It is expected that some of the services will be more heavily used if users are explained in a personal way about their existence and the benefits the users will be able to derive out of their use. Once the users are able to grasp the utilities of services and master the techniques of searching, they may provide useful feedback to librarians for the improvement of information services.

5.2 *Course Contents*

What should be taught to users? Users should be taught what they do not know and require to know. A number of studies regarding users information problems, needs and awareness of resources, etc., have been conducted in the country. Presently, many of such studies are lying scattered. The reports of such studies should be collected, collated and analyzed. The major findings of various reports should be blended to develop guidelines which may help to draft course contents of a users' education programme workable under Indian conditions of scientific and technical information resources and services.

5.3 *Provision of Fees*

Should the users' education in India be free or fee based? The NAL, Bangalore charges a fee of Rs. 200 from the participants who attend the three-day online demonstrations organized by it. Since India requires to create an awareness of importance of information among users, free-based demonstrations and courses will not be a helpful practice. Experience gained from users' education and training programmes at IIT, Madras, indicates that many users are not prepared to learn from even free programmes. The provision of fees may further discourage them.

5.4 *Computer Literacy Campaign*

Keeping in view developments in information and communication-technologies in developed countries and the increasing trend of use of microprocessors in the country, India should start making efforts in preparing users to make a cost effective use of such technologies. To those who do not know much about computers, computer systems appear to be a phobia. A large-scale computer literacy campaign is, therefore, desirable for the users of scientific and technical libraries in India.

REFERENCES

1 TOFFLER Alvin: *Future Shock*, London, Pan Books, 1971, p 321.
2 Personal Interview with N V Sathyanarayana, Managing Director, Informatics, India Ltd, Bangalore, July 1, 1987.

Q 1

Delhi Library Association: A Living Monument of P N Kaula

H R Chopra

1. Foundation laid by Kaula

Delhi Library Association (DLA) was established on August 16 1953, as a result of the efforts of Prof P N Kaula who collected some 200 librarians of Delhi at the Marwari Public Library, the oldest Public Library of the city and laid the foundation of this organization. It was inaugurated by Ch Brahm Prakash, Chief Minister of the State and was addressed by Dr S R Ranganathan. It elected Miss Shanta Vashist, the then Education Minister, as the President and P N Kaula as General Secretary. Shanta Vashist has continued to be its President all these years. Aims and objectives of DLA are similar to those of any other Library Association in India. Its main aim is to provide a common forum for the Librarians working in different types of libraries in Delhi. It also aims at imparting training in Librarianship and to bring out serial and monograph publications for furtherance of the cause of the profession. Cooperation and coordination of library activities within the State and at national level has been emphasized. It also aims at working for the improvement of service conditions of this profession.

2. Structure

Membership of the Delhi Library Association is open to the working librarians, teachers of Library and Information Science and anyone having interest in libraries and librarianship. The present membership of DLA is 517, comprising 295 Life members; 219 Ordinary members and three Institutional members.

2.1 *General Body and Executive Committee*

The highest body of this association is "General Body" which consists of all its members. It meets biennially for transaction of business and to elect its office-bearers and members of the Executive Committee. The Executive Committee comprises the President; one Senior Vice-President; two Vice-Presidents; one General Secretary; one Treasurer; two Secretaries; one Public Relation Officer; and 14 members (including six coopted members). The Executive Committee is responsible for the transaction of day-to-day business of the association under the overall supervision and directions of the President and according to policies laid down by the General Body. At present Shanta Vashist a former Member of Parliament, and H C Jain, Librarian, South Delhi Campus Library are its President and General Secretary, respectively.

2.2 *Other Authorities*

Four Regional Secretaries are also appointed by the DLA for a period of two years, who look after the coordination of activities of the association in different parts of Delhi. An Administrative Committee of the School of Library Science of the Association is also appointed for a period of two years (which consists of one Honorary Director, one Honorary Registrar and five members) which looks after the management of training classes of Post-matric Certificate Course in Library Science and Post-graduate Diploma Course in Library Science, both of one year's duration, run by the Association.

2.3 *Own Building*

The headquarters of the Delhi Library Association were in the beginning at the Marwari Public Library when its former librarian, K S Pareek, worked as Secretary and for some years as Treasurer of the Association. In 1960 the office was shifted to the Hardyal Municipal Public Library premises in Delhi. Its own new building, "Rabindra Bhavan", is in Naraina, New Delhi.

2.4 *Finances*

At present the association has a budget of about Rs. 90,000 per year. Its main source of income is membership fee, training courses fee and sale proceeds of its publications. It also gets an amount of Rs. 2500 as grant-in-aid from the Delhi Administration every year. The budget for one of its publications, namely, "*Indian Press Index*", is operated separately, which is presently about Rs. 35,000 per annum. For this purpose, an annual grant of Rs. 10,000 is provided by the Indian Council of Social Science Research, while the balance is met out of the sale proceeds (Subscription charges) of this publication.

3. Varied Activities

Ever since its inception in 1953, DLA has been actively engaged in various activities in accordance with its aims and objectives foundation for which was laid by P N Kaula. Some of the significant activities of the Delhi Library Association are as under:

3.1 *Conferences*

DLA organizes conferences biennially on the occasion of its General Body meeting and election of office-bearers. The first Delhi Library Conference was organised by P N Kaula in 1957 which resulted in the publication of *Library Movement in India*, edited by Kaula. On these occasions, members of DLA discuss their professional problems and exchange their views.

3.2 *Seminars*

Various professional seminars and symposia are organized by the Association from time to time on different themes such as "Indian "Reference Sources", "Library Classification at Crossroads", "Acquisition of Reading Material", "School Libraries: Problems and Prospects", etc. These seminars and symposia have proved very useful for the working librarians in Delhi.

3.3 *Lectures*

Delhi Library Association invites, from time to time, experienced librarians and educationists to deliver lectures on different themes for the benefit of its members. More than two dozen experts from abroad and quite a large number of prominent speakers from India have delivered lectures to the members of DLA on topics of varying interest.

Since 1972 "Das-Gupta Memorial Lectures" are also organized.

3.4 *Training Programme*

3.41 *Certificate Course*: In order to meet the demand for trained librarians in the school libraries, public libraries and semi-professional positions in large libraries, P N Kaula instituted, with effect from 1955, a one-year post-matric training programme leading to "Certificate in Library Science". He organised its Academic Committee with the late Prof S Das Gupta as Director and himself as Registrar. In 1959 Prof Kaula became Director of the School with C S Krishnamurti as Registrar. This position changed with the shifting of Kaula to Banaras in July 1960 when he joined Banaras Hindu University. His mantle was taken over by late N K Goil continued the work with dedication. Classes are conducted in the morning and evening in the Hardayal (Hardings) Municipal Public Library, Delhi. About 200 students are admitted. Teaching is done by honorary staff, who are working in various institutions in Delhi. The Certificate awarded by the association was got recognized by the Delhi Administration and the Government of India, Ministry of Education, for employment purpose. This was again done through the effects of P N Kaula. In order to encourage the trainees, "Das Gupta Memorial Medal" was instituted in 1967, which is awarded every year to a person who secures highest marks in the Certificate Course in Library Science conducted by DLA.

3.42 *Diploma Course*: Since 1972, the Association has started another one-year course namely, "Post-graduate Diploma in Library Science", which is primarily meant for the working librarians who may be interested to improve their professional qualifications. To start with only 20 students were admitted, but keeping in view the increasing demand, now 20 students are admitted every year. Arrangements for internship or practical training in librarianship for the trainees have also been made in 14 reputed libraries in Delhi.

3.5 *Publication Programme*

The Delhi Library Association has been bringing out some serial and monographic publications ever since its inception. The initial publications were started by Prof P N Kaula followed by late N K Goil. Some of the important publications are :

(a) *Serial Publications*

(i) *Library Herald : Library Herald* as the organ of DLA was started in 1958 by P N Kaula who remained its editor for four years (1958–62). It is a quarterly journal and publishes learned papers pertaining to all fields of Library Science and Librarianship. The pattern and features set out by Kaula have been continued till this day. A few special issues of the *Library Herald* have also been brought out from time to time, viz. "Acquisition of Reading Material", "University Libraries in India", "S Das Gupta Memorial Issue", "S R Ranganathan Memorial Issue", "N K Goil Memorial Issue", etc.

(ii) *Indian Press Index (IPI)*: It is a monthly publication, being published regularly since 1968. It indexes articles, special writeups, editorials, important statements and letters published in 17 daily English newspapers of India. It covers about 26,000 entries per year and is very well used throughout the world. It has a separate budget of Rs. 35,000 per year, out of which Rs. 10,000 are provided by the Indian Council of Social Science Research, Delhi, and the balance is met out of the sale proceeds (Subscription) of the publication.

(iii) *Book Review Supplement* : It is a quarterly publication, which was started in 1968. It covers book reviews published in 17 English newspapers of India mentioned above.

(iv) *Annual Report* : The association's annual report and statement of accounts is also published every year since 1953-54, which includes results of the "Cert. Lib. Sc." and "P.G. Dip. Lib. Sc." examination conducted by DLA, and also various activities of the Association during the period under review.

(b) *Monographs*

DLA has published more than eight monographic publications ever since its establishment. Some of the important publications are "Directory of Librarians and Who's Who in Library Profession in India"; "Library Movement in India"; "Indian Library Literature : A Bibliography"; "Directory of Pseudonyms in Indian Literature", etc. It has plans to bring out a few more such publications in the near future.

3.6 *Library Legislation*

P N Kaula drafted a Library Bill for Delhi on behalf of DLA and submitted to the Delhi Administration. The Bill was referred to the Select Committee after being whetted by the Law Committee, the Select Committee had also approved it with some modifications. It was going to be presented to the State Legislature (Delhi was then Part C State), when due to States Reorganization Commission Report (1956) Delhi State was abolished. Thus the Bill could not be enacted into a law in 1955. Even afterwards followup work has been undertaken and the Administration and Corporation persuaded for enacting the Library Act for the Delhi area. The outcome is still awaited.

3.7 *Extension Programmes*

DLA organizes book exhibitions in Delhi from time to time, which are quite useful for the librarians, publishers, book suppliers and the library users. The first All-India Book Exhibition on "Indian Library Literature" was organized by P N Kaula in 1956. He also organized an all-India exhibition on "Gandhiana" as the General Secretary of DLA.

3.8 *Cultivation of Reading Habits*

The Association is very keen to cultivate reading habits in the general public, especially school students. In order to give incentive in this regard, DLA organizes an "Essay Competition" on different topics every year and awards prizes to the winners.

3.81 *Cooperation and Coordination Activities*: DLA has been engaged in close cooperation with various agencies, within Delhi and outside it, for professional achievements. It negotiates with the Good Officers Committee of the Delhi State Book-Suppliers Association and fixes the rate of discount, conversion rates of foreign currency for purchase of books by different types of libraries in Delhi.

3.82 *Projects*: DLA has undertaken various projects which could be useful for the profession in Delhi. In 1966, it undertook the compilation of "Union Catalogue of Periodicals in Social Science and Humanities available in Delhi Libraries". Later on this work was taken over by the Social Science Documentation Centre of the Indian Council of Social Science Research, Delhi.

It is evident from the preceding pages that the Delhi Library Association has been engaged in a variety of professional activities for the benefit of its members. Its many pronged activities were spearheaded by Prof P N Kaula when he was the moving spirit behind this organization (1953–60).

4. Achievements

Keeping in view the financial position and geographical jurisdiction of the Delhi Library Association, it is doing reasonably good work. But such small associations at local level can do much more for the profession. A library association at State or Union Territory level like DLA is expected to get the library legislation passed from the concerned and competent authority. DLA has not been able to achieve this goal initiated in December 1954 by P N Kaula as the Library Act has not so far been enacted in the Union Territory of Delhi. No doubt DLA has been organizing conferences, seminars, symposia, training courses and also bringing out both serial and monographic publications very regularly, but it is lacking behind so far in standardization of library services, equipment and appliances. It has yet to draw a code of ethics for its members planned originally by Kaula in 1956. It has not done anything for the autonomy of the profession.

5. School of Library Science

Since 1955, DLA School of Library Science has been conducting a one-year Post-matric Certificate Course in Library Science. The classes are held in the morning and evening in order to accommodate the working persons. The Faculty is also honorary. The trained persons are absorbed in the junior positions in various types of libraries as the above-mentioned course has been recognized by the Ministry of Education, Government of India and the Delhi Administration for employment purposes solely through the efforts of Kaula.

DLA has imparted training to a very large number of persons and a majority of them are employed in various capacities in the field of librarianship. They all owe a sense of gratitude to Prof P N Kaula who laid the foundation for the Association, its School of Library Science, and its organ, the *Library Herald*.

6. Tribute to the Work of Prof Kaula

The Association which has become one of the most active organizations in the country, owes much to the dynamic, far-sighted and multi-pronged leadership of Prof P N Kaula who gave it a foundation, base, structure, school and publication activities. Prof Kaula left Delhi in July 1960 to join Banaras Hindu University as University Librarian and Head, Department of Library Science. The Executive Committee of DLA authorized Prof Kaula to edit and publish the *Library Herald* from Varanasi which he did till 1962. Before his departure, the grateful Association paid high tributes to Prof Kaula for his dedicated work and multi-pronged activities of the Association that put Delhi on the "Library Map of India". The Farewell Address was presented to him in the Constitution Club, New Delhi, on July 5, 1960. It was presented to him by Miss Shanta Vashist, President, DLA. Ch. Brahm Prakash, former Chief Minister of Delhi who had inaugurated the Association on August 16, 1953, presided over the function. He said that while being associated with Prof Kaula, he became a protagonist of library cause, but he could not influence Kaula to join the political forum. The Address was read out by Mr C S Krishnamurti, General Secretary of the Association. Since the new generation of librarians who have qualified from DLA's School of Library Science may not know much about the contributions of Prof Kaula, the Address presented to his is reproduced below:

Farewell Address

Presented to

Shri P. N. KAULA

Our Dear Kaulaji,

We, the members of the Delhi Library Association have great pleasure in greeting you on your elevation to one of the important positions in a Premier University of the country. Though we have ventured to bid you farewell, it is not without a feeling of void in our hearts and agony in our minds, that your absence from the capital may not retard the progress of library movement in Delhi.

It is superfluous on our part to recapitulate the rise, growth and development of this Association and the part you played in its many pronged activities. It has indeed been a matter of great pride to us that you have secured a place for Delhi on the library map of India. Your adriot piloting of the Association by blending the conflicting opinions and interests of diverse groups into harmony, relieved the Association from the pangs of birth and saved it from many an infantile mortality. The leopard's stride of progress in the membership of the Association speaks volumes of your ability to attract and hold men together around you.

Your zeal and enthusiasm for promoting libraries and the interests of librarians are well known. It was your ardent desire to see a network of libraries functioning in Delhi that prompted you to draft a Library Bill for Delhi. It had every prospect of becoming a law but for the abolition of the Delhi State. The organisation of the two All-India Book Exhibitions–Gandhiana and Indian Library Literature–in 1953 and 1956, and the Library Conference in 1957, bear testimony to your amazing organising capacity. The holding of the Library Convention soon after the release of the Report of the Pay Commission is a further proof of your abiding interest in the profession. The starting of the School of Library Science in 1955 which has filled a long felt desideratum in Delhi is yet another notable achievement of yours. Your sustained efforts in obtaining recognition to the school from the Government have infused new hopes to our trainees employed in various libraries in Delhi.

Your active participation at a young age in the activities of the Indian Library Association as member of the Council, Research Circle and Managing Editor of the *ABGILA* under the guidance of Dr S R Ranganathan, were sufficient indications of your subsequent achievements. Your activities in creating professional interest among the members may perhaps be formidable to be catalogued.

Starting of the LIBRARY HERALD, a publication series, and instituting incentive awards for librarians are only a few among the many. Your far-sightedness in building a literate body-politic in Delhi is demonstrated by your instituting prizes for inculcating reading habit in children.

It is very encouraging to note that your activities are not selfishly concentrated in Delhi. Your cherished desire to see the Indian Library Association function actively integrating all the State Associations as its branches is only one example of your lofty ambitions. The image of your desire is unfurled in your wish to have many Carnegies for India. You are a pioneer in the library field who is destined to keep alive the trail blazed by Dr. Ranganathan.

First to leave Kashmir for Madras to study Library Science, first to forge library movement in Kashmir, first to draft a Library Plan for that state, first to be awarded the Master's degree in Library Science in

India, first to initiate a systematic documentation service and bibliographical series in the Government of India, and first to occupy the Readership in Library Science in the East, you stand *unique* among the librarians. Yours is a versatile personality endowed with peerless industry, indefatigable energy, intellectual acumen, gifted tongue and above all irrepressible enthusiasm and zeal for library cause. It has been a matter of pride for the profession to watch the progress of your career with your varied talents as a student, worker, organizer, administrator, bibliographer, documentalist, author, journalist and a teacher. It is no wonder that in a very short time you have by dint of hard work and devotion, attained maturity and a position of rank and leadership in the profession.

That you may be long spared and your efforts may prosper more and more is the fervent prayer of our humble selves.

Constitution Club, We are Members of
New Delhi DELHI LIBRARY ASSOCIATION
5 July, 1960

Mr C S Krishnamaurti conferred that it was Mr. Kaula who had inducted him into the work of DLA. So also he had inducted a dedicated band of colleagues like N K Goil, who not only continued the work initiated by Prof Kaula but gave new dimensions and extensions to its activities. That itself is a matter of tribute to the leadership of Prof Kaula.

R 1

Prof Kaula and Assam Library Movement

Alaka Buragohain and **Narendra Lahkar**

0. Introduction

Prof Prithvi Nath Kaula, the first UGC Emeritus Fellow Professor in Library and Information Science and also the first Reader in Library Science in the country, although settled down at present in Lucknow, carries the feeling of this part of the country that he was much to Assam and the North-East. It is Prof Kaula who has been continuously bothering why the Assam Library Association is not functioning and reviving its activities. It is Kaula who has been trying to inject some motion into the minds of the Professionals of Assam and the North-East, "the land of lahe lahe" (slowly and slowly) to work hard and make a vigorous movement in this field. And the professionals of the North-East are acquainted with the style of working of Kaula Saheb right from 1964.

1. Life with Manifold Experience

Prof P N Kaula, the distinguished library scientist, is an administrator, a teacher, an organizer, a thinker and scholar, a planner, builder and promoter of libraries/Information, centres and library and information science education, has a long professional experience of more than 40 years to his credit since he joined first as a librarian in a college in 1944 in Srinagar. Prof Kaula is fortunate also for being a student and co-worker of Dr S R Ranganathan the Father of Library Science in India. He is an excellent teacher and has a rare quality of convincing people by his oratory and tenacity.

Besides, Prof Kaula, a multi-faceted personality, is a prolific writer with a large number of books and monographs, bibliographies, more than 400 articles and 400 book reviews, 18 depth classification schedules and editing the most popular journal, *Herald of Library Science*, and also *International Information, Communication and Education* and *Granthalaya Vijnana.*

Prof Kaula, besides being an international expert and UNESCO Advisor, has received several international awards. Prof Kaula Endowment has instituted Kaula Gold Medal also for international library experts.

2. Visit to Assam and the North-East

2.1 *8th Conference of Assam Library Association*

Prof Kaula, with all the aforesaid rare qualities and experience, has visited Assam and the North-East several times with professional interest and needs. It was in 1964 when Prof Kaula, along with late Dr S R Ranganathan, Mr P N Gaur, the then President of the Indian Library Association, and Dr A K Ohdedar, Librarian of Jadavpur University in Calcutta, first came to undivided Assam in order to attend the 8th Conference of Assam Library Association at Guwahati and at the invitation of its Reception Committee, mostly at the initiative of G N Phukan, the then Librarian of Guwahati High Court and Secretary of the Association. Assam Library Association till then was essentially a voluntary socio-cultural organization of undivided Assam having taking birth at the initiative of a rare personality like late Kumudeswar Barthakur in 1938 in a spirit, devoted to India's National Movement. People who had seen Kaula Saheb that time speaking in a non-stop, spontaneous way cannot forget his spirit, his mastery, his devotion to the profession and its service, and his scholarship.

2.2 *Other Remarkable Visits to the N.E. Region*

Prof Kaula's other remarkable visits to the North-eastern Region were his participation in the North-Eastern Council seminar on "Library System, Data Collection and Dissemination of Information for N E Region", held at Guwahati in March 1981; his visit to Guwahati and Shillong in February, 1985 along with other national experts in connection with regional discussion on National Policy on Library and Information System; his participation in the second NEC seminar in May, 1986 on "Improvement of Library and Information System in the N E Region" offering the most wise suggestion for establishment of a

Regional Information Centre as a coordinating, funding and planning agency; his participation as a resource personnel in June, 1986 in the UGC-sponsored Refresher Course for Academic Librarians, organized by the Department of Library and Information Science, Gauhati University and lastly, his visit to NEHU as a member of the UGC Review Committee for Central Universities in December 1986; besides occasional visits to the N E Region on professional duties.

3. Prof Kaula and the Public Library Movement in Assam

Prof Kaula addressed the open session of the 8th Assam Library Conference in 1964 along with Dr S R Ranganathan, which was inaugurated by Mr Dev Kanta Baruah, the then Education Minister of Assam and presided over by Dr Maheswar Neog, the then President of the Assam Library Association and a scholar who had later been gracing several honourable positions as President of the Assam Sahitya Sabha, Jawaharlal Nehru Professor of Gauhati University, Sankardev Professor of Punjabi University, etc. Prof Kaula took the opportunity to introduce Dr S R Ranganathan, the doyen of library and information science to the audience and the people of Assam. He chaired the seminars on "Public Libraries", "Library Legislation", etc.

Kaula Saheb long since 1964 has been with the professionals of Assam in attempting to create viable units under a uniform permanent network of free public library system backed by legislation in order to educate, enlighten and inform the people at large in a continuous non-formal way. Prof Kaula on different occasions of the conference pointed out the various hurdles to an organized public library movement. He contributed a paper on "Responsibility of the State and Library Law" in the seminar. Prof Kaula while presenting the recommendations of the seminar in the form of resolutions got a resolution passed for adoption of a library Bill for undivided Assam. He as well as Dr S R Ranganathan approached and impressed upon the Minister concerned the need for its enactment. Unfortunately, not a single State in the Region has yet enacted a library Bill.

The conference could create, due to the presence of the aforesaid doyens of the profession, a stir among the professionals and the public about what could librarians do with the Government's support for culture, education and progress of the people and development of the State. Mr S C Rajkhowa, then D P I of Assam, immediately after the conference convened a meeting of the officials in Shillong to discuss along with Prof Kaula an effective library service in the State.

3.1 *NEC Seminar*

Prof Kaula when he came to attend the N E C (North-East Council) seminar in March 1981, brought up the issue again but in the second N E C seminar on "Improvement of Library and Information System in the N E Region", his paper had hinted on the past attempts for a library Act in the region and strongly recommended for free public library service and *free* flow of information to each and every person of the region in order to ensure culture, education and progress of the region. Kaula Saheb did not miss the chance to impress upon the scholars, ministers and officials of the region whom he could contact about the need of a library Act; while he came for regional discussion on "The National Policy on Library & Information System", he along with Prof B D Nagchowdhury (former V C of J N U), Prof P B Mangla, Prof Ashin Dasgupta (ex-Director of the National Library), Mr T S Rajagopalan, Mr Girja Kumar and Dr B P Baruah (Director of Raja Ram Mohan Roy Library Foundation) met the Governor, Vice-Chancellors, Ministers and officials of both Assam and Meghalaya at Guwahati and Shillong respectively and pleaded for the cause of a free public library service based on legislation. Prof Kaula took the opportunity once again to press for the need of library legislation while he came to Guwahati for the UGC sponsored Refresher Course in June 1986. It is Kaula Saheb whose well reasoned arguments had at last appeared to convince Mr Kamaleswar Borah, then Education Commissioner of Assam and present Vice-Chancellor of Dibrugarh University, of the cause of the public library service backed by legislation as an essential aspect for consideration in the developmental schemes for the State. Prof Kaula's pleading has not yet been forgotten by those who were with him. Although no State of this region has yet enacted a library Bill, the ground appears to be fertile, only a strong initiative is the need of the time.

4. Kaula and Academic Library Movement in Assam

Prof Kaula chaired the first important seminar on "School and College Libraries in Assam" at the 8th Assam Library Conference in 1964 at Guwahati, which was aptly inaugurated by Mr S C Rajkhowa, then D P I of Assam and later Vice-Chancellor of Gauhati University. Prof

Kaula, while emphasized that education should be library-centred rather than classroom-centred, he brought out what the librarians could do for the success of the education system. Having received good response from the D P I, Prof Kaula suggested certain important matters like provision of trained full-time librarians in colleges, establishment for teaching of library science at Gauhati University. (Department of Library Science, Gauhati University started in 1966); full-time librarians with a Certificate course in schools instead of teacher-librarians; the certificate course to be conducted by the Government in cooperation with the Assam Library Association; circulation of reading lists; starting of open access system, organizing periodical seminars on use of books and use of libraries by teachers and librarians etc.

Prof Kaula took the opportunity to address the staff and students of the Department of Library and Information Science at Gauhati University on 3rd Feb, 1985 along with Prof P B Mangla from Delhi University, Mr Rajagopalan, the then President of the Indian Library Association, and Mr Girja Kumar from Jawaharlal Nehru University.

4.1 *UGC sponsored Refresher's Course*

Prof P N Kaula's real thrust in the field, however, was first felt while he came to participate as a resource personnel in the U G C- sponsored refresher course on "Organization, Administration and Service of Academic Libraries for the N E Region", June 6-26, 1986, organized by the Deptt. of Library and Information Science, Gauhati University. His presence had made the refresher course a really successful one from different angles. Kaula Saheb's academic sessions demonstrated his scholarship and long experience in the field and long association with Banaras Hindu University and Delhi University. His lectures had greatly educated and participants and inspired them for service.

4.2 *Meeting with Education Commissioner*

It was Prof Kaula who could properly apprise the Education Commissioner the delicate situation faced by the College librarians in Assam who had long been deprived of U G C recommended status and salary and pinpointed the fact that UGC pay-scales had long been implemented in other states including few of the N E States also. It was Kaula Saheb who in the presence of A C Borkotoky, the then Director of Assam Library Service and N Lahkar, Lecturer of the Department of Library Science, Gauhati University could befittingly convinced the Commissioner at Dispur of the real role of library-oriented education policy for the all round development of the State.

4.3 *Other Efforts*

Prof Kaula's this visit to the Department of Library and Information Science, Gauhati University along with other personnel like Jnyanpith award winner and ex-President of the Assam Sahitya Sabha, Dr Birendra Kr Bhattacharya, ex-M P and President of Assam College Librarians Association, Prof Ajit Kr Sharma, President and Secretaries of the Assam College Teachers Association and Gauhati University Teachers Association respectively, and other dignitaries have largely contributed to creating an atmosphere of appreciation for academic librarianship as an essential part of an educational programme. This ultimately has made the Government of Assam to decide and declare to implement the U G C pay-scales for college librarians w.e.f. August 5, 1987.

5. **Kaula and Assam Library Association**

Assam Library Association which took birth in 1938 fell ill at its 10th Conference in November, 1971 held at Nowgong, and has stopped functioning altogether since several years now. Prof P N Kaula recalling his association with the Eighth most successfully Assam Library Conference held in 1964 at Guwahati in the presence of Dr S R Ranganathan, the makes him feel pain at this silence and inactivity of the Assam Library Association. It is Kaula Saheb who is bothering for its revival along with a few local professionals, although old office-bearers with a few exceptions appear to have lost all enthusiasm. So, it is Kaula Saheb who is trying with his little link with the old fellows like Mr Gojendra Nath Phukan to revive its functioning. He is still writing on this matter to who so ever he could approach. Unfortunately, the Assam Library Association is still a history to the new-comers in the profession.

6. **Assam Felicitates Prof Kaula**

Prof P N Kaula, UGC Emeritus Fellow Professor, and an internationally renowned library scientist, was felicitated with a "*Fulam Gamoche*" (embroidered handwoven towel, symbol of affection) and a "*Sarai*" (plate with stand, symbol of honour) by Library and Information Science Student's Forum of Gauhati University on June 26, 1986; Kaula Saheb was honoured and felicitated in the presence of the participants and guests attending the Valedictory function of the Refresher Course for academic librarians of the North-East Region for his outstanding contributions to India and abroad, his dedication to the profession, and the well-deserved eminence he had attained in the field.

6.1 *Tribute paid by Phukan*

On this occasion Mr Gojendra Phukan, a Veteran Librarian and Vice-President of the Assam Library Association, paid tributes to Prof Kaula for his services to Assam. He said :

> While thanking the organizers of the Seminar for giving me an opportunity to be associated with the fellow librarians, I must congratulate them for inviting Prof P N Kaulaji as the Chief Guest, an Emeritus Professor of International repute and doyen of Library Science, endowed with international honours and awards to his credit, to grace the occasion. To honour him with Assamese traditional *Sarai* and *Fulam Gamocha* is a great privilege for us all and it has enhanced the dignity of the function. Many distinguished scholars and professors of Gauhati city and the university have attended the function including Dr D Barua, Vice-Chancellor of the Gauhati University.
>
> Mr Phukan recalled "the sterling qualities of head and heart of my *Guruji* – Prof Kaula – and the tremendous achievements made by him in the field of Library Science in India and the world over. Prof Kaula was instrumental and a guiding spirit along with Dr S R Ranganathan, the Father of Library Science, in convincing the then Chief Minister Bimala Prasad Chaliha, the Education Minister Deva Kanta Barua, and the Gauhati University authorities in 1964 to open the Bachelor of Library Science Course in the university and also for enactment of library law. We must remain ever grateful especially to Prof Kaula for his love and affection to the people of Assam and the splendid services still being rendered for the improvement of library service in the State by contacting the Education Secretary and Commissioner and other officials of the Depart-

ment for enactment of Library Legislation for Assam, while visiting Gauhati for the said conference.

7. Conclusion

Prof P N Kaula is a dynamic personality. Barring all other things, what we find in him, is his dedication for the profession which keeps him always preoccupied, alive and young with hopes for the future in the field. The profession in Assam and the North-East would always need guidance from people like Prof Kaula. Long live Prof Kaula Saheb!

R 2

Prof P N Kaula and Bihar

U M Thakur

1. Versatile Library Educator

Prof P N Kaula has been a distinguished librarian, bibliographer, documentalist, information scientist, organizer, planner, innovator, editor, writer, speaker, educator, a doyen of librarianship, a great son of India and a scholar of international repute – all combined in one. His manifold contributions have earned for him a unique place in the world.

He has been the recipient of several International awards – the one coming from Brazilian Academy of Humanities for "International Understanding". He has been also honoured with "Kaula Festschrift" through an International Festschrift Volume Committee in 1974. An Endowment established in his name awards "Kaula Gold Medal" since 1975.

2. Fruitful Contact

Writing something about such a great personality is not an easy task for me. I know from the very first day I joined the "noble profession of Library Science", which is now almost 25 years in span of time. During this period, I had the privilege to come in very close contact with him. He has not only quenched my thirst to drink deep the great knowledge of Library and Information Science, but also has given all the affection of a real Father.

3. Visit to Bihar

For the past three decades, he has taken all the pains for the library development in the State of Bihar.

It was in 1969 when the great historian late Dr K K Datta was the Vice-Chancellor of Patna University, that Prof Kaula was felicitated by all the professional librarians of the State in the Wheeler Senate Hall, Patna. It was through his sincere efforts only that the teaching of the Library and Information Science was started in Patna University in 1980.

His visits and ardent desire for the library development have always inspired the professionals of Bihar State. He is a person of such magnitude that all true professionals adore him. He is a true friend of them all indeed.

4. Bihar Felicitates Kaula

Representatives from 22 library organizations and institutions from Bihar felicitated Prof P N Kaula, at a special function held at Srikrishna Vigyan Hall, Patna, on February 24, 1986. Prof Kaula was presented an "Address of Tribute" eulogized him for his outstanding contributions as librarian, bibliographer, writer, thinker, organizer, journalist and educator. The Address duly framed was presented to him at a large gathering of librarians, educationists, public men and students of library science from all over Bihar. Twentytwo organizations and their representatives garlanded Prof Kaula who was drowned in garlands. There were speakers who spoke about his work and contributions. Dr S F Rab, Librarian, A N Sinha Institute of Social Studies, said that Dr S R Ranganathan was "Father of Library Science in India" and Prof Kaula was "Patriarch of Library Movement in India". He spoke about Prof Kaula's love for Bihar and the Address presented to him in 1969 at the Wheeler Senate Hall of Patna University.

4.1 *Address of Tribute*

The Address read out by Dr U M Thakur was as under:

Embodiment of Library Science

Respected Sir!

We, the students and the working professionals in the field of Library and Information Science, are filled with the feelings of gratitude and honour to ourselves, by your benign presence in this historical city of

Patliputra. Sir, kindly permit this assembly of the citizens of the first order, the respectable teachers and devoted students of library science of 22 organizations and institutions to express their deep regards and heart-ful greetings on this occasion which has become graceful by your auspicious presence. We beseech your honour to kindly accept our salutations.

(1) *Earlier Felicitation at Patna*

Sir, allow us to recollect that your outstanding personality was also felicitated in the year 1969 at the Wheeler Senate Hall, Patna, by an assembly which was presided over by Dr K K Datta, the then Vice-Chancellor of Patna University. On that occasion the Governor of Bihar and the Chancellor of the universities of the State, Mr Ananthasayanam Ayyangar, offered a grand and memorable welcome to your Honour. Perhaps not satisfied by his kind gesture on the occasion, the Hon'ble Governor expressed his warm feelings for your personality which were published in *Library Science Today* and which have remained a source of inspiration to the new generation of librarians.

(2) *Shining Star of the World of Library and Information Science*

Professor Kaula, Sir, we see in you a distinguished library scientist, the librarian of the highest possible order, the learned author, the original thinker, a successful promoter, organizer and builder of libraries and schools of library and information science. This has been recognized as such and highly acknowledged by the library profession in our country and abroad. Your cap is full with the feathers of honours, such as PRO MUNDI BENEFICIO MEDAL of Brazilian Academy of Humanities, SAO Paulo, Brazil; DEUTSCHE BUCHEREI MEDAL of the German Democratic Republic; INTERNATIONAL BIOGRAPHICAL ROLL OF HONOUR PLAQUE of American Biographical Institute in recognition of your "Distinguished Service in Education and Library Science" and many others. All-India Radio has described Professor Kaula as the "first Indian to have received such high honours and awards". We feel a great pride in you, Sir.

Your Honour, we know that you were the only Indian among the two distinguished representatives selected the world over at the International Conference on Information Science held in Tel Aviv in the year 1971 to participate in the TV programme. Your contributions as

UNESCO Expert in Library and Information Science are recognized more than once by the august bodies at the international level. The librarians in every corner of the world have been ever eager to quench their thirst of knowledge and information on library and information science in the presence of your person and through your discourse, a moving encyclopaedia on the subject. Authenticity and depth of your masterly knowledge have been quite often felt by the community of librarians in various countries, such as Belgium, Cuba, Denmark, Egypt, France, Hungary, Germany, GDR, Mexico, Thailand, UK, USA and USSR.

(3) *Prolific Author*

You have made the library literature richer by innumerable writings on libraries, library services, and librarians. So far 48 books and monographs, 800 articles and book reviews and about 5,000 valuable items of "Notes and News" have come into existence from the facile flow of your pen. You have been successfully editing three journals of international repute, viz *Herald of Library Science, Granthalaya Vijnana* and *International Information, Communication and Education.* Besides, you have founded a number of academic societies and bodies in the field of library science.

(4) *Matchless Organizer of Libraries*

The *Times Literary Supplement* (London) stated in 1971 that Prof Kaula was "one of the most influential librarians in the world". The *Library World*, London, a journal of long standing, has recognized you as one of the World-famous contemporaries", and counted you among the "galaxy of the Great". *Bulletin Bibliotica* (Cuba) has named you a Specialist Professional in the international field. Thus, you are the rightful heir of rare human qualities of dutifulness, wisdom, intelligence and simplicity of Dr S R Ranganathan, Father of Library Science in India. Dr Ranganathan, at a much early stage, could see an unparallel personality hidden in your goodself.

(5) *Worldwide Felicitations*

An International Committee consisting of 215 members from 30 different countries dedicated KAULA FESTSCHRIFT "March of Library

Science" in your honour. Prof Kaula Endowment Trust has been established by your admirers, friends and students that has been awarding KAULA GOLD MEDAL and Citation to a distinguished professional on the recommendations of the International Awards Committee having representatives of seven countries. Seventeen Library Associations jointly felicitated you in the city of Hyderabad in 1974.

(6) *Distinguished Educations*

After your superannuation from the position of Head of the Department of Library and Information Science, Banaras Hindu University, the University Grants Commission of India got you attached to the Lucknow University as Visiting Professor. In 1985 you were awarded the honour of Emeritus Fellow Professor by the University Grants Commission, a rare distinction given to only a few educationists in the country and the lone one in the field of Library and Information Science.

(7) *Our Affinity*

We all know that Prof Kaula's affection and affinity to the librarians of the State of Bihar has flown unhindered. Whenever we have needed you, you have been kind enough to be present among us. We express our deep feelings of gratitude for your ever kind and affectionate response. While felicitating your honour today, we pray to the Almighty to shower upon your august person good health and long life so that we can march ahead under your able guidance and command.

Ever Grateful Yours
Librarians of Bihar

4.2 *Tribute Paid by Colleges*

Dr R P Poddar, Superintendent of Libraries, Government of Bihar, who presented the "Address of Tribute" to Prof Kaula, in his Presidential remarks emphasized that Prof Kaula was speaking about Dr S R Ranganathan's greatness out of his love and regard to him. But he did not agree with Prof Kaula when he said that the honour that was done to him by his professional colleagues and bodies should be done to his *Guru*. Prof Kaula had brought a name to the profession by his own contributions and as per Sanskrit proverb, he had brought greater dimensions to the profession and the contributions of his Guru by his own work. Dr R S P Singh, Librarian, State Central Library and Secretary, Bihar State Library Association, said that Prof Kaula had always helped the librarians of Bihar. It was through his efforts that library science education was instituted in Patna and it was again because of his efforts that the Library Bill was drafted and presented to the Government. He wanted Prof Kaula to shift to Patna which was a land from where Lord Buddha preached Buddhism. Among those who spoke were Duryodhan Singh, Dr S Dwivedi, Dr Bhawnath Mishra, and B P Mishra who eulogized the work of Prof Kaula quoting Dr S R Ranganathan that he was "second to none in the country". Later Prof Kaula spoke to Mr L N Jha, State Education Minister, urging for the enactment of the Library Bill for the State.

5. Humility Personified

His role in the development of library movement has been significant. He has got remarkable grasp of extensive knowledge, scholarship and his roaring voice and is an excellent orator.

Prof Kaula's understanding nature, pleasing personality, broad mindedness and vision has often been a matter of surprise to many. I have always wondered at his depth of knowledge, his dedication to the profession, even at this advanced age.

Prof Kaula's reputation and fame has not touched his simplicity. The charming simplicity in him is the true Indian spirit. He is the most prolific writer in library science and in the words of Dr S R Ranganathan, "Second to none in the profession in the country".

I am afraid that I have skipped lot of Prof P N Kaula's rare qualities at this moment. To express such a great personality in a few words is impossible. I can only express my gratitude and convey my respect and reverence to Prof Kaula, who, to me, is not only a *Guru*, educator and guide but also an affectionate father. Not only Prof Kaula but Didijee (Mrs Kaula) also treated me like her son. I will never forget her affection and kind love in my life. I pray to lord, let him be the same P N Kaula for a long, long time to come!

S 1

An Essay on Professor Kaula's Contributions to Library Journalism

Mohinder Partap Satija and **Sukhdev Singh**

1. Rare Confluence of Qualities

Professor Prithvi Nath Kaula, a most noted of the contemporary Indian librarians, has carved a secure niche for himself in the Indian library history. An eminent scholar, a teacher who inspires respect, a versatile writer, a library leader of repute, and a successful library journalist, he is a rare confluence of so many qualities at once. With his single-minded devotion to the cause of library and information science profession, he has earned a name in the national and international library world. His patron and *Guru* Dr S R Ranganathan, the acknowledged Father of Indian library science, declared him as "*second to none in the profession*". Among the contemporaries, he is certainly among the top notches, and no wonder that he figures amongst the most famous of Indian librarians of all times. This article, however, dwells only on one aspect of his life — his contribution to Indian library journalism. To him goes the credit of founding six journals, and successfully running three journals of his own, now sponsored by the Trust bearing his name. His success in and far-reaching contributions to library journalism can be better understood in the perspective of his other achievements.

2. Some Aspects of His Life

Prithvi Nath Kaula, born on March 13, 1924, strayed into librarianship by mere chance – as in those days it was hardly a known career. But his constant rise in the profession is not a chance; it is a story and a citable example of the success of single-minded devotion and dedication to the profession. For him only the sky has been the limit. He is an *exemplary* disciple of his great *Guru* Dr S R Ranganathan.

2.1 *A True Apostle*

Kaula received his early education in Kashmir, and came to Madras to study library science under Dr Ranganathan. His first, now a historical event, meeting with Dr Ranganathan at the latter's residence and later accompanying him to Benaras in August 1945 has been vividly described by Kaula himself.[1] Obtaining his Post-graduate Diploma in Library Science, Kaula moved to Delhi in 1948 to be admitted to the country's first Master's degree in Library Science again under his revered teacher Ranganathan. His association with Dr Ranganathan has been life-long, first as a student, then colleague and always his ardent protagonist. He is indeed an *apostle* of Ranganathan. Now, the association of the two names lives eternally in the "*Ranganathan-Kaula (National) Award*" instituted by Professor Kaula Endowment. His obligation to his *Guru* is tangible in the form of a Festschrift entitled *Library Science Today*, edited by him, which still remains unsurpassed in editorial acumen and quality of all the Indian festschrifts that have followed in its wake. It is still a model.[2] Above all Kaula's great and sincere tribute to his *Guru* is manifested in his unique achievements earned by following in Ranganathan's footsteps. In the best of Indian traditions of humility, he has always attributed his achievements to the blessings of Ranganathan and of God. He thus best exemplifies the age of old Indian *Guru-Shishya* tradition.

2.2 *Noble Son of the Soil*

Most travelled both in India and abroad, Prof Kaula's achievements are too numerous. Like Tennyson's *Ulysses* it can be said of him :

> I am become a name;
> For always roaming with a hungry heart.
> Much have I seen and known; cities of men
> And manners, climates, councils, governments,
> Myself no least, but honoured of them all;
> And drunk delight of battles with my peers,
> Far from the ringing plains of windy Troy
> I am a part of all that I have met; . . ."

Many professional organizations in India have vied with one another in honouring him and presenting him addresses of honour. In 1972, he was jointly honoured by 17 professional organizations at a function held at the State Central Library, Hyderabad, for his varied work and contributions to the profession. Dr Ch Devananda Rao, the then State Minister for Public Libraries and Tourism, Andhra Pradesh, in his presidential remarks said of him:

> ". . . Professor Kaula is the son of Mother India, who has brought distinction to his country by his contributions and attainments. It does not matter if he came from Kashmir or Kanyakumari. He is the noble son of the soil to be known everywhere. . . ."

2.3 *Brazilian Honour and After*

In 1979, a unique honour was conferred on him by the Brazilian Academy of Humanities with *Pro Mundi Beneficio Medal* for international understanding. It is a "Cultural Award" conferred on a person of special merit and moral nobility, and who contributes with his outstanding activities to "Promotion of Civilization, Peace and Human Understanding and creation of a better world for the future". Importance of this award to a librarian and to the country is self-evident. Among his other numerous recognitions and honours the latest one includes "Gold Medal of Honor from the American Bibliographical Institute for distinguished achievements in education and library science. The citation reads:

> "This invitation comes to you in view of your outstanding achievements. The Medal of Honor has been designed exclusively for you who has contributed so much to the betterment of the society and the Profession."

Prof Kaula is in fact known as a librarian who has earned many awards, and has given many awards – the national and international awards instituted by Kaula Endowment for Library and Information Science; and the tally of his awards and honours is imposing.

3. **Beginning in the Journalism**

Kaula was attracted to library Journalism by writing on library movement and the role of Kashmir in this movement. He published a series of articles, mostly in Urdu, in the Kashmir Press in 1946-47. During a brief span of one and a half years, the number of such articles rose to 108. Such was the influence of his articles on the people that almost every newspaper be it daily, weekly or even quarterly preferred to publish them. One of his articles, "*Kashmir badal ki zamana badal gaya*" (Change O' Kashmir as the world has changed), became very popular. He also wrote poems on libraries and library movement. This was the period when he had just returned after training under Dr Ranganathan. He also published a small booklet, *Kashmir mein Ilmi Inqlab* (Educational Revolution in Kashmir) with a foreword by Dr S R Ranganathan. Under the influence of Dr Ranganathan, it was such a single-minded devotion to the cause that it is no wonder that some of his relatives and friends thought that he had gone crazy.[3]

4. Matures as a Professional Journalist

Kaula had to leave Kashmir in order to join Birla Central Library to become its Chief Librarian. Library profession in Kashmir in those days was not so developed as to accommodate the genius of Prof Kaula. Later he gave up the post of the Chief Librarian to join Delhi University Library as a Junior Library Assistant on a much smaller salary simply to work under Dr Ranganathan. He learnt the art of editing journals from his *Guru*, who made him later, in December 1989, the Managing Editor of ABGILA – (A)nnals. (B)ulletin and (G)ranthalya of (I)ndian (L)ibrary (A)ssociation – in place of S Das Gupta. It was short-lived (1949–1953), but a journal of high repute. Apart from the printing work, Kaula had to prepare the detailed Index to the three parts of ABGILA. Each part had a half-title page, title page and an Index. Volume I of *Annals* had an Index of eight pages and Volume I of *Bulletin* had an Index of 16 pages. The Index was prepared in standard abbreviated terms. ABGILA ceased publication in 1953 with the change in the Management of the Indian Library Association.[4]

4.1 *Editor of "Sharda"*

Kaula found another forum to express his views and of others of his liking. The Kashmiri Pandit Association, Delhi, invited him to edit its organ "*Sharda*" from October 1952 onwards. He brought out the issues of Vols 1-3 (1952–54) in October 1952, January 1953, October 1953 and March 1954. Though it was not a library journal, it afforded him the experience of independent editing.

4.2 *Founder Editor of "Library Herald"*

Professor Kaula played the key role in founding the Delhi Library Association on August 16, 1953. The Association decided to launch its organ *Library Herald* under the editorship of Kaula in 1958. The first issue of the journal was brought out in April 1958 with the first article by Dr Ranganathan. Prof Kaula edited Vols 1-4 (1958–1962). His association with the ABGILA stood him in good stead in this work. He also brought out the detailed Index of each volume on the pattern of ABGILA. Two new features were included in this journal:

(1) Personalia (Who's Who in Library Science) (Under Personalia, bibliographic description of leading librarians along with their photographs used to be given. It was a valuable feature in India as biographies of Indian librarians are not easily available. Regretfully this feature has been discontinued now).

(2) Library Gazette: This feature brought together the information about appointments, transfers, promotions, etc, of library personnel of Delhi.

4.3 *Disassociates from "Library Herald"*

Kaula had to shift to Varanasi to join Banaras Hindu University as its University Librarian and Head of the Department of Library Science, the position offered to him by that University on his own terms. The Executive Committee of the Delhi Library Association decided to request its founder and successful editor Kaula to take *Library Herald* with him to Varanasi to publish it from there. Kaula agreeing to this proposal brought out the 1960 and 1961 volumes from Varanasi. However, later the new management of the Delhi Library Association set up an Editorial Board for *Library Herald* without taking Prof Kaula into confidence. And, he resigned from the editorship of the journal.

Despite its chequered career, and bereft of punctuality, the *Library Herald* is still continued on the pattern set by Kaula by the DLA and is considered one of the important journals in Library Science for its contents which include articles, reports, lectures, memoranda, reviews of publications, etc.

5. Birth of a New Journal – "Herald of Library Science"

Relinquishing the editorial charge of the *Library Herald*, Prof Kaula embarked upon a new journal of his own named *Herald of Library Science* in 1962. By this time Prof Kaula had gained much experience of professional journalism by editing the *Library Herald* and through his earlier association with Dr Ranganathan in bringing out ABGILA. Dr Ranganathan in the "Foreword" to the first issue of the *Herald of Library Science* wished, "It will . . . live long under his care". He was prophetic. In this Message for the inaugural issue (January 1962) Ranganathan remarked.

> The *Herald of Library Science* is the tenth organ of the librarianship in India. . . . This is the second such organ to be started by my friend Prithvinath Kaula – a bundle of energy-cum-determination. . . . In the English language we have the *Annals of Library Science* as the medium for the nascent thought getting created in the country. We have also other periodicals mainly carrying library news and popular communication. The place of the *Herald of Library Science*, I take it, will be between these two extremes. It will act as the proving ground for the new voices coming up in increasing numbers in Renascent India. . . .

5.1 *Regularity*

Sarada Ranganathan Endowment in Library Science sponsored this journal initially. But on the establishment of Prof Kaula Endowment for Library and Information Science (1975), the sponsorship got inevitably shifted to the latter. This journal is unique for its regularity, style, exhaustive and international news coverage and its regular features. It is among 23 selected core periodicals in the world as mentioned in a report published by the United Nations. Dr Ranganathan regularly contributed to this journal. In fact Ranganathan's autobiography could only get started with the availability of this new medium.

At the initiation of Prof Kaula "A Librarian Looks Back" by S R Ranganathan was serialized in this journal from 1963 till his death in 1972, which will perhaps be published in a book form by Prof Kaula Endowment for Library and Information Science.

5.2 *Salient Feature*

This journal has many salient features. Some of these are :

(1) Papers on various library techniques and library system
(2) Reports on library activities throughout the world
(3) Notes on library education
(4) Extensive Reviews of publications
(5) Library Notes and News–National and International in Library Science (arranged areawise)
(6) Review articles on recent developments
(7) Exchange of library ideas throughout the world
(8) Original papers from librarians
(9) Each article bears an abstract mostly given by the editor
(10) Each feature is assigned a class number according to the Colon Classification; and
(11) Special numbers on different aspects of Library Science from time to time, edited by a guest Editor. For example, the first such issue in 1962 was the Special number of Dr Ranganathan.

5.3 *Special Issues*

An up to date list of all such special issues is given below :

(1) Ranganathan Number (1962)
(2) Documentation Number (1964)
(3) Library Movement Number (1964)
(4) Classification Number (1965)
(5) Library Education Number (1966)
(6) Teaching of Library Science Number (1967)
(7) Ranganathan Memorial Number (1972)
(8) Kaula Felicitation Number (1974)
(9) Dewey Commemoration Number (1976)
(10) Indian Librarianship Number (1976)

(11) British Librarianship Number (1976)
(12) Information Science Number (1979)
(13) Silver Jubilee Number on Library Science Literature (1987)
(14) Kaula Sixtyfirst Birthday Felicitation Number (1987)
(15) Document Processing Number (1989).

5.4 *The Silver Jubilee Issue and Cumulative Index*

The journal observed 1986 as its Silver Jubilee Year. Silver Jubilee issue on Indian Library Science Literature — which it has helped to grow fast--was brought out in the year 1987. Cumulative Index of Vols 1-22 (1962–1983) has been brought out by S S Pal in 1985 as a separate publication.[5] The journal is best known for its numerous book reviews and comprehensive coverage given to library notes and news from India and abroad. Each volume has also got an Analytico-keyword Index (Vols 1-19, 1962–1980 and Vols 24-25 (1985 and 1986).

5.5 *Widely Popular*

Herald of Library Science has indeed something to offer to every reader and is eagerly awaited by all librarians and library professionals. With Prof Kaula as its founder-editor the *Herald of Library Science* is India's ambassador in the world of Library and Information Science. It has a place of pride among the world's core journals in our field. Though its approach is ecumenical and coverage international in some aspects, yet no other journal portrays India's picture as vividly and symbolically as this. This journal with thickly packed contents is known for its regularity and stability in a country where the birth and mortality rate of journals is too high. Blessed by Dr Ranganathan, it is endowed with many qualities which Ranganathan always held high. Not the last among them is to spot talent and encourage the youngsters. Apart from its academic role this journal has played an influential social role for the development of library and information sources in our country.

6. Founder-Editor of "Granthalaya Vijnana"

Kaula has also founded a Hindi periodical in Library Science, *Granthalaya Vijnana*. This periodical with immense scope has been brought out for the development of Hindi and other regional languages. It is a Hindi journal on the subject of Library Science started in 1970 and published half-yearly, in June and December. Each issue is a special number on a specific topic. It covers the following:

(1) Libraries in India (General)
(2) Libraries in India (States)
(3) School Libraries
(4) Functions of Libraries
(5) Ranganathan Memorial Volume
(6) Public Library Service
(7) Library Management
(8) Library Cataloguing
(9) Reference Service
(10) Bibliography
(11) Library Organization
(12) Library Classification
(13) Documentation
(14) Library Standards
(15) College Libraries
(16) Information Service
(17) Academic Libraries
(18) School Libraries

7. Editor of the Research Journal of B H U

Prof Kaula was appointed Dean, Faculty of Arts, in June 1979, while he was away with his programme of lectures and attending meetings in the Federal Republic of Germany. After returning from abroad, he took over the new responsibility and as the Dean, he initiated several academic programmes including initiation of the *Research Journal of the Faculty of Arts*. He induced teachers of the other departments to contribute to this journal. It included a section on Library Science and contained papers on "Research and Research Areas in Library Science". Activities of the Department of Library and Information Science were prominently published besides the various articles contributed by Prof Kaula himself and his colleagues at B H U. He also organized an Exhibition of the works of Faculty members for the first time in the University.

8. Founder-Editor of "Progress in Library and Information Science"

With the efforts of Prof Kaula, the Department of Library and Information Science, BHU, started, in 1980, a departmental journal: *Progress in Library and Information Science*. He shouldered the responsibilities of editing this journal with colleagues in the Department as associate editors. This journal, though issued annually is a notable venture of Prof Kaula in the professional journalism and it has contributed greatly to the fields of librarianship and Library and Information Science. Prof Kaula edited this journal from 1980 to 1983. This journal is also being continued.

9. Founder-Editor of "International Information, Communication and Education" (INICAE)

INICAE is a multidisciplinary journal started by Prof Kaula in 1982. The background of initiating this journal was that the departments conducting library science courses were renamed as the Department of Library and Information Science on the recommendation of a Panel on Library and Information Science of the UGC of which Prof Kaula was a member. This was done to introduce teaching programme on information storage, processing, retrieval and technology. More stress was laid on Information Science than merely on the traditional library science. With this new trend of the development in library science, Kaula decided to launch a new international journal on information technology and service. Some of the friends even from abroad suggested change in the name of the *Herald of Library Science* to *Herald of Library and Information Science*. Kaula with his all foresight did not agree to this and launched a new journal with the title *International Information, Communication and Education* (INICAE) in 1982, a year preceding his retirement. This was a decision fraught with real risks he had taken at that stage. But INICAE was started with full hope and determination with an International Board of Editors and even the contributors to the journal are international with no limitation of country or any other viewpoint. Reviewing the INICAE, the *Library Journal* (New York), the oldest and grand professional journal, commented: "The contributors are international and no way limited to one country or viewpoint. That is what gives the well edited journal a certain zest and fascination rarely formed in library literature." (emphasis ours).

9.1 *Special Features*

INICAE is now a well-established journal on an even keel. It has successfully met international standards and competition; and introduced many new features in Indian library science journalism. This journal is media for bringing into operation the new concepts and advances in communication, information science and technology transfer, research and innovation and management and marketing of information.
Some of the special features of this journal are :

(1) It provides systematic coverage of communication process and channels, media, including mass media of communication and experiences and new developments relating to them.
(2) It serves as a primary source material for all aspects of information science and technology right from the very creation of information through recording, storing, handling and retrieval to its pinpointed, exhaustive and speed dissemination.
(3) It publishes authoritative papers on theory and practice of information and communication sciences written in English. In addition, it encourages and promotes evaluation and criticism of practices.
(4) It is international in coverage and multidisciplinary in nature and is useful to all those concerned with communication, education and dissemination of recorded information in Sciences, Social Sciences and Humanities.
(5) It provides an invaluable source material for libraries, documentalists, information scientists and technologists, communicators, media specialists, educators, archivists and journalists alike.
(6) It is a dependable guide to the documentary sources on information and communication and their education through its unbiased scholarly Book Reviews, Reports, Viewpoints, Digest and other features.
(7) It records reports on research findings, opinions and practical application of information systems, services and technology.
(8) With its International Board of Editors and chief editorial direction of Prof Kaula, it conforms to the international

norms in enabling readers to be abreast of developments in information and communication science and also facilitating the exchange of ideas and materials among users.

(9) It covers Communication Science, Information Science, Applied Information Science, Management Economics and Marketing of Information and the Structure, Development and Change in Education for Information.

9.2 *Assessment*

Prof Kaula now well steeped in library journalism, was initiated in this professional aspect by Dr S R Ranganathan himself. As a farsighted library leader, he recognized the value of new journals especially for nurturing and grooming the library profession in a country like India. With his determination, energy and skill Kaula has made a name for himself in library journalism as much as in the overall library movement of the country. It is no exaggeration to say that he is the most successful and experienced of the living Indian library editors. He has kept his journals surviving and progressing in a country where unpunctuality, irregularity and ultimate demise is the bane of the library journalism. Every year library journals spring up with promises and vanish unnoticed and unceremoniously. He has kept his journals regular in spite of his many engaging and multifarious engagements and commitments to the profession, though to cover delay frequently, two issues are combined in one.

Another service to the library journalism lies in keeping his journals moderately priced. In the days of inflation when prices of journals are fast spiralling, and some profiteers are always looking for an opportunity to raise the price of their journals, he has tried to check this tendency. He never takes them as profit ventures. I recall how he regretted the high price of the Cumulative Index to his journals brought out by a Chandigarh-based publisher. *Granthalya Vijnana*, a financial liability, has been kept going as it is an asset to the vernacular library journalism. It will help in the medium switchover of education in the local languages. It also speaks of his love for the national language.

It is alleged not without substance, that he uses his journals, especially the *Herald of Library Science*, for the eulogies sung in his praise. It is true on its face. But this journal is as much open to him (the editor) as it is to any other member of the Indian library profession. Achievements of other librarians are given due place and importance in the columns of the *Herald*. Many a new established librarians gratefully remember the opportunities provided to them by his journals when they were unknown, uninitiated and unskilled in the art of technical writings. He has always encouraged novices to write in order to spot new talents and to give a fillip to the library movement in the country. True to the hopes of Dr S R Ranganathan, "our young librarians use its pages in full measure to communicate their own nascent thought and use it as a stepping stone to reach towards eminence of fundamental and enduring research". He has skilfully discharged this professional obligation without lowering the standard of his journals. Thus, his journals have played a vital social role in grooming new authors, creating library awareness, and to strengthen library movement and education in India.

REFERENCES

1 KAULA P N: Ranganathan: A study (In : *Library Science Today*: Ranganathan Festschrifted by P N Kaula Vol I, Bombay, Asia, 1965, pp 649-676).

2 KAULA P N Ed : *Library Science Today* : Ranganathan Festschrift", Bombay, Asia 1965, p 832.

3 Letter dated 29-9-1986 from Professor P N Kaula to M P Satija.

4 SATIJA M P Ranganathan in the Fleet Street : Story of Ranganathan's Career in Library Journalism, [*Herald of Lib. Sci.*, Vol 24 (3), July 1985, section p 2]

5 PAL S S : *Herald of Library Science: Trend Report, Citations and Index (1962-1983)*: Chandigarh, Gina House (Publishers), 1985, p 94.

Further Readings

1 SATYANARAYAN N R: :"Survey of Literature in Periodicals in India", (In: *March of Library Science : Kaula Festschrift*", ed by V Venkatappaiah New Delhi, Vikas, 1979, p 110-120),

2 KUMAR R P : Periodicals in Library and Information Science in India : *Origin and Development*", (In: Gupta, P K and Usha Pawan Ed: "*Library and Information Science: Current Trends in India*", Jaipur, R B S A Publishers, 1986, pp 245-256).

3 KUMAR R P : *Research Periodicals of Colonial India (1780—1947)*. Delhi Academic Publications, 1985.

4 MUSHIB S K : Production of Journals in India, (*Indian Library Review*. Vol 19-(4), Oct 1987, pp 423-432).

5 *Herald of Library Science*. Vol 26 (3-4), July-October 1987: pp 161-329 (Kaula Sixtyfirst Birthday Felicitation Number), edited by P S G Kumar.

6 *Herald of Library Science*. Vol 13 (3-4), July-October 1974 (Professor Kaula Special Number) edited by V Venkatappaiah and R N Sar.

7 POLEMAN Horace I : Serial Publications in India. (*Library of Congress Quarterly Journal of Current Acquisitions*, July-Sept 1943, pp 23-29).

[illegible]

[illegible]

[illegible]

[illegible]

[illegible]

[illegible]

S 2

The Sui Generis Educator

Dr S R Gupta and **S S Verma**

0. The Vedic Concept

Indian intelligentsia has accorded to a *Guru* (a teacher-educator) the top important role and position in society. The characteristics of a true *guru* as defined by *Yukti Kalp Taru* include[1]:

"सदाचारः कुशलधीः सर्वशास्त्रार्थपारगः ।
नित्य नैमित्तिकानाञ्च कार्याणां कारकः शुचिः ॥
अपर्व मैथुनपरः पितृदेवार्चने रतः ।
गुरुभक्तो जितक्रोधो विप्राणां हितकृत् सदा ॥
दयावान् शीलसम्पन्नः सत्कुलीनो महामतिः ।
परदारेषु विमुखो दृढ़ संकल्पको द्विजः ॥
अन्यैश्च वैदिकगुणैर्युक्तः कार्यो गुरुः नृपैः ।
एतैरेव गुणै युक्तः पुरोधाः स्यान्मही भुजाम् ॥(१)

The *guru*, thus, needs to be a man of good character, wise, learned, religious minded, devoted to his own *guru*, one who has control over his anger, has strong will-power, etc. In this paper a humble attempt is being made to know Prof Prithvi Nath Kaula in the background of the above-mentioned vedic concept, grown to the extent of "the *Sui Generis Guru*".

1. At Aligarh Muslim University

Those who have known Kaula only in the latter part of his career, as Professor of Library and Information Science, and have heard his roaring voice elucidating the subject under discussion whether in a classroom or in an assembly of professionals, may not know about his humble beginnings in the profession. Kaula has worked in a much junior position of Technical Assistant at Delhi University Library in the years 1948–50 where he could be closely associated with his *Guru*, Dr S R Ranganathan. Prof S Bashiruddin of Aligarh Muslim University was keen to start a School of Library Science at his University. His penetrating eyes caught the hidden quality of the teacher in Kaula's person. He asked Kaula to draft the syllabus of Cert. Lib. Sc. in 1958 , come to Aligarh and organize the course of Certificate in Library Science. Kaula could not say to Prof Bashiruddin. But by that time (1951) he had joined the Ministry of Labour as librarian and according to the conditions of his service, he feared he could not have joined the project of Prof Bashiruddin unless permitted by the Ministry. At this Prof Bashiruddin made Dr Zakir Husain, the then Vice-Chancellor of AMU, to write to the Secretary, Ministry of Labour to help the University in procuring the services of Kaula. Thus, Kaula started going to AMU at weekends straight from his Library. There he having drafted the course for C. Lib. Sc., organized its teaching programme and started teaching as a Visiting Lecturer (Honorary). For this purpose he travelled to and fro Aligarh at his personal expense and taught for five to six hours in a day to cover various papers of the course. This was done by Kaula at the cost of his personal comforts and out of his sheer devotion to his profession. This arrangement continued till 1958 when the University appointed two full time lectures and started B.Lib.Sc. course. In one of his letters written to Kaula in the year 1979, Prof Bashiruddin recollected Prof Kaula's noble gesture by stating, "I feel proud, however, that my choice of a promising young man to help me in starting a Library School at the Aligarh Muslim University in 1951 has been more than justified. Thousands of boys and girls remember you and feel lucky to have sat at your feet and listened to your inspiring lectures".

2. School of Library Science, DLA

Equipped with his basic ideas and encouraged by his experiences at

AMU, Kaula founded in the year 1955 the School of Library Science of the Delhi Library Association. Here, his insight, enthusiasm and experimentation as Registrar of the School provided a sound footing to its C. Lib. Sc., programme and hundreds of students each year continue to enjoy the benefits of this activity of DLA. Prof Kaula even obtained recognition to the course from the Delhi Administration and Government of India.

3. At Delhi University

Kaula was perhaps the right choice when in the year 1958 he was appointed as the first full-time Reader in the Department of Library Science of Delhi University. Kaula's enthusiasm for teaching and his devotion to the profession continued. He was instrumental to restart the M.Lib.Sc. teaching programme in 1959, which was kept under abeyance for a period of four years. It was a tough and challenging task for him and he taught as many as six papers of M.Lib.Sc. course at the Department, teaching also a different paper at Dip. Lib. Sc. level, then treated first year of M. Lib. Sc. Prof Das Gupta, the then University Librarian and Head of the Department of Library Science at Delhi University, has recorded his impressions about Kaula's performance in a testimonial issued to Kaula, (Appendix A to this paper). His students at Delhi University consisted of many would-be renowned librarians in the country including Prof A P Srivastava, Prof P B Mangala, Prof Krishan Kumar and many others. Prof Srivastava has acknowledged his debt and respects, which he has for Prof Kaula, his former senior colleague and teacher, "The major force of my survival at Delhi University was Kaula's company who was Reader in the Department of Library Science. An ordinary person in place of Mr Kaula may also have withdrawn this support to me. But Kaulaji, being a fearless person, gave me much support".[2]

4. At Banaras Hindu University

The Banaras Hindu University offered Kaula the post of University Librarian and Head of the Department of Library Science and waived the condition of probation period in his case. In July 1960 Kaula joined BHU. His stay at BHU constitutes the largest span of his professional career. Here he worked for about 23 years till he attained the age of superannuation in the year 1983.

4.1 *On the Desk of University Librarian*

Kaula's untiring zeal, unflinching dedication, clear vision, keen interest and scientific outlook as librarian were best proved in his work at the BHU Library. His staff remembers him for his hard work and affectionate behaviour till today. K D Tiwari, former Registrar of Lucknow University, and for years the Executive Council Member of BHU, has this to say of Kaula:

> Of the many facets of this rare personality — both enduring and lovable — I have never ceased to be struck by his incessant zeal to scan new horizons and give the best of himself to his students, colleagues and the organization he serves.[3]

B N Ghatak, one of Kaula's deputies, has enumerated Kaula's outstanding contributions to the BHU Library and has called Kaula's association with it as an "era of consolidation". He says

> The Library is the biggest University Library in India. It is situated in the centre of the huge and well-planned campus of the world-famous university. It has a spacious circular type of reading room unique in the country. It has been a laboratory for the study of Library science by the staff and the teachers of the Department of Library Science", and Prof Kaula was appointed full-time Professor of Library Science in March 1971 and he continued to be the University Librarian till December 1971. The university library went back to its original position by appointing an Honorary Librarian and Prof Kaula moved out of the Library and the library building. He and the staff who worked with him as well as the users of the library generally look back to this era of consolidation and activities with pride and satisfaction.[4]

D Subrahmaniam, former, University Librarian of the BHU Library, thus spoke of Kaula:

> The organization of BHU Library consisting of 4,10,000 volumes on the latest techniques is a miracle and speaks of Prof Kaula's vision, interest and scientific outlook.[5]

4.2 *In the Chair of Professor and Head of Department*

After Kaula joined BHU as a University Librarian and Head of Department of Library Science, he successfully carried the burden of the two positions till 1971 when the teaching department got separated from the University Library. Then he became the first full-time Professor and the Head of Department of Library Science and retired from that position in 1983. His achievements in this period of 23 years are described in two parts — first, his innovations in the teaching and, second, the gratitude and tributes by the students, as follows.

4.21 *Innovations in Teaching*: When Kaula joined BHU, the University was running a course of Diploma in Library Science. Soon he realized the professions' demand on the teaching department in the country and to meet the demand he made all-out successful efforts to get the nomenclature of the course changed to B.Lib.Sc. in the year 1963. He surrendered his own teaching allowance to the University to get a post of full-time Lecturer in his Department.

For the purpose of upgrading the status of the Department and also to meet the growing demand of the profession, in the year 1965 he got introduced the higher course of M. Lib. Sc. at BHU. BHU, thus, became the second university in the country, the first being Delhi University, to provide M.Lib.Sc course. Also to keep pace with the changing demands on the teaching department, he got yet more updated nomenclature for the Department, viz. Department of Library and Information Science, and accordingly introduced new courses in the syllabus of the Department by incorporating the new front-lines in the discipline of Library Science.

Before, he left the Department in 1983, though continued to teach the students of M.Lib.Sc for another year at the request of the Vice-Chancellor, Kaula had built a reputation for the Department which attracted students from abroad to do research work leading to Ph.D. in Library Science. At the time of his retirement, he was supervising the research work of eight research scholars and one of them was from Bangladesh and the other from Thailand. As a teacher Kaula experimented in the techniques of teaching. He had introduced and made maximum use of "Class-Interview Methodology" of teaching. He also introduced for the first time theoretical study in Documentation, conducted examinations of practical papers by inviting experts and specialists to conduct examinations and viva-voce, arranged for study tours of students as part of the teaching programme.

4.22 *Gratitude and Tributes by Students*: Ever since Kaula undertook the job of teaching of library Science at AMU, Delhi University and BHU, his love and affection for his students and supreme command over the subjects taught have created a large band of admirers among his students. One may still sit with Prof A P Srivastava and listen to his experience of Kaula's affection and help to students. Out of his unmitigated respect for Kaula, Srivastava calls him in reverence "Panditji", the name affectionately given to Kaula by his *guru* Dr Ranganathan.

Kaula's students are unanimous in pronouncing Kaula as the *best teacher* they could have in their lifetime. Tiwana,[6] Jain,[7] Phookan,[8] Kanwal,[9] and many others have talked about Kaula's qualities *par excellence* of a teacher educator. His students have held that he is a teacher with rare dedication and devotion to his subject, has a strong moral character, superb eloquence in transmission of thoughts, is a path-finder for seekers of knowledge, a celebrated advocate of the profession, and a teacher who moulds his students into higher levels with his unending love, affection and help.

It may be a useful sharing of experiences with many who do know little of Kaula to narrate two experiences of S R Gupta, a student of Kaula in the year 1963-64. At that time Kaula carried the responsibility of dual position at BHU, a University Librarian of the biggest University Library and the Head of the Department of Library Science. His much time and energy were diverted to the needs of his University Library, where he worked till late night hours. He was awfully occupied with the work on Librarian's desk and would often forget the time for his class periods. There was no sounding of bell to declare the class-room periods. His students, though much eager to listen to him, were somewhat hesitant to remind Kaula about his periods. Gupta took the responsibility of reminding Kaula. It was a big surprise for Gupta to find that Kaula had welcomed the arrangement. Yet bigger surprise awaited him when he saw the performance of Kaula. On a short notice of just one to two minutes before the class, Kaula would suspend the work on his desk, which kept him engrossed throughout the day, and would appear in the class-room without any special preparation or with teacher's notes. Even then he would exhibit masterly control over the topics and students' involvement and understanding in the class-room. Gupta could interpret his experience as Kaula having the crystal vision of a *yogi* which encompassed and controlled the Librarian's work, the subjects of his teaching, the class-room needs and his students, and everyone receiving his due. Kaula's work in the Library and his teaching inside and outside the class-room were somewhat like a spiritual experience to Gupta.

Gupta did experience the depth of Kaula's affection and the extent of help for his students. Kaula came to know about the financial hardships of Gupta, a student. Circumstances compelled Gupta to bring his old mother from Delhi to Varanasi. So he had to vacate his room in the hostel and needed a private room in the city. From Delhi he wrote to Kaula to help him in getting a room in the city. Kaula assured him about the arrangement. When Gupta with his mother reached Varanasi, he found that Ugra Mohan Thakur, his class-mate and friend, was sent by Prof Kaula to receive them at the railway station. Thakur informed him that Prof Kaula had sent him with a message that the room had been arranged for them. So Gupta accompanied Thakur who took them to Prof Kaula's residence where Prof Kaula had already got vacated one room for Gupta in his own bungalow. It was a heart-moving experience to Gupta and his mother. Next day, Gupta discussed the arrangement with Prof Kaula. Gupta was insisting for some room in the city. Kaula was affectiontely advising his student to live in the bungalow and to save expenses on another room. It was only when Gupta placed a counter-argument – that Prof Kaula's arrangement would give an opportunity to others to defame both, the teacher and the student and the affectionate relations between the two would be misinterpreted in case Gupta could sustain his merit through the examinatiom results – that Kaula yielded with a heavy heart. Soon Gupta shifted to an independent room in the city. Later when Gupta secured the top position in the University Examinations, Kaula had all appreciation for Gupta's farsightedness and boldness. One may know that Gupta was not known to Kaula through caste, creed, state, etc. The only relationship between the two was that of a student and a teacher.

5. An Emissary in the World of Library Science

Prof Kaula deeply belonged to Ranganathan's School of Thought. He is vocal enough to declare fearlessly and most detachedly his this belonging in the mixed gatherings of admirers of other Schools of Thought. Wherever he worked or went, he carried with him the ideology and philosophy of the Great Master. Kaula's clear understanding of Ranganathan's ideas, techniques, methodology and application clearly reflects in Kaula's teaching, writings and working on several projects, committees, conferences, small gatherings and in the offices held by him. A brief account of such facts is given as follows.

5.1 *Multi-directional Activities in Teaching*

Besides his assignments for teaching in Delhi University and BHU, which were served by him in his official capacity, Kaula made him available to students in many other parts of India and other countries. His additional assignments include :

- Visiting Lecturer in Library Science at AMU (1951–58)
- Founded, and served as Registrar, the School of Library Science at DLA
- Director at the First Refreshers' Course in Library Science for Librarians at Varanasi
- Director and Professor, Training Programme in Library Science and Documentation, University of Hawana
- Lecture-cum-Study Tour of Canada, Paris, Bangkok, Madrid, Mexico, Rome, USA, UK, GDR, Hungary, Isreal, Iran, Germany Cuba and USSR
- Visiting Professor at University of Maryland, Graduate School of Hebrew University.

Extension lectures at Karanataka University, Saugar Unversity, Varanssya Sanskrit University, Marathwada University, AEC Training College (Parchmarhi), Kashmir University, AMU, Vikram University (Ujjain), Jiwaji University (Gwalior) and many more universities.

5.2 *Official Positions*

Many libraries and offices were served by Kaula with his professional acumen and administrative abilities. These include :

- Librarian, D A V College, Srinagar
- Chief Librarian, Birla Central Library, Pilani
- Librarian Consultant, Delhi College, Delhi
- Librarian, Ministry of Labour and Employment, New Delhi
- University Librarian and Head of the Department or LIS, BHU
- Dean, Faculty of Arts, BHU

5.3 *On Various Committees*

As an expert of eminence, Prof Kaula's contributions to various committees are also enormous. Many such contributions of Prof Kaula include :

- Rapporteur, Indian Working Party, International Bibliographical Survey, UNESCO/LC
- Expert Member, Documentation Committee, ISI, New Delhi
- Expert and Adviser, Selection Committees for Librarians, UPSC, New Delhi
- Expert Member, Library Buildings, Furniture and Fittings Committee, ISI, New Delhi
- Member, Technical Committee, INSDOC, New Delhi
- Expert Member, Review Committee on Library Science, UGC, New Delhi
- Founder and Secretary (1961), Ranganathan Commemoration Volume Committee
- Nominee Member, Executive Council, Varanassya Sanskrit University, Varanasi
- Member, Governing Council, National Library of India, Calcutta
- Unesco Expert, Unesco Regional Centre in Western Hemisphere, Hawana
- Member, Library Science Terminology, Commission on Scientific and Technical Terminology, Ministry of Education, New Delhi
- Member, Panel on Library Science for Production of Books in Hindi, Government of India
- Member, Review Committee of Vishva Bharati University Library, Santiniketan
- Chairman, Council of Literacy and Adult Education, World University
- Consultant, National Board of Adult Education, New Delhi
- Expert Member, Documentation Sectional Committee ISI (non Bureau of Indian Standards), New Delhi
- Hony Adviser, Library Committee, Andhra Pradesh.
- Member, State Library Committee, A.P., Hyderabad.
- Member, Standards for Public Libraries, A.P.
- Member, State Library Committee, UP, Lucknow
- Member, Expert Library Committee, Bihar, Patna

5.4 *In Conferences and Seminars*

As a thinker and advocate of various issues concerning the discipline and profession of Library Science, Kaula has effectively participated in a large number of conferences, seminars, workshops, and group discussions of profesionals. Some such significant participation by Kaula includes :

- Student Guide, All India Educational Conference (1942), Srinagar
- Member Delegate, to various All India Library Conferences
- Founder Member, Library Research Circle, Delhi
- Director, Seminar on Library Services in India and America, BHU, Varanasi
- President, Assam Library Conference, Guwahati
- Director Seminar on Public Libraries and Academic Libraries, All Assam Library Conference, Guwahati.
- Director, All-India Seminar on Library Classification, IASLIC, Trivandrum
- President, First Jammu and Kashmir Library Conference
- Director, Seminar on Library Services in Jammu and Kashmir State
- Director, All India Seminar on Education for Librarianship, Varanasi
- Director, Conference on "Planning of Library Services" and "Foundations of Library Classification", Cuba
- Founder, Research Circle on Library Science, Cuba
- Delegate, International Conference on Information Services, Tel Aviv
- President, UP Library Conference, Lucknow
- President, All Rajasthan College Libraries Seminar
- Guest Speaker, All India Seminar on National Integration, Hyderabad
- President, IASLIC Conferences, Jaipur
- Chairman/Director various IATLIS Seminars.

5.5 *With Professional Associations*

The Professional associations help in development of professionals and their professional activities. As a true teacher of Library Science Prof

Kaula has a great love for professional associations to whom he is ever ready to give all help. His working with various library associations may be described in brief as follows:

- Member, ILA, since 1946
- Member, Executive Council, ILA (1945–53 and 1956–62)
- Founder and General Secretary, DLA (1953–55)
- Vice-President, DLA (1956–58)
- Vice-President, GILA (1956–58)
- Founder Chairman, FILA
- Founder, Jammu and Kashmir Library Association
- President, IATLIS (1973–1984), Founder General Secretary (1969–73)
- Patron, Indian Music Academy, Calcutta
- Patron, Indian College Library Association, Hyderabad and Delhi
- Patron, IATLIS
- Chief Patron, Library Council, Jamshedpur
- President, second AP Public Library Conference, Hyderabad.

5.6 *Furthering Library Movement*

As an embodiment of his subject, Kaula has contributed his mite to the development of libraries in the country. He has made his best efforts to take the torch of library movement to such areas where it could not reach earlier. His contributions, as mentioned below, are remembered with respect.

- Published a Scheme for the development of libraries in the State of Jammu and Kashmir and drafted a Library Bill for the State
- Prepared a Development Plan for Libraries for Delhi State and also drafted a Library Bill
- Restructured Uttar Pradesh Library Association and teaching of Library and Information Science at BHU.

5.7 *Publications*

In the world of Library Science, Kaula is known as a prolific writer. He is author of 56 works and about 500 articles. He has published 600 book reviews and 5,000 items of notes and news. He prepared 18 schedules of depth classification. He is the compiler of 43 bibliographies. He brought out a number of publications under Documentation series and Bibliographical series, initiated by him, at the Ministry of Labour, New Delhi (1951–58) and Banaras Hindu University (1961–71). He has edited six professional journals, of which he is the Founder of four. The *Herald of Library Science* and the *International Information, Communication and Education*, the latter he started in the year 1984 at the age of 59, are as dear to him as his two sons. *Granthalaya Vijnana* is the only Hindi journal on library science started by him in 1970.

5.8 *Donations and Endowments*

Kaula was instrumental in the establishment of Ranganathan Endowment for Library Science. He worked as its Secretary during the years 1952–61. Then, an endowment was established in his own name, the Kaula Endowment for Library and Information Science. Kaula has contributed a large part of his hard earned savings to these endowments. The entire amount of royalty on his works earlier went to professional associations and since 1975 goes to the Kaula Endowment for Library and Information Science.

6. **Research Supervisor**

A teacher-educator of high calibre does does confine himself to the knowledge of his subject in the past. He not only updates his knowledge but also creates and helps creation of new ideas through his students. He prepares and supervises his students in stimulating new ideas, new theories, problem-solving and interpretations of the earlier known facts. Kaula encourages research in the field of Library and Information Science beyond mere class-room teaching. As Head of the Department at BHU, Kaula introduced the Ph D courses in Library and Information Science in his Department. Before he retired from BHU, he could make one of his research scholars complete the work on a thesis. There were eight research scholars working under his supervision of which two came from foreign countries, one from Thailand and another from Bangladesh.

Kaula's research students did always find in him a knowledgeable guide and an ever helping human being. His penetrating eyes would never miss the researcher's hidden quality in his students. Then he would make them work hard in the right direction. He would not hesitate a little even approaching a clerk or the Vice-Chancellor to help the researcher whenever he learnt that the researcher is facing problems in completion of office formalities. He would willingly help from his sources the researcher in case he needed financial help. As a matter of fact, a researcher is treated by Kaula as his family member. After being initiated in the research methodology and techniques, the researcher would ever find Prof Kaula at his back at all the stages the research work proceeds and the subject being studied developed.

7. The Paragon

Kaula's students and associates know him for his good conduct, wisdom, learnedness, God fearing, ever helpful, his devotion for his *Guru* Dr Ranganathan, strong will-power and enduring human qualities. All these virtues combined in the personality of Kaula make him "the *Sui generis* Teacher-Educator". Summing up the qualities and capacities of Kaula, Muzaffar Ali says

> Kaula has the qualities and capacities of leadership. He has the superb combination of those characteristics which lift and inspire the human spirit. His cause predominates over his self. Like his *Guru* he has the rare qualities – single-mindedness and selfless dedication to the profession. In reverses he has the fortitude, in arguments he is forceful, in speech he is convincing, in difficulties he is bold and in success he is humble.[10]

Ranganathan's and Dasgupta's observations on Kaula's professional and personal qualities in his earlier professional life are appended to this paper as Appendices-A and B.

REFERENCES

1 *YUKTI Kalp Taru* (In: *Hindu Dharam Kosh* by Rajbali Pandey; Lucknow, Hindi Sansthan, Hindi Samiti Prabhag, 1978).

2 SRIVASTAVAI, A P: Energy Isolates of Kaula. (*Herald of Library Science*, 13, 3-4; July-October 1974, p 302).

3 TIWARI, K D: Tribute to Pathfinder (*Herald of Library Science*, 13, 3-4; July-October 1974, p 315).

4 GHATAK, B N: Metamorphosis of a University Library; Progress in a Decade (*Herald of Library Science*, 13, 3-4; July-Oct 1974; p 269).

5 SUBRAHMANIAM, D: Quoted in Tribute to a Pathfinder by K D Tiwari. (*Herald of Library Science*, 13, 3-4; July-Oct 1974 p 315).

6 TIWANA, Jagpal S: An Institution by Himself: Kaula — My Teacher (*Herald of Library Science*, 13, 3-4; July-Oct 1974; pp 303-05).

7 JAIN, T C: Professor P N Kaula — My Teacher. (*Herald of Library Science*, 13, 3-4; July-Oct 1974; pp 311-12).

8 PHOOKAN, Ramesh: My Teacher — Professor Kaula. (*Herald of Library Science*, 13, 3-4; July-Oct 1974; pp 313-14).

9 KANWAL, D R: An Educator of Library Science. (*Herald of Library Science*, 13, 3-4; July-Oct 1974; pp 317-19).

10 MUZAFFAR ALI: Prithvi Nath Kaula — A Profile (*Indian Librarian*, 20, 4; March 1966; pp 196-98).

APPENDIX A

DELHI UNIVERSITY LIBRARY

University Buildings
DELHI - 6
21 June 1960

I have known Shri P N Kaula since 1948 when, fresh from the University of Banaras, where he had obtained the Diploma in Library Science, he joined the Delhi University Library as a Junior member of the staff. Ever after it has been a source of pleasure and pride to follow his career, to watch him grow to maturity and attain, with the unfoldment of his many talents, a position of leadership and rank in the profession of librarians. Always eager to learn and willing to apply himself, sparing no effort and determined to reach a conclusion, he has successfully progressed from one venture to another gaining new knowledge and practical experience and doing many a useful work which eventually has earned him well deserved recognition — as author, bibliographer, documentalist, editor of a leading library journal and organizer and moving spirit of the Delhi Library Association. In whatever he has attempted or accomplished, he had displayed thoroughness, originality and intellectual acumen. It was most gratifying, therefore, to have him return to the University in 1958, this time as a teacher, to occupy the newly created position of the whole-time Reader in Library Science. The teaching responsibilities of the Reader were diverse and many and Shri Kaula with his versatile experience and pioneering zeal filled the position with distinction. But for him, the Master of Library Science course, which the University had kept in abeyance ever since the retirement of Dr S R Ranganathan in 1955, could hardly have been restarted. And that is a matter of high tribute to Shri Kaula.

Sd/-S Das Gupta,
Librarian and
Head of the Department
of Library Science
University of Delhi, Delhi

APPENDIX B

Padamshri

Dr S R Ranganathan
M.A.,D.Litt.,L.T.,F.L.A.,
Honorary Professor,
Vikram University, Ujjain
Retired Professor of Library Science, Delhi University
Ex-President, Indian Library Association.

775 Seventeenth
Cross Road,
Bangalore
July 1958

Shri P N Kaula, M.A.,B.Lib.Sc. was first my student in the Diploma in Library Science class at the Banaras Hindu University in 1945-46. Again he was my student in the Degree Course in Library Science at the Delhi University. He belonged to the very first batch in the Degree Course when the Degree was called B.Lib.Sc. From the second year of the Course the name of the Degree was changed into M.Lib.Sc. Thus, it is only by accident that he is a B.Lib.Sc. and not M.Lib.Sc., though he took exactly the same Course and examination as the later M.Lib.Sc. candidates had.

Even before he joined the Degree Course, he did considerable work both in Kashmir and in Pilani in developing library service.

He was an active member of the Delhi Library Research Circle. He has several papers and publications to his credit.

He collaborated with me in building the *Union Catalogue of Learned Periodical Publications in South Asia* and in publishing the *Abgila*, the organ of the Indian Library Association from 1949–53 when I was the President of that Association.

In 1951 he became the Librarian of the Ministry of Labour. He has totally transformed the Library of that Ministry. He was the first to initiate a monthly documentation service. I have been closely scrutinizing his monthly documentation lists and I know how steadily it has improved in quality. This improvement is a testimony to his creative ability, singleness of purpose, and tireless industry. While developing documentation service, he has trained a number of documentalists and instilled in them a healthy spirit of team work.

In November 1957 he prepared *Labour Literature: A Bibliography* for presentation to the Fourth Asian Regional Conference of ILO. I have seen and heard the encomia that this classified bibliography has elicited from competent men both in India and abroad. The Documentation experience of Shri Kaula is somewhat unique at the present time in India.

Apart from such intensive technical works, Shri Kaula has also much extra-mural library activity to his credit. He had been the soul behind the Delhi Library Association. The credit for its publishing work, for its organ *Library Herald* and for its scheme of Library Science goes to him to the large extent. I have very high hopes that he will contribute greatly to the future of Indian librarianship — Library Science, Library service as well as education for librarianship. I wish sincerely that our country should utilize his services in the best way possible during this early stage of our renaissance.

Sd/- S R Ranganathan

S 3

The Ideal Librarian and Inspiring Teacher

M A Nayeem

0. Introduction

When Prof Prithvi Nath Kaula was born on March 13, 1924, in Srinagar, Kashmir, a mathematics teacher of Madras University undertook voyage for Great Britain to acquaint himself with modern library methods. After reading the literature on librarianship, he gained experience at the School of Librarianship of the University of London. It was Kaula's *Guru,* Rao Saheb, Padamasri, Dr S R Ranganathan, National Research Professor and Father of Library Science in India.

1. An Ideal Disciple

Kaula graduated from S P College, Srinagar, affiliated to the University of Punjab, Lahore, and was appointed as librarian, D A V College, Srinagar on a salary of Rs 30 p.m. only, in 1944. K G Saiyidain (ex-Secretary, Union Ministry of Education) advised him to take to the library profession. Having gone through the books of Dr S R Ranganathan, he decided to take admission in Madras University for training in Library Science in 1945. His going from North to South was his "Quest for Library Science". He had joined the course but did not find in the lectures the spirit which dominated in the books of Ranganathan. He learnt immediately that "Rao Saheb" had retired a few months earlier and was living at his residence in Madras. The young Kaula managed to get his address and went at the door of Dr Ranganathan's house. Kaula saw a half-clad man inside the room from the entrance. He approached the half-clad man, taking him to be a cook or a domestic servant, and enquired from him as to where "Rao Saheb" was ? No immediately he discovered the man appearing before him was none else but "Rao Saheb" himself.

This was Kaula's dramatic entrance into the library world. Dr Ranganathan knowing Kaula's sincerity used to spend a few hours every day discussing the subject on library science and thus affection and love grew between the *Shishya* and the *Guru*. When the *Shishya* was receiving inspiration, Dr Ranganathan was invited by three outstanding personalities to act as a librarian. Pandit Madan Mohan Malaviya and Dr S Radhakrishnan (then Vice-Chancellor of the Banaras Hindu University), and Sir Maurice Gwyer, (then Vice-Chancellor of Delhi University). Dr Ranganathan chose the holy place Banaras. But Kaula's affection had grown so strong that neither the *Shishya* nor the *Guru* had the strength to discontinue such relation. Dr Ranganathan put one of the conditions to Dr S Radhakrishnan — to secure Kaula's late admission. The late admission of Kaula at Banaras Hindu University was condoned and Dr Ranganathan accepted the offer. In 1945-46 Kaula passed Dip.Lib.Sc. obtaining second position in order of merit. The *Shishya* again joined his *Guru's ashram* at Delhi University for M.Lib.Sc. In 1949, he passed the two-year B.Lib.Sc. of Delhi University (identical to M.Lib.Sc.) obtaining first position in order of merit and the first to qualify with a Degree in Library Science in India.

1.1 *Guru's Appreciation*

In the words of the *Guru*, Kaula is "second to none" in the profession in the country. The *Shishya* took the unchallenged leadership in the profession when Ranganathan's era ended on September 27, 1972.

1.2 *Padmasri I V Ramanayya's Appreciation*

Padmasri Iyyanki Venkata Ramanayya, the "Architect of Public Library Movement in India", while blessing Prof Kaula, narrated the pains he had taken to educate himself under Dr S R Ranganathan and through hard work he had reached the top in the profession. He was recognized as an International Expert. He said that his *Guru* must be showering his invisible blessings from above on this occasion of universal recognition and honour that was being done to his disciple.

2. International Recognitions

Professor Kaula has served with UNESCO in 1967-68 in the UNESCO Regional Centre in Western Hemisphere, Havana, Cuba and has been associated with international organizations like UNESCO, ISO, FID and IFLA.

2.1 *"Times Literary Supplement" and "the Library World"*

Kaula is the first Indian to teach library and information science under the auspices of UGC as full-time Professor at the Banaras Hindu University in 1971. The *Times Literary Supplement*, London, in its issue of May 28, 1971, describes Kaula as "One of the most influential librarians in the World". The oldest British periodicals, the *Library World*, London, regards Kaula among "the World-famous contemporaries and counts him among "the galaxy of the great".

Now the galaxy of Melvil Dewey, Charles Ammi Cutter, James Duff Brown, Henry E Bliss, S R Ranganathan includes P N Kaula. At present Prof Kaula is matcheless in the Library World.

2.2 *First Festschrift Volume*

An "International Professor Kaula Festschrift Volume Committee" was formed consisting of 215 members from 29 countries and several international bodies. It brought out and presented "Kaula Festschrift" containing a selection of 102 papers offered in his honour in 1974.

2.3 *Kaula Endowment and Kaula Gold Medal*

An Endowment has been created in the name of Prof Kaula. The endowment awards since 1975 "Kaula Gold Medal" and citation to a distinguished professional for his contributions in the field of library and information science under an international committee consisting representatives from Canada, France, GDR, India, UK, USA and USSR. It is a matter for great pride for the Indian librarianship that "the International Professor Kaula Festschrift Volume Committee" has published under the title "*March of Library Science*", the Kaula Festschrift, in 1979. Another award called "Ranganathan-Kaula Medal" has been established to recognize the achievements and services of Indian professionals in the field of library science. The awards have been made in 1980, 1984 and 1986.

2.4 *Honoured as an Outstanding Individual*

Prof Kaula has been honoured by the International Biographical Centre of American Biographical Institute, Raleigh, NC (USA) in (version 1984). The Centre presented "International Biographical Roll of Honour Plaque" to Prof Kaula in recognition of his "outstanding achievements in Library and information science" and for being "recognized as an outstanding individual". The Plaque presents a permanent recognition of his achievements through suitable citation and listing of biographical volumes.

2.5 *"Pro Mundi Beneficio Medal"*

Professor Kaula is the first Indian Gold Medal recipient of "Pro Mundi Beneficio Medal" and Diploma by the Brazilian Academy of Humanities for the promotion of "International Human Understanding". He has also been named by the Academy among the World's 50 academicians who are "outstanding people in the field of Human Relationship".

3. **International Expert**

3.1 *Served as* UNESCO expert, UNESCO Regional Centre in Western Hemisphere (1967-68).

3.2 *Invited to* Advanced Study Institute in Information Science, Pittsburgh (USA), International Summer School for Training of Librarians, Copenhagen (Denmark)

3.3 *Attended* Several conferences and seminars of FID, ISO, UNESCO and IFLA.
International Conference on Information Science at Tel Aviv (1971),
World Conference of Librarians in Brussels (1977),
Conference of South-East Asia Librarians in Bangkok (1978),
First Regional Conference on Classificaion in Germany in Konigstein (1979)
First International Conference on Information Science in Egypt at Cairo (1982),

3.4 *Visited* Several countries in Asia, Europe, Latin America and the Middle East and delivered a series of lectures in the library schools of many countries – specially Cuba, Denmark, France, Italy, Iran, Egypt, Israel, GDR, Hungary, Spain, Thailand, Malaysia, Mexico,

Brazil, Germany, UK, USA, USSR and Yugoslavia.

3.5 *International Honours and Awards*

(i) Felicitation by 17 Professional Organizations at Hyderabad (1974).
(ii) Indian Library Movement Award (1974).
(iii) Special Number of Professional Journals – Kaula Number (1974).
(iv) "Pro Mundi Beneficio Medal" and "Diploma for International Understanding", Brazilian Academy of Humanities (1975)
(v) Kaula Festschrift Volume (50th Birthday) (1979).
(vi) Plaque of Honour, International Biographical Institute, Cambridge (1979)
(vii) Deutsche Buchere Medal, GDR (1981)
(viii) "International Roll of Honour", Plaque American Biographical Institute (1983)

4. Ranganathan-Kaula Award

Prof Kaula Endowment for Library and Information Science, Guntur (AP), confers Ranganathan-Kaula Award on an Indian professional who has made distinct contributions in the library and Information science field.

Prof Kaula Endowment also awards Prof Kaula Gold Medal. This award is given to a person who distinguishes himself as librarian, documentalist or teacher of library science.

5. Prolific Writer and Editor

Prof Kaula has written and edited 48 books, 43 Bibliographies, 400 articles, 400 book reviews, 4000 items of Notes, 18 depth classification schedules. He is unique in contributing 107 papers in one and a half years in 1946-47. He has been editing *Herald of Library Science* (HLS), 1962; *Granthalaya Vijnana* (GV), 1970; *Progress of Library and Information Science*, 1980; and *International Information; Communication and Education*, (INICAE), 1982; and he is assoicated with other journals like *Library Today*, organ of A P Public Library Assoication, and *Library Science* organ of the Library Council,

Jamshedpur.

6. **Inspiring Teacher and Dean**

Prof Kaula's service as a teacher in library and information science has no example. His *Guru* Dr Ranganathan taught him dynamic methods of inspired teaching. Prof Kaula never goes to a class with ready-made notes or dictates from textbooks to the students in a classroom. From his Lectures, ideas flow like a fountain showering knowledge with a deep love and blessings on to students. In every forum his extempore lectures have fascinated the audience.

Prof Kaula retired from the Banaras Hindu University on March 31, 1983, after serving the University as University Librarian and Head, Department of Library Science (July 1960-March 1971) Professor of Library and Information Science and Head of the Department (March 1971-March 1983) and also as Dean, Faculty of Arts (April 1979-April 1981). After his retirement, the teachers of Faculty of Arts appreciated his services at a farewell function, presided over by Prof Lallanji Gopal, Dean, Faculty of Arts. Among those who spoke about the outstanding qualities of Prof Kaula were Prof Anjan Kumar Banerjee, Head, Department of Journalism and Mass Communication, Prof R S Mishra, Head, Department of Philosophy, and Prof Anand Krishan, Head, Department of Musicology. Prof Banerjee said that Prof Kaula had the unique qualities of head and heart and he served the Faculty as the "Best Dean" and a great administrator. Prof Gopal said that Prof Kaula was an internationallly recognized authority on library science. He added that in his travels to the Soviet Union and Czechoslovakia, the librarians in those countries mentioned the greatness of Prof Kaula and showed me his works and contributions.

7. **As Visiting Professor**

Prof Kaula was requested by the Vice-Chancellor, Banaras Hindu University, Prof Iqbal Narain, to continue in the University till December 1983. This consideration given by the University is an unique example as no other teacher has been provided this extension in the University. Meanwhile he received invitations to be the Visiting Professor at the following universities:

(1) Sambalpur University
(2) Calicut University
(3) Aligarh Muslim University
(4) Kashi Vidyapith
(5) Kurukshetra University
(6) Lucknow University

Prof Kaula joined the University of Lucknow as its first Visiting Professor in Library and Information Science on February 4, 1984. He has been awarded "Emeritus Fellow" Professorship by the University Grants Commission for his outstanding contributions to Library and Information Science. The scheme has been introduced for the first time and Dr Madhuri Shah, the then Chairperson, UGC asked Prof R S Mishra, Vice-Chancellor, Lucknow University, to provide all academic facilities to Prof Kaula.

8. **Other Activities**

Prof Kaula has been more active even after formal retirement from BHU. During 1984-85 he was invited to the International Conference on Education and Culture held at Philadelphia, USA on July 1-6, 1984, as one of the main speakers. He was invited to the 2nd Congress of IFLA held at Nairobi, Kenya, in August 1984. He was again invited to the 42nd Congress of International Federation for Documentation and its FID/ET workshop held at the Hague from September 17 to 27, 1984. He was one of the main speakers at the workshop. The Vice-Chancellor, Allahabad University, appointed Prof P N Kaula and Prof P K Patil on November 11, 1984, to examine the working of its University Library. Prof Kaula delivered a number of lectures covering all aspects of Library and Information Science at the various universities (December 1984-April 1985), viz. Agra University, Jadavpur University, Calcutta University, Jiaji University; Aligarh Muslim University, National Archives of India, Gujarat University, and DESIDOC, New Delhi. He attended the meeting of the Bureau for Promotion of Urdu-Bibliographical Committee held at Aligarh on May 18, 1985, the meeting of the Raja Ram Mohan Roy Library Foundation and its Administrative Committee held at Calcutta on June 24, 1985, the National Seminar among others on Automation in libraries held at Jabalpur University, Jabalpur from July 15-17, 1985.

With the efforts of the Raja Ram Mohun Roy Library Foundation and the Indian Library Assoication, a National Committee was set up by the Government of India to draft a National Policy on Library and Information System. Prof Kaula has been a member of the Committee to draft the National Policy. In that connection, he met the officials, ministers, Governors and other sections of society at various places along with the other members and participated in seminars and meetings and held discussions in different parts of the country: Calcutta (December 9-10, 1985), Bombay (January 4-5, 1986), Madras (January 7-8, 1986), Bhopal (January 17-18, 1986), Lucknow (January 24-25, 1986), Jaipur (January 31-February 1, 1986), Gauhati (February 3-4, 1986), Shillong (February 5, 1986), Delhi (February 14-15, April 3-4, 1986). He attended, on invitation, the meetings of the International Federation for Documentation in Montreal, Canada, such as FID/ET Seminar, FID/CR Regional Conference and FID Congress during September 7-25, 1986. He was also invited by Dalhousi University to deliver lectures.

The Committee has submitted the Report on the National Policy of Library and Information System *vis-a-vis* National Policy on Education to the Ministry of Human Resource Development on May 30, 1986.

Round the clock, Prof Kaula's activities and his works on national importance and international human understanding as an organizer of professional associations and constant works in various universities, academic units may be recalled in a concluding speech at his farewell function in the campus of the Banaras Hindu University, which is quoted:

> Retirement is a stage in one's life but it does not mean retirement from work which I am going to pursue till this body is able to survive.

T 1

Multifaceted Internationalist : Salutations to Prof P N Kaula

Anis Khurshid

1. Fountain-head of Energy-cum-Determination

A "bundle of energy-cum-determination" that is Prof Prithivi Nath Kaula who completed four decades of a very active and spirited library career in 1984 which also synchronizes a year later with the 61st year of his birthday. It is on this happy occasion that his students, friends and admirers are bringing out a *Festschrift* to honour him which he rightly deserves. This, in fact, is the second *Festschrift*. The first presentation volume [*March of Library Science; Kaula Festschrift. . .*; (ed. by V Venkatappaiah, New Delhi: Vikas Publishing House 1979)] contained papers presented to him on his 50th birthday in 1974.

1.1 *Unabated Energy*

However, the age has neither slowed down his energy, nor weakened his determination. Weather-beatean, Prof Kaula, even in his retired life, seems to be more busy than he ordinarily used to be in his service days. He has been awarded UGC Emeritus Fellow Professorship on his retirement in recognition of his dedicated services and is currently teaching and guiding research at several universities.

2. Distinguished Record

Prof Kaula has a distinguished record of library service and is known the world over for his writings and contributions to library seminars/congresses both at home and abroad. He is perhaps the *most published living library author* of our time. He has written and edited some 56 books, compiled 43 bibliographies and contributed about 400 articles and the same number of book reviews to professional journals and publications. This is besides several thousand items of 'Notes'. He is the founder-editor of six library journals, three of which are still published under his editorship.

3. Widely Travelled Librarian

He is a widely travelled librarian as well. During the four months between July 8, and October 25, 1981, Prof Kaula had visited five cities in India and two cities in the German Democratic Republic and addressed 13 meetings/seminars in those cities.

4. Execllent Promoter of Libraries

He is equally a good organizer and an excellent promoter of a cause. He has founded a good number of library associations in India and held important posts in them. His popularity among the library associations can be gauged from the fact that 17 professional organizations, both of national level, such as the Indian College Library Association, and of State and local levels, such as Andhra Pradesh Library Association and the Library Study Circle, Guntur, joined together in Hyderabad on June 24, 1974, to present an "Address of Tribute" to this great library leader on his completion of three decades of dedicated library service to the library profession in India. In October 1981 Librarians and Library Science Teachers jointly felicitated him at Jiwaji University, Gwalior. In February 1986, 22 library organizations once again collectively felicitated him at Patna with an Address entitled "Embodiment of Library Science". No one else has got this combined professional honour, prestige and universal applause.

5. International Honours and Awards

The benefit of this spirited service is not limited to India alone but its impact is worldwide as is discernible from the international honours and awards that have been bestowed on him. Among them are "Pro Mundi Beneficio Medal" (Brazil, 1975); "Deutsche Bucherei Medal" (GDR, 1981), and "Gold Medal of Honour", (1987) USA.

6. A Living Tribute

The establishment of the Prof Kaula Endowment for Library and Information Science in India and with it the award of "Kaula Gold Medal", since 1975, to eight distinguished library scientists/educators of international repute, from Canada, Denmark, Germany, GDR, Hungary, India, UK, USA and USSR and "Ranganathan-Kaula Medal", since 1980, to Indian librarians, in recognition of their achievements and services, is a living tribute to Prof Kaula for his distinguished services as a librarian, library educator, library philosopher and intellectual, and above all, as a library leader.

7. Salutations from Pakistan

This is Prof Kaula, a disciple of the great S R Ranganathan and a distinguished library internationalist to whom the present Festschrift is dedicated to honour him on his 61st birthday. I on my personal behalf and on behalf of the librarians of Pakistan *salute* him on this happy occasion and pray for his long life and many more professional achievements.

T 2

Roses and Thorns : A View of Kaula's Life

C V Subba Rao

0. See Through "Time"

Admiration for success is natural. But to be cognisant of the core of the man in adversity is rare. The run of the world misses the Man, which has count for *Name*, *Money* and *Position*, and whenever these ingredients are missed, worshipping of New idol begins. In truth there are situations when struggling hard and sincere, the result belies the effort, the atmosphere does not fertilize and seems impervious, cats-on-the-wall gain by "I told-you-so's". There are also situations in life, where for nothing credit is heaped or attributed, the name by itself cashes, rallies and becomes a banner, and fades too likewise, for inscrutable reasons. The person remaining the same, efforts at times succeed, sometimes fail. Success and failure are the magic of time in no one's power. Let us see Kaula through times, how he is tossed up by the waves and how he goes out-of-sight, engulfed at times.

1. Foundation Stone

Kaula went to Madras School of Librarianship at the suggestion of K G Saiyiddain, the well-known educationist. He mistook Dr S R Ranganathan (SRR) in his homely attire to be a domestic servant in the house, and was embarrassed the most to confess so. At that time. Dr SRR was down, having had to step out of Madras University Library before time, with a management and a successor who had least sympathy. With venom, he was ridiculed. Even to get his home address was a difficulty. The instance reveals Kaula, searching for real talent in adversity and sticking to right values throughout. Any other careerist would have cared for the best result and worshipped "paper" Gods. His entire life hinges on this vital decision, firmly made. I believe it is not he who made the decision, nor SRR, but both were unknown participants in the hands of destiny, the charmer and the destroyer, for no reason whatsoever.

1.1 *Untrue Tautology*

The critics opine that Kaula built his career with the first interview as the *Foundation*. Looking back, events of life are given, to be reasoned. Looking forward, from *that present*, the moment to moment, movement of life, is full of emotions, affections, angers, words, visits and actions, that to make them fall into a calculated pattern is monstrosity of life. Living in the present is the total involvement of personality, or is consuming life. One may regret the outcome, or welcome it, but the events are unalterable. Those who do deliberately, and choose a path have no regrets, for the choices were all open, and the die was cast, to cross the Rubicon in full force.

2. Fire-test of Chastity

Dr SRR was not an easy man to get on with. When fate throws down a person, suspicion enters him and at the age of above 50 new relationships are not made and retained so easily as in youth. None would deny that Dr SRR was the hardest task master, who squeezed out talent through work and appreciated only when he was non-claiming. He gave pittances, when anybody else in his place would have bestowed a knighthood. At times one is put back, or shelved temporarily, with growing criticism. Bearing in good cheer, but sticking to the path of work and rejoice in the findings, is a love and loyalty test. Many have fallen from grace at this period of the monastery service in the subject. To deny the dues but expect cheerful work is a firetest to *Loyalty* to the subject, to the career, and to the Revison. Among the monks that surrounded the Great Bishop in Library Science, many were not symbols of virtue and to come out unscathed through the hell-fire, merits a laurel. The Great-man had the virtue of listening to gossip and believe it till disproved. In totality, it amounted to a *test of chastity* in thought, word and deed.

3. Keeping Company

In adversity, if a faithful is found, he is clasped with hoops of steel. Dr

SRR made a special condition that Kaula be allowed to join the Banaras Hindu University in mid-term, for his acceptance of the Librarian's post to the then Vice-Chancellor, Dr S Radhakrishnan. When he moved to Delhi, he took Kaula there, gave him a job at Delhi University and admitted him to the second year Degree course, which is recognized now as Master's Degree. Occasions were when Kaula opted for less money, the only attraction being "to be with Ranganathan" and saw silently many of his colleagues sent for foreign trips.

3.1 *Mr Faithful*

One quality distinguished Kaula's relationship with Dr SRR, that of *abiding faith*. Many kick the ladder before they stand on the wall and some wise men do after reaching the roof, but Kaula did neither. He was the Mr Faithful of Dr SRR. He ran to him, like a helpless child, and never did anything of consequence. In return he had full measure of support. After rise to a level, like that of University Librarian, the loyalty tie was cut between SRR and others and slowly drifting apart started. It was Kaula who could not bear any misunderstanding and his chin quivered in sobs of joy and grief when *Truth* was appreciated by this Master.

4. **Associations, Periodicals and Teaching**

Kaula did *dedicated work* for Ranganathan in Librarianship. Dr SRR had the handicap, not being able to move about actively and Kaula filled the gap. Working for *Abgila* (*A*nnals, *B*ulletin and *G*ranthalaya of the *I*ndian *L*ibrary *A*ssociation), *Union Catalogue* and other publications at Delhi: starting Delhi Library Association and establishing its school of library science; activizing UP Library Association; starting of and working for IATLIS (Indian Association for Teachers of Library and Information Science; holding of All-India Conventions and founding of FILA; running of library science periodicals like *Library Herald* of the Delhi Library Association, *Herald of Library Science Granthalya Vijnana* and *INICAE*; promotion of Ranganathan Endowment and Ranganathan Festschrift; introduction of documentation in libraries of the Government of India are monumental pieces that stand the test of time, that there was a KAULA in Indian librarianship. The photographs are in plenty in the periodicals he ran, for verification.

5. Fighter Who Bore the Brunt

When the 21st century would dawn, people who have lived through 1942–1972, the Ranganathan-Keswan Era, and have left their footprints would be valued most. Both have been eminent speakers and quick silver thinkers, who rose to positions of power and honours. Dr SRR's restraint and *sattvic* powers lacked flamboyant flourishes that regaled shallow supporters, though his razorsharp brain always won. But he did not invest his powers to battle day-to-day bureaucratic back-sliding and attitude of proving the Best to be the worst. Dr SSR's refusal to go to Calcutta as the Librarian of the National Library, his refusal to contest Presidentship of the Indian Library Association (1953), his stepping down from the editorship of the *Annals of Library Science*, his tight-lipped silence on financial irregularities of the Indian Library Association, left his followers reining standstill, without smashing up the conspiracies, a let-down that caused tears. "Rao Sahib" (SRR) cannot be dictated to. For people who fought, like Kaula, he was a disappointment, when so-called victory was sure. Kaula who fought bore the brunt.

5.1 *Check-mating*

Dr SRR was a retired person having intellectual powers, and hence influence, nationally and internationally. Administrative power was not with him, except when somebody who venerated him was in position of power in Government hierarchy. His critics had administrative power, large following that regaled in gossips. SRR's students, unless they became acidic of him, were not acceptable. One tactic applied was to see that the small band of Ranganathan followers grew smaller and then the "king" is "check-mated". As a *follower* Kaula roamed like an elephant on the chessboard, and roared like a lion on platforms; innumerable efforts were made to chain him, to finish him, perhaps to bribe too. To his credit, he succumbed to *none*.

5.2 *Lion of Delhi*

For instance, he fought tooth and nail to get CC (Colon Classification) numbers in INB (*Indian National Bibliography*) in the ILA (Indian

Library Association) Conference at Calcutta in 1956. He veered the majority on the issue, but the cunning leadership seemed to give in, but retained DC (Decimal Classification) for filing order, thus taking the wind out of the sails, by bureaucratic manoeuvres. Those who attended remember "Kaula" as "Sher-i-Delhi" (the "Lion of Delhi"). The battle was a rare feat. He was from then on well marked to be effective in any toppling game or score a cheeky goal.

6. **Embarrassing Critics**

Many lamented the inactivity of ILA (Indian Library Association) and the end of the journal of ILA, but few raised their voice. Kaula did not mince words, and he became all the more unpopular; Opponents decried him, the friends-turned-critics knowing Dr SRR as well as Kaula, if not more than him, flung the charge that he misinterprets his *Guru*, in the after-dinner conversations, after the event. Such a situation is highly embarrassing and Kaula *bore* it. Dr SRR knew, is spite of the stories, that the critics were spineless, who would neither protest nor support Kaula. This led to a situation that the greater unpopularity Kaula courted, the greater was SRR's love for him. It was equally true that SSR's other followers, who turned critics of Kaula, and hence SRR too, did not accept his leadership. The battles were waged at Calcutta (1960,1962), at Patna (1964), at Chandigarh (1966) and at Indore in 1968. Kaula has halted his battles, realizing the ILA situation irremediable and the majority of members impervious to the state of affairs in ILA. Society takes such a stance, for no fault of the reformers. The times refuse to move. That honest, sincere efforts were made at tremendous personal cost is to be recognized.

6.1 *Work Triumphs*

Kaula won against his critics in running the Delhi Library Association and later, the U P Library Association for a time. In these two moves, he caught the spirit of the times. At the start of the Delhi Library Association, he was unmarked and the revival of UPLA took place during the rising tide of ascendancy. His dynamism was felt successfully, but his efforts to get the North Indian States have Library Bills have fallen on deaf years. He was in it as he himself drafted the Bills for Delhi and Kashmir. A great part of his success is due to the editing of Library Science periodicals – *Library Herald* at Delhi, and *Herald of Library*

Science and *Granthalaya Vijnana* from Varanasi.

6.2 *Editing a Labour of Love*

Kaula's editing needs a special word of praise. From scratch he started, when the atmosphere in Indian librarianship was that only a discovery should be reported in a paper. He put his own money into the ventures, and by hard work built up circulation and goodwill for the periodicals. Innumerable letters he wrote persistently till he got the subscription. He prevailed on his friends, old students, and Ranganathan circle to contribute successfully. Advertisements do not seem to be his strong point, but *News* and *Index* are. Scanning, editing, writing, printing, etc., are done admirably and no other library science journal contains such good News section and Index. He has also kept to the time schedule more or less evenly and gained confidence of authors and readers. He does the editing as a labour of love. The Banaras Hindu University library so far has not created many reputations, but Kaula is not *sunk*. The brave swimmer is striking his might, after surviving adverse onslaughts both from his professional colleagues and their benchmen in the development of a growing Department of Library science and the Library.

6.3 *Bed of Nails*

Kaula went abroad as UNESCO expert to Havana (Cuba) and that period of his absence was used to "reorganize" BHU Library and distribute its collections liberally to the departments of the University. He was to be called back, but he fought even from Havana. Soon after he came back, he found the Central Hall of the Library almost empty. Charges were made and rumours and anonymous letters were circulated and sent. Undaunted, he had to fight legal battles. He is still *Alive* in spite of the best efforts of his once "pets" to liquidate him.

6.4 *Disseminator I*

All the adversity was not in vain. His friends sympathized with him and his students rallied round him. He spread CC (=Colon Classification) and CCC (=Classified Catalogue Code) thoughts through his eloquent, humorously called *thundering* lectures. Dr SRR was more than pleased when he found BHU students well posted with his latest thinking and asked intelligent questions. For digging deeper and unraveling "New worlds", Dr SRR did not choose him. For understanding, spreading and explaining his thoughts, Kaula was unparalleled. He became an *All-Rounder*, and in this sense perhaps SRR said *Kaula is second to none in Library Science*, and that *Kaula is the Foskett of India.*

6.5 *Bank Balance*

All summed up and errors rounded, Kaula stood, at mid-fifties, a man of considerable achievements, a *warrior* of many battles. Some he won, some he lost, but he never ran away. Undaunted courage he has in plenty, which keeps him youthful at this age. The Delhi Library Association stands as a mark of his hard work. *Herald of Library Science* and *Library Herald* he has fathered and he should be proud of his new creations born of his brain's powers. He works nights and days with unbounded energy, visits libraries and librarians wherever he be, not a highbrow, but an elderly chum, cheerful, helpful and a person of self-confidence.

6.6 *A Moon or A Sun*

Dr SRR who meant for him so much is no more. If Kaula has something of his own he will survive in the future too, for there is nearly several years of Professorship before him. The last ten years are the period when one collects honours. But let not Kaula grow looking backwards, and indulge in self-pity or get Overjoyed. Not to perch any lower than the larky heights is itself a difficult job. To keep up to one's reputation is a burden. But vision fixed to a noble goal, and gathering the powers within, he should leap for what all he is worth, towards *Kaula's ideal*. Otherwise that he was the Moon to Ranganathan and was eclipsed soon after, having nothing worthy to do, may be the verdict. Ranganathan contributed more after retirement than before. Would the "faithful" belie the Master or ennoble the professional ends with sacrifice and love? After Ranganathan, the eyes of the profession are on Dr SRR's students, especially on Kaula. The times should play their game all the same. With a reverential bow to the spirit of Ranganathan, let the profession March on to new morns of the Future.

7. Postscript

Kaula is over 60 now. Does the assessment hold good even after a decade? How could unalterable past be changed? But the premonitions of "After-Ranganathan" have fallen into a shape.

7.1 *Research Guide*

An exhibition of Master's level dissertations at M.Lib.Sc. showed that Prof Kaula had *originality* and guided valuable and fruitful themes. For instance "Change of terminology used in classification schedules" is in original piece. In general, many dissertations at M.Lib.Sc. level of the Banaras Hindu University are creative and not run-of-the-mill variety. He has guided around half-a-dozen Ph.D. theses also.

7.2 *Propagation–Quasi Research Level*

To understand Dr Ranganathan's ideas, still fresh, and explain them or integrate them, is a difficult task. Many students who have marched backwards after leaving Dr Ranganathan complained of his advances, as they were out-distanced by knowledge levels. Kaula not only kept abreast, but gave popular rendering of the new techniques and was unrelenting in their propagation. At times he went to the extent of advocating before the UGC to adopt Dr Ranganathan freely Faceted structure for survival or exhibiting the dynamism of the depth scheduled in the field of Health Documentation, while at Cuba. ASCOM (Analytico Synthetic Classification of Medicine) is a pioneering example.

7.3 *Heralding Anew*

Not satisfied by the *Herald's* success in India and abroad, he started "*International Information, Communication and Education*" (INICAE) in 1982, at the fag-end of this career. The courage and perseverance have been rewarded with admiration and success. Foreign authors are extending active cooperation. But the question, After Kaula Who? for the orphaned journals haunts many minds.

7.4 *Reflections*

Creating Kaula-Ranganathan Endowments, biography in "Who's Who" collecting International Honours and Citation of Honours, Festschrift Volumes and photographic display in the *Herald*, are all on SRR Model. Though critics embarrass, there is no escape. The bluff is called when critics also have Festschrift volumes and display success, not to be left second in the race. Same FID, same IFLA but between Dr SRR's creativity and mastery, the others are leagues behind, not miles. To the credit of Kesavan, in spite of pall-bearers with decorated chairs, for 60th year, 70th year, etc, he refused to be shown around.

7.5 *After Ranganathan*

A decade and a half has gone by since 1972. Kaula is collecting Honours, delivering acceptance speeches, and framing Felicitation Addresses. Penetrating, discovering Research Thoughts have not reached National or International fora. Nor institutionalization of Research and reward in library and information science. ILA and IASLIC, DRTC he has decided to be a minimal participant. Giving up of personal ambition has made him a respected elder. Friends and students do feel that ILA has given him a raw deal, though he deserves quite an elevated position. Since the period is for carving a small area of effective operation, his resignation not to alter the past is Noble, for he has still energies and influence to have a show-down. Reckless fights have given way to let bygones be bygones, be bygones, a wise distance and a smile.

7.6 *Weakness for Ranganathan*

Ranganathan still means a bundle of overflowing emotions. He is part of Kaula's Psyche, affections overpowering reason. He is not blind to the other sides, but axiomatically it is not for Kaula. To the exclusion of God, he has worshipped at the altar of a Great Man, but after all a Human. Had to selected deep research as the sphere, instead of propagation and broadcasting Ranganathan, he would have had an independent niche. But having chosen his role when young, his *Guru* needing him in the educator's role, after 50 years, change of role had gone beyond him. Is he a Boswell? No; He is Arjuna to his Krishna. He is Kaula of Ranganathan.

T 3

Views and Experiences

Arvind Gurtu

0. Introduction

From obscurity to fame; from a log table in a private college in Srinagar to Professional Chair in a national university; from an insignificant participant in a college committee to an expert in UNESCO, is the story of Prithvi Nath Kaula. Tall, handsome, fair with a strong nose that looks more like a nose of a Roman patrician than a Brahmin from Kashmir, he abounds in indefatigable energy and passion. His life is his work. Author of more than four dozen publications and over 400 papers, over 500 book reviews, he impresses one as a person who takes his work seriously; never himself. His muse is the world of books; the Library Science. With a string of firsts in his own field; first Reader, first to be offered an Endowed Professorship in Madras University, first Professor in a national university, first to obtain a degree in Library Science, first systematic personal bibliographer, he looks and sounds modest to a fault. The *Times Literary Supplement*, London, assessed him as "one of the most influential librarians in the World"; the *Library World*, London, called him as "one of the world-famous contemporaries"; Pittsburgh University thought of him as "one of the World's foremost information scientist".

1. First Meeting with Dr SRR

Here is a very interesting incident in Prof Kaula's own words about his encounter with Ranganathan, the greatest man in Library Science.

> When I reached Madras, I was restlessly trying to meet Dr Ranganathan. I went to the Acting Librarian of the University. He told me, "you are the first Kashmiri to come to Madras". (I thought that

> he was Ranganathan.) I answered that it was only because of his work which had inspired me. He rather looked at me amazingly. He told me, "You mean Ranganathan: You will be disappointed to know that he will not be teaching you.
>
> I was taken aback, but I had got admission in the University. I did not know that he had wide differences with Ranganathan. Later when I met Prof Nilkanta Sastri with an introductory letter, he advised me not to mention to anybody that I am a "Pandit". In the form you had stated you were a Brahmin; and that you have been preferred over a South Indian Brahmin.
>
> Well after this I was quite fortunate to get the address of Ranganathan from a Reference Assistant. He gave me the address on condition that I would not disclose it to anybody in the Library.

And then finally the encounter with the doyen of Library Science, Dr Ranganathan:

> I reached the two-room flat of Ranganathan, and found a half-naked man, barely with a white *dhoti*, sitting on the floor. Unable to understand him, I thought that perhaps he was the servant in the house, but the simple man gave to me his own introduction that he was "Ranganathan', I was quite surprised and could not speak for a few seconds.

"Ranganathan", as it has become the synonym for the Library Science, has contributed much in the field of expanding this neglected subject of the Social Science. Kaula and Ranganathan became interlinked after that meeting and Kaula tried to prove the possibilities of giving thought to what was already "Philosophized" by Ranganathan. Ranganathan didn't go to Banaras, though personally called by the then Vice-Chancellor, Dr S Radhakrishnan, merely because he couldn't leave Madras without his fresh disciple Kaula. What would happen to him if he leaves for Banaras, who had travelled all along to Madras from the other end of India — Kashmir — merely because he wanted to attain the much — bestowed *Padvi* of Noble *Sishya* of Ranganathan.

1.1 *Kaula-Ranganathan Tie*

It is quite insignificant for a modern teacher or student what they should think of each other in all circumstances of life. But this *Guru* and *Shishya* tradition, may be medieval, is permanent in the realm of moral standards of life. Kaula and Ranganathan were *Shishya* and *Guru*, but friends in the actual sense, and that is why what Ranganathan attributed to "Glorious Reformation of Library", Kaula pratically carried out the whole scheme.

2. The Potter

Kaula was asked: "What was the greatest contribution of Dr Ranganathan in the field of Library Science?" He said, "Ranganathan was a Master Educator. He made men out of clay, like a potter sitting at the wheel". That was what he said to the American audience while delivering lectures in USA in 1968.

For a layman, Ranganathan changed the entire system of library, the books which were badly stocked in the steel almirahs of one library, and layers of dust and rust were accumulated in the wealth of knowledge, which should perhaps be in the hands of the knowledge-seekers. As Kaula describes when he reached back his own Library in Srinagar, first thing he did was that he opened all the shelves of library closets. 'The books are for All' — that was his slogan and with this method of achieving results, the student could find easily his books immediately, despite the bureaucratic outcries of the college authorities. The reader read excessively and gained immensely, and true Librarian only became the mediator to find the book for which he may be searching in the rows. Again, Kaula found many difficult situations when at one instance, at the end of a year, 48 books were found missing from the shelves, and he was in great trouble with the college authorities. The college Principal asked for an explanation, and wanted the shelves be locked. Kaula did not agree. He said that simply because the books were sneaked away from the shelves, it would not be correct to lock the shelves. He would, he said, rather compensate from his meagre salary, but never, would close the doors of the library shelves.

2.1 *Ranganathan's Last Wish*

Dr Ranganathan after completing his 80 years on August 12, 1972, expressed his last desire to Kaula about the immediate need to enact a Library Act at the Centre and in each of the Constituent States. In spite of his failing health, he prepared the Drafts of Union Library Act, the State Library Act, National System of Service Libraries and National

System of Copyright Library and urged Prof Kaula before his death on September 27, 1972, to publish them in the form they are presented. The letter said:

> I am obliged to you for agreeing with my suggestion about the articles on library legislation, which should be sent along with your covering letter to officers occupying vantage positions and to others to help in the initiation of library legislation in each of the States within this year.

And then finally his letter to Kaula, his greatest disciple, about his closing chapters of life:

> I am mortal like anyone else. When I say mortal, I have to say that by 12th August 1972 I shall be completing 80 years of the journey in this body and very soon thereafter this body may have to be sloughed off.

I could ask much about Ranganathan but as this interview only centred on Kaula, I could very well imagine how much the great respect and admiration he has for his "*Guru*" as he could write extensively on this particular subject.

3. One of the Top Specialists

A staunch Kashmiri, as Prof Kaula is, now he is ranked as one of foremost information scientists in the world and has reached the top of the Library Science ladder in the country. He has written extensively on Library Science. He has also founded and edited several journals including the journal "*Herald of Library Science*" which he is bringing out till now along with his wife. The most dominant contribution lies, like his *Guru* Ranganathan, both in his capacity as practical teacher, and in the position of Library Educationist. It is on account of his pioneering activities in the field of libraries and documentation that Marquis 'Who's Who', Chicago (USA) has included the biographical sketch of Prof Kaula in its "*Who's Who in the World*". Besides, Kaula was quite fortunate enough that he prepared a Festschrift volume for Ranganathan. Likewise *Kaula Festschrift* was presented to him on completing 50 years of his dedicated life by an International Festschrift Volume Committee consisting of 215 members from 30 countries and international bodies.

4. An Applied Science

On my inquiry on the scope of the subject, Prof Kaula said that Library Science — is an "applied science". It cannot be taken like any academic subject in social sciences. Since the inception in training in Library Science — apprenticeship in Baroda — by W C Borden in 1911, short training course was introduced in 1915 by A Dickenon where booksellers and publishers were also invited. First systematic training was started by Dr Ranganathan in 1929 and under the auspices of Madras University in 1931. Dr Ranganathan started a training course leading to Post-graduate Diploma in 1937 in Madras itself. This course had a tremendous impact on Library Science, as it was introduced in three universities in the successive years, i.e. Banaras 1942, Bombay 1943, Delhi 1947. Delhi University started the first Master's degree course in 1948, when Sir Maurice Gwyer was the Vice-Chancellor. Delhi University course was the only course at Post-graduate level leading to M.Lib.Sc. in the entire Commonwealth till 1963. The Banaras Hindu University was the second University to institute Post-graduate training leading to M.Lib.Sc in 1965 through Kaula's efforts. There are 46 universities now conducting M.Lib.Sc. course and 66 universities are conducting the first Professional Degree Course, i.e. B.Lib.Sc. Also, there are two institutions which provide specialized training in documentation. These institutions are Documentation Research and Training Centre, Bangalore and INSDOC, New Delhi. There are a number of polytechnics and government institutions which are equipped to train at an elementary level. Some professional associations are also conducting short-term training courses for various durations. The Delhi Library Association is conducting one-year training programme leading to certificate which was introduced by Prof Kaula himself. There is also provision of research at Delhi, Banaras and Panjab Universities and after 1968 at 15 others also.

5. The Information Science

Library Science has in general given its due emphasis to democratization of knowledge, mass book production, intensive research activity, varied specialized studies, more educational research institutions, and personnel of higher academic calibre. But with the changed situation, Library Science has incorporated within its boundary Information Science. Book is no longer considered as a unit of investigation for research, but it is the information recorded in any document, which is considered essential for research purpose. This shift of emphasis from traditional book to articles, monographs, reports, editorial comments, contributed material, news and notes in a particular field has made the study of this subject more complex and specialized. As Prof Bernal says: "It is not difficult these days to invent a new idea, but it is impossible to find out whether the same idea has been given out by someone at some time, and recorded in some document". New technologies in information and communication have yet to be introduced in our libraries to provide speed, comprehensiveness, storage and retrieval of information.

6. Out-of-Date Books

Prof Kaula was quite disappointed about the recent trends in libraries, where out-of-date books were stored and the new documents and books were not acquired. It has been investigated by a survey that 80 per cent of the books in sciences go out of date within a span of five years while 40 per cent become out of date in social sciences during that period. Thus majority of the documents in most of the libraries contain out-of-date information and no steps were being taken to weed out such materials to provide space for new acquisitions and up to date materials. In many libraries the rare materials were not organized. Prof Kaula felt that these rare documents should be reproduced and a union catalogue of such rare and research materials should be brought out. He particularly emphasized the need for reproduction of books that made India famous written by Western scholars.

7. Library Legislation

Prof Kaula claimed that library legislation could automatically solve such problems, but he regretted that in spite of the efforts made by him and Ranganathan, many of the Indian States were still without proper library service. Only five States in India, viz., Tamil Nadu, Andhra Pradesh, Mysore, Maharashtra and West Bengal had passed a Public Libraries Act. The original Bills in three States were drafted by Ranganathan. Kaula has drafted the library Bills for Delhi and Jammu and Kashmir State. Recentrly three states — Manipur, Kerala and Haryana — have enacted library laws.

Prof Kaula suggested that under a library law, a system of libraries would be formed with the National Central Library at the apex of the entire system, followed by the State Central Library at the apex of the State system, followed by districts, city branch rural and delivery stations served by mobile libraries. There are some subjects for national libraries as well. There is need to coordinate the activities of all the National Libraries by forming the National Library Board. He emphasized the need for setting up of a commission on Library and Information Service on the lines of the USA.

8. Proposal for a Council

There is a vital need, he continued, that a Council of Scientific and Technical Information should be formed which will have a department of Library and Information Science. This Council should help in the establishment of the Ranganathan Foundation as a Research Wing, which has become the Indian School of Thought. This Council should be directly under the charge of the Prime Minister's Secretariat. The Council should also coordinate and develop the information activities in various government organizations in the centre, setting up branches in constituent States. Describing the activities of this Council, Prof Kaula explained that this council should be responsible for establishment, maintenance and development of diverse Information Services in various fields. It should be able to promote new areas of information science and assist the various programmes by up to date indexing and abstracting services. It is also to keep the people informed about the measures taken by the government in the various fields. He quoted the example of Cuba where 97.3% of literacy was achieved within five years by enacting such a Central Library System. United States and the USSR have also some such councils or commissions to assist the Government programmes and policies. Cuba believes in the gospel — "Books for All" — which was adopted by UNESCO in 1972 to promote book production and distribution activities. In a poor country like ours, the need for "Free book service for all" is necessary, Kaula emphasized.

9. Low Priority for Libraries

Kaula lamented that under the National Education Policy some steps have been taken to set up 48% Administrative Staff Colleges to refresh the education of teachers/lecturers, but libraries have received no priority at all. The National Policy on Library and Information System which has been drafted by a committee with which Kaula was associated and submitted to the Government on May 30, 1986, has yet to be implemented. While India has close relations with the Soviet Union and other socialist countries, it has yet to learn the priority these countries have given to eradicating illiteracy and promotion of education backed by a network of libraries.

While India is keen to adopt new technologies in information like computer, the Government has yet to think of developing a network of libraries or establishing national data banks for the good of the people, Kaula concluded.

T 4

Kaula and Ranganathan : A Perspective

P S G Kumar

1. Journey to South

During his student days, P N Kaula associated himself with his college library. His experience in working in the library made him to recognize the potentiality in librarianship, prompted him to take up a course in Library Science and adopt the same as his career. Having heard about Dr Ranganathan and his contribution to Library Science, Kaula decided to go to Madras and get himself trained under him. As against the normal practice in those days, he went all the way from Kashmir to down South for his education.

2. At Madras University

After a long journey, Kaula reached Madras on June 30, 1945. When he went to the University Library and met the Librarian in connection with his admission, he asked him as to how he came all the way from Kashmir to Madras, when there were courses at Lahore and Banaras. Kaula believing that he was talking to Ranganathan, replied that he had heard of his work and contribution in the field, and that is why he made up his mind to come to Madras and not to go anywhere else. The Librarian's was mixed reaction. He was surprised and upset on hearing Kaula. He asked whether he meant Ranganathan? Then he informed Kaula that Ranganathan had retired and that if he came to be trained under Ranganathan, he better return the admit card and go back to Kashmir. Though disappointed, Kaula pleaded and got admitted to the course. It was with great difficulty that Kaula could also get the address of Ranganathan.

3. Kaula with Ranganathan

3.1 *First Encounter with Ranganathan*

When Kaula knocked at the door of Ranganathan's residence, a young lad, Yogeshwar (Ranganathan's son) opened the door and directed him to go up the stairs. Kaula went up the stairs and there he found a person semi-nude sitting with a plank at his elbow. Thinking that he must be the domestic servant, Kaula went further to another room and found no one there. He then went back to the first room and inquired about the whereabouts of Mr Ranganathan. The person replied that he himself was Ranganathan. Kaula being perplexed offered his apologies. Seeing Kaula so nervous, Ranganathan asked why he offered his apology and Kaula said because he thought of Ranganathan as someone quite different. Ranganathan was not satisfied with this answer and kept on asking the same question. Kaula could not speak. Then Ranganathan told him that he would not talk to him until he had disclosed what he had thought of Ranganathan. At this Kaula said that he had thought him to be the "domestic servant". Ranganathan had a hearty laugh. Thus was the first meeting of Kaula with Ranganathan. Thereafter Kaula kept visiting Ranganathan and every visit helped to strengthen the bonds of friendship.

3.2 *To Banaras*

When Ranganathan decided to go to Banaras now called Varanasi at the invitation of Dr S Radhakrishnan, Vice-Chancellor, Banaras Hindu University, Kaula decided to follow Ranganathan and to go with him to Banaras Ranganathan noticing Kaula's devotion got him admitted as a very special case, as the admissions were practically over long before at BHU. When Kaula was at Banaras, he used to spend almost all the waking hours in the company of his *Guru*.

3.3 *To Delhi*

Soon after his training, Kaula got the position of Chief Librarian in the Birla Central Library, under the Birla Education Trust, Pilani, in the scale of Rs 250-400. But, when Ranganathan offered him the post of Junior Library Assistant in Delhi University in the scale of Rs 100-10-200, without any hesitation, he left the job at Pilani and joined

Delhi University Library just to have the opportunity to work with the Master.

3.4 *The Personal Touch*

While at Banaras, Kaula used to go with Ranganathan to the Ganges for a bath in the early morning hours; he used to be with him in the class in the noon; he used to work with him in the Library in the evening; and stay with him at his residence till late in the nights as his steno. Ranganathan used to dictate letters, papers, reports, etc., to Kaula. He was like his personal assistant. He made him write technical papers. He used to correct mistakes in his notings and writings in his presence. Guided him in the art of technical writing. While in Delhi, Kaula was made the Managing Editor of ABGILA, organ of the Indian Library Association. This gave Kaula an opportunity to master the art of editing. Kaula was to stay during nights in the printing press for proof correction and distribute the copies of the journal personally by carrying the load on his bicycle. There were instances when Ranganathan was very stiff with Kaula. But all this helped Kaula to master many things in his professional life. This association continued for over a decade, till Ranganathan left Delhi. The work of Kaula impressed his "Master" so well that once he declared publically that "Kaula is second to none in the profession".

4. Ranganathan's Impact on Kaula

4.1 *As Librarian*

Kaula made a mark as Librarian at the Ministry of Labour, Government of India, Delhi. He for the first time introduced "documentation services" in the government departments. He started indexing and abstracting services, and bibliographical services both at the Ministry and in the Banaras Hindu University. Dr Ranganathan guided Kaula in all these ventures.

4.2 *As Teacher*

Kaula is one of the *most popular and effective* teachers of his time. It was again Ranganathan who moulded Kaula as an excellent speaker and a great orator. He made him speak in the classes, discuss at seminars, debate in symposia and deliver talks. He started teaching at Aligarh Muslim University in the early 1950s and had the honour of being selected as the first full-time Reader at Delhi University in 1958. He is one of the most widely travelled and extensively lecturing professional in the country. He is superb in his lectures and has the talent and tact of taking away the hearts of the audience with him.

4.3 *As Editor*

As Managing Editor of *ABGILA*, (1950–53) Kaula gained experience in professional journalism. This was handy when he started the *Library Herald* in 1958 on behalf of the Delhi Library Association; and later his own journals — *Herald of LIbrary Science*, (1962); *Granthalaya Vijyana* (Hindi) (1970); and the latest one *International Information, Communication and Education* in 1982. The journals being edited by him have a mark of quality, uniqueness in the format and uniform method in editing. He also started *Progress of Library and Information Science* at the Banaras Hindu University in 1980.

4.4 *In Other Areas*

Ranganathan is known as "Father of Library Movement in India" because of his multi-faceted contributions in the field of library science. He worked on several national and international committees. Kaula worked on the Editorial Board of the *Union Catalogue of Learned Periodicals in the Libraries of South Asia*. Kaula was also a member of UNESCO's Bibliographical Survey Committee for India; Documentation Committee, and Buildings, Fittings and Furniture Committee of the Indian Standards Institution (now called Bureau of Indian Standards); Expert Member of the Review Committee on Library Science of UGC, Governing Council of the National Library of India; Terminology Committee of the Ministry of Education, Government of India; Bureau for Promotion of Urdu, Panel on Library Science; UGC Panel on Library and Information Science; Raja Rammohan Roy Library Foundation; Committee on National Policy on Library and Information System, etc. He has been on several committees of IFLA, FID, ISO and UNESCO.

5. **Kaula's Loyalty**

In fact Kaula has been a *unique* example of loyality and dedication of a pupil towards his master.

5.1 *Popularizing Ranganathan's Ideas*

Wherever Kaula served, he tried to put into practice the ideas of Ranganathan. His ideas of depth classification and indexing were adopted in the Ministry of Labour Library. He introduced Colon Classification and Classified Catalogue Code in the Banaras Hindu University, whereby a huge collection of about 500,000 vols was reclassified and recatalogued – in a unique and challenging adventure. He carried out this herculean task most efficiently, the professionals calling it a "miracle".

5.2 *Ranganathan Endowment*

By August 12, 1951, Ranganathan had completed 60 years and Kaula proposed to celebrate the 61st birthday on a grand scale. Many of the students, disciples and admirers of Ranganathan approved the idea. Work was started but, when Ranganathan came to know about this, he opposed the move. Then, whatever amount that was collected was invested in creating "Ranganathan Endowment for Library Science" with late S Dasgupta as Chairman and Mr Kaula as Secretary. This amount was later handed over to Ranganathan to make it the corpus of "Sarada Ranganathan Endowment for Library Science", of which Kaula was a trustee for many years.

5.3 *Ranganathan Series in Library Science*

It was Kaula who initiated the "Ranganathan Series in Library Science" in 1957. The first one in this series is *Library Movement in India*, edited by him. This work contains the papers presented at the symposium held at the First Delhi Library Conference, organized by Kaula himself.

5.4 *Festschrift to Ranganathan*

The irrepressible inner urge of Kaula to prepare and present a Festschrift Volume to Dr Ranganathan took shape only in 1962. He formed an International Committee consisting of top persons in library profession to contribute to the commemoration volume to be presented to S R Ranganathan on his 71st birthday in 1963. He contacted all top intellectuals and professionals in the library field. He toiled day and night to make it a masterpiece in library literature. The volume was presented in 1965 to Dr Ranganathan under the presidentship of Mr V V Giri (the then Governor of Mysore).

5.5 *Autobiography*

In 1962, Kaula started the *Herald of Library Science* from Banaras. This was sponsored initially by the Sarada Ranganathan Endowment. It was at the request of Kaula that Ranganathan agreed to contribute his autobiography serially in this journal. This was published under the title *A Librarian Looks Back* till Ranganathan breathed his last in 1972.

5.6 *Ranganathan Memorial Volume*

With the passing away of Dr Ranganathan, the main Era in Indian librarianship came to close. Kaula lost his mentor. He brought out the "Ranganathan Memorial Number" of the *Herald of Library Science* in 1973. This volume has contributions from the world over. The paper by Kaula in this volume, "Some less known facts about Dr Ranganathan", speaks out the love and regard he had for his *Guru* in his lifetime.

6. **Ranganathan's Appreciation and Assessment**

The above discussion has given an idea of the deep association and powerful impact of Ranganathan on Kaula. Dr Ranganathan had a great admiration for the indefatigable energy, unbounded enthusiasm and single-mindedness of Kaula. The following extracts take us into a deeper vision of Ranganathan for Kaula:

1946, January 19

"He (Kaula) is *unexampled* industry and in the interest he takes in pursuing the subject. During the few months he has been with me, he has covered an unusually large ground. He will be an acquisition for any library which wants to work on the highest level."

1946, April 23

"Pt Prithvi Nath Kaula is one of the most industrious and sincere students of library science that I have *ever* come across during my experience as a teacher of the subject. In the year he spent with me first at Madras and later at Banaras, he has made considerable progress. . . . His remarkable grasp of the details, unusual enthusiasm for the subject and genial manners make him a real acquisition to the library profession."

1948, May 29

Ranganathan's introduction to Kaula's book on *The Library Development Plan of Kashmir* :

> . . . I have been having ample opportunity to watch his development in library science. I have been impressed by his earnestness and industriousness. . . .
>
> He wields a *prolific* pen. The fact that he wrote nearly a hundred articles within two years gives the measure of his capacity. . . .

1951, February 17

"His devotion to the subject was of a higher order. He has acquired a *mastery* of most of the branches of library techniques. . . . His good physique, grasp of details of library science, untiring energy and industry for library cause, makes him an asset to the newly emerging library profession in India."

1956, July 1

". . . I have been closely scrutinizing monthly documentation lists and I know how steadily it has improved in quality. This improvement is a testimony to his *creative ability*, singleness of purpose and his tireless industry. . . . The documentation experience of Shri Kaula is somewhat *unique* at the present time in India. . . . I have very high hopes that he will contribute greatly to the future of Indian librarianship, library science, library service as well as education for librarianship. I wish sincerely that our country should utilize his services in the best way possible during this early stage of our renaissance."

7. Kaula lives up to the Expectations of Ranganathan

7.1 *A Multi-faceted Personality*

Today there is hardly anyone in the field of library and information science in India who is not aware of the manifold contributions of Prof Kaula who has gained universal reputation by his numerous and varied contributions as a librarian, bibliographer, documentalist, theoretician, writer, editor, speaker, organizer, thinker and educator of library science. He has indeed proved to be the faithful and versatile disciple of his *Guru*, Dr Ranganathan.

7.2 *Created a Library of his own Writings*

During a period of over 40 years of his professional career, Kaula has created a library of his own writings in the field of library and information science. He has to his credit 56 publications, over 500 technical papers, and many more reviews. He was associated with ABGILA (of ILA); *Sarada; Library Herald* (of the Delhi Library Association for vols 1-4); and presently is bringing out three prestigious journals namely *Herald of Library Science* (Which is listed by UN Experts as one among the world's selected 23 periodicals theoretically concerned with "international documentation"); *Granthalaya Vijnana* the only journal on the subject in Hindi); and the latest one *International Information, Communication and Education* (INICAE), a multi-disciplinary journal. He designed 18 depth classification schemes; drafted 14 developmental plans for various institutions in India, drafted two library Bills and has produced 43 bibliographical and documentation works. His publications have appeared in about 60 journals and 30 publications. The "Notes and News" and "Digests and Notes" — regular features of his journal — number over 5,000.

7.3 *Widely Travelled Person*

Among the professionals in India today, Prof Kaula is undoubtedly the most widely travelled person in the field of library science. He has visited several places in various parts of the country and has participated in various conferences, seminars, workshops and delivered lectures extensively. He contributed a great deal through DLA, UPLA,

FILA and IATLIS. He was UNESCO Expert in Cuba in 1967-68. He has visited and lectured in the USA, GDR, France Hungary, Great Britain, USSR, Philippines, Israel, Canada, Egypt; Denmark, Belgium, Yugoslavia, Thailand, Brazil, Mexico, Indonesia and Singapore, Italy, Iran, Federal Republic of Germany, and addressed a number of library schools and gatherings of librarians.

7.4 *Recognitions and Honours*

As early as in 1963, Dr Ranganathan declared that "Kaula is second to none in the profession today". *The Times Literary Supplement*, London, described him in 1971 as "one of the most influential librarians in the world". He was honoured and felicitated by a number of organizations on many occasions both in India and abroad. His profiles have appeared in more than a dozen journals. His bio-data is covered in international biographical works like *Who's Who in the World*, New York: *International Who's Who*; London, *Dictionary of International Biography;* London, *Men of Achievement,* Cambridge etc. In the year 1975 Prof Kaula was presented the coveted "Pro Mundi Beneficio Medal" by the Academia Brasileira de Ciencias Humanas for his "outstanding activities . . . in international understanding and creation of a better world for the future". He was awarded the "exclusive Gold Medal of Honor" by the American Biographical Institute for his "distinguished achievements in the field of library science". He has been the recipient of "*Deutsche Bucherei Medal*" from the GDR. Prof Kaula has been the recipient of the plaque from International Biographical Centre, Cambridge, England, engraved with the citation "For Distinguished Service", and "International Biographical Roll of Honor" Plaque for his "Distinguished Services to Education and Library Science."

7.5 *Kaula Festschrift*

On his 51st birthday, an International Festschrift Volume Committee was formed with representation from over 30 countries. A Festschrift under the title *March of Library Science* was presented to him. This was published by the Vikas Publishing House and all the copies were sold out in about 6 months : Another volume to commemorate his work on his 61st birthday is under print. It is entitled "*Dimensions of Library and Information Science*" Concept Publishing Co., New Delhi, to which this paper is a contribution.

7.6 *Endowment for Library and Information Science*

Prof Kaula Endowment for Library and Information Science was formed on March 13, 1975, the 51st birthday of Prof Kaula with Guntur as its headquarters. The Endowment has instituted "Prof Kaula Gold Medal and Citation". This is being awarded annually to a distinguished library and information scientist abroad. Apart from Kaula Gold Medal, another award named as "Ranganathan-Kaula award" was also instituted by the Endowment for an Indian Librarian. So far three persons have been honoured with this Award. Medals/Trophies were instituted at IT College, Lucknow, Library Council, Jamshedpur and Jiwaji University, Gwalior. Very recently, the Endowment instituted the "Best Librarian Award" with ILA and has also donated to the institution of an award to be executed by IATLIS. The *Herald of Library Science* is being sponsored by the Endowment. The Endowment is planning to initiate some research projects.

7.7 *Kaula Series in Library and Information Science*

Mr O P Uppal, a student of Prof Kaula, initiated the "Kaula Series in Library and Information Science" in 1974. So far eight books have come out in this Series.

7.8 *More Active after Retirement*

Prof Kaula has more time now to devote for the profession. His travels both in India and abroad have increased. He was requested by Lucknow University to serve as a Visiting Professor initially and then he was awarded, Emeritus Fellow Professorship of UGC at the same University. He is working on a UGC project of "evaluating library collections in Indian universities". He is associated with UGC Panel on Library and Information Science for the last so many years and is presently its Chairman. He is actively associated with Raja Rammohan Roy Library Foundation, and many other professional organizations at different levels.

8. Characteristics of Great Man

Kaula has an unfailing faith and devotion towards Ranganathan. He regarded him as his philosopher and guide. He did dedicated work for Ranganathan in Librarianship. Many students of Ranganathan used him (Ranganathan) as a ladder to reach the top and kicked him there-after. But it was diferent with Kaula. Even when Ranganathan kicked him, his loyalty remained unchanged. Of course, Ranganathan realized his mistake later. He made Ranganathan and Ranganathan's works popular. He was responsible in Ranganathan getting the National Research Professorship and many other honours, which very few know or realized. Kaula repeatedly mentions that "Ranganathan made me a man out of clay like a potter sitting at the wheel". This is the characteristic of a great men. Kaula is in no way less he also turned out a number of his students in the same fashion — this author is one among the many.

T 5

Work and Impact of Prof Prithvi Nath Kaula : A Study

Bana Bihari Shukla

1. Early Life and Education

Before we venture upon a study of ideas, ideals and contributions made by Prof P N Kaula, it is essential to have a background knowledge of his birth, his upbringing, the influence his parents and teachers had on him, and the inspirations that contributed to make him what he is now.

Born of a middle class family and of high aristocratic Hindu Brahmin family of Kashmir, he had all that could provide him an excellent education within India. He was the only son of his parents and was born on March 13, 1924 at Srinagar. As such it is but natural that his father Pandit Damodhar Kaula then a school teacher, was anxious to give his son the best education that was possible; and under his careful guidance he guided Kaula in his educational career. Kaula's intelligence and aptitude for acquiring knowledge was so high that one would be astonished to see his intellectual capacity even at the primary school stage. Solving the critical problems without rest, answering questions intelligently and without mistake was the general phenomenon in Kaula's early educational career that indicated Kaula's outstanding intellectual ability of the years ahead.

Arnold Toynbee in his illuminating *Study of History* writes that in every age civilization throws some challenges and if they do not get a favourable response, civilization gets a jolt. Since the students are the architect of the nation, they have to equip themselves to face the challenges and to shoulder the responsibilities of the nations. In the same manner Kaula's father too wanted his son to face the challenges of the world and to brighten the light of civilization by trying to get a teacher's job for his son, after his graduation from SP College,

Srinagar.

The father's aim was that his son by becoming a teacher would in his turn be able to train the youth of the country to be responsible citizens shouldering the responsibilities of the Nation. But God had his mysterious plans for Kaula. Kaula dedicated himself to a mission to serve the suffering humanity by lighting the candle of knowledge in the darkness of ignorance. He worked hard and suffered much and faced many a challenges as librarian of DAV College, Srinagar in 1944. This was the beginning of Kaula's career in the library profession. Later as librarian, he worked hard to put into practice all that he learnt from Dr Ranganathan. Kaula was the first librarian in Kashmir State in 1945 who introduced "Open Access System" and long reading hours for the users of the library, although he was a librarian without a training in the art of librarianship at that time. It was but instrumental that the senior members of the college advised Kaula to get himself traine ind Library Science. Mr B L Pathak, Lecturer-in-charge of the Library, D A V College, Srinagar and Mr K G Saiyiddain, Director of Education, Jammu and Kashmir State advised Kaula to get himself trained under S R Ranganathan at Madras University. But his father was not in favour of Kaula being a librarian. He was eager that his son should get the training in Physical education.

1.1 *As Library Science Student*

At this critical juncture and in this trying circumstance, Kaula took admission in Diploma course in Library Science at Madras University. Kaula's departure from Kashmir to Madras was a turning point in his life, which changed the pattern of his whole life for the advancement of knowledge and culture. By that time Dr Ranganathan had already retired and on the invitation of Dr S Radhakrishnan, Ranganathan joined the BHU as the Librarian-cum-Professor in Library Science. After 45 days of study at Madras, Kaula accompanied Ranganathan, his *Guru* from Madras to Banaras to get himself trained in Librarianship under Ranganathan and thus secured the Diploma in Library Science at BHU being placed in second position in order of merit. In 1949, Kaula was the first to receive the Master's Degree in Library Science from Delhi University under Dr Ranganathan and stood first in order of merit.

1.2 *As College Librarian*

With Librarianship as his career at DAV College, Srinagar, Kaula through his great enthusiasm for the profession, opened a new vision in the field of education for the people of Kashmir. Kaula's contribution containing the germs of literary fervour not only filled the nerveless, spineless and gutless masses with the ardent zeal and patriotic fervour to dedicate themselves to the cause of dissemination of knowledge and literature but also it marked the end of a barren period in the whole history of library hemisphere. It was the beginning of twilight of modern and ultra-modern period of library science.

2. **Kaula's Works**

Library literature in India has not achieved its adulthood as yet. Unlike most of the contemporary modern subjects whose history does not pass beyond two or three hundred years, library science has a History of some hundred years and it has evolved in the course of time through the intelligence of enthusiastic librarians all over the world, like Melvil Dewey, the father of modern librarianship, Dr S R Ranganathan, the father of library science in India, and Prof P N Kaula. After Ranganathan, the rich contributions of Prof Kaula through literature, science, documentation and other works in the field, has given a great push to library education in India. Briefly to recall his works, Kaula contributed 4 papers for professional journals (*ILA Bulletin* and *Modern Librarian*) and contributed 3 papers to the Seventh All India Library Conference held at Baroda during that period. In 1946-47, Kaula promoted library movement in Jammu and Kashmir State and published 108 articles in the press of Kashmir including a scheme for library development in the State. His poems on libraries and library movement have helped to make a great impact on the people of Kashmir for the development of libraries in the State. In 1949, Kaula's first profile was published in the daily *Martand*, Srinagar. Kaula published *Tasvir-e-Kashmir*, the first concise history of Modern Kashmir in 1948. In the same year Kaula drafted the plan of Jammu and Kashmir University Library at the invitation of the Vice-Chancellor of the University, drafted the plan for the re-organisation of the Sri Pratap Public Library, Srinagar at the invitation of the Education Secretary, Srinagar.

2.1 *Pioneering Work in Documentation*

In 1951, as librarian in the Ministry of Labour and Employment, Government of India in New Delhi, Kaula started a systematic bibliography and documentation work for the first time in the Government of India libraries and published the monthly classified list of *Documentation on Labour Literature. Labour Literature: A Classified Bibliography* was brought out by him within a period of three months at the time of Regional Conference of International Labour Office (ILO) in 1957. In 1952 Kaula proposed and established the Ranganathan Endowment in Library Science. In 1954, Kaula drafted the library development plan and library bill for the then Delhi State and after its approval by the Delhi Library Association, submitted it to the Chief Minister of Delhi. In 1962, Kaula published the first classified personal bibliography in India under the title *Malviyana.* In 1967, while at Cuba, he established the research circle in Library Science and at Havana, he designed the Analytico-synthetic Classification of Medicine — Ascom. In addition, Professor Kaula has 56 books and monographs, 43 bibliographies and about 500 articles, over 600 book reviews, over 5000 items and notes, 18 depth classification schedules on Library Science, books on labour problems and student unrest in 5 volumes to his credit.

In all his contributions, there was an invisible spark of international understanding and brotherhood which was intended to rouse the millions and millions of searchers for knowledge and truth of this country and abroad to stimulate for the cultivation of knowledge and literature. His writings, contained an exhaustive library literature for the library users. The critical analysis of Kaula's writings indicate the influence they had on literature, and in the socio-economic motives for library development, the library movements and the users in the country.

3. **Professional Career**

Kaula left DAV College, Srinagar in 1947 and joined the Birla Central Library, Pilani, Rajasthan on October 31, 1947. He could not stay at Pilani for long since Dr Ranganathan who had joined Delhi University wanted Kaula (his disciple) to join there as a Junior Library Assistant on much less pay and grade than what he was drawing at Pilani. Due to his devotion to his *Guru*, love for the profession and his faith in hard work, he did not reveal this monetary loss even to his father for a number of years till he was deputed as Librarian to organize the Delhi College Library in November 1950 with a higher start in lecturers' grade. At Delhi, Kaula had to work hard with Ranganathan, on professional matters especially on research in various aspects of library science. Ranganathan was a hard task master and the person who could complete the given tasks could satisfy Ranganathan but Kaula did much more than this to please Ranganathan. He had unbounded energy and courage, devotion to duty and hard work. Even at Delhi, Kaula had to work hard with his *Guru* Ranganathan. In turn Ranganathan tested Kaula for a number of years like a goldsmith testing pure gold by putting it into concentrated nitric acid. Ranganathan was astonished to see the unbounded energy in Kaula and told Kaula that "God had given him many of the qualities he himself was having and even much more and that if he worked in the way he had worked, he would gain recognition in the professional world in half the time it had taken for himself.

3.1 *Relentless Fighter*

Each step in Kaula's life has been a relentless testing ground where he had to fight and face many struggles in his efforts to further the library cause. His strong character impelled him on towards something beyond the confines of a routined and mediocre life.

3.11 *An Episode*: While at Delhi, Kaula presented a copy of his publication *Kashmir Speaks* to his *Guru*, Dr Ranganathan. But when he placed the copy in his hands, Ranganathan without looking into the book flew into a rage. Ranganathan told Kaula that there were two ways open for him, one was the line he had started in which he had immediate limelight and instant recognition; the other line was the professional line in which there was no immediate recognition, no financial gain and no influence with power. He then asked Kaula to choose any of these as he could not ride on two horses at the same time. With tearful eyes and quivering lips Kaula promised Ranganathan to follow the professional line with devotion and dedication and give up writing and thinking seriously on non-professional subjects.

Kaula had great faith in Ranganathan and in his work. In course of time, Ranganathan developed filial interest in him and Kaula reached the top in the hierarchy of his discipleship. He had championed the cause of library profession and had won laurels for himself by his successful achievements based on hard labour, hard work and chastity.

The odds were against him but he fought without flinching for nearly three decades and achieved astonishing results.

4. Versatile Personality

Kaula has achieved distinction both in India and abroad. He is a distinguished academician, a prolific writer, an inspiring teacher par excellence, a humanitarian of high order, a philanthropist second to Ranganathan in the library profession and a saint with missionary zeal. It is almost humanly impossible for an ordinary human being to fully understand and appreciate the qualities of head and heart of Prof P N Kaula, the great and multifaceted personality of India who has proved his excellence in almost every aspect of library field. By his complete devotion, work chastity and hard labour towards the profession, his works have lifted the discipline of library and information science in India and abroad like that of his *Guru* Ranganathan. He was the first to introduce the Open Access System in Kashmir State (DAV College, Srinagar), and followed the same practice at the Birla Central Library Pilani, at Delhi College, and at the Banaras Hindu University while at Banaras Hindu University library he has reclassified and recataglogued over 400,000 volumes of books of the library almost single handed with the support of about half-a-dozen staff whom he trained in new technologies by organizing Refresher Course in May-June 1961. This has been described as a "miracle" by the professional colleagues. That explains the magnanimity of a personality and enormity of a multifaceted brain of Prof P N Kaula. The positions and honours he has received in the library field are immense.

4.1 *Positions Held*

In brief, we can sum up a few of his extra ordinary brilliant achievements. He has been the member of the Council of Indian Library Association from 1949 to 1953 and 1956 to 1962; Managing Editor, *Annals, Bulletin and Granthalaya of the Indian Library Association* from 1949 to 1953, Editor, *Library Herald* of DLA, 1958-62; Editor, *Herald of Library Science*, 1962; *Granthalaya Vijnana*, 1970, *International Information Communication and Education*, 1982, Secretary, Ranganathan Endowment for Library Science from 1951 to 1961, General Secretary, Delhi Library Association, 1953–55 and 1958–60, and its Vice-President, 1956–58. He has been an expert member of the Indian

Standards Institution, 1957–62, Committee on Scientific Terminology, 1962, Reader, Department of Library Science, University of Delhi, 1958–60, Vice-President, Government of Indian Libraries Association from 1958 to 1961, Member, Review Committee on Library Science, UGC 1961–63. He has been the Chairman, Federation of Indian Library Associations from 1966 and its President from 1974. He has been member of the Governing Council of the National Library 1966–69, General Secretary, IATLIS from 1969–72, and its President from 1973–85.

4.2 *At the International Scene*

In the International organisations too, he has been the UNESCO expert at the UNESCO Regional Centre in the Western Hemisphere, Havana, from 1967-68. In the professional capacity too, he has been the librarian, professor and Head of the Department of Library Science, Banaras Hindu University and Dean of the Faculty of Arts, BHU from 1971 and 1979–81 respectively, Emeritus Fellow Professor of Library and Information Science instituted by UGC from 1985, Emeritus Professor at Kashidyapith, 1984. He is the Chairman, Council of Literacy and Adult Education since 1971, Expert member of the UNESCO Advisory Group on Comparability of Higher Degree in Library Science from 1973. He is also on the panel of Library and Information Science of UGC. He has been the visiting Professor of 29 Indian Universities, 7 American Universities, University of Havana, Hebrew University, Jerusalem and selected Universities of Canada, France, Denmark, Federal Republic of Germany, GDR, Hungray, Mexico, Spain, Thailand, UK and USSR. He has been the consultant on library science to several international organiZtions and National Associations, OrganiZng Secretary and President of numerous conferences and the international member of the American Biographical Institute Research Association from 1983, he has been associated with Kaula Endowment in Library and Information Science established since 1975, and of the Kaula Gold Medal an Annual award made through the International Award Committee since 1975. He was invited to the Advanced Study Institute in Information Science, Pittsburgh, USA, International Summer School for Training lbrarians, at Copenhagen (Denmark). He also visited several countries in Asia, Europe, Latin America, and Middle East and delivered a series of lectures in the library schools of several countries specially in Cuba,

Belgium, Denmark, France, Italy, Iran, Egypt, Israel, GDR, Hungary, Spain, Thailand, Malayasia, Mexico, Spain, Brazil, Germany, UK , USA, USSR and Yogoslovakia. He has also attended the International Conference on Information Science at Tel Aviv in 1971, World Congress of Librarians at Brussels in 1977, Conference of South-East Asian Librarians at Bangkok in 1978, First Regional Conference on Classification in Germany in Konigstein in 1979, First International Conference on Information Science in Egypt at Cairo in 1982. In addition, he has attended several conferences and seminars of FID, IFLA, UNESCO and ISO.

5. International Honours and Awards in Recognition of Contributions

It will not be out of place here to honour Kaula by saying that he has been a 'Responsible' educator, and a library scientist who could foresee the future.

It has been rightly observed, "Liberty does not descend upon a people, a people has to rise to attain it". And Prof Kaula's attempts, in various directions, had a single paramount consideration. Hardly any librarian in the world has been so lucky and fortunate so as to earn as much name and fame as well as recognition for his works as Professor Kaula. Both his works and services have been very much appreciated all over the world. He was honoured by the International Festschrift Committee in 1974, in India on completion of his 50 years of life and 30 years of dedicated work to the library and information science. This international committee was formed comprising 215 members form India and 29 other countries. It brought out and presented *Kaula Festschrift* containing a selection of 102 papers offered in his honour. Special numbers in library science journals have also been brought out as a mark of respect to this gigantic personality. He has also been honoured with a number of addresses of tributes in several parts of the country. Eighteen professional organizations collectively honoured him at Hyderabad in 1974. Many library Associations, Departments of Library Science, Librarians, students felicitated Prof Kaula for his dynamic activities to the cause of Library and Information Science. Prof Kaula has been the recipient of international honours and awards for his outstanding contributions for the promotion of civilization, peace and human understanding and creation of a better world for the future. The great honour accorded to him was by the Brazilian

Academy of Humanities Sao Paula, Brazil in 1975 who awarded him "Pro Mundi Beneficio Medal" and "Diploma" for "International understanding". He is the first Indian to receive this international award. Professor Kaula has been named by the Academy among the world's 50 Academicians who are outstanding people in the field of human relationship.

Many library science associations, educationists and professional bodies had felicitated Prof Kaula on this unique distinction conferred on him. Here we quote a few lines from the felicitation address given to him by FILA (Orissa Unit):

> A great scientist as you are, you did your utmost to foster a scientific aptitude among generations of students who passed through the portals of Delhi and Banaras Hindu University and came under the spell of all enveloping influence of your towering personality. Today you are not only a great *Guru,* of all those who are guiding the destiny of India, but you are also there amongst us as second to none in the library profession in India after your own *Guru*, the late Dr S R Ranganathan, and you are a living symbol of the learned *Rishis*. On this memorable day of your attaining international recognition, we pray for your long life, so that you continue to emanate the beconlight of a luminous star in our country's firmament.

Professor Kaula has been honoured in 1981 with "Deutsche Bucherei Medal" from the German Democratic Republic. The medal was presented to him at Leipzig for his outstanding contributions to the development of libraries and information services. He has also been the recipient of the "International Roll of Honour Plaque" from American Bibliographical Institute[9] for his distinguished service in education and library science. Recently Prof Kaula received "Commemorative Medal of Honor" from U S A.

6. **Kaula Endowment and Kaula Awards in Library Science**

In honour of Prof Kaula, an Endowment named Professor Kaula Endowment in Library and Information Science was instituted on March 13, 1975, the birthday of Kaula. The Endowment awards "Kaula Gold Medal" and a Citation to distinguished professionals of the world for their contributions in the field of library and information science. Bernard I Palmer, formerly Education Officer, British Library Association, London, was the first to receive the "Kaula Gold Medal" and Citation in 1975. Mr Palmer's contribution to professional education has been recognized resulting in the fulltime courses and establishment of several library schools in Great Britain. Dr Jesse H Shera, the Dean Emeritus, School of Library Science, Case Western Reserve University (USA) was the second specialist to receive the Kaula Gold Medal and Citation in 1976. Iyyanki Venkata Ramanyya, the known architect of public library movement in India, was the third recipient of Prof Kaula Gold Medal and Citation in 1977. Then this Honour for 1978 was conferred on Dr Peter Lazar, former Director-General, Hungarian Central Technical Library and Documentation Centre, Budapest. Other recipients of the Kaula Gold Medal and Citation are Prof Dr Helmut Arntz, a German (for 1979), Prof Mikhailov, a Russian (for 1981), Prof P Kirkagaard, a Danish (for 1982), Prof Dr Horst Kunze of GDR (for 1983), Harry Campbell, a Canadian (for 1984), Principal Frank Hogg (1985) and Dr Nasir Sharify, an American (for 1986).

The Endowment has instituted in 1980 Ranganathan-Kaula Award for Indian Librarians and Information Specialists. The first "Ranganathan-Kaula" Award for 1980 was conferred on Prof S Bashiruddin. The other recipients are Prof A K Mukherjee and Dr I N Sengupta of the Indian Institute of Chemical Biology, Calcutta.

7. A Shining Star

Prof Kaula's impact is of a wider significance. His enthusiasm for library profession, library service, his crusade for international brotherhood and understanding, his honesty in public duty, his impartial approach to religion and above all his pragmatic nationalism, profound concern with problems, human and social, cultural and intellectual make him a man, an situation and a leader in the profession. According to *Times Literary Supplement* (London) Prof Kaula is "one of the most influential librarians of the world". The *Library World*, London depicts him among the "World's famous contemporaries" and "galaxy of the Great". We can very well understand the magnitude of work of this great man, Prof P N Kaula. If we look into the International Who's Who and Year books of different countries of the world, we find the profiles of Prof Kaula, that describe Kaula's robust imagination, symbolic gesture of his personality and imaginative leadership in the profession. We find the blueprints of reformers like Prof Kaula in *International Who's Who* London, *Dictionary of International Biography (London), Men of Achievements* (Cambridge). *Who's Who in the World* (New York), *Who's Who in Asia and Far East* (London), *Times of India Year Book and Who's Who* (Bombay).

8. Conclusion

The mind of Prof P N Kaula is moulded by the thoughts of the present and future generations of the people of the world. Even in the quest of knowledge he is a bold adventurer of the spirit unmindful as to where he might land or what consequences might follow. What makes him great is his vision, his humility, his tolerance and above all, a termperament that is not ruffled by ill fortune or good.

U 1

Friend, Philosopher and Guide of Librarians

M B Konnur

0. Introduction

My first meeting with Prof P N Kaula was only a few years back, i.e. in the beginning of 1984. In January of the same year, our Department at Poona University had organized a national seminar on 'Management Trends in Library and Information Science'. Many stalwarts in the profession in India were given invitations for the seminar and Prof Kaula was one among them. However, on the inaugural day of the seminar, we were disappointed as he did not turn up, making us think that such a stalwart in the profession, who extensively travels within the country and abroad, might not find time to come to Pune. But to our great surprise, he did come in the afternoon, as he arrived late in the town. When he came into the hall, the seminar was going on, hence he quietly took his seat in the last row. Participants in their excitement became aware of his presence, particularly when he rose to offer his comments at the invitation of the Chairman of the session. This was the first occasion when I saw him.

Just at this time I happened to be busy with my doctoral work *Transnational Library Relations : The Indo-American Experience*. The topic being a historical one, covered the events of about 75 years which took place in the library cooperation between the USA and India. So far as India's role was concerned, I was to write about Dr S R Ranganathan's contributions. And for getting information about Dr Ranganathan's contribution, I found in Prof Kaula an appropriate person.

1. Profoundity and Depth of Knowledge

After the session was over, I introduced myself to him with a request to give me an interview on the subject. I was doubtful whether he would accept my request. But to my surprise, he immediately consented to meet me. I wanted him to spare from his busy schedule, half an hour for me answering a few questions which I posed to him in connection with my research topic. I was taken by surprise when he waited for me at my residence and came the next three days of the seminar to give an extensive interview on the subject and spend considerable time to have discussions with me. I managed to record his conversation with me on tapes. This was my first encounter with Prof Kaula giving me a glimpse of his profundity and depth of his knowledge.

Prof Kaula answered not only those five questions which I posed to him, but spoke at length on various historical aspects of the Indian librarianship. He gave me to understand that he loves to help researchers without making one feel that he is a *Pandit*. As in a flower, the fragrance is already there which spreads out; so has been the fragrance of the exposition of the subject by Prof Kaula. One should be lucky enough to get a favourable wind and possess a sensitive nose to know and to understand Prof Kaula more intimately.

1.1 *Another Experience*

Dr Ravindra Nath Sharma, who has settled in the USA, had come to India a few years back in connection with his doctoral work. He, too, like me, wanted to interview Prof Kaula. He was recording Prof Kaula's views on Dr Ranganathan at his residence at the Banaras Hindu University. He exhausted all the unacted tapes filled inside the tape recorder, because of which, ultimately Prof Kaula was compelled to stop providing further information. This shows Prof Kaula's intimate and vast knowledge on Dr Ranganathan and his willingness to help researchers.

2. A Friend in Action

In Prof Kaula, I find a friend of librarians. I am here reminded of one incidence. During the time of the seminar, the local librarians of Pune organized a function to give a warm welcome and reception to a few stalwarts in the profession including Prof Kaula. During the meeting, somebody posed a question about the non-availability of the book *Colon Classification*. They said the sixth edition of the book was out of print and the seventh edition had not come out as yet. How was one to carry out the daily routine in the classification work ? How could one teach Colon Classification in the Library schools ? Prof Kaula listened and returning to the Guest House, he wrote a letter to Dr M A Gopinath of DRTC which was posted the very next morning. This action of Prof Kaula showed us how prompt he was to solve the problems of the library profession. His philosophy of librarianship can be seen in his deep respect for Dr S R Ranganathan and his deep concern over the Indian librarianship for its improvement. If anybody wants some information about Dr Ranganathan or Indian Librarianship, let him approach Prof Kaula. He will get so much information on the relevant point that it will be difficult for him to decide where to stop.

3. A Philosopher

Here I am again reminded of another incidence. During his lecture-tour of selected universities in the USA in 1968, Prof Kaula was asked in his lectures at UCLA, in an audience of about 500 persons, to mention what he would rate No. 1 about Dr Ranganathans's contributions. Whether it would be facet analysis, chain indexing, fundamental categories or the five laws. Prof Kaula thought for a moment and then, suddenly enlightened by the God of Wisdom, replied that "he would rate Ranaganathan's contribution as No. 1 — Ranganathan as an Educator; Ranganathan was a Master Educator". Dr Ranganathan being alive in those days, Prof Kaula referred this matter to him. Dr Ranganathan replied saying; "Except Kaula, no one would have been able to interpret that in that way".

4. A Guide Par Excellence

Prof Kaula has guided many library professionals in their doctoral works. I happened to meet one such professional colleagues – Dr S P Mehta, Librarian of the National Defence Academy, Pune. During Prof Kaula's short stay at Pune, Dr Metha accompanied him whenever possible. Prof Kaula has many *bhaktas* like Dr Mehta spread throughout the country. The great disciple of Dr Ranganathan has a chain of disciples of his own indeed.

5. A Karamyogi

In addition to guiding his students in their doctoral works, Prof Kaula is busy also travelling extensively within the country and abroad, delivering lectures on various aspects of librarianship, editing *Herald of Library Science* and *International Information, Communication and Education*. One has only to be by his side and watch his work. One feels exhausted by the magnitude of it. Yet there is an equal amount of pleasure too. It is like watching a sculptor chiselling out a statue out of hard stone. I believe, this is due to a certain breeziness and ease in the manner in which Kaula approaches and tackles the problems that face him in his day-to-day work.

6. Matchless Voice and Oratory

One more thing which attracted me towards Kaula is his impressive voice. Voice is not a mere vehicle of words. It brings along with it a distinct personality of its own. There is a natural quality of persuasion in Prof Kaula's voice. Even a casual *Namaste* from him suggest a sincere concern about others. When he addresses a meeting of librarians or other people, apart from the conviction which he carries about what he says, this endearing quality of his voice makes one want to listen to him all the more. He is superb in transmission and is a matchless orator.

7. Allied Interests

Prof Kaula has interest not only in library matters, butn other things too. During his stay in Pune, I arranged for his visit to Raja Kelkar Museum. He spent nearly two hours in the Museum, watching all the historical articles there with keen interest and finally at the end of his visit, he discussed many things with Mr Kelkar, the Proprietor of the Museum.

8. Conclusion

Prof Kaula has already completed 60 years of life and has retired officially from the position of the Head of the Department of Library and Information Science, Banaras Hindu University. Ordinarily, after formal retirement, people do reading, join some club for playing cards, take evening walks, etc. But these things are not applicable to Prof Kaula. After retirement from the Banaras Hindu University, he has joined Lucknow University as the Visiting Professor, and Emeritus

Fellow Professor of UGC — a distinct honour made by UGC to Kaula. He travels extensively within the country and abroad, attending meetings, giving lectures, etc. Besides, he continues writing books, articles for journals and editing works of his journals etc. In short, he is equally busy even after his retirement which shows that he has not retired at all.

Prof Kaula! Nay, and who benefits from plenum of his activities ? It is the library profession. On this occasion, I will simply pray to God that let Prof Kaula complete a century providing help to younger generation in library matters and bringing the library profession deep respect from society. And I am sure that even in the hundredth year of his life, Prof Kaula will be carrying out all the activities with the same vigour and energy as at present.

U 2

An Institution by Himself

Sister M Esperanza A C

1. A Rare Combination of Virtues

I have known Prof P N Kaula personally for the past seven years. My first impression of him was formed when I listened to his address to the students of B.Lib.Sc. course at Patna University in 1981. He seemed to exude the eminence of his predecessor and *Guru*, Dr S R Ranganathan. The spirit of Dr Ranganathan was in his words as he spoke to the students of Library Science.

1.1 *Kaula-Ranganathan : Shishya-Guru*

Dr S R Ranganathan and Prof P N Kaula are so very closely linked that they cannot be separated. Their lives seem to be entwined in the field of library science and in the library profession. They have lived and worked together as *Guru* and *Shishya* for 25 years to make the library movement an important component of the education system in our country. As time went on, Prof Kaula got more and more involved into the various activities of the profession. This made him forget even his social life. He left his dear ones early in the day for his iibrary work to return only after midnight. Prof Kaula is truly a devoted *shishya* of a worthy *Guru*, Dr Ranganathan, in every way and has imbibed everything from him.

1.2 *Kaula and Iyyanki*

Nor can we forget here Mr Iyyanki Venkata Ramanayya, the predecessor of Dr Ranganathan and who was very intimately connected with Prof Kaula for several years even after the death of Dr Ranganathan. Prof Kaula came in contact with Mr Iyyanki at Andhra

Pradesh when the latter moved with him to various places and addressed conferences and meetings with Mr Iyyanki by his side. Prof Kaula developed a deep friendship with Mr Iyyanki from 1961 as Editor of the *Herald of Library Science*. It was Mr Iyyanki who led Prof Kaula deeper into the library field in Andhra Pradesh by his affection, enlightenment and encouragement. Prof Kaula's efforts to make the profession grow had been much appreciated by Mr Iyyanki as by Dr Ranganathan. Prof Kaula has indeed risen to his *Guru*'s size and stature and Mr Iyyanki's drive and perseverance. He in short is a combination of both.

2. **Professional Life**

Prof Kaula came into the library profession in 1944. He started his service as a librarian as early as in 1944 in Kashmir, his native land, when the library profession was still in its infancy. It was this work experience that took him further in seeking admission into the Library Science course at Madras and later at the Banaras Hindu University. As a trained librarian, Prof Kaula worked in Kashmir and tried to create library consciousness through his writings in the Press of Kashmir, dedicated services and by putting into practice the teachings of Dr Ranganathan. Since then, Prof Kaula's one aim has been to further the cause of libraries in our country through visits to the various institutions and through lectures, etc. Library Science became so much a part of his life that involvement in its works was his mission. He was never tired of being a learner and, as in early years, he still stands as a learner in his years of retirement. He still feels that there is yet so much more to learn and to do for the development of libraries in the country.

2.1 *Contributions Pour In*

From his obscure beginnings, he was later to go beyond what he learnt from Dr Ranganathan in certain areas, such as in the works of Classification, Bibliographical and Indexing Works. The "Malviyana" – a classified Personal Bibliography – has been considered to be a most praiseworthy piece of work which Prof Kaula brought out while at Banaras Hindu University Library in 1962. Dr Ranganathan called it a "formidable and pioneering piece of work".

His work for the completion of his mission was the outcome of his dedication and toil. In order to achieve what he aimed at in the profession, Prof Kaula had to learn a lot from his *Guru,* Dr Ranganathan who discovered and understood his great potentialities. Prof Kaula, as remarked by Dr Ranganathan, has indeed been a *bundle of energy-cum-determination.* This gave him a great push to be a learner and to work hard to upgrade the profession. Prof Kaula with all his knowledge in the field of Library and Information Science is an "Institution in himself".

The concept of Information Science today are integrally linked with Library Science. Due to advancement of science and technology, computers and telecommunication developments have been, in particular, taking place at a faster pace than ever before.

2.2 *His Patience and Curiosity to Learn*

Prof Kaula's boundless energy and enthusiasm to improve the prospects of his profession called for a lot of struggle and an intensive training under Dr Ranganathan. For Prof Kaula, to work under Dr Ranganathan was not an easy apprenticeship. All the years that he spent with Dr Ranganathan were years of patiently going through the day's hard work. But he did this cheerfully and perseveringly, for he had the inclination to learn and the faith in the guidance of Dr Ranganathan, his *Guru.* Today he has his reward for the great joy he experiences in the profession. His efforts made possible the beginnings of the Library Movement. As a prolific writer, he has not only contributed greatly to the Library Movement but has also initiated several projects for its growth. The spread of this Movement became his goal and he has been working tirelessly to achieve it.

2.3 *Unending Zeal and Enthusiasm*

With unending zeal and enthusiasm he has been visiting various organizations with a view to establishing in every State a Grid of Libraries and Information Services. Retirement from regular service has not deterred Prof Kaula from making professional contributions. The spirit of Dr Ranganathan still keeps him alive in the profession. He is working with every aim to uplift both, the librarians and the profession. He actively moves with the changing times and misses no chance to stress the need for an open mind.

2.4 *Efforts for Spread of Library Legislation*

With the efforts of Dr Ranganathan, library legislation has been implemented in five States, namely, Tamil Nadu, Andhra Pradesh, Karnataka, Maharashtra and West Bengal. But Prof Kaula is still very keen that besides these five States and other States in India too should welcome Library Legislation and thus a "Free-Book Service" be introduced. A "Free-Book Service" is very much needed in a poor country like ours to educate its masses.

3. A Scholar and an Educator

Prof P N Kaula who today is regarded as a distinguished scholar of Library and Information Science began his teaching career as early as in 1951, when as a visiting lecturer he conducted on weekends C.Lib.Sc. classes for the students of Library Science at the Aligarh Muslim University. He has been instrumental in reviving the M.Lib.Sc course at the University of Delhi and the starting of B.Lib.Sc. and M.Lib.Sc. courses both at Aligarh University and at Banaras Hindu University. Besides, he has also laid the foundation of the Certificate and Diploma Courses for Library Science in several other parts of the country. To further the Library Education in India, he has made very valuable contribution in our country.

As Educator of Library Science, Prof Kaula remarks that Library Science involves practical, observational and experimental knowledge. Modern libraries exist not only for use of books, but play a very important role in Education and in the life of the society today. Libraries are agencies of not only ideas but also of communication supported by mechanical devices including the computers. The development of modern libraries opens the way towards the National Education and Free-Book Service through a network of libraries.

It has been Prof Kaula's mission in the profession not only to know Dr Ranganathan but to interpret his ideas and techniques and to make them known in several parts of the world through library education.

4. His Works

4.1 *Initiator and Promoter of Documentation Work*

Prof Kaula's documentation work at the Ministry of Labour Library at

Delhi in 1951 onwards and the *Labour Literature* brought out by him in the form of a Comprehensive Micro-Bibliography in 1957 won for him a great appreciation. He also initiated a number of projects like Documentation of Labour Awards, the First Classified Indexing of Awards on labour disputes given by Courts and Tribunals, Classified Union Catalogue and Classified Subject Bibliographies. During these active years of service at the Ministry of Labour and Employment, Government of India, Prof Kaula started "Documentation on Labour Economics". This was his first attempt in Systematic Documentation Work in Government of India Libraries. Prof Kaula was a Do-All Librarian in the Ministry at that time. He had a huge library which he had organized on Colon Classification. A printed catalogue was also published. Yet he started Documentation Service on his own initiative. Fortnightly lists and later monthly lists of Labour Literature were prepared and indexed according to Depth Classification Schedule designed by Prof Kaula himself. These lists were circulated in the Ministry and outside the Ministry. These lists were also sent to labour organizations including ILO (International Labour Organization), Geneva, and to other Ministries in the Government of India concerned with Economics, Commerce, Productivity, Finance, Industries, etc. Prof Kaula's contributions and reaction of professional colleagues have been recorded by Dr Ranganathan in his work *Documentation: Genesis and Development.* Since it involves the attitude of other librarians towards a pioneer in Documentation, it is recorded hereunder:

> The Librarian of the Ministry of Labour, Prof P N Kaula, unfortunately for him, started publishing a Documentation List periodically. His Minister, who was a voracious reader, appreciated this, and often sent for the librarian and got the benefit of his documentation service. This latter event reached the notice of the librarians of the other Ministries. This made some of them use their new status to go to the room of the Under Secretary of the Ministry of Labour, spend an hour or two in chatting and ejecting some venom into his mind against the Librarian of that Ministry. But that Librarian was not second to anybody else in putting the Under Secretary in good humour. However, the documentation list proved to be a real red-rag to the other librarians. The librarian of the Ministry of Labour was regularly sending copies of his documentation list to the Chief Officers in the other Ministries. This made some of the officers ask their respective librarians to

give similar service. This was too much to bear after having become gazetted officers.

Results: The Librarian of the Ministry of Labour was boycotted. No other Librarian of the Secretariat would speak to him.[1]

At Banaras Hindu University, Prof Kaula was the first to introduce a paper on the theory of Documentation at the M.Lib.Sc. teaching curriculum in India while he was the Head of the Department of Library and Information Science there. To make the students respond better to the teaching of this paper, he conducted practicals and test exercises for admission to the B.Lib.Sc. and M.Lib.Sc. courses. Later these tests were also conducted for the admission of the working librarians. A three-year work experience was also introduced as a requirement into the M.Lib.Sc. Course in order to qualify these students to be better teachers of Library Science.

Documentation is essential to obtain an uptodate information from the recorded material. This is done through compilation of bibliographies and various publications using various forms of micro-literature, reviews, tape-recorded materials, etc. The government departmental libraries have also taken up documentation work as part of their library work. The Ministry of Labour Library stimulated other libraries to introduce documentation work by its doing systematic documentation work in Labour Economics and allied problems. The Indian Council of World Affairs Library has been doing useful work on Documentation in International Affairs. The other libraries in Delhi too are engaged in various documentation works.

Realizing the importance of documentation, UNESCO has since set up a Committee of Experts on Documentation in the Social Sciences. This Committee provides finances and technical aid to organizations engaged in this work. Today we have in our country documentation work in several areas including irrigation, defence, diverse scientific and technological disciplines, textiles, statistics, social sciences, planning, agriculture, community development, education and industrial problems.

Thus Prof Kaula has been the initiator of the systematic documentation work and bibliographical activities in Government of India libraries. As a result, various centres like INSDOC (Indian National Scientific Documentation Centre, Delhi), DRTC (Documentation Research and Training Centre, Bangalore) and NISSAT (National Information System for Science and Technology), have been established in our country to conduct the work of information dissemination and to help in the bibliographical control of information. Due to increase in the research activities, documentation and bibliographical services have helped an important branch of information science. The problems of bulk of printed material, the procurement of varied literature out of limited funds, limited storage capacity and also limited methods of processing and retrieval system, continue till date and need solutions through inspired and new techniques of documentation.

4.11 *INSDOC*: Apart from the pioneering work of Prof Kaula, the documentation in India got impetus with the establishment of INSDOC in 1952. Dr Ranganathan succeeded in establishing INSDOC with the initial help from UNESCO and thus brought India within the International documentation sphere. The Insdoc list of Current Scientific Literature started in 1954, was the documentation work in anticipation. It fulfilled two purposes: (i) as a stimulant; and (ii) enabled the research worker to lay hands on the required material without any waste of time. Unfortunately this useful work was stopped by the newly appointed Director of INSDOC in 1963.

4.12 *Other Libraries*: Where documentation is concerned, the library profession in India has a very important role to play. In the absence of a centre, even the individual libraries can fulfil the demand through reference service and make the recorded micro-literature available to those concerned. It is the librarians who have to take the lead in this work and not to allow non-librarians to take it into their own hands as is done in the West. UNESCO is anxious to start this work and has already established a Research Centre for South Asia at Calcutta.

In keeping with the changing times, Prof P N Kaula's "Trends in System of Information Handling" argues that the principal agency for handling information is the library. The traditional method of Documentation Handling System has undergone a great change today. Science has become so complicated and has grown to such an extent that Library and Information Science has to meet the needs of the ever advancing knowledge. Information Management which originated in 1950 today has to control the information scattered in documents, in magazines and in periodicals. This activity has brought in the use of computers, micro-films, micro-fische and other automation services in the libraries. These non-traditional documents have yet to take a firm root in library services in our country.

4.2 *Works on Classification*

Besides being the first to initiate documentation work, Prof Kaula has done pioneering work on Classification too. The Colon Classification had been one of the seminal contributions of Dr Ranganathan. He wished its interpretation, its application and its authoritative *Help-Book* to explain its mechanism and its working to librarians of all ranks. He wanted Prof Kaula, his faithful disciple, to accomplish this task.

Even when the design of Depth Classification methodology had not been evolved, Prof Kaula had designed and prepared a number of Depth Schedules of Colon Classification and conducted useful research studies on the subject. As Librarian at the Banaras Hindu University Prof Kaula brought about many functional changes for the reorganization of the biggest university library in India. He not only trained the skeleton staff how to run the library using the modern tools of classification and other techniques, but organized refresher courses to train the library staff and to keep them in the know of the latest theory and techniques of Library Science relating to classification and cataloguing work. Thus under his dynamic organizing capacity, Prof Kaula was able to reclassify and recatalogue about 500,000 books in the library and bring the collections in line with the new system and techniques within a short period. This was acknowledged by the profession as a "Miracle". Prof Kaula also provided many facilities in the use of library materials, including the construction of 64 research cubicles, reduction to only three days the closing of the library in a year.

Prof Kaula received regular communications from professionals – seniors and juniors – to which he attended and is also in possession of seven bound volumes of communication from and to Dr Ranganathan on various subjects. Prof Kaula himself is the author of no less than 32 articles pertaining to different aspects of the Colon Classification Scheme. Classification schemes keeping changing to suit the requirements of a particular period and do not provide flexibility and techniques to incorporate new classes and isolates. Prof Kaula has designed 18 Depth Schedules of Colon Classification. Some other works on classification include.

- Schedules for the Depth Classification of Students' Unrest in 5 volumes.
- How to use your Classification Scheme (1963).

- Analytico-Synthetic Classification (1964).
- A Treatise on Colon Classification (1985).

Prof Kaula has also been making all out efforts to urge the Government to promote the extension of Dr Ranganathan's System of Colon Classification. He wrote to the Director of the Indian Standards Institution (now called Bureau of Indian Standards) Dr Lal C Verman, in 1958, to provide for the editing and extension of two works of Dr Ranganathan – *Colon Classification* and *Classified Catalogue Code* like the one provided by the British Standards Institute for UDC. But the Director of ISI wrote back only to say that since INSDOC was a better laboratory for this type of responsibility and as they had adopted Colon Classification and Classified Entries for documentation work, the matter may be taken up by them. This was not possible as Dr Ranganathan was on the Technical Committee of INSDOC and the then Director of INSDOC was a person who would not like to provide these facilities for the study of Ranganathan's School of Thought.

Prof Kaula then wrote to the Prime Minister and to the Education Minister to take up this national responsibility. There being no response, both the Prime Minister and the Education Minister were approached again with the same request, but to no avail. A few years back, Prof Kaula again attempted to write to the Ministry of Education and also to the librarian of the Central Reference Library which also brings out the *Indian National Bibliography* with Colon Numbers, to be the laboratory for developing the work of Colon Classification and the Classified Catalogue Code as important constitutions by India.

4.3 *Professional Efforts in UK and USA*

In 1901, the Royal Society of London started indexing scientific literature in a comprehensive way. In the USA the special librarians worked independently and established a Bibliographical Society of America. In Great Britain Special librarians started their own independent organization, Association of Special Libraries and Information Bureaux. Side by side, in 1927, a British Society for International Bibliography came into existence but it got merged into ASLIB in 1949.

In India, this approach of voluntary professional organization was not supported. Here the librarians became Documentalists, Bibliographers and, Information Scientists and were considered outside the library profession.

4.4 *In the Thick of Library Movement*

Further, Prof Kaula also introduced the Urdu System of Cataloguing at Dar-ul-Aloom, Srinagar, to build up a Classified Catalogue for the first time in Urdu language in India. However, the Urdu Catalogue for the Delhi Public Library System could not materialize. In his enthusiasm for the library movement, Prof Kaula not only wrote 108 papers in the Press of Kashmir in a span of one and a half years, but also recited verses in Urdu on libraries and the library movement. This alone marks him out as most prolific and creative writer. But it was during his early years of career (1946-1947).

4.5 *A New Work*

In compliance and in fulfilment of the desire of Dr S R Ranganathan, Prof Kaula devoted his first year of retirement to bring out a *Help Book* in order to explain and to interpret the mechanism and the working of the Colon Classification to librarians of all ranks. This publication entitled *A Treatise on Colon Classification* in January 1985 is one of Kaula Series in Library Science, No. 8 and is the first publication after his retirement from service in 1984. This book which is a theoretical analysis of the System brings out a combination of the theory of the Scheme with the process of Number Building. Prof Kaula is an authority on Colon Classification and is the author of no less than 32 articles pertaining to different aspects of the Colon Classification Scheme. *International Classification*, edited by Dr I Dahilberg from Frankfurt, Germany, has published an article entitled "Classification in India". It reveals that Prof Kaula ranks third in his writings on Classification.

Prior to this and when still in active service, Prof Kaula had brought out many publications relating to classification besides being engaged in his teaching work.

5. Experiences in Libraries

With all the training Prof Kaula had undergone under Dr Ranganathan and through his self-study in later years and with the undiluted zeal in his works as librarian, he has been able to transform many libraries in our country, bringing them to proper working standards. These libraries include DAV College, Srinagar; where he initially worked, Birla Central Library where he was Chief Librarian, Delhi College Library (now called Zakir Husain College Library), where the furniture designed by him is still a model for a college library, Ministry of Labour library, a model Government Departmental Library and the Banaras Hindu University Library. The Banaras Hindu University Library is the last of these, where much of his ability, hard work and talent have been displayed. His hard and sincere work brought about many changes in this library. The functional innovations now introduced promoted growth and development of the library all round. His hard work and total dedication, and the energetic zeal of a perfectionist also won him enemies who became envious of his good name and brought down the image of the library after he shifted to the full time teaching in the Department of the Library and Information Science in 1971.

6. Founder of Library Association

Prof Kaula being the Founder of the Delhi Library Association (established in 1953) strengthened its many sided activities and has been a landmark in his efforts. He has further conducted several conferences in Delhi, Varanasi, Srinagar and other places. He has organized many professional bodies in various places and has boldly put forth his viewpoints in spite of many obstacles. He also rejuvenated Uttar Pradesh Library Association by changing its structure and constitution in December 1960, convened All India Conventions in Delhi and in Bhubaneswar in 1975 having the mandate from all the 45 library associations in India, founded library associations like J & K Library Association, Federation of Indian Library Associations at Chandigarh in 1966 and Indian Assoication of Teachers of Library and Information Science (IATLIS) in 1969. To quote Dr S R Ranganathan: "Prof Kaula has indeed been the 'Live Wire' of the Library Movement through all his works and activities for the profession".

7. As UNESCO Expert

As UNESCO Expert, Prof Kaula has directed several training programmes and has visited several countries and schools of Library Science. In 1967, he directed a Training Programme on Documentation at Havana, Cuba and in 1973 he was invited to direct a Training Programme at Denmark at the Royal School of Librarianship, Copenhagen. In 1974, he visited Budapest and delivered lectures on "Library Development and Planning". Touring Eastern Europe, Prof Kaula has delivered lectures on Library and Information Science. He also conducted a workshop on Modern Developments in Information Science at Bangkok, Thailand in 1978. He lectured on Short Term Training Programme at fourth Congress of Southeast Asian Librarians.

As UNESCO Consultant and Advisor on Library Service, Prof Kaula was invited to visit the socialist countries. He has thus become an international figure in the library profession. He has indeed been declared by Dr Ranganathan as "Second to none in the country and in the library profession". His lectures both in India and abroad as well as his writings have brought credit to India.

Prof Kaula has also made a great impact on the international bodies when he was invited to visit various countries in the capacity of an International Expert by UNESCO and other international organizations like IFLA (International Federation of Library Assoications), FID (Federation of International Documentation) and ISO (International Standards Organization). In 1971, Prof Kaula also visited Tel Aviv as an International Specialist to participate in Inter-national Conference on Information Science to speak on Information Science. He was also one of the two experts interviewed by Television. In 1980, he attended the Forty-sixth General Conference organized by IFLA at Manila. At this time he also visited Latin America where he observed the functioning of the American Library and attended the Documentation Congress held at El Salvador.

In 1970, Prof Kaula participated in FID/ET Seminar held at Copenhagen. He also availed of the opportunity offered him to attend the Lecture-cum-Study Programme held at Budapest by the Hungrian Institute for Cultural Relations. In 1982, Prof Kaula addressed the Fourth International Conference on Classification at Germany which was organized by the combined effort of IFLA, FID and ISO. Again he was privileged to attend a conference at Cairo along with other library and information science experts from Egypt. The theme of this conference being "Information".

8. As Journalist

Since 1950, Prof Kaula has been the Managing Editor and

Founder-Editor of a number of professional journals in India, and among them are *ABGILA (Annals, Bulletin and Granthalaya* of *Indian Library Association)* (1950–53), *Library Herald* of Delhi Library Association (1958–62), and the *Herald of Library Science* (1962) (a well-known professional journal). Again INICAE (*International Information, Communication and Education*), a journal on recent technologies (1982) is yet another contribution of his literary genius. Both these journals (*Herald* and *INICAE*) have international recognition. There is yet another journal *Progress of Library and Information Science* started by him in 1980. He has also been editing *Granthalaya Vijnana*, the only Hindi journal in India since 1970. Prof Kaula has also prepared classified Indexes to periodicals and has published bibliographies, documentation lists and several other publications dealing with the progress of the profession. Books dealing with scientific methods and knowledge of library classification, cataloguing, legislation, etc., have also been published to further the library education in our country. All these works show the greatness of his intellectual ability and zeal in the work of the profession.

Prof Kaula's aim all along has been to gear the libraries in our country to meet the ever-increasing demands of the times; to introduce new techniques and new services and to prepare the librarians to face the challenges of the rapidly changing modern society.

9. **Learning on the Move**

In the capacity of the Visiting Professor, Prof Kaula has visited several libraries abroad and has observed their functioning. These visits have proved beneficial and helped guide the working of the Library System in our country and raise the standard of services in our libraries. Some of the libraries visited by Prof Kaula and worth mentioning are :

- The Public and University Libraries of U S A
- The Vatican Library at Rome
- The Bibliotheque Nationale at Paris
- The UNESCO Library, Paris
- Libraries in Cuba, GDR, Hungary, Yugoslavia, Spain, Mexico, Thailand, Egypt, Denmark, Belgium, Iran, Great Britain, France, Germany, Israel, Brazil and USSR.

Both in the capacity of a Librarian and Consultant, Prof Kaula had the privilege to visit the UNESCO Regional Centre in Western Hemisphere at Havana. Comparing the Indian librarianship with the librarianship abroad, Prof Kaula feels proud of the pioneering efforts of Dr Ranganathan who through his dedication and hard work succeeded in maintaining a high standard in the functioning of libraries in India.

10. Contributions to ISI and Various Committees

Further, Prof Kaula has also been on the Library Science Expert Committee for Standardizing Scientific and Technical Terms. This appointment was given to him by the Union Ministry of Education, Delhi. He has been a member of the Documentation Secional Committee of ISI (Indian Standards Institution), where he has formulated several standards for the use of library works. He has been on the Committee for Buildings and Furniture of ISI, and has served as a member on the Committee for Terminology of Library Science in Hindi and the Committee for Terminology of Library Science in Urdu. He was appointed a member of these two Committees by the Ministry of Education, Government of India. Prof Kaula has served on the Technical Committee of INSDOC also which is related to the work of classification and documentation.

11. Kaula and Endowments

In 1954, Prof Kaula had been instrumental in the founding of the First Executive Committee to guide the Delhi Library Association which he had started in 1953. He himself had been its General Secretary. Besides, he has also founded the Ranganathan Endowment for Library Science and worked as its Secretary up to 1961. As a Trustee of the Endowment, he has arranged for lectures to be delivered in India and abroad.

Asha Kaula, the soft-spoken wife of Prof Kaula, is one of the Trustees of the Kaula Endowment which began a Festschrift Volume Committee and has been registered under the Charitable Endowment Act of 1966. The Endowment has started a series of publications and awards of Gold Medals. For the past several years it has risen to be an international body of eminent persons in the library profession.

The Endowment has awarded Kaula Gold Medal to :

1 Mr Bernard I Palmer (UK);
2 Dr Jesse H Sherz (USA);
3 Mr Iyyanki V Rammanaya (India);
4 Dr Peter Lazar (Hungary);
5 Prof Dr Helmat Arntz (Germany);
6 Prof A I Makhailo (USSR);
7 Prof P Kinkegard (Denmark);
8 Prof Dr Hoonst Kunze (GDR);
9 Mr Harry Campbell (Canada);
10 Principal Frank Hogg (UK); and
11 Dr Nasir Sharify (USA).

12. **Tribute to Asha Kaula**

Behind the success of every great man there is a women. In the case of Prof Kaula it is not the "other" woman but his own wife Asha Kaula. She is a trained librarian having got Certificate in Library Science from Aligarh Muslim University and Diploma in Library Science from Banaras Hindu University. She is a graceful lady who understand men and matters. Apart from looking after the secretariat work of the journals that her husband is editing, she has relieved Prof Kaula of running a home, a family, and social life. As confessed by Mr J S Tiwana who is now serving in Halifax, Canada, "She welcomes students of Kaula even at odd hours and serves them with tea, coffee and refreshment. She asks them about their welfare and those of their families with a cheerful disposition. She is a pillar of strength to Kaula and silently participates in all he does".[2]

I have had the good fortune of visiting the house of Prof Kaula in connection with the writing of his biography. I found in Mrs Kaula a women of unusual understanding, sobriety, faith, dignity and affection. Prof Kaula acknowledges her contribution by dedicating his 48th work to Ashaji "to whom I owe a debt of gratitude for her ungrudging support and silent participation in my professional work".[3]

13. **Moving Star Unabated**

Recently in 1986 the Government of India appointed Prof Kaula as member of the newly constituted Committee on the New Education Policy. As member of this Committee, he has strongly pointed out the neglect of the importance of libraries in the framing of the New

Education Policy for our country.

After the late Iyyanki and Dr Ranganathan, Prof Kaula has been the leading pioneer in our country and holds a unique position of leadership in the profession today. In 1975, all the 45 professional organizations in India, had acknowledged his unique leadership when he decided to convene the All India Library Convention at Bhubaneswar, Orissa. Prof Kaula can well be considered in today's significance and work which he has put in for the growth of libraries in our country, as the "Live wire of the Library Movement in India". After Dr S R Ranganathan, Prof Kaula, having achieved proficiency in several branches of library science, is the only one who can talk on several aspects of library and information science with confidence and reference to without notes, to the satisfaction of the listeners.

Today all the efforts and energies of his retired years are directed not only towards the growth of library association and various professional bodies, but he aims to strengthen them further through various government financial aids. This will surely result, in the years to come, in creating a nation-wide programme of educational and cultural development in our country.

In his constant efforts and appeals, Prof Kaula has been trying to draw the attention of the Government to the effective library development in our country. Although this development started in 1948, it has not yet been able to build a National Grid of Public Libraries in our country.

Prof Kaula is very much concerned to develop National Library Services for special classes of readers in the country and to establish a national net-work of libraries for the backward and the weaker sections of society. He is working to establish National Programmes for Special Users which include the illiterate and the semi-illiterate as well.

14. Conclusion

As a result of Prof Kaula's hard work and his complete and selfless dedication, the librarianship in India can look forward to a brighter future when the library services will be considerably improved and libraries will add to their role of information centres or service points to disseminate knowledge, the *key-role* in determining the ethos of a *New Society*.

REFERENCES

1 RANGANATHAN S R: *Documentation : Genesis and Development*, 1973, pp 125-26.

2 *Herald of Library Science: Kaula Felicitation Number*, Vol 13, 1974, p 305.

3 KAULA, P N: *Treatise of Colon Classification*, 1985.

V 1

Portrait of Professor P N Kaula in Verse

Inder Vir Malhan

Kashmir is considered as Paradise on Earth,
Prof Kaula here on March 13, 1924 took birth.
His father who was a teacher in some school,
Wanted his son to be a teacher as a rule.

Kaula got attached with library while studying in college,
As he always had desire to increase his knowledge;
So during studies became member of library and reading room,
And from member to secretary's position soon he could bloom.

In that S P College he was also a Rover Scout,
And every student in Kaula's favour would shout;
So he was adult education leader at Anantnag,
And a Certificate he received for social service cause.

A post of librarian fell vacant in D A V College,
As Kaula was learned and had library knowledge;
So at Srinagar he was appointed on Rs 30 a month,
To organize and administer the college library's *granth*.

To render good service to readers he was keen,
And in library administration very clean;
The books he arranged on open-shelves,
So that readers may browse by themselves.

So Kaula changed this college library's fate,
When introduced open-access without any wait;
Though afterwards book-loss he had to compensate,
But Ranganathan's works on Kaula had great influence.

He got first library training at Madras and then at Banaras,
Immediate transfer of Ranganathan to Kaula did harrass;
As most of the money in such a move he could spend
And always felt shy to ask any friend to lend.

In Diploma of Library Science second position he secured,
And very soon with library ideas he matured;
So in Master's degree first position he got,
And by then many articles of his were sought.

In Chief Librarian's capacity he went to Pilani,
But never told his father how much was the money.
Here determined one thing that during his future life,
Better facilities for readers and libraries he will strive.

With Ranganathan he always worked till midnight,
Who encouraged him to discuss, read, edit and write;
To work with his *Guru* from Pilani to Delhi he came,
On a junior assistant's post just for Ranganathan's name.

To remain always on top is in Kaula's horoscope,
So in every field for Kaula there was great scope;
Is it not evident from his books on Kashmir,
Kashmir Speaks, *Kashmir Darshan* and *Tasvir-e-Kashmir*.

So when still very young he wrote his first book,
To give about Kashmir history a wider outlook,
Such a document so informative by his pen,
Was also taken for discussion to United Nations then.

With Kashmir-history book Kaula rushed to his *Guru* great,
So as to receive his congratulations without any wait;
But Ranganathan flew into rage and called him names,
And asked why Kaula has developed such non-professional aims.

Ranganathan said on the one hand he had the immediate gain,
On the other public service, hard work and pain;
Which side he was to adopt, asked Kaula, to at once decide,
As at one time two horses he could not ride.

Kaula demanded some time to think but guru said nay,
Thus he at once wanted to hear Kaula's decision that way;
He asked Kaula to then and there decide,
Only then further guidance he would provide.

Kaula acted on his *guru*'s advice and made up his mind,
To write only that which he for library science could find;
So here was a turning point towards single-mindedness,
To achieve in the library science field great success.

Within one year Kaula many papers wrote,
So in professional contributions an example to guru quote;
About 40 books, 300 papers and same number of reviews
Many hundred "Notes and News", is the printed record of his views.

Soon praise came to Kaula from far and wide,
And Ranganathan blessed him like his own child;
So with a single motto he went East and West,
That is the gospel of library science and service so abreast.

Then established Delhi Library Circle to Library problems discuss,

To solve many new problems so as to achieve success;
To apprise with library science was now the theme,
And to make library media great was the dream.

In 1953 from records we can well gather,
Kaula formed a librarians get-together;
That body D L A with two hundred members to start,
A library movement rose in this country's part.

Then he prepared a draft bill for Delhi State,
For government to consider and legislature to discuss and celebrate.
A good library in every part, he said.
Will make the people well informed and well read.

So Kaula in the Kashmir State his own birth land,
Created a library association to make libraries expand;
He introduced longer library hours and open access,
For the first time in Kashmir and achieve success.

And he prepared for state a Library Development Plan,
With state library committee to project and man;
Many other development plans he drafted,
And Library bills for various states he opted.

Kaula convened at Bhubaneswar All India Library meet,
So as to revive ILA with new life and heat;
In association's Joint Council many changes he brought,
So always won the acclaim with major support.

Foundation of IATLIS is another feather in his cap,
And with U P Library Associations with govt., he could clap;
All 45 library associations in our country together he brought,
And everybody stood up at Convention to Professor Kaula's support.

For librarians' higher scales he is first to stress,
And for better facilities he will always press;
So in various capacities he could well plead,
Librarian's case before various committees to heed.

Kaula advocates summer schools for practising librarian's need,
So as to current biblio-techniques to them feed;
For profession's welfare and to improve professionals' plight,
This great man of library profession would courageously fight.

A strong appeal to Government he always made,
To set up free public libraries and to others upgrade;
Maximum study facilities for public is the aim main,
So wrote to Railway Minister for libraries and biblio-train.

Herald of Library Science and *Library Herald*,
At Varanasi and Delhi due to his efforts could bud. Like them editor of
Abgila and *INICAE* he acted,
For editorship of many other publications Kaula was selected.

Kaula has got great courage to take initiative,
So first to compile many bibliographies so informative;
He is first to set up Indian Library Literature exhibition,
To attract librarians, scientists and men of other occupation.

Many a times Kaula delivered radio talk,
So different library fields so nice to hark;
Some programmes were also shown on television,
To explain Kaula's lectures with wit and vision.

India's first Reader and UGC's first Professor of Library Science,

For ever will be noted in history for coming years to glance;
Adviser of UPSC and UGC, government bodies you must remember,
Such as National Library, ISI, Review Committees he served as expert member.

In 1960 took Banaras University Library's work in hand,
And started the work of reorganization and to actively expand;
Here University Librarian and Head, Library Science appointed,
And authorities from Kaula had no application and probation period wanted.

Granthalaya Vigyan is under his editorship another journal,
So as to communicate the ideas through Hindi channel;
And *Herald of Library Science* is as good as should be,
So UNESCO included it among the world's best twenty-three.

Kaula is Chairman of Literacy Council and Adult Education,
For which a landmark is to be done by our Nation.
In shortest time prepared a bibliography when in Labour Ministry served,
And did lot of work in documentation as a *pioneer* in the field he deserved.

Many seminars and short courses as Director he did inaugurate,
Inspector of libraries was also appointed in Kashmir State;
Here Vice-Chancellor and Education Secretary his expertise sought,
As a masterman in library planning to him they could talk.

Whenever need arose, Kaula contributed money also,
So in library philanthropy some contribution he could show;
And surrendered monetary gain for a teaching post to create,
So that in library faculty full-time teachers may participate.

Bald headed, tall and with fair complexion,
Handsome, smiling face but not an American;
In every sphere of librarianship and education, he has well done,
With untiring energy and dedication this reputation he has won.

Another notable point which must be told,
Is that, he is a man of many folds;
A poet, a scholar, good administrator and educationist,
Such combination of qualities in professor Kaula exist.

Writer, editor, organizer and good speaker,
Fights for justice and stands for the weaker;
For the poor and the suffered he fearlessly fought,
And those who spoke against profession were lessons taught.

Now Kaula is considered as librarian of world fame,
Throughout the world professionals know his name;
You read about him in *Men of Achievement,*
International Who's Who and *Times Literary Supplement.*

All professionals abroad for him have great regard,
And professional services too brought many awards;
He got awards of Indian Library movement,
Medals, plaques and honours from abroad were sent.

With *Sham-e-Danish*, he was honoured by his own state,
As a stir in library field he could create.
And many organizations invite him as chief guest,
In seminars and conferences his presence is considered as must.

As an international expert Kaula often goes abroad,
As visiting professor in universities we must feel proud.
At international meets he is first to get invitation,
To hear his views on library science and information.

So in his field of study he is very alert,
That is why UNESCO also appointed him its expert;
And got invitations from countries East and West,
In lectures and conferences he taught with zest.

Librarians and teachers from all over the world,
Have now instituted Kaula International Award;
And instituted a Gold Medal after his name,
To honour the library scientists of world-fame.

C-1, Banaras Hindu University, Who did not know ?
And library experts who visit India there first go;
Thus to see Professor Kaula here many librarians arrive,
To seek expertise and inspiration from his views they derive.

From All India Radio an announcement came,
That Professor Kaula for our Nation has won name;
To award him *Pro Mundi Beneficio Medal*, Brazilian Academy
thought,
And Kaula is the first Indian who this international award got.

"Among the galaxy of great" the *Library World* has written down,
To describe Kaula "Librarian of Repute", ABP, Calcutta is proud;
Statesman highlights his views in the column 'In Town',
And *Bulletin Biblioteca*, Cuba, handsome tributes has shown.

Founded library schools, centres, bodies and trusts,
To convince authorities about information work he is the first;
Recently the External Affairs Minister wrote this thing,
That in all our embassies information centres we must bring.

From Kaula Endowment *March of Library Science* appeared,
And world-famous librarians their views well cleared;
A meeting of world's topmost library scientists has set,
This endowment for the profession Kaula has done the best.

V 2

Tribute to Professor P N Kaula at Sixty-one

G L Trehan

This poem is composed on receipt of an invitation from Dr V Venkatappaiah, Secretary, Professor Kaula 61st Birthday Felicitation Committee, Eluru (A P) as a humble tribute to one whom the late Dr S R Ranganathan acknowledged as *Second to none in the profession.*

1 Hail Blithe spirit : Thou've crossed 61 to know And're still going strong with guts and go. What a great speaker thou're verily to lead And to carry an aura of bliss around thee indeed.

2 Thou're on inspiring educator and a dedicated soul and as a dynamic personality thou play a leading role. As a prolific writer on library science and creative thought. Thou in thy books and papers have contributed a lot.

3 *Herald of Library Science* mirrors library literature of the time And portrays thee as library luminary of the clime. It covers scholarly articles, addresses and book reviews And also features Awards, Reports, Interviews, 'Notes and News'.

4 A recipient of international honours and awards first rate Thou're counted among the galaxy of the Great. Thou're now emeritus Fellow Professor, an image to boost, And to bring to the profession a glory and repute.

5 Thou've build bridges of understanding betwixt East and West And the library journals are a link line so best. Thou travel a glory road in countries far and near. As International Expert in library science, O Kaula dear !

6 A powerful library blood flows in thy veins so clear That it vitalizes and makes thee a beacon without peer; Mayest thou always be up and doing by God's grace, And attain *Moksha** by doing impersonal service with pace.

**Moksha* means "eternal bliss". Late Dr S R Ranganathan advised young men and women to adopt library profession if they want to attain *Moksha.*

Theme W
The Significance

PROF KAULA
GOLD MEDAL

RANGANATHAN-KAULA
GOLD MEDAL

W 1

Works of Professor Kaula

P.S.G. Kumar and **S.R. Gupta**

[Prof Kaula's life is imbued with many colourful events of significance. Such events are recollected in the chronology. Several significant events, already placed more apporpriately in chapters "W 1" and "W 2", have, however, not been repeated and should be waded through for *tout ensemble*. — S R Gupta, Associate Editor]

A. Publications (Books and Monographs written/compiled/edited)

A Librarian Looks Back : Autobiography of S R Ranganathan, appended with a Biography. ABC Publishing House, New Delhi, 1990.

Adarsh Granthalayi. 1953. Delhi Library Association, Delhi.

Analytico-Synthetic Classification. 1964. C-1, Banaras Hindu University, Varanasi.

Bibliografica : Bibliotechnologia, Documentacion. 1967. Faculty of Technology, University of Havana, Havana.

Bibliographical Services : A Report submitted to UNESCO (Indian Working Party, International Bibliographical Survey). 1953. Unesco, Paris.

Bibliography of Current Labour Problems. 1958. Ministry of Labour and Employment, New Delhi.

Bibliography on Labour Relations in India. 1958. Ministry of Labour and Employment, New Delhi.

Bibliography on Workers' Eduction. 1958. Ministry of Labour and Employment, New Delhi.

Bibliogrphy on Wages. 1958. Ministry of Labour and Employment, New Delhi.

Classified Index to Labour Gazette. Vols I-17, 1943-59. 1959. Ministry of Labour and Employment, New Delhi.

Documentation of Labour Awards. Vol. 1. 1958. Ministry of Labour and Employment, New Delhi.

Documentation of Labour. Vols 1-5; 1951-56, 1957. Ministry of Labour and Employment, New Delhi.

Edificio de la Bibliotecas la Facultad de Technologia. (Unesco Plan CUB 2). 1967. University of Havana, Havana.

Eduction and Libraries. 1969. C-1, Banaras Hindu University, Varanasi.

Essentials of a Classification Scheme and Decimal and Colon Classifications. 1964. C-1, Banaras Hindu University, Varanasi.

Festschrift to Dr. Ranganathan. C-1, BHU, Varanasi.

Free Book Service for All. 1973. Sri Sanmati Pustakalaya Trust, Jaipur.

Government of India Libraries and their Working. 1971. C-1, Banaras Hindu University, Varanasi.

Government of India Libraries and Salary Scales of Librarians. C-1, BHU, Varanansi.

How to Choose Your Classification Scheme? 1963. C-1, Banaras Hindu University, Varanasi-5.

Indian Library Literature. 1956. Delhi Library Association, Delhi.

Indian Library Manifesto. ABC Publishing House, New Delhi, 1989.

Kashmir Darshan. 1951. Raja Ram Kumar Book Depot, Lucknow.

Kashmir men Ilmi Inqlab : 1948. Library Club, Srinagar.

Kashmir Speaks. 1950. S Chand and Co., Delhi.

Kutub Khanaun ki Darja Bandi (Classification for Libraries). 1950.

Labour Literature. 1957. Ministry of Labour and Employment, New Delhi.

Librarian Consultant to the Faculty of Technology. University of *Havana : Final Report*, Feb. 1967-Jan. 1968.

Library Building of the Faculty : *Basic Principles* and *Primary Elements of Design*. 1967. University of Havana, Havana.

Library Buildings : *Planning and Design*. 1971. Vikas Publishing House, Delhi.

Library Legislation: England, ILA, Delhi. 1952.

Library Movement in India. 1958. Delhi Library Association, Delhi.

Library Science Today (Ranganathan Festschrift). Vol 1. 1965. Asia Publishing House, Bombay.

Library Services in India : An Outline, BHU, Varanasi.

Malaviyana. 1962. Banaras Hindu University (Library), Varanasi.

National Grid of Public Library System of India. 1972. C-1, Banaras Hindu University, Varanasi.

National Library of India : A Critical Study. 1970. Somaiya Publications Ltd., Bombay.

Pictorial Education of Students' Unrest. 1969. Banaras Hindu University, Varanasi.

Plan for the Development of Banaras Hindu University Libraries. 1971. Banaras Hindu University (Library), Varanasi.

Rethinking on Enigma Infested Profession. IASLIC, Calcutta, 1989.

Select Labour Problems. 1958. Ministry of Labour and Employment, New Delhi.

Sino-Indian Border Question : Pilot Fascicule. 1962. Banaras Hindu University (Library), Varanasi.

Student Unrest in BHU. Part 1: 1965 Unrest (October 1965 to December 1965) 1969.

Student Unrest in BHU. Part 2: 1966 Unrest (Phase 1). 1969.

Student Unrest in BHU. Part 3: 1966 Unrest (Phase 2). 1969.

Student Unrest in BHU. Part 4: 1968 Unrest (November 1967 to January 1968). 1969.

Student Unrest in BHU. Part 5: 1968 Unrest (August 1969 to March 1969). 1969.

Study of the Working of the Library of the Faculty of Technology, Havana, 1967. University of Havana, Havana.

Subject Guide to the Book Collections, BHU Library, Varanasi. 1963.

Survey of Library Science Education in Banaras Hindu University. 1971. Department of Library Science, BHU, Varanasi.

Tasvir-e-Kashmir. 1949. Zinat Kitab Ghar, Delhi.

Training Programme in Library Science and Documentation. 1967. Unesco Regional Centre, Havana.

Training Programme of Librarians and Documentationalists in Eight Phases for Latin America. Faculty of Technology, University of Havana. 1967.

Treatise on Colon Classification. New Delhi, Sterling Publishers. 1985.

Union Catalogue of Learned Periodical Publications in South Asia. Vol. 1 : Physical and Biological Sciences (UNESCO/ILA Project). 1953. Indian Library Association, Delhi.

Union Catalogue of Periodical Publications in South Asia: Pilot Fascicule (UNESCO/ILA Project). 1950. UNESCO South Asia Science Cooperation Office and Indian Library Association, Delhi.

Universe of Knowledge : Its Sections and Cross Sections, Vikram University, Ujjain, 1974.

Use Your Library. 1964. Banaras Hindu University (Library), Varanasi.

What They Say. 1964. Ranganathan Commemoration Volume

B. Periodicals Edited

Abgila (Annals, Bulletin and Granthalaya of the Indian Library Association), Indian Library Association, Delhi.Vols 1-3; 1949-53 (Managing Editor)

Granthalaya Vijnana, Varanasi. Vol 1-; 1970-;

Herald of Library Science, Varanasi. Vol 1-; 1962-.

International Information, Communication and Education (INICAE). Vol 1-; 1982-.

Library Herald (Delhi Library Association, Delhi). Vols 1-4; 1958-61.

Progress of Library and Information Science. (B.H.U.) Vols 1-3, 1980-1983.

Research Journal of the Faculty of Arts (B.H.U.). 1979-82.

Sharada (K P Association, Delhi), Delhi. Vols 1-3; 1953-55.

C. Schedules of Depth Classification

Classification for Devaluation, 1950.
Classification for Five Year Plans of India, 1965.
Classification for Higher Education, 1970.
Classification for Indo-China Relations, 1962.
Classification for Industrial Relations, 1958.
Classification for Labour Awards, 1958.
Classification for Labour Economics, 1953.
Classification for Library Science, 1965.
Classification for Marketed Foodgrains, 1968.
Classification for Military Science, 1964.
Classification for National Integration, 1962.
Classification for National Productivity, 1968.
Classification for Personal Bibliography, 1962.
Classification for Planning Literature, 1959.
Classification for Socialism, 1966.
Classification for Student Unrest, 1968.
Classification for Wages, 1958.
Classification for Workers' Education, 1958.

D. Library Development Plans

Building Plan of Kanpur University Library.

Development Plan for Agricultural Institute, Allahabad, 1966.
Development Plan for Banaras Hindu University Libraries, 1971.
Development Plan for Development of Library Science, Banaras Hindu University, 1970.
Development Plan for Jammu and Kashmir University Library, 1949.
Development Plan for the S P Public Library, Srinagar, 1949.
Development Plan of Delhi College, Delhi, 1950.
Development Plan of the Birla Central Library, Pilani, 1948.
Library Building and the Reorganisation Plan for the Birla Central Library, Pilani, 1947.
Library Development Plan for Jammu and Kashmir State, 1951.
Library Development Plan for Delhi, 1954.
Library Service and Staff Pattern of the Kashmir University Library, 1971.
Norms and Standard for College Libraries (1980, 1983).
Norms and Standard for Public Libraries (1979).
Plan for the Library System of Jammu and Kashmir State, 1949.
Reorganisation Plan of the Andhra University Library, 1973.
Report on the Reorganisation of State Central Library, Hyderabad (1978).
Staff Pattern of Vishwa Bharati University Library, Santiniketan, 1968.

E. Draft Library Bills

Delhi State, 1954
Jammu and Kashmir State, 1951

F. Memoranda Submitted

On Departmental and Faculty Libraries, 1972
On the National Library, 1968
To the Central Pay Commission, 1957
To the Third Pay Commission, 1970

G. Articles/Reviews/Notes and News Published in Periodicals

Abgila, Delhi
Ajkal, Delhi
AMULA Bulletin, Aligarh
Annals of Library Science, Delhi

Bahar-i-Kashmir, Lahore
BHU Gazette, Varanasi
Boletin Biblioteca, Havana
Ceylon Library Review, Colombo
Chand, Jammu
Desh, Srinagar
Education Forum, Delhi
Granthalaya Sarvaswamu, Vijayawada
Granthalaya Vijnana, Varanasi
Granthapal, Nagpur
Hamdard, Srinagar
Herald of Library Science, Varanasi
Hindustan Times, New Delhi
ILA Bulletin, Calcutta
Indian Jorunal of Information, Janatry and Society, Cuttack
Indian Librarian, Jalandhar
International Classification, Frankfurt
International Forum on Documentation, Moscow
International Information Communication and Education, Varanasi
Jid-o-Jahad, Delhi
Journal of Indian Library Association, Delhi
Journal of Library Science, Nagpur
Kashmir Chronicle, Srinagar
Kashmir, Srinagar
Khidmet, Srinagar
Kram Vir, Khandwa
Lala Rookh, Srinagar
Leader, Allahabad
Libra, Jaipur
Library Herld, Delhi
Library Journal, Jamshedpur
Library Review, Agartala
Library Today, Hyderabad
Library World, London
Lucknow Librarian, Lucknow
Martand, Srinagar
Mazdoor Jagat, New Delhi
Modern Librarian, Lahore
Nai Disha, Nagpur
Nav Yug, Srinagar

Noolagam, Madras
Noor, Srinagar
Northern India Patrika, Allahabad
Pakistan Library Review, Karachi
Prajna, Varanasi
Pratap, Srinagar
Progress of Library and Information Science, Varanasi
Pustakalaya Sandesh, Patna
Pustakalaya Sandesh, Ujjain
Pustakalaya, Patna
Pym-i-Taleem, Delhi
Ranbir, Jammu
Research Journal of the Faculty of Arts, Banaras Hindu University, Varanasi
Reveue Internationale de la Documentation, The Hague
Sharad, New Delhi
Sidhant, Varanasi
Sudharak, Srinagar
Timeless Fellowship, Dharwar
Unesco Bulletin for Libraries, Paris
Yojana, New Delhi

Over 400 papers, 400 reviews and over 6000 Notes and News written by Prof. Kaula have been published in various periodicals/journals in India and abroad.

H. Series in Library Science and Documentation Initiated

Bibliographical Series, Ministry of Labour and Employment, New Delhi;
Bibliogrpahical Series, Banaras Hindu University;
Documentation Series, Banaras Hindu University;
Documentation Series, Ministry of Labour and Employment, New Delhi;
Ranganathan Series in Library Science

J. Foreword/Preface Written

Catalogue Entries and Procedure by S.S. Agrawal, Lakshmi Book Store, New Delhi, 1972.

Colon Classification : Its Structure and Working by M P Chand, New Delhi, Sterling Publishers, 1978. Ed. 2. 1984.

Fundamental Theories in Abstracting, By B.B. Shukla Bharati Publications. 1984

Handbook of Pseudonymous Authors in Telugu by A.A.N. Raju, Booklinks Corporation, Hyderabad, 1974

Light of the Library by V. Venkatappaiah. World Federation of Wisdom, Vijayawada, 1973

Public Libraries System by Gopal Rao Ekbote, Ekbote Bros. Hyderabad 1987

Pustakalaya Jagat by P K Jayaswal, Santulal Pustakalaya, Ranchi, 1966

Pustakalaya Prakriya by Anuj Shastri, Pustak Sadan, Patna, 1962

Sandarbh Sewa (Reference Service) by K S Sundareshwaran Bhopal Hindi Granth Academy, 1980

Theory of Knowledge Classification in Libraries by A P Srivastava, Lakshmi Book Store, New Delhi, 1964

K. Memorial Lectures Delivered

Master Motilal Memorial Lectures (Rajasthan Library Association), 1972

Ranganathan Memorial Lectures (Marathwada University, Aurangabad), 1973

Ranganathan Memorial Lectures (University of Saugar, Sagar), 1973

Ranganathan Memorial Lectures (Vikram University, Ujjain), 1974

Ranganathan Memorial Lecture (Andhra Unniversity, Waltair), 1974

Ranganathan Memorial Lecture (M P Library Association, Bhopal), 1974.

Ranganathan Memorial Lecture (Banaras Hindu University), Varanasi, 1981.

As a Professor of Library and Information Science, Prof. Kaula delivered a series of extension lectures in forty-two university in India:

L. Visiting Lectures (Delivered Abroad)

All Union Institute for Scientific and Technical Information (VINITI), Moscow (USSR)

American Library Association Midwinla Meeting at Miami, Florida

California University, Los Angeles (USA)
Case Western Reserve University, Cleveland (USA)
Catholic University, Washington (USA)
Chulalongkorn University, Bangkok (Thailand)
Columbia University, New York (USA)
Detroit Public Library, Detroit
Deutsche Bibliothek, Frankfurt (Germany)
Deutsche Bucherei, Leipzig (GDR)
Deutsche Staatisbibliothek, Berlin (GDR)
Enoch Pratt Free Library, Baltimore
German Documentation Institute, Frankfurt (Germany)
German Research Society, Bonn (Germany)
Hebrew University, Jerusalem (Israel)
Hungarian Central Technical Library and Documetation Centre, Budapest (Hungary)
Institut fur Wirtschaftsforchung, Hamburg (Germany)
John Hopkins University, Washington
Library of Congress, Washington, DC
Library School, Hamburg (Germany)
Mahchula Buddhist University, Bangkok (Thailand)
Malaysia University, Kuala Lumpur (Malaysia)
National Agricultural Library, Washington DC
National Library, Bangkok (Thiland)
National Library, Singapore
Pan American Union, Washington DC
School of Library and Information Science, Paris (France)
School of Library Science, Berlin (GDR)
Smithsonian Institution, Washington DC,
Soviet Academy of Science, Moscow (USSR)
Timmasat University, Bangkok (Thailand)
University Library School, Cologn (Germany)
University of Florida, Miami
University of Havana, Havana (Cuba)
University of Maryland, Baltimore (USA)
University of Michigan, Ann Arbor
University of Pittsburgh, Pittsbuurgh (USA)
University of Tubingen, Tubingen (Germany)
Wayn University, Detroit (USA)
Wayne State University, Datsoit
Wurttemberg Ladesbibliothek, Stuttgast (Germany)

M. Participated in Formulation of Library Standards

Rules for Abbreviation of Periodicals
Rules for Alphabetical Arrangement
Rules for Making Alphabetical Index

P. International Conferences (Participated/Conducted)

Conference on Foundations of Classification, 1967
Conference on Planning of Library Services, 1967
Conferences and Congresses organised by (1967, 1977, 1982), International Federation of Library Associations and Institutions (IFLA) (1971, 1977, 1980, 1981, 1982); International Federation for Information and Documentation (FID) (1980, 1982, 1986), International Standards Organisation (ISO) (1981)
First Conference of International Federation of Classification Societies, Aachen, Germany (29 June-1 July, 1987)
First International Conference on Information in Egypt, Cairo Egypt December, 1983
First Regional Conference on Classification, Konigstein Germany, October, 1979
Fourth International Conference on Classification Research, Augsberg, Germany, September 1982.
Hungarian Central Tech Library & Documentation Centre, Budapest, 4 September, 1980.
ILO Regional Conference, 1957
International and Regional Seminars conducted by FID/ET (1980, 1981, 1982, 1986), FID/CR (1979, 1980, 1982, 1986) and FID/CCC (1982, 1983)
International Conference on Information Science, Tel Aviv, 1971
International Conference on Information Work, Rome, 1971
International Conference on Classification Theory and Computer Age at New York, 18-19 November, 1988.
International Congress on Terminology and Knowledge Engineering, Trier, Germany, 20 Sept-10 Oct. 1987
International Seminar on Application of Standards in Information, Budapest, Hungary, 2-10 Sept. 1980.
International Seminar on Resource Sharing, Antwerp, 1977
International Study Institute, Pittsburgh, 1971
International Training Programme on Library Science, Copenhagen, 1973

Panelist on Education and Learning. 50th Anniversary of IFLA, Brussels, 1977

Resource person at the International Training Course in Library Science for Developing Countries held at Copenhagen, Denmark in 1973

Second International Conference on Terminology, Vienna, Austria (1981).

Third International Conference on Classification Research, Bombay, January, 1975.

Training Programme in Library Science and Documentation at the University of Havana, Cuba in 8 phases for four months in 1967

Unesco Regional Conference, 1956

White House Conference on Information Science, Washington DC, 1979

Workshop on Modern Techniques in Information Science held at the National Library, Bangkok, Thailand in 1978.

World Congress of Librarians, Brussels, 1977

Q. Research Guide

Prof Kaula guided 103 dissertations of M Lib Sc candidates at Banaras Hindu University and acted as supervisor of doctoral theses of 9 candidates including one each from Bangladesh and Thailand.

R. Plea/Proposals for the Profession

Evaluation of Teaching and Research in Library Science in Indian Universities to UGC (Dec. 1965).

Plan for setting up Book Museum to Ministry of Education, Social Welfare and Culture (Sept 1981).

Plea to External Affairs Minister to provide for a chain of Contact Libraries in several countries managed through Indian Librarians (1964).

Plea to Ministry of Education for bringing out Colon Classification and Classified Catalogue Code as national projects (July 1965).

Plea to the Director, Indian Standards Institution for taking over the editing and publication of Colon Classification and Classified Catalogue Code as national projects (1951).

Plea to the Minister for Railways to introduce "Bibliotrain" for the reading public travelling in trains (1957).

Plea to the Prime Minister to take up development of national and state grid of libraries based on legislation as national project through Planning Commission in the Silver Jubilee Year in (1972).
Proposal on establishment of National Colleges to UGC (July 1985).
Proposal on Role of Libraries to Promote Literacy to Ministry of Education (July 1988).
Study on Social Science Research and its Problems to Chairman, Research and Programme Committee, Planning Commission (Feb 1986).

S. Innovations in Library Education/Work

Analytico-keyword index to periodicals
Class assignment programme after every lecture delivered
Class interview methodology in teaching
Classified index to legal decisions and awards
Designing of ASCOM (Analytico-Synthetic Classification of Medicine) with the assistance of two medical specialists and two librarians under the auspices of National Information Centre of Medical Sciences, Havana, Cuba. The special scheme within the framework of UDC (Universal Decimal Classification) was presented to the World Congress of Medicine held in Brussels, Belgium in 1969.
Introduction of Urdu System of Cataloguing in Darul Aloom, Srinagar

T. Kaula Gold Medal*

Prof Kaula Endowment for Library and Information Science was formed on 13th March, 1975. The donations made to the Festschrift Volume Committee by its members has been converted into the Endowment Fund. The Trustees of the Endowment decided to award annually "Prof Kaula Gold Medal" and citation to a distinguished professional/person for his contributions in the field of Library and Information Science.

The following are the recipients of the International Gold Medal:

Bernard I Palmer (UK), 1975
Dr Helmut Arntz (Gernamy), 1979
Dr Jesse H Shera (USA), 1976

---

* Replica on Page 582

Dr Nasser Sharify (USA), 1985
Dr Peter Lazar (Hungary), 1978
Henry Campbell (Canada), 1984
Iyyanki Venkata Ramanayya (India), 1977
Prof A I Mikhailov (USSR), 1981
Prof Dr Horst Kunze (GDR), 1983
Prof Frank Hogg (UK), 1986
Prof Kroben Kirkegaard (Denmark), 1982

V. Ranganathan-Kaula Gold Medal*

Ranganathan-Kaula Gold Medal has been instituted by Prof Kaula Endowment for Library and Information Science to recognise the contributions of a distinguished professional from India.

The following are the recipients of the Medal:

Dr I N Sengupta, 1986
Prof M K Mukherjee, 1984
Prof S Bashiruddin, 1980

Y. Other Awards Instituted

Damodar Scholarship
I T College — Kaula Award
IATLIS — Kaula Best Teacher Award in India
ILA — Kaula Endowment Best Librarian Award in India
Jiwaji University — Kaula Award
Library Council — Kaula Award, Jamshedpur

Z. Pioneer and Pathfinder in Library Science

First among the professionals engaged in editing of professional journals for more than 37 years

First full time Professor in Library Science provided by UGC at the Banaras Hindu University in 1971

First full time Reader in Library Science in India at the University of Delhi in 1958

* Replica on Page 582

First Indian professional to be felicitated jointly by 17 professional organisations at Hyderabad in 1974 and 22 organisations at Patna in 1986

First Indian Specialist Invited to deliver lectures in Socialist countries (GDR, Hungary, USSR, Yugoslavia) in 1974

First Indian to act as Specialist on UNESCO Assignment in a Socialist Country, 1967-68

First Indian to receive DEUTSCHE BUCHEREI MEDAL from GDR

First Indian to receive PRO MUNDI BENEFICIO MEDAL from Brazilian Academy of Humanities for "International Understanding"

First professional Editing three professional journals simultaneously.

First professional Endowment for Library Science (Ranganathan Endowment for Library Science) established in 1952

First Rapporteur of the Indian Working Party, International Bibliographical Survey of UNESCO, 1950-51

First Specialist from India to participate in the International Conference in Information Science in Tel Aviv in 1970

First to apply Modern Theory on Classification to Universal Decimal Classification for Medical Sciences and designed ASCOM in 1967

First to be offered full time Professorship in Library Science in India (Sarada Ranganathan Chair in Library Science) in 1961

First to compile a Bibliography on India's Contribution to Library Science (Indian Library Literature) published in 1956

First to compile Classified Index to (Indian Labour Gazette) published in India in 1958

First to convene the First All India Library Convention sponsored by 35 professional organisations in India, 1974

First to compile a Classifised Bibliography in India (Indian Labour Literature) in 1957

First to draft Library Development Plan and the Library Bill for the Jammu and Kashmir State in 1951

First to draft Library Development Plan and the Library Bill for the then Delhi State in 1954

First to organise All India Exhibition on Indian Library Literature as a programme of UNESCO Regional Conference in New Delhi in 1956

First to organise in 1953 the All India Exhibition on Gandhiana by a professional organisation (Delhi Library Association) organised

First to publish over 100 articles in the press within one year period during 1946-47

First to qualify in 1946 with a Post-graduate Diploma in Library Science

First to start Systematic Documentation Series in the Government of India Libraries in 1951

First UNESCO Expert from the East to the UNESCO Regional Centre in Western Hemisphere in Havana, 1967;

W 2

Felicitations and Honours Conferred and Works on Prof. Kaula

Poonam Chaudhary

1. Addresses to Felicitate Kaula in India

Farewell Address by BHU Library Science Association on 21 January 1967

Farewell Address by Cuban Disciples in Havana on 14 December 1967

Farewell Address by Delhi Library Association, Delhi on 5 July 1960

Felicitation Address by 22 Organisations at Patna on 24 February 1986

Felicitation Address by A P Public Library Associations on 4 November 1978

Felicitation Address by A P College Librarians Association on 23 February 1980

Felicitation Address by Andhra Pradesh Public Libraries Association on 16 August 1974

Felicitation Address by BHU Library Science Association on 26 April 1971

Felicitation Address by Federation of Indian Library Associations, Orissa Branch on 24 October 1978

Felicitation Address by Kashmir University Library Science Association on 27 May 1974

Felicitation Address by Librarians of Bihar, Patna on 3 January 1969

Felicitation Address by Librarians and Teachers of Library Science of India at Gwalior on 25 October, 1981

Felicitation Address by Staff and Students of Library Science, Kurukshetra University, Kurukshetra on 27 Oct. 1985

Felicitation Address by the Department of Library Science, Varanasya Sanskrit University on 16 April 1968

Felicitation Address by the Librarians of East and West Godavari Districts of Andhra Pradesh on 23 March 1972

Felicitation Address by the public and social organisations of

Hyderabad on 25 June 1974

Felicitation Address by the Staff and Students of Nav Nalanda Mahavihar on 16 November 1981

Felicitation Address by U P Library Association, Gorakhpur Branch, Gorakhpur on 16 October 1983

Felicitation Address by Vidarbha Academic Libraries Association, Nagpur on 27 June 1974

Tribute paid by 17 professional organisations on 24 June 1974

Innumerable organisations/bodies in India have expressed their regards and gratitute by offering citation addresses and organising functions to felicitate Prof Kaula in recognition of his works and contributions to the profession. For obvious reasons of space, etc., it is not possible be to reproduce original text of all the addresses. However, extracts from the first (1960) and the recent (1986) are being reproduced.

> It is superfluous on our part to recapitulate the rise, growth and development of this Association and the part you played in its many pronged activities. It has indeed been a matter of great pride to us that you have secured a place for Delhi on the library map of India. Your adriot piloting of the Association by blending the conflicting opinions and interests of diverse groups into harmony, relieved the Association from the pangs of birth and saved if from many a infantile mortality. . . .
>
> The starting of the School of Library Science in 1955 which has filled a long felt desideratum in Delhi is yet another notable achievement of yours. Your sustained efforts in obtaining recognition to the school from the Government have infused new hopes to our trainees employed in various libraries in Delhi. . . .
>
> Your activities in creating professional interest among the members may perhaps be formidable to be catalogued. Starting of the LIBRARY HERALD, a publication series, and instituting incentive awards for librarians are only a few among the many. . . .
>
> You are a pioneer in the library field who is destined to keep alive the trail blazed by Dr. Ranganathan. . . .
>
> Yours is a versatile personality endowed with peerless industry, indefatigable energy, intellectual acumen, gifted tongue and above all irrepressible enthusiasm and zeal for library cause.
>
> Delhi Library Association, 1960

Authenticity and depth of your masterly knowledge have been quite often felt by the community of librarians in various countries, such as, Belgium, Cuba, Denmark, Egypt, France, Hungary, Germany, GDR, Maxico, Thailand, UK, USA and USSR.

Twenty-two Organisations, 1986

2. Honours from Abroad

Prof Kaula was honoured by the International Biographical Centre, Cambridge, England with a "Plaque" engraed with the Citation "For Distinguished Service".

Prof Kaula was honoured by the Brazilian Academy of Humanities, Sao Paulo, Brazil which awarded him the PRO MUNDI BENEFICIO MEDAL and Diploma for "International Understanding". He is the first Indian to receive this International Award. The Chancellor of the Academy has expressed his appreciation of the work of Prof Kaula in the following words:

Prof Kaula was presented *"Deutsche Bucherei Medal"* (German Book Medal) at Leipzig for "Distinguished Service in Library Science".

3. Profiles/Bio-data Published

Profiles

Amrit Bazar Patrika, Calcutta (22 December 1971)
Boletin Biblioteca, Havana (September-October 1967)
Business Standard, Calcutta (29 May 1983) under the heading "Librarians and Libraries"
Granthalaya Sarvasvamu, Vijayawada (May-June 1971)
Herald of Library Science, Varanasi (July 1971; April 1972)
Hindustan Times, New Delhi (13 Dec, 1976) under the heading "Medalist Kaula wants chain of Information Centres"
Indian Librarian, Jalandhar (March 1966)
Indian Library Movement, Ambala (November 1974)
Khidmet, Srinagar (31 May 1951)
Library Herald, Delhi (April 1959; July 1960)
Library Review, Agartala (May 1973);
Martand, Srinagar (7 October 1949)

Nantional Herald, New Delhi (25 January 1988) under the heading "Doyen of Librry Science"

Statesman, New Delhi (17 February 1969)

The Pioneer, Lucknow (7 March 1987) under the heading "Literate India is far away"

The Statesman, New Delhi (8 Nov. 1987) under the heading "Prophet of Library Power"

Bio-Data in Reference Books

Asia: Who's Who, New Delhi

Biographical Information of Eminent Men and Women of India, Delhi

Dictionary of International Biography, London (UK)

Directory of Booksellers, Libraries and Librarians of India, Delhi

Famous India, New Delhi.

Fareast and Australasia, London

India : Who's Who, New Delhi

International Who's Who, London (UK)

Learned Asia, New Delhi

Men and Women of Distinction, Cambridge England

Men of Achievement, Cambridge (UK)

Men of Library Science and Libraries of India, Delhi

Reference Asia : Asia's First Who's Who of Men and Women of Achievement and Distiction, Delhi

Times of India Directory and Who's Who, Bombay

Who's Who in India, Bombay

Who's Who in the World, New York (USA)

Who's Who of Men and Women of Achievement and Distinction of Asia, Delhi

4. Work on Kaula

"Kaula Felicitation Number" of *Herld of Library Science*, Vol 13, Nos. 3-4, 1974.

"Kaula sixty-first Birthday Felicitation Number" of *Herald of Library Science*, Vol 26, Nos. 3-4, 1987.

Festschrift to Prof. P.N. Kaula by Dr. V. Venkatappaiah

March of Library Science : "Kaula Festschrift", New Delhi, Vikas Publishing House.

What They Say about P N Kaula, ed by Velaga Venkatappaiah

5. Kaula Series in Library Science

To perpetuate the recognition of the professional contributions of Professor Kaula "Kaula Series in Library Science" was instituted in 1974 — Eight books has been published in this sersies.

Sitting: (Extreme right) Pt Damodar Kaula, father of Kaula

Mrs P Kaula, a lady of saintly habits and pious thought
Mohini Saraf, sister of Prof Kaula is standing

With Mrs. Asha Kaula — who gave full support in all the activities of Kaula — An intimate life-long partnership

W 3

Going Up the Ladder: A Chronology of Events in Kaula's Life

Sister M Esperanza, A.C.

1924, March 13

— Born in a middle class Hindu family at Bana Mohalla, Srinagar (Kashmir).

Father: Pt Damodar Kaula; a School Teacher. Mother: Smt. Posh Kiy Kaula.

1939-1942

* Student Member, Library and Reading Room Committee, and Secretary (1941-42), S P College, Srinagar.
* Rover Scout, SP College, Srinagar; was and awarded Certificate of Merit for "good work" done in the Library and at the Kumbha Mela, Shadipora, Srinagar.
* Group Leader, Adult Education Campaign programme at Anantnag (Kashmir).
* Student Guide, All India Educational Conference held in Srinagar, 1942.
* Passed graduation from S P College, Srinagar, affiliated to the University of Punjab, Lahore.

1944-47

* Librarian, D A V College, Srinagar. Introduced "open access", and long of reading.

1945-46

* Joined Dip Lib Sc Course at the University of Madras, but when Dr S R Ranganathan joined BHU, Kaula also left Madras and joined Lib Sc course under Ranganathan at BHU.
* Passed Dip Lib Sc from Banaras Hindu University obtaining second position in order of merit.
* Publication of four papers in professional journals.

* Contributed, while as a student 3 papers to the Seventh All India Library Conference held at Baroda.
* Became member of the Indian Library Association.

1946-47

* Promoted Library Movement in Jammu and Kashmir State. Published some poems on libraries and library movement.
* Chief Librarian, Birla Central Library, Pilani (Rajasthan).

1948-50

* In order to be able to work with Dr Ranganathan assigned Chief Librarian's post at Pilani, and joined as Technical Assistant, Delhi University Library.

1949

* Publication of *Tasvir-e-Kashmir*, a concise history of modern Kashmir.
* Passed M Lib Sc at Delhi University obtaining First position in order of merit.
* Rapporteur, Indian Working Party International Bibliographical Survey (UNESCO/LC) — project on International Collaboration.
* Drafted Plan Jammu and Kashmir University Library at the invitation of the Vice Chancellor of the University.
* Drafted Plan for the Re-organisation of the Sri Pratap Public Library, Srinagar.

1949-53

* Member of the Executive Council of the Indian Library Association.

1950-53

* Managing Editor, *Abgila*, organ of the Indian Library Association.

1950-55

* Founder Member, Library Research Circle, Delhi.

1951

* Librarian, Ministry of Labour and Employment, Government of India, New Delhi.

1951-1958

* Visiting Lecturer in Library Science, Aligarh Muslim University, Aligarh.

1951

* Starting of systematic Documentation Service in the Government of India Libraries and the beginning of Documentation on Labour (Monthly Classified List).

1952

* Establishment of Ranganathan Endowment for Library Science.

1952-61

* Secretary, Ranganathan Endowment for Library Science.

1953-1955

* Founder and General Secretary of Delhi Library Association.
* Editor, *Sharada*, organ of K P Association, Delhi.

1953

* Organised All India Exhibition on Gandhiana (Literature by and on Mahatma Gandhi) in Delhi.

1954

* Founder and Registrar, School of Library Science, Delhi Library Association. Starting of one-year Certificate in Library Science Course.

1955

* Posted as Librarian of Ministry of Labour elevated into a gazetted post.

1956-1958

* Vice President, Delhi Library Association and Vice President, Government of India Libraries Association, New Delhi.

1956

* Acted as Specialist in Documentation with ILO for a period of 3 years.
* Organiser, 'First All India Exhibition on Indian Library Literature' in New Delhi.
* Publication of *Indian Labour Literature* from Ministry of Labour, classified bibliography on the subject.

1956-62

* Member of the Council, Indian Library Association.

1957

* Organising Secretary, First Delhi Library Conference.

1957-61

* Expert Member, Documentation Committee, Indian Standards Institution, New Delhi.

1958-1960

* Reader in Library Science at the University of Delhi.

1958-1961

* Founder Editor, *Library Herald*, organ of the Delhi Library Association.

* Expert and Advisor, selection committees for librarians, U P S C, New Delhi.

1958

* Starting of Ranganathan Series in Library Science.
* Director, School of Library Science, Delhi Library Association.

1958

* Gave evidence before the Advisory Committee for Libraries.

1958-61

* Expert Member, Library Buildings, Furniture and Fittings Committee, ISI (now Bureau of Indian Standards), New Delhi.
* Member, Technical Sub-Committee, Indian National Scientific Documentation Centre, New Delhi.

1959

* Organising Secretary, First National Library Convention, Delhi.

1960

* Accepted the offer of the post of University Librarian and Head Department of Library Science, Banaras Hindu University (without probation) in a permanent capacity.

1960

* Organising Secretary, All U P Library Conference, Varanasi, and Director, Seminar on Libraary Cataloguing.
* Starting of integrated training programme of UP Library Association as Director of the programme.

1961-1963

* Expert Member, Review Committee on Library Science, University Grants Commission, New Delhi.

1961

* Sarada Ranganathan Endowment Professorship at the University of Madras was offered.
* Founder and Secretary, Ranganathan Commemoration Volume Committee.
* Director, First Refresher Course in Library Science for Librarians at Varanasi.
* Re-organisation of Banaras Hindu University Library (with about 5 lakh volumes) initiated.

1962

* Founder Editor, *Herald of Library Science*, Varanasi, sponsored by Sarada Ranganathan Endowment for Library Science.
* Visiting Professor, Documentation Research and Training Centre, Bangalore.

* Publication of *Malaviyana*, a classified personal bibliography.
* Director, Seminar on Public Libraries, U P, Allahabad.

1963

* Surrendering of teaching allowance of BHU for getting an additional full time lecturer in the Department of Library Science and starting of Lib Sc in place of Dip L Sc at BHU.

1964

* Nominated to Executive Council of Varanaseya Sanskrit University, Varanasi.
* Presided Assam Library Conference and directed its seminar.
* Instituted Ranganathan Gold Medal in Library Science and donated Rs 5,000. Acted as Secretary, Ranganathan Commemoration Volume Committee.

1965

* Visiting Professor, DRTC, Bangalore.
* UNESCO offer for the post of Technical Librarian, Kabacan Institute of Technology, Mindanas (Philippines).
* Introduction of M Lib Sc course at Banaras Hindu University (Second University to institute this training in India).
* Presentation of "Ranganathan Festschrift" (Volume I) entitled *Library Science To-day*, edited by Kaula, to Dr Ranganathan at Bangalore by Dr V V Giri, the then Governor of Karnataka, later the President of India.
* Director, All India Seminar on Library Classification, Trivandrum.

1966-69

* Member, Governing Council, National Library, Calcutta.

1966

* Founder and Chairman, Federation of Indian Library Associations (FILA), Chandigarh.
* Organised and presided, First Jammu and Kashmir Library Conference and Founder, J and K Library Association.
* Director, Seminar on Library Science in Jammu & Kashmir State.
* Director, All India Seminar on Education for Librarianship, Varanasi.
* President, Golden Jubilee of Punjab Library Convention.

1967

* UNESCO Expert, UNESCO Regional Centre in Western Hemisphere, Havana; Librarian-Consultant to the University of Havana, Faculty of Technology; Director and Professor, Training

Programme in Library Science and Documentation, University of Havana;

* Director, Conferences on "Planning of Library Services" and "Foundations of Library Classification"; Visit to libraries and lecture tour of France, Italy, Spain and UK; Visit to Libraries in Washington, Baltimore and Maryland (USA).

1967-68

* Lecturer-cum-Study tour of Madrid, Mexico, Rome.

1968

* Guest Speaker, Association of American Library Schools, Miami, Florida (USA).

1968-1970

* Member, Library Science Terminology, Commission on Scientific and Technical Terminology, Ministry of Education, New Delhi.
* Member, Panel on Library Science for Production of Books in Hindi, Government of India, New Delhi.

1970

* Founder Editor, *Granthalaya Vijnana,* Varanasi, sponsored by Sarada Ranganathan Endowment of Library Science.
* Member, Review Committee of Visvabhararti University Library, Santiniketan.
* Chairman, Council of Literacy and Adult Education (World University).

1971

* Professor of Library Science, BHU (full time post sanctioned by UGC).
* Presentation of the first Personal Bibliography — Writings by and on Kaula by BHU Library Science Association.
* Participation in the International Conference on Information Science held at Tel Aviv (Israel).
* Visiting Professor at the Graduate Library School, Hebrew University, Jerusalem.

1972

* Consultant, National Board of Adult Education, New Delhi.
* Visiting Professor, Karnataka University for extension lectures.
* President, 12th U P Library Conference, and Director, Seminar on Library Legislation, Lucknow.
* President and Director, All Rajasthan College Librarians Seminar.

1973

* President, IATLIS (Indian Association of Teachers of Library Science)

* Visiting Professor, Karnataka University, AEC Training College and Centre, University of Sauger, Marathwada University and Varanasya Sanskrit University for extension lectures.

1974

* Introduction of class interview methodology of teaching.
* Celebration of 51st Birthday and three decades of professional career by different organisations.
* Celebrations of "*Shame-e-Danish*" in Kashmir University and Felicitations
* Guest Speaker, All India Seminar on National Integration in Hyderabad.
* Library Tour of GDR, Hungary, Yugoslavia, and USSR.

1975

* Member, Review Committee of ILA, Bhubaneshwar.
* Founder of NACILA to Convened the Convention on behalf of NACILA.
* Established Foundation to award Gold Medal on distinguished librarians, Documentalists or teachers in the profession in any part of the world.
* Director and Resource Person of a Seminar, Department of Extension Services, Faculty of Education, Varanasi.

1976

* Presided over a Seminar of Post-Graduate College and University Librarians, Agra.

1977

* Delivered extension lectures, University of Kashmir, Srinagar.

1978

* Extension lectures at Aligarh Muslim University
* Main speaker at CONSAL IV (Congress of South East Asian Librarians, Bangkok) and President of Special Session of the Teachers of Library Science.
* Lectures at 5 Universities of Thailand in Bangkok
* Inaugurated the Workshop on Modern Techniques in Information Service at the National Library of Thailand.
* Conducted Training Programme on Modern Techniques in Cultural Information Services.
* Reception by Thai-Bharat Cultural Lodge, Bangkok

1979

* Presided over the 2nd Conference of Public Libraries at Andhra Pradesh.

* Presided over the 58th Annual Celebration of Kanya Kumari Vidyalaya, Varanasi.
* Inaugurated one-week Refresher Course for staff of the Library at BHU Central Library, Varanasi.
* Chief Guest at the 4th Annual Day of Library Council, Jamshedpur.

1980

* Inaugurated Chess-playing Competition at the Rotary Club, Varanasi and lectured on 'Problems of Higher Education'
* Delivered a talk on 'Standards for College Libraries at Narasaraopet", A.P.
* Introductory speech highlighting Problems of Journalism and the Freedom of Press at a National Seminar of Indian Press at Varansai.
* Inaugurated a 'Seminar on Library Services' in Bihar and 'Need of Library Legislation' at the State Central Library, Patna.
* Talk on 'Role of Library and Documentation in increasing Managerial Effectiveness' 'Use of Library & Inf. Sc. in changing situations', at Gorakhpur.

1981

* Honoured with DEUTSCHE BUCHEREI MEDAL for outstanding contributions to development of libraries and information Services.
* Lecture on 'New Dimensions of Library Science' to the librarians, Patna
* Lecture on 'Management Development' and 'From Librarianship to Library Science', at Jamshedpur.
* All India Seminar on 'Information & Communication', organised by the Deptt of Journalism & Mass Communication, BHU, Varanasi.
* Inaugurated Seminar on 'Library Legislation' at Nalanda.
* Lecture on 'Perspective of Library Science' at the Institute of Lib. Sc, Patna University, Patna.
* Persided over the Conference sponsored by Bihar Library Conference Committee, Nalanda.
* Lecture on 'Libraries and Readers', Varanasi.
* Lecture on Current Trends in Library Classification, Panjab University, Chandigarh.
* Addressed the teachers and students of the Faculty of Lib Sc, Calcutta University.
* Inaugurated a National Seminar on Lib Sc at Calcutta.
* Speaker at the 3rd All India Kasmiri Samaj Conference, Bombay

1982

* Presidential Address at the All India Seminar, Jamshedpur.
* Chairman at a session on Staff Pattern, at the Conference of Indian Association of Academic Librarians, Delhi.
* Lecture on 'Libraries and Book Trade' at Delhi.
* Attended 'All India Workshop' at Jiwaji University, Gawalior.
* Visited USSR and participated in the presentation of "Kaula Gold Medal" to Prof. A.I. Mikailov, Director, VINITI, Moscow.
* Lecture on 'Challenges of the Profession' at DRTC, Bangalore.
* Lecture at the Defence Science Documentation Centre, Delhi.
* Inaugurated the 3rd A.P. Library Conference at Tirupati.
* Lecture at the 4th All India KS Conference at Jodhpur.

1983

* Lecture on Problems of College Libraries' at Poona.
* Speaker at Seminar on Research Methods, Poona.
* Lecture at the U.P. Library Association Convocation, Lucknow; Lecture on 'Recent Development in Library Science', "Recent Trends in Library & Inf. Sc.", Lucknow.
* Attended 11th National Book Fair and Conference on 'Role of Libraries in Promoting National Integration' at Chandigarh.
* Lecture at the State Conference on Planning of Library Services Jamshedpur.
* Lecture to Librarians of Orissa.
* Lecture at Isabella Thoburn College, Lucknow.
* Retired from the post of Head, Deptt. of Lib. Inf. Sc. B.H.U.
* Lecture on 'Development of Lib. Sc. in India', at DRTC, Bangalore.
* Addressed the staff and students of Patna Women's College, Patna.
* Keynote Address at a workshop "On Libraries organised as an Aid to Higher Teaching and Research," at Gwalior.
* Presided over a meeting of the Classification Society of India, Nagpur
* Inaugruated as Chief Guest the Deptt. of Lib. Sc. at Kashi Vidyapith, Varanasi.
* Addressed the students of Lib. Sc., Mithila University
* Delivered a lecture on 'Processs of Change in Information Activities' at Moscow.
* Chief Guest at the Kaula Presentation to Prof. A.I. Mikhailov, Director of VINITI, USSR.

1984

* Joined Lucknow University as Visiting Professor in Lib. & Inf. Sc.
* Lecture on 'Challenges of the Profession' at Lucknow University.
* Received an International Bibliographical Role of Honour Plaque by American Bibliographical Institute (USA).
* Chairman, Library Staff Cadre Review Committee of UGC, New Delhi.
* Lecture on 'Library Development in Bihar' at British Council, Ranchi.
* Entrusted with the Project on Evaluation of Book Stock in University Libraries by UGC.
* Chief Guest at UPLA function, Lucknow.
* Appointed as Honorary Professor and Director of Library & Inf. Sc. Deptt. of Kashi Vidyapith, Varanasi.
* Member, Advisory Council of National Resource and Documentation Centre for Physical Education, Gwalior.
* Lecture on 'Changing Concepts of Libraries' at I.T. College, Lucknow.

1985

* Chairman at UGC Seminar, Mysore.
* Lecture at the National Archives of India on 'Role of Library in Archival Studies'.
* Lectures at B.Lib. Sc. & M.Lib. Sc. level at Aligarh Muslim University.
* Received "Emeritus Fellow" Professorship by UGC.
* Lecture at Gujarat University, Ahmedabad. Lecture at Gujarat Seva Sangh, Ahmedabad. Lectures at Gujarat Vidyapith, Ahmedabad
* Lecture at DESIDOC, Delhi, on 'Classification and Emerging Technologies.'
* Lectures at Agra University, Agra.
* Attended meeting of Bibliographical Committee of Bureau for Promotion of Urdu at Aligarh.
* Attended meeting of Administration Committee of Raja Rammohun Roy Library Foundation, Calcutta.
* Speaker and Chairman, National Seminar on Automation at University of Jabalpur, Jabalpur.
* Lecture on 'Situation of Libraries and Librarianship in India' at Lucknow. A talk on 'International Library Day' at Lucknow University.

* Member, Advisory Committee, School of Archival Studies, New Delhi.
* Member, Organisng Committee of International Conference on Ranganathan's Philosophy, ILA, Delhi.
* Member, Standing Council of Central Institute of Lib. Sc., Hyderabad.
* Presided over the National Seminar on Library & Information, Manpower Development, Nagpur.
* Member, National Policy on Library & Information System Committee for Bihar.

1986

* Lecture at I.T. College, Lucknow, on Library Movement and its Growth.
* Lecture on 'Documentation Activity in India' at Rajasthan University, Jaipur.
* Lecture on 'Library Development and Professional Responsibility' at Agra University, Agra.
* Lecture on 'Role of Library in Archival Organistion' at National Archives of India, New Delhi.
* Lecture on 'Challenge of Information', Patna.
* Lecture on 'Need to Vitalis Library Movement' at Rajasthan Library Association meeting at Jaipur.
* Lectures at Jiwaji University, Gwalior on 'Documentation and Classification'.
* Seminar and Meeting of North Eastern Council, Shillong, for the establishment of Regional Documentation Centre and Lib. Inf. Board under the Council.
* Attended meeting at the International Development Research Centre for cooperation between India and Canada in Lib. & Inf. Sc. Education and for setting Regional Centre for LIS training personnel in South Asia.
* Lectures at University of Halifax, College of Education, Truro and other institutes.
* Reception by Indian Community at Truro, Halifax, Canada.
* Presided over inaugural function of National Seminar on 'Manpower Resources in Lib. & Inf. Sc.', Nagpur.
* Worked out a plan for development of National Resource & Documentation Centre at Gwalior.
* Addressed the 4th Public Library Conference of Andhra Pradesh.

* Lecture on 'Education and Information Revolution' at NGRI, Hyderabad.
* Presided over the Workshop of Application of Computer to Libraries, Lucknow.
* Guided professionals of 7 universities in research work and research projects.

1987

* Speaker at Seminar on 'Social Relevance' Delhi, organised by Foundation for Amity and National Solidarity.
* Chairman of the Panel on Library & Information Science of UGC, New Delhi.
* Attended the Extraordinary World Congress of Philosophy, Argentina.
* Meeting of Documentation Sectional Committee EC2 of Bureau of Indian Standards, Delhi.
* Attended International Congress on Terminology and Knowledge Engineering at Trier, Germany.
* Attended meeting of Task Force Sub-Group for Implementation of National Policy, UGC.
* Lecture on 'Recent Library Development in India', at Kashmir University, Srinagar.

1988

* Presided over the Valedictory function of Workshop and Panel discussion on Scientific Communication and Bibliometric at Calcutta.
* Kaula Endowment and ILA instituted annual Award for "best librarian."
* Speaker at the Workshop on Computer Applications to Library and Information Activities organized by CDRI, Lucknow.
* Attended National Library meeting for development of its services, Calcutta.
* Attended meeting of the Central Reference Library, Calcutta, to update the publication of *I.N.B*.
* Lectures at the Academic Staff College, Kurukshetra University.
* Lecture on "Book Culture and Nehru" at the Central State Library, Chandigarh. Lecture at Punjab University Library, Chandigarh.
* Inaugurated the State Seminar on Standards for School and Public Libraries organised by U P Library Association at Nainital.
* Speaker on Panel Discussion on the National Library, Calcutta.

* Addressed the Joint Veledictory Session of ILA and IASLIC Conference at Calcutta.

1989

* Lectures at Marathwada University, Aurangabad.
* Inaugural lecture on 'Education and Our Never Failing Friends', at Aligarh Muslim University to motivate the students for the use of books and libraries. Series of lectures, Deptt. of Lib. Sc., Aligarh Muslim University.
* Lecture on Classification, I.T. College, Lucknow.
* Lectures at Marathwada University, Aurangabad.
* Attended International Conference on Bibliographical Databases & Networks, organised by DESIDOC, Delhi.
* Meeting of the Panel under Banking Service Commission, Dehradun.
* Lectures on Notation in Classification, I.T. College, Lucknow.
* Addressed the National Seminar on Local History Librarianship and chaired the last session at Pune.
* Attended National Seminar on Library Legislation and chaired the session on 'Factors Problems in Lib. Legislation', at Aligarh Muslim University.
* Lecture on Standards of College Libraries at the Workshop on User Education in Academic Libraries at G N D University, Amritsar.
* Lecture at Academic Staff College, Banaras Hindu University, Varanasi.
* Lecture on "Libraries and Democracy" at A N Sinha Institute of Social Studies, Patna.
* Lecture on 'Role of Libraries and Right to Information' organised by Maharashtra Grantha Mandal, Nagpur.
* Chief Guest at State Seminar on Library Legislation in Bihar.
* Chaired the meeting of UGC Panel on Library and Information Science at New Delhi.
* President of the 17th All India Conference organised by IASLIC at Jaipur.

1990

* Lectures at Marathwada University, Aurangabad.
* Guest Speaker, Workshop on New Technologies organised by Bengal Library Association at Jadavpur University, Calcutta. Lecture on 'Public Library Situation in India' organised by Indian Association of Special Libraries and Information Centres at Calcutta.

* Lectures at Manipur University, Imphal.
* Lectures at Aligarh Muslim University, Aligarh.
* Lectures at Jiwaji University, Gwalior.
* Lectures at Sampurnanand Sanskrit University, Varanasi.
* Chairman, Concluding Session of National Seminar on INFLIBNET organised by U P Library Association at Lucknow.
* Lectures at Osmania University, Academic Staff College, Hyderabad.

INDEX